Final Report of the Thirty-fifth Antarctic Treaty Consultative Meeting

ANTARCTIC TREATY
CONSULTATIVE MEETING

Final Report
of the Thirty-fifth
Antarctic Treaty
Consultative Meeting

Volume II

Hobart, Australia
11 - 23 June 2012

Secretariat of the Antarctic Treaty
Buenos Aires
2012

Antarctic Treaty Consultative Meeting (35th: 2012: Hobart)
  Final Report of the Thirty-fifth Antarctic Treaty Consultative
  Meeting. Hobart, Australia, 11 – 23 June 2012.
  Buenos Aires: Secretariat of the Antarctic Treaty, 2012. 288 p.

ISBN 978-987-1515-46-2 (v.II)

                1. International law – Environmental issues. 2. Antarctic Treaty System. 3.
                Environmental law – Antarctica. 4. Environmental protection – Antarctica.

DDC 341.762 5

ISBN 978-987-1515-46-2

9 789871 515462

Contents

VOLUME I

2. Decisions

Decision 1 (2012) Measures on Operational Matters designated as no longer current
    Annex: Measures on Operational Matters designated as no longer current
Decision 2 (2012) Secretariat Report, Programme and Budget
    Annex 1: Audited Financial Report 2010/11
    Annex 2: Estimate of Income and Expenditures 2011/2012
    Annex 3: Secretariat Programme, Budget for 2012/13 and Forecast Budget for 2013/14
Decision 3 (2012) The Development of a Multi-Year Strategic Work Plan for the Antarctic Treaty Consultative Meeting
    Annex 1: Principles
Decision 4 (2012) Electronic Information Exchange System

3. Resolutions

Resolution 1 (2012) Strengthening Support for the Protocol on Environmental Protection to the Antarctic Treaty

Resolution 2 (2012) Cooperation on questions related to the exercise of jurisdiction in the Antarctic Treaty area

Resolution 3 (2012) Improving Cooperation in Antarctica

Resolution 4 (2012) Site Guidelines for visitors

Resolution 5 (2012) Barrientos Island – Aitcho Islands Visitor Site Guidelines

Resolution 6 (2012) Antarctic Conservation Biogeographic Regions
    Annex: Antarctic Conservation Biogeographic Regions
Resolution 7 (2012) Vessel Safety in the Antarctic Treaty Area
Resolution 8 (2012) Improved Coordination of Maritime, Aeronautical and Land-Based Search and Rescue
Resolution 9 (2012) The Assessment of Land-Based Expeditionary Activities
    Annex: Questions to consider as part of the authorisation process for non-Governmental land-based activities in Antarctica
Resolution 10 (2012) Yachting Guidelines
    Annex: Checklist of yacht specific items for preparing safe Antarctic voyages
Resolution 11 (2012) Checklist for visitors' in-field activities
    Attachment: Checklist for visitors' in-field activities

Picture and picture diagram

VOLUME II

Acronyms and abbreviations

ACAP	Agreement on the Conservation of Albatrosses and Petrels
ASOC	Antarctic and Southern Ocean Coalition
ASMA	Antarctic Specially Managed Area
ASPA	Antarctic Specially Protected Area
ATS	Antarctic Treaty System or Antarctic Treaty Secretariat
ATCM	Antarctic Treaty Consultative Meeting
ATCP	Antarctic Treaty Consultative Party
CAML	Census of Antarctic Marine Life
CCAMLR	Convention on the Conservation of Antarctic Marine Living Resources and/or Commission for the Conservation of Antarctic Marine Living Resources
CCAS	Convention for the Conservation of Antarctic Seals
CEE	Comprehensive Environmental Evaluation
CEP	Committee for Environmental Protection
COMNAP	Council of Managers of National Antarctic Programmes
EIA	Environmental Impact Assessment
HCA	Hydrographic Committee on Antarctica
HSM	Historic Site and Monument
IAATO	International Association of Antarctica Tour Operators
ICG	Intersessional Contact Group
ICSU	International Council for Science
IEE	Initial Environmental Evaluation
IHO	International Hydrographic Organization
IMO	International Maritime Organization
IOC	Intergovernmental Oceanographic Commission
IP	Information Paper
IPY	International Polar Year
IPCC	Intergovernmental Panel on Climate Change
IPY-IPO	IPY Programme Office
IUCN	International Union for Conservation of Nature and Natural Resources
RFMO	Regional Fishery Management Organisation
SATCM	Special Antarctic Treaty Consultative Meeting
SCAR	Scientific Committee on Antarctic Research
SCALOP	Standing Committee for Antarctic Logistics and Operations
SC-CAMLR	Scientific Committee of CCAMLR
SP	Secretariat Paper
SPA	Specially Protected Area
UNEP	United Nations Environment Programme
UNFCCC	United Nations Framework Convention on Climate Change
WG	Working Group
WMO	World Meteorological Organization
WP	Working Paper
WTO	World Tourism Organization

PART II

Measures, Decisions and Resolutions (Cont.)

4. Management Plans

Management Plan for Antarctic Specially Protected Area No. 109
MOE ISLAND, SOUTH ORKNEY ISLANDS

Introduction

The primary reason for the designation of Moe Island, South Orkney Islands (Latitude 60°44'S, Longitude 045°41'W), as Antarctic Specially Protected Area (ASPA) No. 109 is to protect environmental values, and primarily the terrestrial flora and fauna within the Area.

The Area was originally designated in Recommendation IV-13 (1966, SPA No. 13) after a proposal by the United Kingdom on the grounds that the Area provided a representative sample of the maritime Antarctic ecosystem, that intensive experimental research on the neighbouring Signy Island might alter its ecosystem and that Moe Island should be specially protected as a control area for future comparison.

These grounds are still relevant. Whilst there is no evidence that research activities at Signy Island have significantly altered the ecosystems there, a major change has occurred in the low altitude terrestrial system as a result of the rapidly expanding Antarctic fur seal (*Arctocephalus gazella*) population. Plant communities on nearby Signy Island have been physically disrupted by trampling by fur seals and nitrogen enrichment from the seals' excreta has resulted in replacement of bryophytes and lichens by the macro-alga *Prasiola crispa*. Low-lying lakes have been significantly affected by enriched run-off from the surrounding land. So far Moe Island has only been invaded by fur seals to a limited extent and its topography makes it less likely that seals will penetrate to the more sensitive areas inland. Moe Island has been visited on few occasions and has never been the site of occupation for periods of more than a few hours.

Resolution 3 (2008) recommended that the "Environmental Domains Analysis for the Antarctic Continent", be used as a dynamic model for the identification of Antarctic Specially Protected Areas within the systematic environmental-geographical framework referred to in Article 3(2) of Annex V of the Protocol (see also Morgan et al., 2007). Using this model, ASPA 111 is contained within Environment Domain G (Antarctic Peninsula off-shore islands geologic). The scarcity of Environment Domain G, relative to the other environmental domain areas, means that substantial efforts have been made to conserve the values found within this environment type elsewhere: other protected areas containing Domain G include ASPAs 111, 112, 114, 125, 126, 128, 145, 149, 150, and 152 and ASMAs 1 and 4.

The three other ASPAs present within the South Orkney Islands (ASPA 110 Lynch Island, ASPA 111 Southern Powell Island and adjacent islands and ASPA 114 Northern Coronation Island) were designated primarily to protect terrestrial vegetation and bird communities. Moe Island complements the local network of ASPAs by protecting a representative sample of the maritime Antarctic ecosystem including cryptogam-dominated terrestrial and coastal communities.

1. Description of values to be protected

Following a visit to the ASPA in February 2011, the values specified in the earlier designation were reaffirmed. These values are set out as follows:

- The Area contains exceptional environmental values associated with the biological composition and diversity of a near-pristine example of the maritime Antarctic terrestrial and littoral marine ecosystems.

- Moe Island contains the greatest continuous expanses of *Chorisodontium-Polytrichum* moss turf found in the Antarctic.

2. Aims and objectives

Management of Moe Island aims to:

- avoid major changes to the structure and composition of the terrestrial vegetation, in particular the moss turf banks;
- prevent unnecessary human disturbance to the Area;
- prevent or minimise the introduction to the Area of non-native plants, animals and microorganisms;
- allow scientific research in the Area provided it is for compelling reasons which cannot be served elsewhere and which will not jeopardise the natural ecological system in that Area
- allow visits for management purposes in support of the aims of the management plan;
- minimise the possibility of introduction of pathogens which may cause disease in bird populations within the Area;

3. Management activities

The following management activities are to be undertaken to protect the values of the Area:

- Visits shall be made as necessary to assess whether the ASPA continues to serve the purposes for which it was designated and to ensure management and maintenance measures are adequate.

- The Management Plan shall be reviewed at least every five years and updated as required.

- Markers, signs or other structures erected within the Area for scientific or management purposes shall be secured and maintained in good condition and removed when no longer required.

- In accordance with the requirements of Annex III of the Protocol on Environmental Protection to the Antarctic Treaty, abandoned equipment or materials shall be removed to the maximum extent possible provided doing so does not adversely impact on the environment and the values of the Area.

- A copy of this Management Plan shall be made available at Signy Research Station (UK; 60°42′30″ S, 045°36′30″ W) and Orcadas Station (Argentina; 60°44′15″ S, 044°44′20″ W).

- Where appropriate, National Antarctic Programmes are encouraged to liaise closely to ensure management activities are implemented. In particular, National Antarctic Programmes are encouraged to consult with one another to prevent excessive sampling of biological material within the Area. Also, National Antarctic Programmes are encouraged to consider joint implementation of guidelines intended to minimize the introduction and dispersal of non-native species within the Area.

- All scientific and management activities undertaken within the Area should be subject to an Environmental Impact Assessment, in accordance with the requirements of Annex I of the Protocol on Environmental Protection to the Antarctic Treaty.

4. Period of designation

Designated for an indefinite period.

5. Maps

Map 1. The location of Moe Island in relation to the South Orkney Islands and the other protected areas in the region. Inset: the location of the South Orkney Islands in Antarctica. Map specifications: Projection: WGS84 Antarctic Polar Stereographic. Standard parallel: 71 °S. Central meridian 45 °W.

Map 2. Moe Island in greater detail. Map specifications: Projection: WGS84 Antarctic Polar Stereographic. Standard parallel: 71 °S. Central meridian 45 °W.

6. Description of the Area

6(i) *Geographical co-ordinates, boundary markers and natural features*

BOUNDARIES AND CO-ORDINATES

The boundary co-ordinates of the Area, starting with the most north-westerly position and moving clockwise, are shown in Table 1.

Number	Latitude	Longitude
1	60°43'40'' S	045°42'15'' W
2	60°43'40'' S	045°40'30'' W
3	60°43'55'' S	045°40'10'' W
4	60°44'40'' S	045°40'10'' W
5	60°44'40'' S	045°42'15'' W

The Area includes all of Moe Island and unnamed adjacent islands and islets. The Area encompasses all of the ice-free ground, permanent ice and semi-permanent ice found within the boundaries, but excludes the marine environment extending greater than 10 m offshore from the low tide water line (Map 2). Boundary markers have not been installed because the coast itself is a clearly defined and visually obvious boundary.

GENERAL DESCRIPTION OF THE AREA

Moe Island, South Orkney Islands, is a small irregularly-shaped island lying 300 m off the south-western extremity of Signy Island, from which it is separated by Fyr Channel. It is about 1.3 km from the northeast to southwest and 1 km from northwest to southeast. It should be noted that the position of Moe Island on Admiralty Chart No. 1775 (60°44'S, 45°45'W), does not agree closely with the more accurate coordinates in Map 2 (60°44'S, 45°41'W).

The island rises precipitously on the north-eastern and south-eastern sides to Snipe Peak (226 m altitude). There is a subsidiary summit above South Point (102 m altitude) and lower hills on each of three promontories on the western side above Corral Point (92 m), Conroy Point (39 m) and Spaull Point (56 m). Small areas of permanent ice remain on the east- and south-facing slopes with late snow lying on the steeply dipping western slopes. There are no permanent streams or pools.

GEOLOGY

The rocks are metamorphic quartz mica schists, with occasional biotite and quartz-rich beds. There is a thin bed of undifferentiated amphibolite on the northeastern coast. Much of the island is overlain with glacial drift and scree. Soils are predominantly immature deposits of fine to coarse clays and sands intermixed with gravels, stones and boulders. They are frequently sorted by freeze-thaw action in high or exposed locations into small-scale circles, polygons, stripes and lobes. There are deep accumulations of peat (up to 2 m thick on western slopes), considerable expanses of the surface of which are bare and eroded.

TERRESTRIAL BIOLOGICAL COMMUNITIES

The dominant plant communities are *Andreaea-Usnea* fellfield and banks of *Chorisodontium-Polytrichum* moss turf (the largest known example of this community type in the Antarctic). These moss banks constitute a major biological value and a reason for the designation of the Area. The cryptogamic flora is diverse. The majority of these moss banks have received little damage from fur seals, and show few visible sign of degradation. However, the exception to this observation is the northern-most banks located around Spaull Point. Here, although still extensive, the moss turf was estimated to have suffered about 50% damage from Antarctic fur seal (*Arctocephallus gazella*) activity during a survey in January 2006. One sub-adult male Antarctic fur seal was present on this area of moss turf during the survey in January 2006. Almost certainly fur seals gain access to this plant community via the gentle slope leading inland from the small shingle beach located at the north-eastern corner of Landing Cove.

The mites *Gamasellus racovitzai* and *Stereotydeus villosus* and the springtail *Cryptopygus antarcticus* are common under stones.

VERTEBRATE FAUNA

There were five colonies of chinstrap penguins (*Pygoscelis antarctica*) totalling about 11,000 pairs in 1978-79. A visit in February 1994 noted fewer than 100 pairs on the northern side of Landing Cove and more than a thousand on the southern side. A visit in February 2011 noted c. 75 pairs on the northern side of Landing Cove and c. 750 pairs on the southern side. Approximately 100 breeding pairs were observed on Spaull Point during a visit in January 2006. Numerous other birds breed on the island, notably about 2,000 pairs of cape petrels (*Daption capensis*) in 14 colonies (1966) and large numbers of Antarctic prions (*Pachyptila desolata*).

Weddell seals (*Leptonychotes weddellii*), crabeater seals (*Lobodon carcinophaga*) and leopard seals (*Hydrurga leptonyx*) are found in the bays on the west side of the island. Increasing numbers of fur seals (*Arctocephalus gazella*), mostly juvenile males, come ashore on the north side of Landing Cove and have caused some damage to vegetation in that area. However, it is possible that the nature of the terrain will restrict these animals to this small headland where damage may intensify.

6(ii) Access to the Area

- Where possible, access shall be by small boat. There are no restrictions on landing from the sea. Landings are usually most safely made at the northeast corner of Landing Cove (Lat. 60°43'55" S, Long. 045°41'06" W; Map 2). If Landing Cove is inaccessible due to the ice conditions, an alternative landing site is at the western-most point of Spaull

Point (Lat. 60°43'54" S, Long. 045°41'15" W), directly opposite an offshore rock of 26 m altitude.

- Under exceptional circumstances, necessary for purposes consistent with the objectives of the Management Plan, helicopters may be permitted to land within the Area.
- Helicopters may land only on the col between hill 89 m and the western slope of Snipe Peak (Lat. 60°44'09" S, Long. 045°41'23" W, Map 2). Landing on vegetation in the col should be avoided to the maximum extent practicable. To avoid overflying bird colonies, approach should preferably be from the south, though an approach from the north is permissible.
- Within the Area the operation of aircraft should be carried out, as a minimum requirement, in compliance with the 'Guidelines for the Operation of Aircraft near Concentrations of Birds' contained in Resolution 2 (2004). When conditions require aircraft to fly at lower elevations than recommended in the guidelines, aircraft should maintain the maximum elevation possible and minimise the time taken to transit the Area.
- Use of helicopter smoke grenades is prohibited within the Area unless absolutely necessary for safety. If used, all smoke grenades should be retrieved.

6(iii) Location of structures within and adjacent to the Area

A marker board is located at the back of the small shingle beach in the northeast corner of Landing Cove, beyond the splash zone on top of a flat rock, to which it is bolted (Lat. 60°43'55" S, Long. 045°41'05" W). During periods of heavy snowfall, the marker board may be buried and difficult to locate.

There is a cairn and the remains of a survey mast, erected in 1965-66, on Spaull Point (Lat. 60°43'49" S, Long. 045°41'05" W). This mast is of interest for lichenometric studies and should not be removed. There are no other structures on Moe Island.

6(iv) Location of other Protected Areas in the vicinity

ASPA No. 110, Lynch Island, lies about 10 km north-north-east of Moe Island. ASPA No. 114, North Coronation Island, lies about 19 km away on the northern side of Coronation Island. ASPA No. 111, Southern Powell Island and adjacent islands, is about 41 km to the east (Map 1).

6(v) Special zones within the Area

None

7. Permit conditions

7(i) General permit conditions

Entry into the Area is prohibited except in accordance with a Permit issued by an appropriate national authority as designated under Article 7 of Annex V of the Protocol on Environmental Protection to the Antarctic Treaty.

Conditions for issuing a Permit to enter the Area are that:

- it is issued for a compelling scientific purpose which cannot be served elsewhere; or
- it is issued for essential management purposes such as inspection, maintenance or review;
- the actions permitted will not jeopardise the natural ecological system in the Area;
- any management activities are in support of the objectives of this Management Plan;
- the actions permitted are in accordance with this Management Plan;
- the Permit, or an authorised copy, must be carried within the Area;
- permits shall be issued for a stated period;
- a report or reports are supplied to the authority or authorities named in the Permit;
- the appropriate authority should be notified of any activities/measures undertaken that were not included in the authorised Permit.

7(ii) Access to and movement within or over the Area

- Land vehicles are prohibited within the Area

- Movement within the Area shall be on foot.

- Pilots, helicopter or boat crew, or other people on helicopters or boats, are prohibited from moving on foot beyond the immediate vicinity of their landing site unless specifically authorised by Permit.

- Pedestrian traffic should be kept to the minimum consistent with the objectives of any permitted activities and every reasonable effort should be made to minimise trampling effects, i.e. all movement should be undertaken carefully so as to minimise disturbance to the soil and vegetated surfaces, walking on rocky terrain if practical.

7(iii) Activities which may be conducted in the Area

- Compelling scientific research which cannot be undertaken elsewhere and which will not jeopardize the ecosystem of the Area
- Essential management activities, including monitoring

7(iv) Installation, modification or removal of structures

No new structures are to be erected within the Area, or scientific equipment installed, except for compelling scientific or management reasons and for a pre-established period, as specified in a permit. Installation (including site selection), maintenance, modification or removal of structures and equipment shall be undertaken in a manner that minimises disturbance to the values of the Area. All structures or scientific equipment installed in the Area shall be clearly identified by country, name of the principal investigator and year of installation. All such items should be free of organisms, propagules (e.g. seeds, eggs) and non-sterile soil, and be made of materials that can withstand the environmental conditions and pose minimal risk of contamination of the Area. Removal of specific structures or equipment for which the Permit has expired shall be a condition of the Permit. Permanent structures or installations are prohibited.

7(v) Location of field camps

Camp in the Area is not normally permitted. If camping is essential for reasons of safety, tents should be erected having regard to causing the least damage to vegetation or disturbance to fauna.

7(vi) Restrictions on materials and organisms that may be brought into the Area

No living animals, plant material or microorganisms shall be deliberately introduced into the Area. To ensure that the floristic and ecological values of the Area are maintained, special precautions shall be taken against accidentally introducing microbes, invertebrates or plants from other Antarctic sites, including stations, or from regions outside Antarctica. All sampling equipment or markers brought into the Area shall be cleaned or sterilized. To the maximum extent practicable, footwear and other equipment used or brought into the Area (including bags or backpacks) shall be thoroughly cleaned before entering the Area. Further guidance can be found in the CEP Non-native Species Manual (Edition 2011) and COMNAP/SCAR Checklists for supply chain managers of National Antarctic Programmes for the reduction in risk of transfer of non-native species. In view of the presence of breeding bird colonies within the Area, no poultry products, including wastes from such products and products containing uncooked dried eggs, shall be released into the Area or into the adjacent sea.

No herbicides or pesticides shall be brought into the Area. Any other chemicals, including radio-nuclides or stable isotopes, which may be introduced for scientific or management purposes specified in the Permit, shall be removed from the Area at or before the conclusion of the activity for which the Permit was granted. Release of radio-nuclides or stable isotopes directly into the environment in a way that renders them unrecoverable should be avoided. Fuel or other chemicals shall not be stored in the Area unless specifically authorised by Permit condition. They shall be stored and handled in a way that minimises the risk of their accidental introduction into the environment. Materials introduced into the Area shall be for a stated period only and shall be removed by the end of that stated period. If release occurs which is likely to compromise the values of the Area, removal is encouraged only where the impact of removal is not likely to be greater than that of leaving the material in situ. The appropriate authority should be notified of anything released and not removed that was not included in the authorised Permit.

7(vii) Taking of, or harmful interference with, native flora and fauna

Taking of or harmful interference with native flora or fauna is prohibited, except by Permit issued in accordance with Annex II to the Protocol on Environmental Protection to the Antarctic Treaty. Where taking of or harmful interference with animals is involved, the *SCAR Code of Conduct for the Use of Animals for Scientific Purposes in Antarctica* should be used as a minimum standard.

7(viii) The collection or removal of materials not brought into the Area by the Permit holder

Collection or removal of anything not brought into the Area by the permit holder shall only be in accordance with a Permit and should be limited to the minimum necessary to meet scientific or management needs.

Other material of human origin likely to compromise the values of the Area which was not brought into the Area by the permit holder or otherwise authorised, may be removed from the Area unless the environmental impact of the removal is likely to be greater than leaving the material in situ; if this is the case the appropriate Authority must be notified and approval obtained.

7(ix) Disposal of waste

As a minimum standard, all waste shall be disposed of in accordance with Annex III to the Protocol on Environmental Protection to the Antarctic Treaty. In addition, all wastes shall be removed from the Area. Liquid human wastes may be disposed of into the sea. Solid human waste should not be disposed of to the sea, but shall be removed from the Area. No solid or liquid human waste shall be disposed of inland.

7(x) Measures that may be necessary to ensure that the aims and objectives of the Management Plan continue to be met

- Permits may be granted to enter the Area to carry out scientific research, monitoring and site inspection activities, which may involve the collection of a small number of samples for analysis, to erect or maintain signboards, or to carry out protective measures.

- Any long-term monitoring sites shall be appropriately marked and the markers or signs maintained.

- Scientific activities shall be performed in accordance with *SCAR's environmental code of conduct for terrestrial scientific field research in Antarctica.*

7(xi) Requirements for reports

The principal permit holder for each visit to the Area shall submit a report to the appropriate national authority as soon as practicable, and no later than six months after the visit has been completed. Such reports should include, as appropriate, the information identified in the visit report form contained in the Guide to the Preparation of Management Plans for Antarctic Specially Protected Areas. If appropriate, the national authority should also forward a copy of the visit report to the Party that proposed the Management Plan, to assist in managing the Area and reviewing the Management Plan. Wherever possible, Parties should deposit the original or copies of the original visit reports, in a publicly accessible archive to maintain a record of usage, for the purpose of any review of the Management Plan and in organising the scientific use of the Area.

8. Supporting documentation

Harris, C. M., Carr, R., Lorenz, K. and Jones, S. 2011. Important Bird Areas in Antarctica: Antarctic Peninsula, South Shetland Islands, South Orkney Islands – Final Report. Prepared for BirdLife International and the Polar Regions Unit of the UK Foreign & Commonwealth Office. Environmental Research & Assessment Ltd., Cambridge. Available at: http://www.birdlife.org/datazone/userfiles/file/IBAs/AntPDFs/IBA_Antarctic_Peninsula.pdf

Longton, R.E. 1967. Vegetation in the maritime Antarctic. In Smith, J.E., *Editor*, A discussion of the terrestrial Antarctic ecosystem. *Philosophical Transactions of the Royal Society of London*, B, 252, 213-235.

Morgan, F., Barker, G., Briggs, C., Price, R. and Keys, H. 2007. Environmental Domains of Antarctica Version 2.0 Final Report, Manaaki Whenua Landcare Research New Zealand Ltd. 89 pp.

Ochyra, R., Bednarek-Ochyra, H. and Smith, R.I.L. *The Moss Flora of Antarctica*. 2008. Cambridge University Press, Cambridge. 704 pp.

Øvstedal, D.O. and Smith, R.I.L. 2001. *Lichens of Antarctica and South Georgia. A Guide to their Identification and Ecology*. Cambridge University Press, Cambridge, 411 pp.

Peat, H., Clarke, A., and Convey, P. 2007. Diversity and biogeography of the Antarctic flora. *Journal of Biogeography*, 34, 132-146.

Poncet, S., and Poncet, J. 1985. A survey of penguin breeding populations at the South Orkney Islands. *British Antarctic Survey Bulletin*, No. 68, 71-81.

Smith, R. I. L. 1972. British Antarctic Survey science report 68. British Antarctic Survey, Cambridge, 124 pp.

Smith, R. I. L. 1984. Terrestrial plant biology of the sub-Antarctic and Antarctic. In: Antarctic Ecology, Vol. 1. Editor: R. M. Laws. London, Academic Press.

Map 1. The location of Moe Island in relation to the South Orkney Islands and the other protected areas in the region. <u>Inset</u>: the location of the South Orkney Islands in Antarctica.

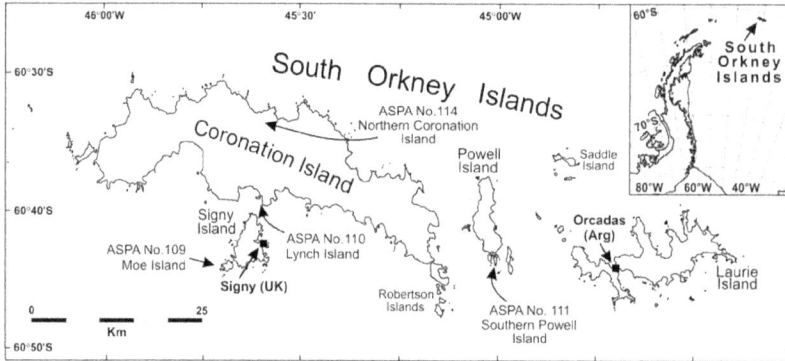

Map 2. Moe Island in greater detail.

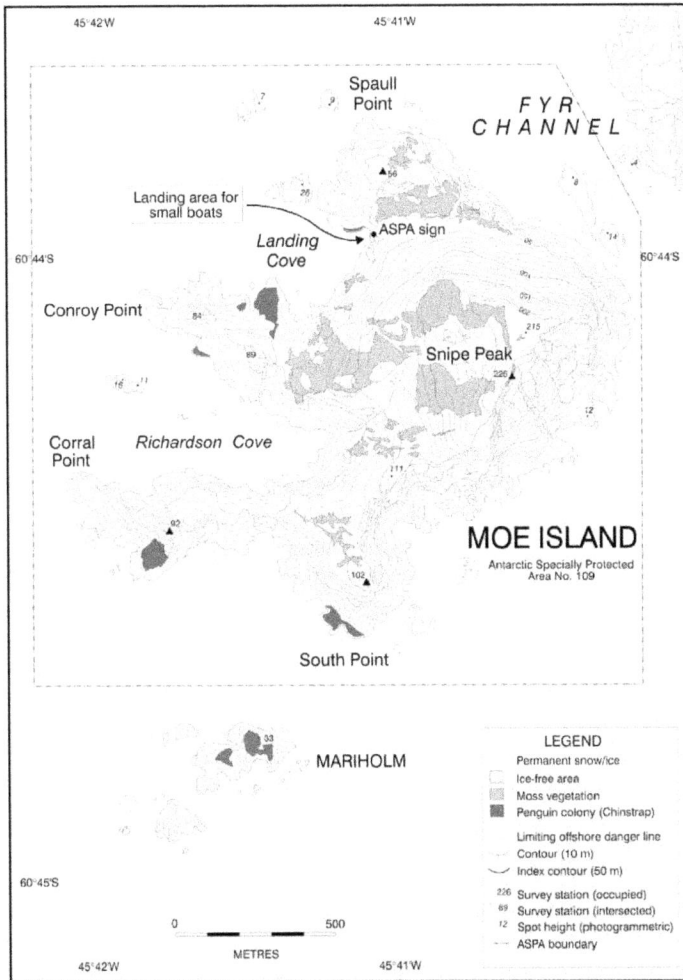

Management Plan for Antarctic Specially Protected Area No. 110

LYNCH ISLAND, SOUTH ORKNEY ISLANDS

Introduction

The primary reason for the designation of Lynch Island, South Orkney Islands (Latitude 60°39'10'' S, Longitude 045°36'25'' W; 0.1 km²), as Antarctic Specially Protected Area (ASPA) 110 is to protect environmental values, and primarily the terrestrial flora within the Area.

Lynch Island, Marshal Bay, South Orkney Islands, was originally designated as a Specially Protected Area through Recommendation IV-14 (1966, SPA No. 14) after a proposal by the United Kingdom. It was designated on the grounds that the island "supports one of the most extensive and dense areas of grass (*Deschampsia antarctica*) known in the Treaty Area and that it provides an outstanding example of a rare natural ecological system". These values were amplified and extended by Recommendation XVI-6 (1991) when a management plan for the site was adopted.

Lynch Island is 2.4 km from Signy Island, the location of Signy Research Station (UK), and about 200 m from Coronation Island, the largest of the South Orkney Islands. The Area has been afforded special protection for most of the modern era of scientific activity in the region, with entry permits having been issued only for compelling scientific reasons. Thus, the island has not been subjected to frequent visits, scientific research or sampling. Since 1983, the numbers of Antarctic fur seals in the South Orkney Islands as increased significantly, with consequent destruction of accessible areas of vegetation where the seals come ashore. Some vegetated areas on Lynch Island have been damaged, for example, accessible *Polytrichum* and *Chorisodontium* moss banks and *Deschampsia* on the north-eastern and eastern sides of the island have been extensively damaged in some locations. A visit in February 2011 reported fur seals were present over the eastern side of the island [roughly drawing a line between the boat landing site (Lat. 60°39'05" S, Long. 045°36'12" W; Map 2) and the island's summit (Lat. 60°39'05" S, Long. 045°36'12" W)]. Seals were present to the highest point of the island with about 30 seals on the summit. Despite this, both the Antarctic hair grass; *Deschampsia Antarctica* and *Colobanthus quitensis* appeared to be thriving. The area covered by *Deschampsia*, as reported in February 2011, is more extensive than in the previous report (February 1999). The grass has now increased its abundance and distribution range in an area to the east of the island, extending west to the highest point on the island with good cover to the summit and all over the area around the summit cairn (Map 3). During a visit in February 1999 it was observed that the most luxuriant areas of grass on the northern and north-western slopes had not yet been affected and this observation was confirmed during a visit in February 2011. Notwithstanding some localised destruction, to date the primary values of the island, as noted above, have not been significantly compromised by either human or seal access to the island.

Resolution 3 (2008) recommended that the "Environmental Domains Analysis for the Antarctic Continent", be used as a dynamic model for the identification of Antarctic Specially Protected Areas within the systematic environmental-geographical framework referred to in Article 3(2) of Annex V of the Protocol (see also Morgan et al., 2007). ASPA 110 is not categorised within Morgan et al.; however, ASPA 111 is likely to be contained within Environment Domain G (Antarctic Peninsula off-shore islands geologic). The scarcity of Environment Domain G, relative to the other environmental domain areas, means that substantial efforts have been made to conserve the values found within this environment type elsewhere: other protected areas containing Domain G include ASPAs 109, 111, 112, 114, 125, 126, 128, 145, 149, 150, and 152 and ASMAs 1 and 4.

The three other ASPAs present within the South Orkney Islands (ASPA 109 Moe Island, ASPA 111 Southern Powell Island and adjacent islands and ASPA 114 Northern Coronation Island) were designated primarily to protect terrestrial vegetation and bird communities. Lynch Island complements the local network of ASPAs by protecting a representative sample of the maritime Antarctic ecosystem including phanerogam-dominated terrestrial communities.

1. Description of values to be protected

Following a visit to the ASPA in February 2011, the values specified in the earlier designation were reviewed. Values within the Area are set out as follows:

- The Area contains luxuriant swards of Antarctic hair grass *Deschampsia antarctica* and the only other Antarctic flowering plant, Antarctic pearlwort (*Colobanthus quitensis*), is also abundant. It is also one of few sites where the grass *Deschampsia* is known to grow directly on *Polytrichum-Chorisodontium* moss banks.
- The cryptogamic vegetation is typical of the region; however, several species of moss found on the island (*Polytrichastrum alpinum* (=*Polytrichum alpinum*) and *Muelleriella crassifolia*) are unusually fertile for their southerly location. It is also possibly the only known location in Antarctica where *Polytrichastrum alpinum* develops sporophytes in profusion annually. Furthermore, *Polytrichum strictum* (=*Polytrichum alpestre*) occasionally produces male inflorescences in local abundance, which is a rare occurrence in this species in Antarctica and the rare moss *Plagiothecium ovalifolium* occurs in moist shaded rock crevices near the shore.
- The shallow loam-like soil associated with the grass swards was contains a rich invertebrate fauna. The population density of the arthropod community associated with *Deschampsia* on Lynch Island appears unusually high, with some measurements suggesting it is one of the highest in the world. The site also shows unusual diversity for an Antarctic site. A rare enchytraeid worm was also found in moist moss in rock crevices on the northern side of the island. One arthropod species (*Globoppia loxolineata*) is near the northernmost limit of its known distribution, and specimens collected from Lynch Island exhibited unusual morphological characteristics compared to specimens collected elsewhere in the South Orkney-Antarctic Peninsula region.

- *Chromobacterium* bacteria, yeasts and fungi are found in higher densities than on Signy Island, thought to be a result of the lower acidity of the soils associated with *Deschampsia* and the more favourable microclimate at Lynch Island.
- The shallow gravelly loam-like soil beneath the dense swards of *Deschampsia* may represent one of the most advanced soil types in the Antarctic.

2. Aims and objectives

Management at Lynch Island aims to:

- avoid major changes to the structure and composition of the terrestrial vegetation;
- prevent unnecessary human disturbance to the Area;
- prevent or minimise the introduction to the Area of non-native plants, animals and microorganisms;
- allow scientific research in the Area provided it is for compelling reasons which cannot be served elsewhere and which will not jeopardise the natural ecological system in that Area;
- ensure that the flora and fauna are not adversely affected by excessive sampling within the Area;

- allow visits for management purposes in support of the aims of the management plan;
- minimise the possibility of introduction of pathogens which may cause disease in vertebrate populations within the Area;

3. Management activities

The following management activities shall be undertaken to protected the values of the Area

- Visits shall be made as necessary to assess whether the ASPA continues to serve the purposes for which it was designated and to ensure management and maintenance measures are adequate.

- The Management Plan shall be reviewed at least every five years and updated as required.

- Markers, signs or other structures erected within the Area for scientific or management purposes shall be secured and maintained in good condition and removed when no longer required.

- In accordance with the requirements of Annex III of the Protocol on Environmental Protection to the Antarctic Treaty, abandoned equipment or materials shall be removed to the maximum extent possible provided doing so does not adversely impact on the environment and the values of the Area.

- A copy of this Management Plan shall be made available at Signy Research Station (UK; 60°42'30" S, 045°36'30" W) and Orcadas Station (Argentina; 60°44'15" S, 044°44'20" W).

- Where appropriate, National Antarctic Programmes are encouraged to liaise closely to ensure management activities are implemented. In particular, National Antarctic Programmes are encouraged to consult with one another to prevent excessive sampling of biological material within the Area. Also, National Antarctic Programmes are encouraged to consider joint implementation of guidelines intended to minimize the introduction and dispersal of non-native species within the Area.

- All scientific and management activities undertaken within the Area should be subject to an Environmental Impact Assessment, in accordance with the requirements of Annex I of the Protocol on Environmental Protection to the Antarctic Treaty.

4. Period of designation

Designated for an indefinite period.

5. Maps and photographs

Map 1. The location of Lynch Island in relation to the South Orkney Islands and the other protected areas in the region. Inset: the location of the South Orkney Islands in Antarctica. Map specifications: Projection: WGS84 Antarctic Polar Stereographic. Standard parallel: 71 °S. Central meridian 45 °W.

Map 2. ASPA No. 110, Lynch Island, South Orkney Islands, topographic map. Projection: Lambert Conformal Conic. Standard parallels: 1st 60°40'00'' W; 2nd 63°20'00'' S. Central Meridian: 045°26'20'' W. Latitude of Origin: 63°20'00'' S. Spheriod: WGS84. Datum: Mean Sea Level. Horizontal accuracy of control points: ±1 m

Map 3. ASPA No. 110, Lynch Island, South Orkney Islands, vegetation map. Map specifications as for Map 2.

6. Description of the Area

6(i) Geographical co-ordinates, boundary markers and natural features

BOUNDARIES AND CO-ORDINATES

The Area encompasses all of Lynch Island but excludes all unnamed adjacent islands and islets. The Area encompasses all of the ice-free ground, permanent ice and semi-permanent ice found within Lynch Island, but excludes the marine environment extending greater than 10 m offshore from the low tide water line (Map 2). Boundary markers have not been installed because the coast itself is a clearly defined and visually obvious boundary.

GENERAL DESCRIPTION

Lynch Island (Latitude 60°39'10" S, Longitude 045°36'25" W; area) is a small island situated at the eastern end of Marshall Bay in the South Orkney Islands, about 200 m south of Coronation Island and 2.4 km north of Signy Island (Map 1). The 500 m x 300 m island has low cliffs of up to 20 m in height on the south, east and west sides, dissected by boulder-filled gullies. The northern side has a low cliff below a rock terrace at about 5-8 m altitude, above which moderate slopes rise to a broad plateau at about 40-50 m, with a maximum altitude of 57 m. A beach at the eastern end of the northern coast affords easy access to relatively gentle slopes leading to the central plateau area. The coastal cliffs generally make access to the upper island by other routes difficult, although access is feasible via one or two of the gullies on the eastern and northern sides. Small temporary melt-streams occur on the slopes in summer, but there are no permanent streams or pools, and only a few small late-lying snow patches occur on the southern side of the island. No meteorological data are available for Lynch Island, but conditions are broadly expected to be similar to those experienced at Signy Research Station. However, anecdotal observations suggest that significant microclimatic differences exist on Lynch Island, as the more profuse growth of plant communities would seem to attest. The island is exposed to the south-west and to katabatic and föhn winds descending from Coronation Island to the north. However, in other respects the island is relatively sheltered from regional northerly, easterly and southerly winds by Coronation Island, Cape Hansen and Signy Island respectively. The föhn effect can briefly raise local air temperatures by as much as 10°C at Signy Island. Lynch Island has often been observed to receive sunshine when the surrounding region is shrouded in low cloud. The angle of solar incidence is also relatively high on the northern side of the island because of its general slope and aspect. The above factors may be important reasons for the abundance of the two flowering plants found on the island.

GEOLOGY

The bedrock of Lynch Island consists of quartzo-feldspathic and micaceous schists of the Scotia metamorphic complex, but is poorly exposed and equivalent rocks are much better displayed in the Cape Hansen area, to the east on Coronation Island.

PEDOLOGY

Three main soil types have been identified on Lynch Island:

(i) An acidic (pH 3.8 – 4.5) moss peat, formed by the tall turf-forming mosses *Chorisodontium aciphyllum* and *Polytrichum strictum* (=*Polytrichum alpestre*), occurs mainly at the north-eastern end of the island. This peat reaches a depth of about 50 cm and is similar to peat on Signy Island where it reaches a depth of 2 m. Where the peat depth exceeds about 30 cm there is permafrost. In a few places where the substratum is moist, shallow peat of 10-15 cm depth (pH 4.8 - 5.5) has accumulated beneath the carpet-forming mosses *Warnstorfia laculosa* (=*Calliergidium austro-stramineum*) and *Sanionia uncinata* (=*Drepanocladus uncinatus*).

(ii) A shallow, gravelly loam-like soil resembling tundra brown soil occurs beneath dense swards of the grass *Deschampsia antarctica*. It is seldom more than about 30 cm in depth (pH 5.0 – 5.8) and probably represents one of the most advanced soil types in the Antarctic.

(iii) A glacial till with material ranging from fine clay (pH 5.2 – 6.0) and sand to gravel and larger stones. This covers the summit plateau and occurs in rock depressions throughout the island, as well as on parts of the rock terrace. On the plateau cryoturbation has in several places sorted the material into patterned features with small stone circles and polygons on level ground and stone stripes on sloping ground. At the north-eastern end of the island, the deposition of limpet shells (*Nacella concinna*) by gulls (*Larus dominicanus*) has resulted in a more calcareous mineral soil in rock depressions with a pH of 6.5 - 6.8.

TERRESTRIAL FLORA

Cryptogamic and phanerogamic vegetation typical of the maritime Antarctic is found over much of the island (Map 3). The most significant aspect of the vegetation is the abundance and reproductive success of the two native Antarctic flowering plants, the Antarctic hair grass (*Deschampsia antarctica*) and Antarctic pearlwort (*Colobanthus quitensis*), found especially on the northern slopes (Map 3). Both species flower in profusion and seed viability appears to be much greater than on Signy Island. Lynch Island possesses the largest stands of *Deschampsia* and the greatest abundance of *Colobanthus* known in the South Orkney Islands and one of the most extensive anywhere in the Antarctica Treaty area.

On the rock terrace and moist slope rising above the northern coast, the grass forms extensive swards of up to 15 × 50 m. These swards range from continuous stands of relatively luxuriant plants on the moister sites and ledges to small, yellowish, more isolated plants on the drier, stonier and more exposed terrain. *Colobanthus* is generally associated with the grass, but here the plants do not coalesce to form closed patches. This is one of very few sites where *Deschampsia* is known to grow directly on *Polytrichum-Chorisodontium* moss banks. Elsewhere on the island, the grass and, to a lesser extent, the pearlwort are frequent associates in other communities, especially stands of denser fellfield vegetation where there is quite high cover afforded by various mosses and lichens (particularly towards the western end of the northern terrace).

Shallow but occasionally extensive (about 50 m^2) banks of *Chorisodontium aciphyllum and Polytrichum strictum* are frequent at the north-eastern end of the island and, to a lesser extent, on the southern side. These are typical of the moss banks which occur on Signy Island and elsewhere in the northern maritime Antarctic, with several fruticose and crustose lichens growing epiphytically on the moss surface. In small moist depressions, there are carpets of *Warnstorfia laculosa* and *Sanionia uncinata*, with some *Warnstorfia sarmentosa* (=*Calliergon sarmentosum*) and *Cephaloziella varians* (= *C. exiliflora*). On wet soil and rock ledges, *Brachythecium austro-salebrosum* is common. On the drier, more windswept, stonier soils and rock surfaces – notably in the plateau area – a typical open fellfield community of many bryophyte and lichen taxa form a complex mosaic. The dominant species in this locality are the lichens *Usnea antarctica* and *U. aurantiaco-atra* (=*U. fasciata*) and the moss *Andreaea depressinervis*; *Sphaerophorus globosus* and other species of *Alectoria, Andreaea, Cladonia,* and *Stereocaulon* are also common, while *Himantormia lugubris* and *Umbilicaria antarctica* are infrequent. Crustose lichens are abundant on all rock surfaces. The mosses and macrolichens in this area are loosely attached on thin soils and are easily damaged. Large thalli of *Usnea spp.* and *Umbilicaria antarctica* are found on moist sheltered boulders and rock faces, especially on the southern side of the island.

Communities of crustose lichen occur in the cliffs above the high water mark, especially where the rock is influenced by breeding or roosting birds. The distribution of several species forms distinctive zones in relation to inundation by sea spray and exposure to wind. The best developed communities of brightly coloured ornithocoprophilous taxa occur at the western end of the island where *Caloplaca spp.*, *Haematomma erythromma*, *Mastodia tesselata*, *Physcia caesia*, *Xanthoria candelaria*, *X. elegans*, and species of *Buellia* and *Verrucaria* are frequent. The uncommon halophilous moss *Muelleriella crassifolia* also occurs within the spray zone around the island.

The only rare moss recorded on Lynch Island is *Plagiothecium ovalifolium*, found in moist, shaded rock crevices near the shore. However, the island is possibly the only site known in the Maritime Antarctic where the moss *Polytrichastrum alpinum* develops sporophytes in profusion each year; this occurs among *Deschampsia*, *Colobanthus* and cryptogams on the northern side of the island; elsewhere in the Antarctic sporophytes are in some years very rare. Also, *Polytrichum strictum* produces male inflorescences in local abundance, a rare phenomenon in this species in the Antarctic. While the thalloid liverwort *Marchantia berteroana* is locally common on Signy Island, Lynch Island is one of very few other localities where it is known in the South Orkney Islands. Several cryptogamic species of very restricted distribution in the Antarctic, but which are locally common on Signy Island and the mainland of Coronation Island only a few hundred metres away, have not been observed at Lynch Island.

TERRESTRIAL INVERTEBRATES

The microinvertebrate fauna associated with the rich *Deschampsia* swards described thus far comprises 13 taxa: three springtails (*Cryptopygus antarcticus*, *Friesea woyciechowskii* and *Isotoma* (*Folsomotoma*) *octooculata* (=*Parisotoma octooculata*), one mesostigmatid mite (*Gamasellus racovitzai*), two cryptostigmatid mites (*Alaskozetes antarcticus* and *Globoppia loxolineata*), and seven prostigmatid mites (*Apotriophtydeus sp.*, *Ereynetes macquariensis*, *Nanorchestes berryi*, *Stereotydeus villosus*, and three species of *Eupodes*). The number of taxa identified is likely to increase with greater sampling. The community is dominated by the Collembolla, especially *Cryptopygus antarcticus* (84% of all arthropods extracted), with relatively large numbers of *I. octooculata*; the principal mite was an undetermined species of *Eupodes*. *Globoppia loxolineata* is near the northernmost limit of its known distribution. In general, the population density of the arthropod community of grass stands on Lynch Island appears unusually high, with some measurements suggesting it is one of the highest in the world. It also shows considerable diversity for an Antarctic site, although this observation was based on a small number of sample replicates and further sampling would be required to establish densities with greater reliability: this is difficult to achieve on Lynch Island given the very limited extent of communities available for sampling.

Lynch Island was the first site in the Antarctic where a terrestrial enchytraeid was found (in soil beneath a moss *Hennediella antarctica* on a rock ledge above the northern shore); only in a few other sites in the South Orkney Islands have these worms been found – although few samples have been gathered and the species has yet to be identified. Of the tardigrade fauna, most of the 16 individuals isolated from a sample of *Brachythecium* were *Hypsibius alpinus* and *H. pinguis* with some *H. dujardini*, while of 27 isolated from a *Prasiola crispa* sample, almost all were the latter species with a few that were other species of *Hypsibius*.

MICROORGANISMS

The mineral and organic soils of Lynch Island have a slightly higher pH than corresponding soils on nearby Signy Island. This higher base and nutrient status, together with the more favourable microclimate, is reflected in larger numbers of bacteria (including *Chromobacterium*), yeasts and fungi than occur in comparable soils on Signy Island. Bacterial numbers in the *Polytrichum* peat on Lynch Island are about eight times, and in the *Warnstorfia* peat about six times, greater than in corresponding Signy Island peats; yeasts and fungi are similarly much more abundant. Soil associated with the two flowering plants yielded several nematophagous fungi: in *Deschampsia* soil *Acrostalagmus goniodes*, *Cephalosporium balanoides* and *Dactylaria gracilis*; in *Colobanthus* soil, *Cephalosporium balanoides*, *Dactylaria gracilis*, *Dactylella stenobrocha* and *Harposporium anguillulae* were found. The basidiomycete fungi *Galerina antarctica* and *G. longinqua* occur on moist moss.

VERTEBRATES

The island has no penguin colonies or substantial breeding colonies of other birds. Groups of chinstrap (*Pygoscelis antarctica*), Adélie (*P. adeliae*) and gentoo (*P. papua*) penguins and, sometimes, blue-eyed cormorants (*Phalacrocorax atriceps*) often congregate at the north-eastern and the western ends of the island. Several pairs of brown skuas (*Catharacta lonnbergii*) and at least two pairs of kelp gulls (*Larus dominicanus*) were observed in the early 1980s to nest at the north-eastern corner. A small colony of Antarctic terns (*Sterna vittata*) may also occur in this vicinity, although in February 1994 breeding was not observed. Cape petrels (*Daption capense*) and snow petrels (*Pagodroma nivea*) breed on the higher cliffs at the eastern end and along the north-western coast of the island. A few pairs of snow petrels and Wilson's storm petrels (*Oceanites oceanicus*) nest on ledges and beneath boulders on the south side of the island.

Weddell seals (*Leptonychotes weddellii*), crabeater seals (*Lobodon carcinophgus*), occasional leopard seals (*Hydrurga leptonyx*), and small groups of southern elephant seals (*Mirounga leonina*) are regularly seen on the coast and on ice floes in the vicinity; none have been known to breed on Lynch Island. Since the early 1980s increasing numbers of Antarctic fur seals (*Arctocephalus gazella*), virtually all being immature non-breeding males, have been observed on Lynch Island, some gaining access up the more gentle north-eastern slopes to vegetated areas, where they have caused local, but severe, damage to *Polytrichum-Chorisodontium* moss banks and other communities.

Seal access to the island is principally from a beach on the northeast coast. Once seals have gained access, there are no further substantial geographical impediments to their more extensive travel over the island. Groups of seals have been observed near the summit. Destruction of swards of *Deschampsia* was first reported in 1988. At the time of the most recent inspection of the island (February 2011), it was observed that the most luxuriant areas of *Deschampsia* and *Colobanthus* on the northern and north-western slopes had not yet been affected. Accessible areas of vegetation in the eastern and north-eastern sides of the island, particularly *Polytrichum* and *Chorisodontium* moss banks, have been severely damaged by Antarctic fur seals. In some eastern and north-eastern areas that have been heavily impacted by fur seals, *Deschampsia and Colobanthus* have either been damaged or have died, but at less impacted locations at higher altitudes, these plants continue to grow and may be increasing their abundance and extending their distribution range on the island (see Map 3).

6(ii) Access to the Area

- Where possible, access shall be by small boat. Landings from the sea should be at the beach on the eastern end of the northern coast of the island (Lat. 60°39'05" S, Long. 045°36'12" W; Map 2), unless specifically authorised by Permit to land elsewhere, or when landing at this location is impractical because of adverse conditions.
- Under exceptional circumstances, necessary for purposes consistent with the objectives of the Management Plan, helicopters may be permitted to land within the Area.

- Landing of helicopters within the Area shall be at the designated location on the rock platform (8 m) on the north-western end of the island (Lat. 60°39'04.5" S, Long. 045°36'12" W; Map 2).

- Within the Area the operation of aircraft should be carried out, as a minimum requirement, in compliance with the 'Guidelines for the Operation of Aircraft near Concentrations of Birds' contained in Resolution 2 (2004). When conditions require aircraft to fly at lower elevations than recommended in the guidelines, aircraft should maintain the maximum elevation possible and minimise the time taken to transit.

- Use of helicopter smoke grenades is prohibited within the Area unless absolutely necessary for safety. If used, all smoke grenades should be retrieved.

6(iii) Location of structures within and adjacent to the Area

There are no structures present in the Area apart from several cairns marking sites used for topographical survey. The island's summit cairn is located at Lat. 60°39'05" S, Long. 045°36'12" W. A sign notifying the protected status of Lynch Island was erected on a prominent rock outcrop above the recommended landing beach in February 1994, but this was destroyed by strong winds.

Signy Research Station (UK) is 6.4 km south at Factory Cove, Borge Bay, on Signy Island.

6(iv) Location of other protected areas in the vicinity

The nearest protected areas to Lynch Island are North Coronation Island (ASPA No.114) which lies about 5 km to the north, Moe Island (ASPA No. 109) which is about 10 km SSW, and Southern Powell Island and adjacent islands (ASPA No. 111) which is about 35 km to the east (Map 1).

6(v) Special zones within the Area

None.

7. Permit conditions

7(i) General permit conditions

Entry into the Area is prohibited except in accordance with a Permit issued by an appropriate national authority as designated under Article 7 of Annex V of the Protocol on Environmental Protection to the Antarctic Treaty.

Conditions for issuing a Permit to enter the Area are that:

- it is issued for a compelling scientific purpose which cannot be served elsewhere; or
- it is issued for essential management purposes such as inspection, maintenance or review;
- the actions permitted will not jeopardise the natural ecological system in the Area;
- any management activities are in support of the objectives of this Management Plan;
- the actions permitted are in accordance with this Management Plan;
- the Permit, or an authorised copy, must be carried within the Area;
- permits shall be issued for a stated period;
- a report or reports are supplied to the authority or authorities named in the Permit;
- the appropriate authority should be notified of any activities/measures undertaken that were not included in the authorised Permit.

7(ii) Access to, and movement within or over, the Area

- Land vehicles are prohibited within the Area

- Movement within the Area shall be on foot.

- Pilots, helicopter or boat crew, or other people on helicopters or boats, are prohibited from moving on foot beyond the immediate vicinity of their landing site unless specifically authorised by Permit.

- Pedestrian traffic should be kept to the minimum consistent with the objectives of any permitted activities and every reasonable effort should be made to minimise trampling effects, i.e. all movement should be undertaken carefully so as to minimise disturbance to the soil and vegetated surfaces, walking on rocky terrain if practical.

7(iii) Activities which may be conducted in the Area

- Compelling scientific research which cannot be undertaken elsewhere and which will not jeopardize the ecosystem of the Area
- Essential management activities, including monitoring

7(iv) Installation, modification or removal of structures

No new structures are to be erected within the Area, or scientific equipment installed, except for compelling scientific or management reasons and for a pre-established period, as specified in a permit. Installation (including site selection), maintenance, modification or removal of structures and equipment shall be undertaken in a manner that minimises disturbance to the values of the Area. All structures or scientific equipment installed in the Area shall be clearly identified by country, name of the principal investigator and year of installation. All such items should be free of organisms, propagules (e.g. seeds, eggs) and non-sterile soil (see Section *7(vi)*), and be made of materials that can withstand the environmental conditions and pose minimal risk of contamination of the Area. Removal of specific structures or equipment for which the Permit has expired shall be a condition of the Permit. Permanent structures or installations are prohibited.

7(v) Location of field camps

Camping should be avoided within the Area. However, when absolutely necessary for purposes specified in the Permit, camping is allowed at the designated site at the north-western end of the island (Lat. 60°39'04" S, Long. 045°36'37" W; Map 2).

7(vi) Restrictions on materials and organisms which may be brought into the Area

No living animals, plant material or microorganisms shall be deliberately introduced into the Area. To ensure that the floristic and ecological values of the Area are maintained, special precautions shall be taken against accidentally introducing microbes, invertebrates or plants from other Antarctic sites, including stations, or from regions outside Antarctica. All sampling equipment or markers brought into the Area shall be cleaned or sterilized. To the maximum extent practicable, footwear and other equipment used or brought into the Area (including bags or backpacks) shall be thoroughly cleaned before entering the Area. Further guidance can be found in the *CEP Non-native Species Manual* (Edition 2011) and *COMNAP/SCAR Checklists for supply chain managers of National Antarctic Programmes for the reduction in risk of transfer of non-native species.*

No herbicides or pesticides shall be brought into the Area. Any other chemicals, including radio-nuclides or stable isotopes, which may be introduced for scientific or management purposes specified in the Permit, shall be removed from the Area at or before the conclusion of the activity for which the Permit was granted. Release of radio-nuclides or stable isotopes directly into the environment in a way that renders them unrecoverable should be avoided. Fuel or other chemicals shall not be stored in the Area unless specifically authorised by Permit condition. They shall be stored and handled in a way that minimises the risk of their accidental introduction into the environment. Materials introduced into the Area shall be for a stated period only and shall be removed by the end of that stated period. If release occurs which is likely to compromise the values of the Area, removal is encouraged only where the impact of removal is not likely to be greater than that of leaving the material in situ. The appropriate authority should be notified of anything released and not removed that was not included in the authorised Permit.

7(vii) Taking, or harmful interference with, native flora or fauna

Taking or harmful interference with native flora or fauna is prohibited, except by Permit issued in accordance with Annex II to the Protocol on Environmental Protection to the Antarctic Treaty. Where taking or harmful interference with animals is involved, the *SCAR Code of Conduct for the Use of Animals for Scientific Purposes in Antarctica* should be used as a minimum standard.

7(viii) The collection or removal of materials not brought into the Area by the Permit holder

Collection or removal of anything not brought into the Area by the permit holder shall only be in accordance with a Permit and should be limited to the minimum necessary to meet scientific or management needs.

Permits shall not be granted if there is a reasonable concern that the sampling proposed would take, remove or damage such quantities of soil, native flora or fauna that their distribution or abundance within the Area would be significantly affected.

Other material of human origin likely to compromise the values of the Area which was not brought into the Area by the permit holder or otherwise authorised, may be removed from the Area unless the environmental impact of the removal is likely to be greater than leaving the material in situ; if this is the case the appropriate Authority must be notified and approval obtained.

7(ix) Disposal of waste

As a minimum standard, all waste shall be disposed of in accordance with Annex III to the Protocol on Environmental Protection to the Antarctic Treaty. In addition, all wastes shall be removed from the Area. Liquid human wastes may be disposed of into the sea. Solid human waste should not be disposed of to the sea, but shall be removed from the Area. No solid or liquid human waste shall be disposed of inland.

7(ix) Measures that may be necessary to continue to meet the aims of the Management Plan

- Permits may be granted to enter the Area to carry out scientific research, monitoring and site inspection activities, which may involve the collection of a small number of samples for analysis, to erect or maintain signboards, or to carry out protective measures.

- Any long-term monitoring sites shall be appropriately marked and the markers or signs maintained.

- Scientific activities shall be performed in accordance with *SCAR's environmental code of conduct for terrestrial scientific field research in Antarctica.*

7(xi) Requirements for reports

The principal permit holder for each visit to the Area shall submit a report to the appropriate national authority as soon as practicable, and no later than six months after the visit has been completed. Such reports should include, as appropriate, the information identified in the visit report form contained in the Guide to the Preparation of Management Plans for Antarctic Specially Protected Areas. If appropriate, the national authority should also forward a copy of the visit report to the Party that proposed the Management Plan, to assist in managing the Area and reviewing the Management Plan. Wherever possible, Parties should deposit the original or copies of the original visit reports, in a publicly accessible archive to maintain a record of usage, for the purpose of any review of the Management Plan and in organising the scientific use of the Area.

8. Supporting documentation

Convey, P. 1994. Modelling reproductive effort in sub- and maritime Antarctic mosses. *Oecologica* **100**: 45-53.

Block, W. and Christensen, B. 1985. Terrestrial Enchytraeidae from South Georgia and the Maritime Antarctic. *British Antarctic Survey Bulletin* **69**: 65-70.

Bonner, W.N. and Smith, R.I.L. (Eds) 1985. *Conservation areas in the Antarctic.* SCAR, Cambridge: 73-84.

Bonner, W.N. 1994. Active management of protected areas. In Smith, R.I.L., Walton, D.W.H. and Dingwall, P.R. (Eds) *Developing the Antarctic Protected Area system. Conservation of the Southern Polar Region I.* IUCN, Gland and Cambridge: 73-84.

Booth, R.G., Edwards, M. and Usher, M.B. 1985. Mites of the genus Eupodes (Acari, Prostigmata) from maritime Antarctica: a biometrical and taxonomic study. *Journal of the Zoological Society of London (A)* **207**: 381-406. (samples of Eupodes analysed)

Buryn, R. and Usher, M.B. 1986. A morphometric study of the mite, *Oppia loxolineata*, in the Maritime Antarctic. *British Antarctic Survey Bulletin* **73**: 47-50.

Chalmers, M.O. 1994. Lynch Island fur seal exclosure report 01/01/94. Unpublished British Antarctic Survey report BAS Ref AD6/2H/1993/NT2.

Greene, D.M and Holtom, A. 1971. Studies in *Colobanthus quitensis* (Kunth) Bartl. and *Deschampsia antarctica* Desv.: III. Distribution, habitats and performance in the Antarctic botanical zone. *British Antarctic Survey Bulletin* **26**: 1-29.

Hodgson, D.A. and Johnston, N.M. 1997. Inferring seal populations from lake sediments. *Nature* **387**(1 May).

Hodgson, D.A., Johnston, N.M., Caulkett, A.P., and Jones, V.J. 1998. Palaeolimnology of Antarctic fur seal *Arctocephalus gazella* populations and implications for Antarctic management. *Biological Conservation* **83**(2): 145-54.

Hooker, T.N. 1974. Botanical excursion to Lynch Island, 13/03/74. Unpublished British Antarctic Survey report BAS Ref AD6/2H/1973-74/N12.

Jennings, P.G. 1976. Tardigrada from the Antarctic Peninsula and Scotia Ridge region. *British Antarctic Survey Bulletin* **44**: 77-95.

Shears, J.R. and Richard, K.J. 1994. Marking and inspection survey of Specially Protected Areas in the South Orkney Islands, Antarctica 07/01/94 – 17/02/94. Unpublished British Antarctic Survey report BAS Ref AD6/2H/1993/NT5.

Smith, R.I. Lewis 1972. Vegetation of the South Orkney Islands. *BAS Scientific Report* **68**, British Antarctic Survey, Cambridge.

Smith, R.I. Lewis 1990. Signy Island as a paradigm of environmental change in Antarctic terrestrial ecosystems. In K.R. Kerry and G. Hempel. *Antarctic Ecosystems: ecological change and conservation.* Springer-Verlag, Berlin: 32-50.

Smith, R.I. Lewis 1994. Introduction to the Antarctic Protected Area System. In Smith, R.I.L., Walton, D.W.H. and Dingwall, P.R. (Eds) *Developing the Antarctic Protected Area system. Conservation of the Southern Polar Region I.* IUCN, Gland and Cambridge: 14-26.

Smith, R.I. Lewis 1997. Impact of an increasing fur seal population on Antarctic plant communities: resilience and recovery. In Battaglia, B. Valencia, J. and Walton, D.W.H. *Antarctic communities: species, structure and survival.* Cambridge University Press, Cambridge: 432-36.

Star, J. and Block, W. 1998. Distribution and biogeography of oribatid mites (Acari: Oribatida) in Antarctica, the sub-Antarctic and nearby land areas. *Journal of Natural History* **32**: 861-94.

Usher, M.B. and Edwards, M. 1984. The terrestrial arthropods of the grass sward of Lynch Island, a specially protected area in Antarctica. *Oecologica* **63**: 143-44.

Usher, M.B. and Edwards, M. 1986. A biometrical study of the family Tydeidae (Acari, Prostigmata) in the Maritime Antarctic, with descriptions of three new taxa. *Journal of the Zoological Society of London (A)* **209**: 355-83.

Wynn-Williams, D.D. 1982. The microflora of Lynch Island, a sheltered maritime Antarctic site. *Comité National Française Recherche en Antarctiques* **51**: 538.

Map 1. The location of Lynch Island in relation to the South Orkney Islands and the other protected areas in the region. Inset: the location of the South Orkney Islands in Antarctica.

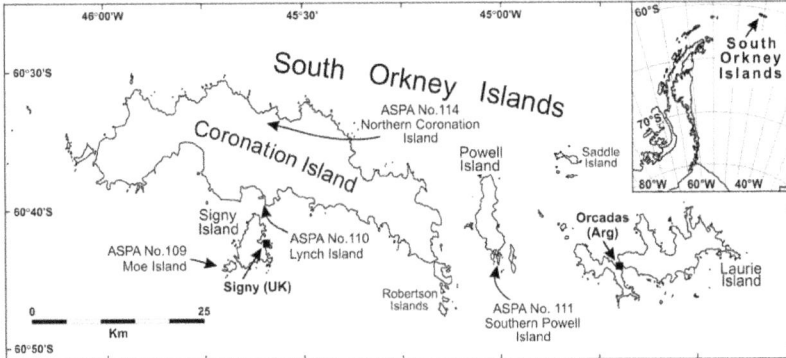

Map 2. ASPA No. 110, Lynch Island, South Orkney Islands, topographic map.

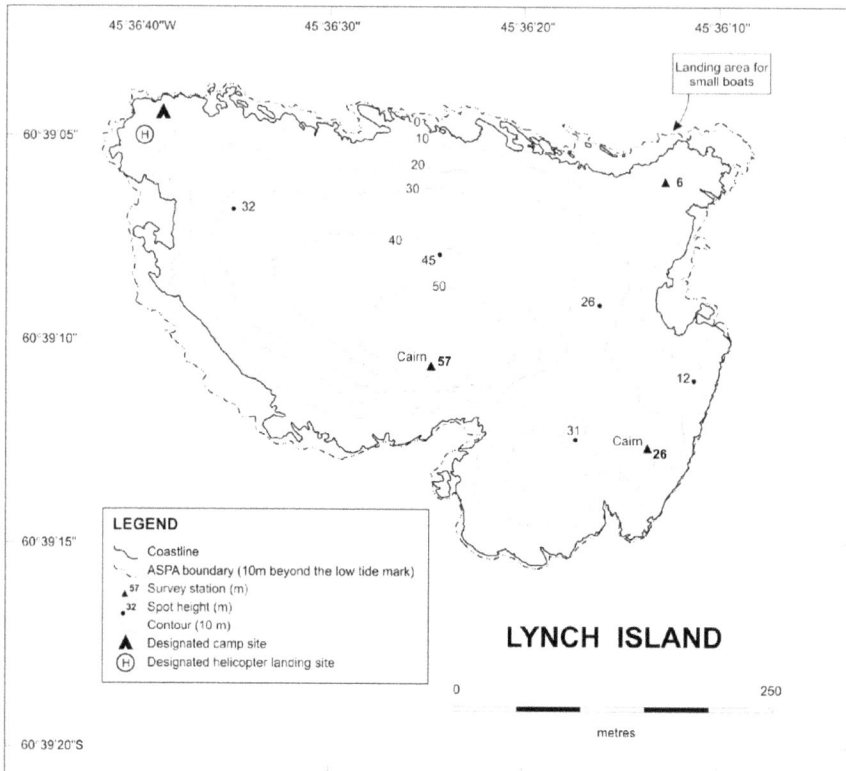

LYNCH ISLAND

LEGEND

- Coastline
- ASPA boundary (10m beyond the low tide mark)
- ▲57 Survey station (m)
- .32 Spot height (m)
- Contour (10 m)
- ▲ Designated camp site
- (H) Designated helicopter landing site

Landing area for small boats

Map 3. ASPA No. 110, Lynch Island, South Orkney Islands, vegetation map.

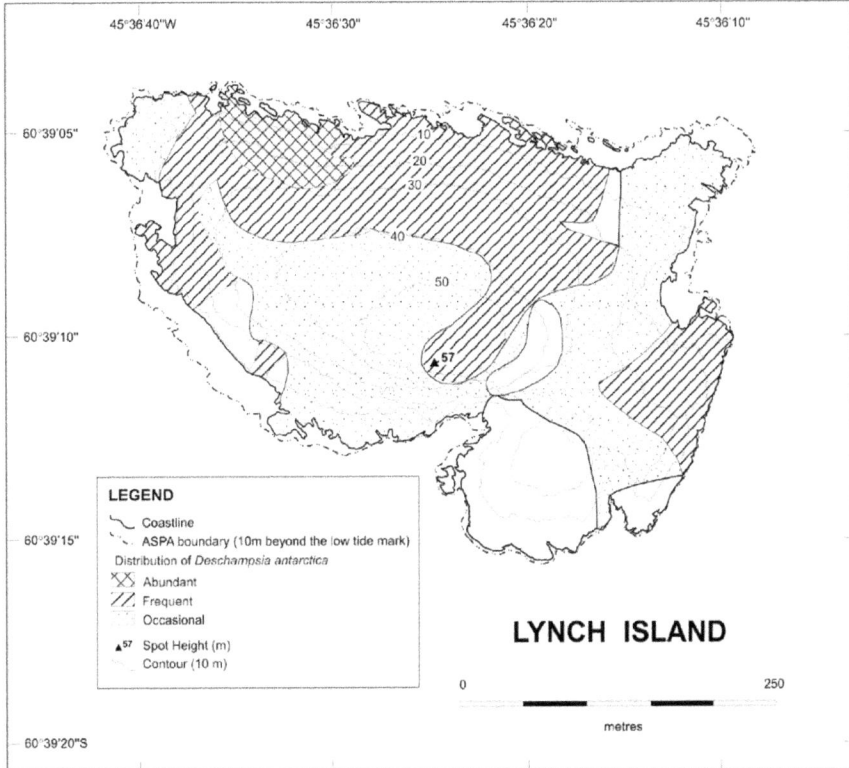

LEGEND

Coastline
ASPA boundary (10m beyond the low tide mark)
Distribution of *Deschampsia antarctica*
Abundant
Frequent
Occasional
▲⁵⁷ Spot Height (m)
Contour (10 m)

LYNCH ISLAND

Management Plan for Antarctic Specially Protected Area No. 111

SOUTHERN POWELL ISLAND AND ADJACENT ISLANDS, SOUTH ORKNEY ISLANDS

Introduction

The primary reason for the designation of Southern Powell Island and Adjacent Islands, South Orkney Islands (Lat. 62°57'S, Long. 60°38'W) as an Antarctic Specially Protected Area (ASPA) is to protect environmental values, predominantly the breeding bird and seal populations, and to a lesser extent, the terrestrial vegetation within the Area.

The Area was originally designated in Recommendation IV-15 (1966, SPA No. 15) after a proposal by the United Kingdom on the grounds that southern Powell Island and the adjacent islands support substantial vegetation and a considerable bird and mammal fauna. The Area was representative of the natural ecology of the South Orkney Islands, and was rendered more important by the nucleus of an expanding colony of Antarctic fur seals (*Arctocephalus gazella*). These grounds are still relevant, though the expansion of the fur seal colony is progressing only slowly.

The Area is also recognised as having scientific value. It is now well established that climate change is affecting the Southern Ocean, and that the region around the Antarctic Peninsula, Scotia Sea and South Orkney Islands is showing some of the most evident impacts of climate change. Air temperatures and ocean temperatures have increased, some ice shelves have collapsed and seasonal sea ice is now much reduced. This has important consequences for biological communities with some of the most obvious consequences of environment change have been reported for pygoscelid penguins. In particular, Adélie penguins, a species of the pack ice, are now though to be declining at most localities along the Peninsula and at the South Orkney Islands. Chinstrap penguins, a species of the more open ocean, are now also thought to be in decline. Consequently, understanding penguin foraging behaviour in an attempt to relate it to their preferred foraging habitat is particularly important. Understanding how pygoscelid penguins utilise the ocean around them is critical if we are to adequately protect their breeding colonies, including in highly biodiverse protected areas such as southern Powell Island.

Resolution 3 (2008) recommended that the "Environmental Domains Analysis for the Antarctic Continent", be used as a dynamic model for the identification of Antarctic Specially Protected Areas within the systematic environmental-geographical framework referred to in Article 3(2) of Annex V of the Protocol (see also Morgan et al., 2007). Using this model, ASPA 111 is contained within Environment Domain G (Antarctic Peninsula off-shore islands geologic). The scarcity of Environment Domain G, relative to the other environmental domain areas, means that substantial efforts have been made to conserve the values found within this environment type elsewhere: other protected areas containing Domain G include ASPAs 109, 112, 114, 125, 126, 128, 140, 145, 149, 150, and 152 and ASMAs 1 and 4. Environment Domain A is also present (Antarctic Peninsula northern geologic). Other protected areas containing Environment Domain A include ASPAs 128, 151 and ASMA 1.

The three other ASPAs present within the South Orkney Islands (ASPA 109 Moe Island, ASPA 110 Lynch Island and ASPA 114 Northern Coronation Island) were designated primarily to protect terrestrial vegetation. Therefore, Southern Powell Island and Adjacent Islands complements the local network of ASPAs by protecting primarily breeding bird and seal populations, but also terrestrial vegetation.

1. Description of values to be protected

Following a visit to the ASPA in February 2012, the values specified in the original designation were reaffirmed and expanded. These values are set out as follows:

- The breeding avifauna within the Area is diverse, including up to four species of penguin [chinstrap (*Pygoscelis antarctica*), gentoo (*P. papua*), Adélie (*P. adeliae*) and macaroni penguins (*Eudyptes chrysolophus*)], Wilson's storm petrels (*Oceanites oceanicus*), cape petrels (*Daption capense*), Dominican gulls (*Larus dominicanus*), southern giant petrels (*Macronectes giganteus*), black-bellied storm petrels (*Fregetta tropica*), blue-eyed cormorants (*Phalacrocorax atriceps*), brown skuas (*Catharacta loennbergi*), sheathbills (*Chionis alba*), snow petrels *(Pagodroma nivea)* and possibly Antarctic prions (*Pachyptila desolata*)

- The longest known breeding site of fur seals in the Antarctic, since their near extermination in the nineteenth century, is found within the Area.

- A diverse flora, typical of the region, including moss banks with underlying peat, moss carpet in wet areas, snow algae and the nitrophilous macroalga *Prasiola crispa* associated with the penguin colonies, is found within the Area.

- The Area has scientific value as a location for the collection of telemetry data in order to explore penguin foraging behaviour. This information will contribute to the development of habitat models that will describe the relationship between penguin foraging behaviour and seasonal sea ice extent.

2. Aims and objectives

Management of southern Powell Island and adjacent islands aims to:

- avoid degradation of, or substantial risk to, the values of the Area by preventing unnecessary human disturbance to the Area;

- allow scientific research in the Area provided it is for compelling reasons which cannot be served elsewhere and which will not jeopardise the natural ecological system in that Area;

- prevent or minimise the introduction to the Area of non-native plants, animals and microorganisms;

- minimise the possibility of introduction of pathogens which may cause disease in bird populations within the Area;

- preserve the natural ecosystem of the Area as a reference area for future comparative studies and for monitoring floristic and ecological change, colonisation processes and community development;

- allow visits for management purposes in support of the aims of the management plan;

- allow for the gathering of data on the population status of the resident penguins and seals on a regular basis and in a sustainable manner

3. Management activities

- Visits shall be made as necessary to assess whether the ASPA continues to serve the purposes for which it was designated and to ensure management and maintenance measures are adequate.

- The Management Plan shall be reviewed at least every five years and updated as required.

- Markers, signs or other structures erected within the Area for scientific or management purposes shall be secured and maintained in good condition and removed when no longer required.

- In accordance with the requirements of Annex III of the Protocol on Environmental Protection to the Antarctic Treaty, abandoned equipment or materials shall be removed to the maximum extent possible provided doing so does not adversely impact on the environment and the values of the Area.

- A copy of this Management Plan shall be made available at Signy Research Station (UK; 60°42′30″ S, 045°36′30″ W) and Orcadas Station (Argentina; 60°44′15″ S, 044°44′20″ W).

- Where appropriate, National Antarctic Programmes are encouraged to liaise closely to ensure management activities are implemented. In particular, National Antarctic Programmes are encouraged to consult with one another to prevent excessive sampling of biological material within the Area. Also, National Antarctic Programmes are encouraged to consider joint implementation of guidelines intended to minimize the introduction and dispersal of non-native species within the Area.

- All scientific and management activities undertaken within the Area should be subject to an Environmental Impact Assessment, in accordance with the requirements of Annex I of the Protocol on Environmental Protection to the Antarctic Treaty.

4. Period of designation

ASPA 111 is designated for an indefinite period.

5. Maps

Map 1. The location of southern Powell Island and adjacent island in relation to the South Orkney Islands and the other protected areas in the region. Inset: the location of the South Orkney Islands in Antarctica. Map specifications: Projection: WGS84 Antarctic Polar Stereographic. Standard parallel: 71 °S. Central meridian 45 °W.

Map 2 shows the Area in greater detail.

6. Description of the Area

6(i) Geographical coordinates and natural features

BOUNDARIES AND CO-ORDINATES
The corner co-ordinates of the Area are shown in Table 1.

Corner	Latitude	Longitude
northwest	60°42'35'' S	45°04'00'' W
northeast	60°42'35'' S	44°58'00'' W
southwest	60°45'30'' S	45°04'00'' W
southeast	60°45'30'' S	44°58'00'' W

The Area includes all of Powell Island south of the southern summit of John Peaks (415 m altitude), together with the whole of Fredriksen Island, Michelsen Island (a tidal peninsula at the southern tip of Powell Island), Christoffersen Island, Grey Island and unnamed adjacent islands. The Area encompasses all of the ice-free ground, permanent ice and semi-permanent ice found within the boundaries, but excludes the marine environment extending greater than 10 m offshore from the low tide water line. All but the Crutchley Ice Piedmont of southern Powell Island are ice-free in summer, though there are patches of semi-permanent or late-lying snow in places.

GEOLOGY

The rocks of southern Powell Island, Michelsen Island and Christoffersen Island are conglomerates of Cretaceous-Jurassic age. The two promontories to the west of John Peaks are Carboniferous greywacke-shales. There are boulders containing plant fossils in the glacial deposits around Falkland Harbour. Much of central and southern Fredriksen Island is composed of sandstone and dark phyllitic shales. The north-east and probably most of the north of this island is highly sheared conglomerate with laminated mudstone. The Area has a thick mantle of glacial till, strongly influenced by seabird guano.

BIOLOGICAL COMMUNITIES

Michelsen Island is almost devoid of land vegetation, although on the rocks there are extensive communities of lichens dominated by nitrophilous crustose species. These are also widespread on Fredriksen Island and elsewhere on bird-influenced cliffs and rocks near the shore. The most diverse vegetation on Powell Island occurs on the two promontories and associated scree west of Falkland Harbour. Here, and on Christoffersen Island and the northern part of Fredriksen Island, moss banks with underlying peat occur. Wet areas support stands of moss carpet. There are extensive areas of the nitrophilous macroalga *Prasiola crispa* associated with the penguin colonies in the area. Snow algae are prominent on the ice piedmont and snow patches in late summer.

No information is available on the arthropod fauna, but this is probably very similar to that at Signy Island. The springtails *Cryptopygus antarcticus* and *Parisotoma octoculata* and the mites *Alaskozetes antarcticus*, *Stereotydeus villosus* and *Gamasellus racovitzai* occur in great numbers beneath stones.

There are few observations on marine invertebrates and biota in the Area, but this is likely to be very similar to the well-researched Signy Island area. The relatively enclosed Falkland-Ellefsen Harbour area and the bay on the east side of the peninsula are highly influenced by glacial run-off from the ice piedmont.

Large numbers of penguins and petrels breed throughout the Area. There are many thousand pairs of chinstrap penguins (*Pygoscelis antarctica*), mostly on Fredriksen Island. Similarly large numbers of Adélie penguins (*P. adeliae*) occur principally on the southern Powell-Michelsen Island area. Here there are also several thousand pairs of gentoo penguins (*P. papua*) and a very few scattered pairs of macaroni penguins (*Eudyptes chrysolophus*) breeding among the gentoos.

Other breeding birds include southern giant petrels (*Macronectes giganteus*), cape petrels *(Daption capensis)*, snow petrels *(Pagodroma nivea)*, Wilson's storm petrels (*Oceanites oceanicus*), blue-eyed shags (*Phalacrocorax atriceps*), Dominican gulls (*Larus dominicanus*), brown skuas (*Catharacia lonnbergi*), sheathbills (*Chionis alba*), and possibly Antarctic prions (*Pachyptila desolata*) and blackbellied storm petrels (*Fregetta tropica*).

Michelsen Island is the longest known breeding site in the Antarctic in fur seals since their near extermination in the nineteenth century. The number of pups born annually has increased slowly but fairly steadily from 11 in 1956 to about 60 in 1989. Thirty-four live pups were recorded in January 1994. Many non-breeding males visit the Area during the summer. Other seals are frequent on the beaches, mainly elephant seals (*Mirounga leonina*) and Weddell seals (*Leptopychotes weddelli*). Leopard seals (*Hydrurga leptonyx*) and crabeater seals (*Lobodon carcinophagus*) are occasionally seen on ice floes.

6(ii) Access to the Area

- Access shall be by small boat.
- There are no special restrictions on boat landings from the sea, or that apply to the sea routes used to move to and from the Area. Due to the large extent of accessible coast around the Area, landing is possible at many locations. Nevertheless, if possible, landing of cargo and scientific equipment should be close to the recommended field camp at 60°43'20''S, 045°01'32''W.
- Under exceptional circumstances necessary for purposes consistent with the objectives of the Management Plan helicopters may be permitted to land at the designated landing site located beside the recommended field camp at 60°43'20''S, 045°01'32''W. Helicopters shall not land elsewhere within the Area.
- To prevent disturbance of breeding avifauna, helicopters landings are prohibited within the Area between the period 1 November to 15 February.
- Within the Area the operation of aircraft should be carried out, as a minimum requirement, in compliance with the 'Guidelines for the Operation of Aircraft near Concentrations of Birds' contained in Resolution 2 (2004). When conditions require aircraft to fly at lower elevations than recommended in the guidelines, aircraft should maintain the maximum elevation possible and minimise the time taken to transit.
- Overflying helicopters should avoid sites where there are concentrations of birds (e.g. southern Powell-Michelsen Island area or Fredriksen Island).
- Use of helicopter smoke grenades is prohibited within the Area unless absolutely necessary for safety. If used all smoke grenades should be retrieved.

6(iii) Location of structures within and adjacent to the Area

Marker boards denoting the Area's protected status are positioned in the following locations:

- Southern Powell Island: on top of a small rock outcrop at the back of the shingle beach on the east side of the southern promontory of the island (60°43'20''S, 045°01'40''W).

- Michelsen Island: on a low-lying rock about 50 m from the shoreline at the back of a high shingle beach at the southern tip of the island (60°44'06''S, 045°01'25''W).

- Christoffersen Island: on a small promontory on the north-eastern shore of the island at the entrance to Falkland Harbour. The board is located at the back of the beach just below a small Adélie penguin rookery (60°43'36''S, 045°02'08''W).

- Fredriksen Island: at the northern end of the pebble boulder beach on the western side of the island, below a small chinstrap penguin rookery. The board is at the back of the beach on top of a small rock outcrop (60°44'06''S, 044°59'25''W).

There are no other structures within the Area, but various mooring chains and rings associated with the use of Ellefsen and Falkland Harbours by floating whale factories in the 1920s are to be found on the shore.

6(iv) Location of other protected areas within close proximity of the Area

ASPA No. 109, Moe Island, and ASPA No. 110, Lynch Island, are located approximately 35 km west of the Area. ASPA No. 114, North Coronation Island, is located around 35 km west-north-west of the Area on the northern side of Coronation Island (see Map 1).

6(v) Restricted zones within the Area

None.

7. Permit Conditions

7(i) General permit conditions

Entry into the Area is prohibited except in accordance with a Permit issued by an appropriate national authority as designated under Article 7 of Annex V of the Protocol on Environmental Protection to the Antarctic Treaty.

Conditions for issuing a Permit to enter the Area are that:

- it is issued for a compelling scientific purpose which cannot be served elsewhere;
- it is issued for essential management purposes such as inspection, maintenance or review;
- the actions permitted will not jeopardise the natural ecological system in the Area;
- any management activities are in support of the objectives of this Management Plan;
- the actions permitted are in accordance with this Management Plan;
- the Permit must be carried within the Area;
- permits shall be issued for a stated period;
- a report or reports are supplied to the authority or authorities named in the Permit;
- the appropriate authority should be notified of any activities/measures undertaken that were not included in the authorised Permit.

7(ii) Access to and movement within or over the Area

- Land vehicles are prohibited in the Area.

- No pedestrian routes are designated within the Area, but persons on foot should avoid walking on vegetated areas or disturbing wildlife wherever possible.

- To reduce disturbance of bird species, anchoring within Falkland Harbour and Ellefsen Harbour is strongly discouraged, except in an emergency.

- Pilots, air and boat crew, or other people on aircraft or boats, are prohibited from moving on foot beyond the immediate vicinity of their landing site unless specifically authorised by Permit.

7(iii) Activities which may be conducted in the Area

Activities include:

- compelling scientific research which cannot be undertaken elsewhere
- essential management activities, including monitoring.

7(iv) Installation, modification or removal of structures

No new structures are to be erected within the Area, or scientific equipment installed, except for compelling scientific or management reasons and for a pre-established period, as specified in a permit. Installation (including site selection), maintenance, modification or removal of structures and equipment shall be undertaken in a manner that minimises disturbance to the values of the Area. All structures or scientific equipment installed in the Area shall be clearly identified by country, name of the principal investigator and year of installation. All such items should be free of organisms, propagules (e.g. seeds, eggs) and non-sterile soil (see Section *7(vi)*), and be made of materials that can withstand the environmental conditions and pose minimal risk of contamination of the Area. Removal of specific structures or equipment for which the Permit has expired shall be a condition of the Permit. Permanent structures or installations are prohibited.

7(v) Location of field camps

In order to minimise the area of ground within the ASPA impacted by camping activities, tents should be erected at the designated field campsite, located at 60°43'20''S, 045°01'32''W. When necessary for purposes specified in the Permit, temporary camping beyond the designated field campsite is allowed within the Area. Camps should be located on non-vegetated sites, such as on the drier parts of the raised beaches, or on thick (>0.5 m) snow-cover when practicable, and should avoid concentrations of breeding birds or mammals.

7(vi) Restrictions on materials and organisms which may be brought into the Area

No living animals, plant material or microorganisms shall be deliberately introduced into the Area. To ensure that the floristic and ecological values of the Area are maintained, special precautions shall be taken against accidentally introducing microbes, invertebrates or plants from other Antarctic sites, including stations, or from regions outside Antarctica. All sampling equipment or markers brought into the Area shall be cleaned or sterilized. To the maximum extent practicable, footwear and other equipment used or brought into the Area (including bags or backpacks) shall be thoroughly cleaned before entering the Area. Further guidance can be found in the CEP Non-native Species Manual (Edition 2011) and COMNAP/SCAR Checklists for supply chain managers of National Antarctic Programmes for the reduction in risk of transfer of non-native species. In view of the presence of breeding bird colonies within the Area, no poultry products, including wastes from such products and products containing uncooked dried eggs, shall be released into the Area or into the adjacent sea.

No herbicides or pesticides shall be brought into the Area. Any other chemicals, including radio-nuclides or stable isotopes, which may be introduced for scientific or management purposes specified in the Permit, shall be removed from the Area at or before the conclusion of the activity for which the Permit was granted. Release of radio-nuclides or stable isotopes directly into the environment in a way that renders them unrecoverable should be avoided. Fuel or other chemicals shall not be stored in the Area unless specifically authorised by Permit condition. They shall be stored and handled in a way that minimises the risk of their accidental introduction into the environment. Materials introduced into the Area shall be for a stated period only and shall be removed by the end of that stated period. If release occurs which is likely to compromise the values of the Area, removal is encouraged only where the impact of removal is not likely to be greater than that of leaving the material in situ. The appropriate authority should be notified of anything released and not removed that was not included in the authorised Permit.

7(vii) Taking or harmful interference with native flora and fauna

Taking of or harmful interference with native flora or fauna is prohibited, except by Permit issued in accordance with Annex II to the Protocol on Environmental Protection to the Antarctic Treaty. Where taking of or harmful interference with animals is involved, the *SCAR Code of Conduct for the Use of Animals for Scientific Purposes in Antarctica* should be used as a minimum standard.

7(viii) Collection and removal of materials not brought into the Area by the Permit holder

Collection or removal of anything not brought into the Area by the permit holder shall only be in accordance with a Permit and should be limited to the minimum necessary to meet scientific or management needs.

Other material of human origin likely to compromise the values of the Area which was not brought into the Area by the permit holder or otherwise authorised, may be removed from the Area unless the environmental impact of the removal is likely to be greater than leaving the material in situ; if this is the case the appropriate Authority must be notified and approval obtained.

7(ix) Disposal of waste

As a minimum standard, all waste shall be disposed of in accordance with Annex III to the Protocol on Environmental Protection to the Antarctic Treaty. In addition, all wastes shall be removed from the Area. Liquid human wastes may be disposed of into the sea. Solid human waste should not be disposed of to the sea, but shall be removed from the Area. No solid or liquid human waste shall be disposed of inland.

7(ix) Measures that may be necessary to ensure that the aims and objectives of the Management Plan continue to be met

- Permits may be granted to enter the Area to carry out scientific research, monitoring and site inspection activities, which may involve the collection of a small number of samples for analysis, to erect or maintain signboards, or to carry out protective measures.

- Any long-term monitoring sites shall be appropriately marked and the markers or signs maintained.

- Scientific activities shall be performed in accordance with *SCAR's environmental code of conduct for terrestrial scientific field research in Antarctica.*

7(xi) Requirements for reports

The principal permit holder for each visit to the Area shall submit a report to the appropriate national authority as soon as practicable, and no later than six months after the visit has been completed. Such reports should include, as appropriate, the information identified in the visit report form contained in the Guide to the Preparation of Management Plans for Antarctic Specially Protected Areas. If appropriate, the national authority should also forward a copy of the visit report to the Party that proposed the Management Plan, to assist in managing the Area and reviewing the Management Plan. Wherever possible, Parties should deposit the original or copies of the original visit reports, in a publicly accessible archive to maintain a record of usage, for the purpose of any review of the Management Plan and in organising the scientific use of the Area.

8. Supporting documentation

Cantrill, D. J. 2000. A new macroflora from the South Orkney Islands, Antarctica: evidence of an Early to Middle Jurassic age for the Powell Island Conglomerate. Antarctic Science 12: 185-195.

Harris, C. M., Carr, R., Lorenz, K. and Jones, S. 2011. Important Bird Areas in Antarctica: Antarctic Peninsula, South Shetland Islands, South Orkney Islands – Final Report. Prepared for BirdLife International and the Polar Regions Unit of the UK Foreign & Commonwealth Office. Environmental Research & Assessment Ltd., Cambridge. Available at: http://www.birdlife.org/datazone/userfiles/file/IBAs/AntPDFs/IBA_Antarctic_Peninsula.pdf

Holmes, K. D. 1965. *Interim geological report on Matthews and Powell islands.* British Antarctic Survey AD6/2H/1965/G2. 2pp

Longton, R.E. 1967. Vegetation in the maritime Antarctic. In Smith, J.E., *Editor,* A discussion of the terrestrial Antarctic ecosystem. *Philosophical Transactions of the Royal Society of London,* B, **252**, 213-235.

Morgan, F., Barker, G., Briggs, C., Price, R. and Keys, H. 2007. *Environmental Domains of Antarctica Version 2.0 Final Report.* Manaaki Whenua Landcare Research New Zealand Ltd, 89 pp.

Ochyra, R., Bednarek-Ochyra, H. and Smith, R.I.L. *The Moss Flora of Antarctica.* 2008. Cambridge University Press, Cambridge. 704 pp.

Øvstedal, D.O. and Smith, R.I.L. 2001. *Lichens of Antarctica and South Georgia. A Guide to their Identification and Ecology.* Cambridge University Press, Cambridge, 411 pp.

Peat, H., Clarke, A., and Convey, P. 2007. Diversity and biogeography of the Antarctic flora. *Journal of Biogeography,* 34, 132-146.

Poncet, S., and Poncet, J. 1985. A survey of penguin breeding populations at the South Orkney Islands. *British Antarctic Survey Bulletin,* No. 68, 71-81.

Smith, R. I. L. 1972. *British Antarctic Survey science report 68.* British Antarctic Survey, Cambridge, 124 pp.

Smith, R. I. L. 1984. Terrestrial plant biology of the sub-Antarctic and Antarctic. In: *Antarctic Ecology,* Vol. 1. Editor: R. M. Laws. London, Academic Press.

Thomson, J. W. 1973. The geology of Powell, Christoffersen and Michelsen islands, South Orkney Islands. *British Antarctic Survey Bulletin,* Nos. 33 & 34, 137-167.

Thomson, M. R. A. 1981. Late Mesozoic stratigraphy and invertebrate palaeontology of the South Orkney Islands. *British Antarctic Survey Bulletin,* No. 54, 65-83.

Map 1. The location of Southern Powell Island and adjacent island in relation to the South Orkney Islands and the other protected areas in the region. Inset: the location of the South Orkney Islands in Antarctica.

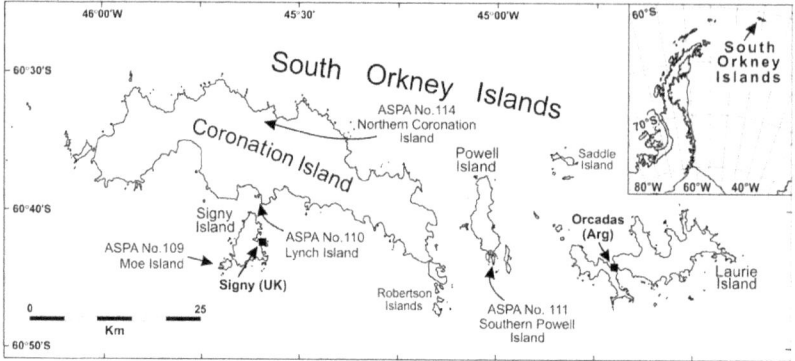

Map 2. Southern Powell Island and adjacent islands Antarctic Specially Protected Area No. 111.

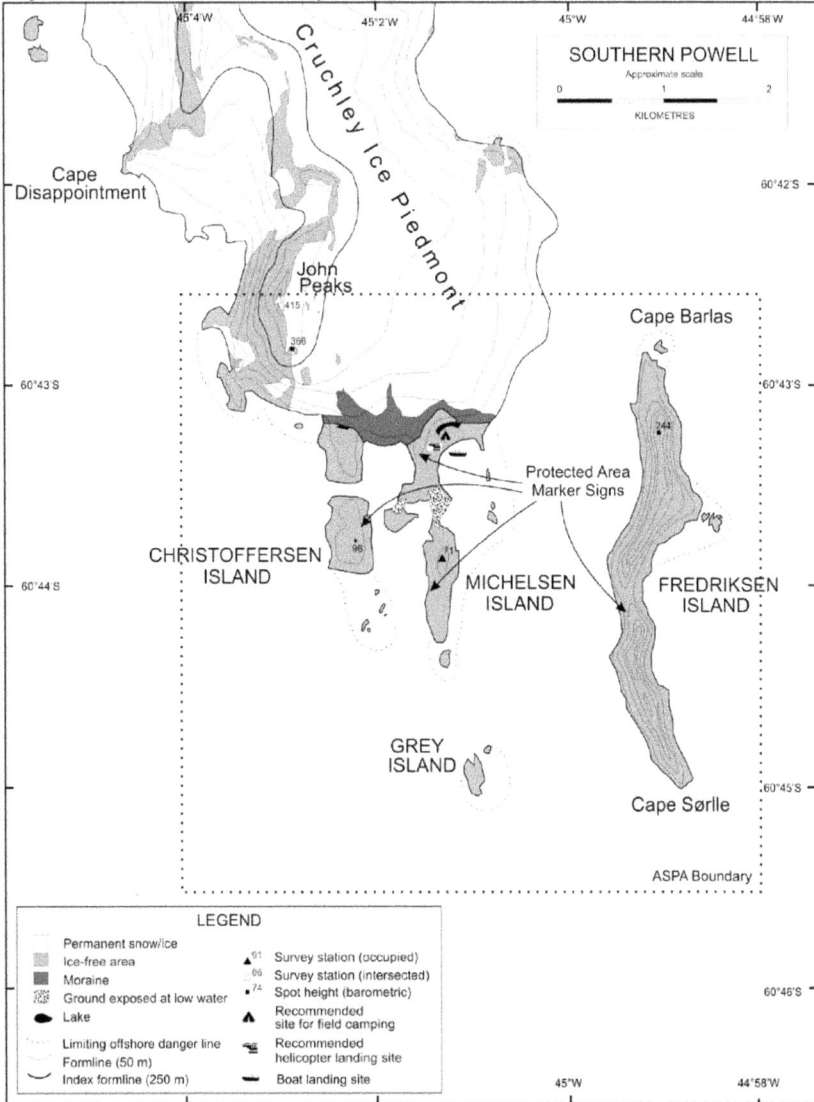

SOUTHERN POWELL
Approximate scale
0   1   2
KILOMETRES

Cape Disappointment

Cruchley Ice Piedmont

John Peaks

Cape Barlas

Protected Area Marker Signs

CHRISTOFFERSEN ISLAND

MICHELSEN ISLAND

FREDRIKSEN ISLAND

GREY ISLAND

Cape Sørlle

ASPA Boundary

LEGEND

Permanent snow/ice
Ice-free area
Moraine
Ground exposed at low water
Lake

Limiting offshore danger line
Formline (50 m)
Index formline (250 m)

▲ 91 Survey station (occupied)
06   Survey station (intersected)
▪ 74 Spot height (barometric)
▲   Recommended site for field camping
      Recommended helicopter landing site
—   Boat landing site

Management Plan for
Antarctic Specially Protected Area No. 112

COPPERMINE PENINSULA, ROBERT ISLAND
SOUTH SHETLAND ISLANDS

Introduction

Coppermine Peninsula (62°24'S; 59°30'W) is located in the north western coast of Robert Island, South Shetland Islands, in front of the English Strait. The Area was designated as Specially Protected Area SPA No. 16 through Recommendation VI-10 (1970). The first Management Plan was approved by Recommendation XVI-6 (1991). In accordance with Decision 1 (2002), the Area came to be called Antarctic Specially Protected Area No. 112.

The Area is mainly protected due to its significant terrestrial ecosystem, with the presence of large Antarctic flora and fauna colonies, which are of special interest for scientific research.

1. Description of values to be protected

Coppermine Peninsula is a biologically rich area with a diverse biota typical of the South Shetland Islands. It supports a wide range of plant communities with associated invertebrate fauna; the vertebrate fauna is also particularly well represented.

Much of the higher ground is permanently ice-covered. There are numerous small streams and pools in summer.

The principal value of the Area is the vegetation, which is characterised by a vast moss carpet, together with hepatic, lichen and algæ species. One of the Antarctic vascular plant species is also present in the Area. The Area is also renowned for the presence of bird colonies nesting here, mainly the giant petrel, *Macronectes giganteus.*

Scientific studies have been developed in the Area in order to know the composition of its biological communities, and identify the impacts that may affect them.

2. Aims and objectives

Management at Coppermine Peninsula aims to:

- Protect the terrestrial ecosystem and the community of birds that breed in the Area;
- Avoid degradation or substantial risk to the values of the Area by preventing unnecessary human disturbance;
- Avoid major changes in the structure and composition of the flora and fauna communities;
- Allow scientific research in the terrestrial environment, while ensuring protection from over-sampling;
- Allow for the development of other scientific research in the Area, provided they do no compromise the values for which the Area has been protected; and
- Allow visits for management purposes in support of the aims of this Management Plan.

3. Management Activities

The following management activities are to be undertaken to protect the values of the Area:

- The staff authorised to access the Area shall be specifically instructed on the conditions of this Management Plan.
- Approach distances to fauna must be respected, except when the scientific projects may require otherwise and this is specified in the relevant permits.
- Collection of samples will be limited to the minimum required for the development of authorised scientific research plans.
- Wherever possible, cloths, shoes and equipment shall be sanitised before visiting the Area, in order to avoid the introduction of microorganisms.
- Signs may be placed (markers, boards or other information structures) in places that do not disturb the values protected or the development of research, either for scientific, management or dissemination purposes, which shall be maintained in good condition.
- The signs or structures to be installed in the Area for scientific or management purposes shall be maintained in good condition.
- The equipment and materials to be installed in the Area shall be removed when no longer required.
- The entry of any type of vehicles to the Area is strictly prohibited.
- Visits shall be made as necessary to assess whether the Area continues to serve the purposes for which it was designated and to ensure management measures are adequate.

4. Period of designation.

The Area is designated for an indefinite period.

5. Maps

Map 1: Part of South Shetland Islands, showing the location of Nelson, Robert and Greenwich Islands, as well as the Antarctic Specially Protected Areas located there, including ASPA No. 112, Coppermine Peninsula.

Map 2: Coppermine Peninsula, Robert Island. ASPA No. 112 is marked in grey. Based on the Chart of the Hydrographical Institute of the Chilean Army (Instituto Hidrográfico de la Armada de Chile), English Strait and Lautaro Channel, scale 1:40,000.

6. Description of the Area

6(i) Geographical co-ordinates, boundary markers and natural features

GENERAL DESCRIPTION

Coppermine Peninsula (62°24'S; 59°30'W) is located at the northwestern end of Robert Island. It covers an elongated strip (2 km long by 500 m wide), from the isthmus connecting Robert Island to Cape Fort Williams. It has an irregular relief, with average heights of 30 to 40 masl, and many protrusions reaching over 80 masl, such as the basaltic columns of Neptune's Cathedral and the snout near the facilities at Luis Risopatrón Base (Chile).

The peninsula features Late Cretaceous volcanic rocks, mainly formed by basaltic lavas and olivine, of a prominent cindery red colour at interfaces. The articulated columns at Fort Williams and Neptune's Cathedral are intrusions from the Pliocene or recent periods.

Soil formation through plant decomposition and humus deposit is slow and scarce, but the accumulation of organic matter can reach 85 cm locally. Low-ground soils resemble moss carpets, usually 3 to 10 cm deep.

The topography and weather conditions of the Area favour various types of habitats for plant communities, which are strongly influenced by the marine aerosols.

BOUNDARIES

The Coppermine Peninsula extends from Cape Morris to Triplet Hill, separating Carlota and Coppermine Coves. This peninsula is the westernmost area of Robert Island and ends in the western tip in Fort Williams, a cape with striking features, such as Morris Rock, located in the coastal area. This peninsula represents one of the earlier stages of the Late Cenozoic volcanism of the region.

The peninsula is connected to Robert Island through a terrace-shaped isthmus featuring marine gravel, about 10 m above sea level, and 250 m wide. The isthmus is interrupted to the east by a small horseshoe-shaped hill. At the south-eastern end of Coppermine Cape, the Triplet Hill emerges, with a height of 140 m.

FLORA

The main value of the Area is its vegetation, which is characterised by a vast moss carpet covering around 1.5 ha, representing one of the most important bryophyte communities in Antarctica. The moistest areas of the peninsula are dominated by *Calliergidium austrostramineum* and *Calliergon sarmentosum,* which is merged in the interior of *Drepanocladus uncinatus,* where drainage is higher. In the dryer marginal areas, *Polytrichumalpinum, Bryum algens, Psoroma cinnamomeum, Sphaerophorus globosus, Ceratidon* sp., and *Usnea* sp., together with other lichens, are associated with *Drepanocladus.* In moist slopes near the summit, moss peats have developed with moist peats of about 85 cm wide. Areas with moist ash soils in valley soils and troughs represent vast communities of foliose lichens. Coastal rocks are frequently covered in lichens, mainly *Caloplaca* sp., *Haematomma erythromma, Physcia caesia, Ramalia tenebrata* and *Usnea* sp., which are occasionally associated with moss.

The *Prasiola crispa* alga is present in areas influenced by bird colonies, and the bluish green alga *Nostoc commune* can also be found in some areas. The *Clammydomonas nivalis* and *Scottiella Antarctica* algae can be found in the areas covered by snow, and give a characteristic reddish colour to the ice.

Deschampsia antarctica is frequently located in the sheltered slopes of the peninsula.

Table 1 shows plant species identified in the Area:

Table 1. Plant species present in Coppermine Peninsula, Robert Island.

Vascular plants		
Deschampsia antarctica		
Mosses		
Andreaea depressinervis	*Caratodon* cf. *grossiretis*	*Polytrichum piliferum*
Andreaea gainii	*Caratodon* cf. *purpureus*	*Pottia austro-georgica*
Andreaea regularis	*Chorisodontium aciphyllum*	*Schistidium (=Grimmia) antarcticum*

Bartramia patens	*Dicranoweisia grimmiaceae*	*Tortula* cf. *conferta*
Brachythecium austro-salebrosum	*Drepanocladus uncinatus*	*Tortula excelsa*
Bryum algens	*Pohlia cruda* var. *imbricata*	*Tortula fusco-viridis*
Calliergidium austro-stramineum	*Pohlia nutans*	*Tortula grossiretis*
Calliergon sarmentosum	*Polytrichum alpinum*	

Hepatic	**Algae**
Barbilophozia hatcheri	*Nostoc commune*
Cephaloziella varians	*Prasiola crispa*

Lichens		
Buellia sp.	*Haematomma erythromma*	*Ramalia terebrata*
Caloplaca regalis	*Lecania brialmontii*	*Rinodina* sp.
Caloplaca sp.	*Lecanora* sp.	*Sphaerophorus globosus*
Candelariella vitellina	*Leptogium puberulum*	*Stereocaulon glabrum*
Cladonia balfourii	*Mastodia tesselata*	*Umbilicaria antarctica*
Cladonia cf. *carneola*	*Ochrolechia frigida*	*Usnea aurantiaco-atra* (forma postrada)
Cladonia furcata	*Physcia caesia*	*Usnea fasciata*
Cladonia sp.	*Psoroma hypnorum*	*Xanthoria candelaria*
Cornicularia epiphorella	*Psoroma* cf. *cinnamomea*	*Xanthoria elegans*

FAUNA

Vegetation present in the Area favours habitats for terrestrial invertebrate communities. Coppermine Peninsula habitats include Collembola, mites, nematodes, rotifers, tardigrades and a variety of protozoa. The main specimen in this group is the Collembola *Cryptopygus antarcticus,* usually associated with moss carpets.

The Coppermine Peninsula hosts various seabird colonies, either breeding or resting. Breeding colonies include giant petrels *Macronectes giganteus,* Wilson's storm petrels, *Oceanites oceanicus,* Antarctic terns, *Sterna vittata,* kelp gulls, *Larus dominicuanus,* and brown skuas, *Stercorarius (Catharacta) lonnbergi.*

The Area is also visited by seals and fur seals, which rest on the beaches.

Table 2. Fauna present in Coppermine Peninsula, Robert Island.

Vertebrates
Flying birds

Scientific name	Common name
Macronectes giganteus	Giant petrel
Daption capense	Cape petrel
Oceanites oceanicus	Wilson's storm-petrel
Phalacrocorax bransfieldensis	Antarctic shag
Larus dominicanus	Dominican gull
Sterna vittata	Antarctic tern
Stercorarius (Catharacta) antarcticus	Antarctic skua
Chionis albus	Seathbill

Swimming birds	
Scientific name	**Common name**
Pygoscelis antarctica	Antarctic or chinstrap penguins
Pygoscelis papua	Gentoo penguins
Pygoscelis adeliae	Adélie penguin

Pinnipeds	
Scientific name	**Common name**
Mirounga leonina	Southern elephant seal
Leptonychotes weddelli	Weddell seals
Hydrurga leptonyx	Leopard seals
Arctocephalus gazella	Antractic fur seal

6(ii) Access to the Area

The Area can only be accessed by sea, landing on the Carlota Cove or Coppermine Cove beaches, only in front of the facilities at Luis Risopatrón scientific station (Chile).

Access by air is only permitted by helicopter and in cases of emergency, landing to the east of the isthmus, on Robert Island, outside the Area.

6(iii) Location of structures within and adjacent to the Area

The Luis Risopatrón scientific station (Chile) is located about 100 m west of the Area, in Coppermine Peninsula. The scientific station stands 40 m above sea level, on solid rock surface, located 150 m from the coastal line. It has 5 modules used for accommodation, laboratories and storage areas. The station operates in the austral summer and can currently host 5 people.

6(iv) Location of other Protected Areas within close proximity

The following Protected Areas are located in the vicinity of the Coppermine Peninsula:

- ASPA No. 133, Point Harmony, Nelson Island, 30 km northwest.
- ASPA No. 144, Chile Bay (Discover Bay), Greenwich Island, about 12 km to the south.

6(v) Special zones within the Area

None.

7. Permit conditions

7(i) General conditions

Access to the Area is prohibited except in accordance with a permit issued by an appropriate national authority. Conditions for issuing a Permit to enter the Area are that:

- The permit is issued for essential scientific or management purposes, consistent with the objectives of the plan, such as inspections, maintenance or review tasks, which cannot be served elsewhere;
- The actions permitted will not jeopardise the ecological and scientific values of the Area;
- Any management activity are in support of the objectives of the Management Plan;
- Actions permitted are in accordance with this Management Plan;
- Scientific staff present in the Area carries the Permit or an authorised copy thereof during the specified period; and
- At the end of the period, a report is submitted before the relevant national authority mentioned in the Permit, making reference to any undertaken activity not expressly mentioned in the Permit.

7(ii) Access to and movement within or over the Area

The Area can only be accessed by sea, landing on the Carlota Cove or Coppermine Cove beaches, in front of the Luis Risopatrón scientific station (Chile).

Movement within the Area shall be on foot.

Vehicle access

Access to the Area by any type of vehicles is prohibited.

Overflights

Due to the presence of seabirds breeding on the island, the landing of aircrafts within the Area is prohibited. Access by air is permitted by helicopter and in case of emergency, landing outside Area, to the east of the isthmus. In addition, any overflight operations shall comply with the guidelines established in Resolution 2 (2004), *Guidelines for the Operation of Aircraft near Concentrations of Birds.*

7(iii) Activities which may be conducted in the Area

- Scientific research that will not jeopardise the ecosystem or scientific values of the Area, or affect in any way the value of the Area as a reference site.
- Essential management activities, including monitoring.

7(iv) Installation, modification or removal of structures

- No structures are to be erected within the Area except as specified in a Permit. Permanent structures or installations are prohibited.

- All structures, scientific equipment or markers installed in the Area must be authorised by a permit for a definite period and clearly identified by country, name of the principal investigator and year of installation. All such items should be made of materials that pose minimal risk of contamination to the Area.
- The installation (including site selection), maintenance, modification or removal of structures must be performed in a way that produces minimal disturbance to the flora and fauna present.
- The authority issuing the original permit shall be in charge of removing the specific equipment which permit is overdue, this being a condition for the permit to be granted.

7(v) Location of field camps

Camping in the Area is prohibited. The Luis Risopatrón scientific station offers accommodation to researchers, subject to prior arrangement with the Chilean Antarctic Program.

Tents will be allowed for the sole purpose of storing scientific instruments or equipment, or to be used as an observation post, and shall be removed upon conclusion of the activity.

If camping in the Coppermine Peninsula is absolutely necessary, the tents shall be located near Risopatrón Station. No other locations shall be used for this purpose, in order to restrict the human impact.

7(vi) Restrictions on materials and organisms that may be brought into the Area

- No alien living animals, plants or microbes may be deliberately introduced into the Area, and precautions shall be taken to avoid their accidental introduction. Whenever possible, all clothes, shoes and equipment must be thoroughly inspected and cleaned before entering the Area.
- To ensure that the fauna, flora and ecological values of the Area are preserved, special precautions shall be taken by visitors against accidentally introducing microorganisms or invertebrates from other Antarctic sites or from regions outside Antarctica. All sampling equipment and markers brought into to the Area shall be cleaned or sterilised before use in the Area, to the extent possible.
- In order to protect the avifauna of the island, no poultry meat or derived products may be introduced into the Area for consumption by researchers.
- No herbicides or pesticides shall be brought into the Area. Any other chemicals, including radio-nuclides or stable isotopes, which may be introduced for scientific or management purposes specified in the Permit, shall be removed from the Area at or before the conclusion of the activity for which the Permit was granted.
- All materials introduced into the Area shall remain there only for the period stated in the Permit, shall be removed at or before the conclusion of the stated period, and shall be handled so that the risk of introduction into the environment is minimised.
- If release occurs which may affect the values of the Area, removal is encouraged only where the impact of removal is not likely to be greater than that of leaving the material *in situ.*

7(vii) Taking of, or harmful interference with, native flora and fauna

Taking of or harmful interference with native flora or fauna is prohibited, except under a Permit issued in accordance with Article 3 of Annex II to the Protocol on Environmental Protection to the Antarctic Treaty, by a relevant national authority.

Where taking of or harmful interference with animals is involved, the *SCAR Code of Conduct for the Use of Animals for Scientific Purposes in Antarctica* should be used as a minimum standard.

7(viii) Collection or removal of materials not brought into the Area by the Permit holder

- Material may be collected or removed from the Area only in accordance with a Permit, and should be limited to the minimum necessary to meet scientific or management needs. Permits shall not be granted if there is reasonable concern that the sampling proposed would take, remove or damage such quantities of soil, sediment, flora or fauna that their distribution or abundance within the Area would be significantly affected.
- Material of human origin likely to compromise the values of the Area, and which was not brought into the Area by the Permit holder or otherwise authorised, may be removed unless the impact of removal is likely to be greater than leaving the material *in situ*; if this is the case, the appropriate authority should be notified.

7 (ix) Disposal of waste

All wastes shall be removed from the Area. However, organic human waste can be released into the sea in accordance with article 5, Annex III of the Protocol on Environmental Protection to the Antarctic Treaty.

Waste generated as a consequence of the activities performed in the Area must be temporarily stored near the scientific station, so as to avoid accidental releases. Such waste shall be adequately labelled as litter. Upon conclusion of the activity, it shall be removed from the Area and from the Antarctic Treaty Area.

7(x) Measures that may be necessary to ensure that the aims and objects of the Management Plan continue to be met

Permits may be granted to enter the Area to carry out biological monitoring and site inspection activities, which may involve the collection of limited samples for analysis or review, or to adopt protective measures.

Whenever possible, all sites where long-term monitoring activities are carried out, which are vulnerable to involuntary disturbance, shall be duly marked on the site and Area maps.

7(xi) Requirements for reports

Parties should ensure that the principal holder for each permit issued submits to the appropriate authority a report of the activities undertaken, no later than six months after the visit. Such reports should include, as appropriate, the information identified in the Visit Report form contained in Appendix 2 of Resolution 2 (2011).

Parties should maintain a record of such activities and, in the Annual Exchange of Information, should provide summary descriptions of activities conducted by persons subject to their jurisdiction, which should offer sufficient detail to allow for the evaluation of the effectiveness of the Management Plan. Parties should, wherever possible, deposit originals or copies of such original reports in a publicly accessible archive, to be used both for review of the management plan and in organizing the scientific use of the Area.

The relevant authority shall be informed of any activity undertaken, any measure taken or material released and not removed which are not covered by a permit.

8. Supporting documentation

Bustamante, R., I. Serey y G. Guzmán. 1987. Importancia de península Coppermine (isla Robert) para el desarrollo de un programa de investigación en ecología terrestre. Bol. Antárt. Chileno 7 (2): 5-8.

Bustamante, R., I. Serey y G. Guzmán. 1989. Mortalidad de musgos y distribución de *Usnea aurantiaco-atra*: ¿Efectos alelopáticos?. Ser. Cient. INACH 39: 69-73.

Casanova-Katny, M.A., G.E. Zúñiga, L.J. Corcuera, L. Bravo y M. Alberdi. 2010. *Deschampsia antarctica* Desv. primary photochemistry performs differently in plants grown in the field and laboratory. Polar Biol. 33 (4): 477-483.

Casaretto, J.A., L.J. Corcuera, I. Serey y G.E. Zúñiga. 1994. Size structure of tussocks of a population of *Deschampsia antarctica* Desv. in Robert Island, maritime Antarctica. Ser. Cient. INACH 44: 61-66.

Cuba, M., A. Gutiérrez-Moraga, B. Butendieck y M. Gidekel. 2005. Micropropagation of *Deschampsia antarctica* – a frost-resistant Antarctic plant. Antarctic Science 17 (1): 69-70.

Etchegaray, J., F. Sáiz y E.R. Hajek. 1977. Análisis de las relaciones entre mesofauna antártica y algunos factores climáticos. Ser. Cient. INACH 5 (1): 35-44.

Machado., A., F. Chemale Jr., R.V. Conceição, K. Kawaskita, D. Morata, O. Oteíza y W.R. Van Schmus. 2005. Modeling of subduction components in the genesis of the Meso-Cenozoic igneous rocks from the South Shetland Arc, Antarctica. Lithos 82: 435-453.

Orrego, C. y C. Campusano. 1970. Investigaciones ecológicas en isla Robert (Shetland del Sur). Instituto Antártico Chileno, Boletín No 5: 40-41.

Orrego, C. y C. Campusano. 1971. Temperaturas de nidificación de aves de isla Robert (Shetland del Sur). Ser. Cient. INACH 2 (1): 51-63.

Pefaur, J.E. y R. Murúa. 1972. Estudios Ecológicos en Isla Robert (Shetland del Sur). 7. Aves de la península de isla Robert. Ser. Cient. INACH 2 (2): 11-23.

Sáiz, F. y E.R. Hajek. 1967. Estudios Ecológicos en Isla Robert (Shetland del Sur). 1. Observaciones de temperatura en nidos de petrel gigante. Publicación INACH. 15 pp

Schlatter, R., W. Hermosilla y F. Di Castri. 1968. Estudios Ecológicos en Isla Robert (Shetland del Sur). 2. Distribución altitudinal de los artrópodos terrestres. Publicación INACH. 26 pp.

Schlatter, R., W. Hermosilla, F. Di Castri y R. Covarrubias. 1970. Estudios Ecológicos en Isla Robert (Shetland del Sur). Efecto de filtros microclimáticos sobre la densidad de artrópodos muscícolas en la Antártica. Instituto Antártico Chileno, Boletín No 5: 11-16.

Serrano, E. y J. López-Martínez.1997. Geomorfología de la península Coppermine. Ser. Cient. INACH 47: 19-29.

Torres-Mellado, G.A., R. Jaña y M.A. Casanova-Katny.2011. Antarctic hairgrass expansion in the South Shetland archipelago and Antarctic Peninsula revisited. Polar Biol. 34 (11): 1679-1688.

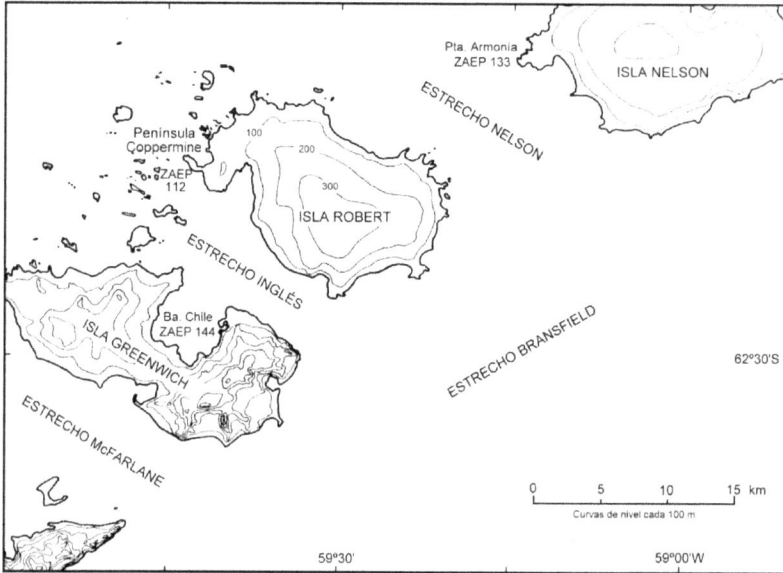

Map 1: Part of the South Shetland Islands, showing the location of Nelson, Robert and Greenwich Islands, as well as the Antarctic Specially Protected Areas located there, including ASPA No. 112, Coppermine Peninsula.

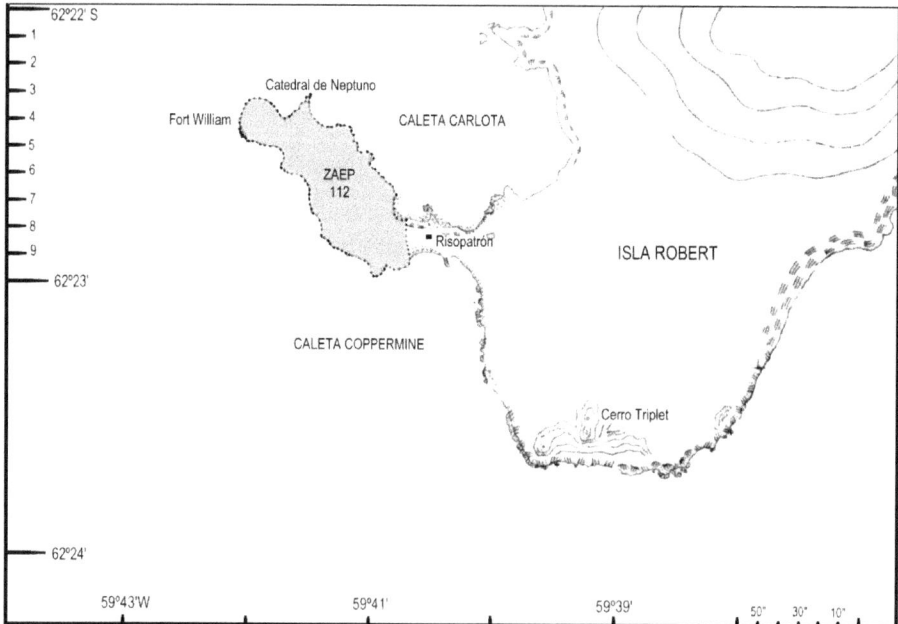

Map 2: Coppermine Peninsula, Robert Island ASPA No. 112 is shown in grey.
Based on the Chart of the Hydrographical Institute of the Chilean Army. English Strait and Lautaro
Channel, scale 1:40,000.

Map 1. Part of South Shetland Islands, showing the location of Nelson, Robert and Greenwich Islands, as well as the Antarctic Specially Protected Areas located there, including ASPA No. 112, Coppermine Peninsula.

Español	English	Français	Русский
Isla Nelson	Nelson Island	Île Nelson	Остров Нельсон
Punta Armonía, ZAEP 133	Harmony Point, ASPA133	Pointe Harmony, ZSPA133	Мыс гармония, ООРА 133
Estrecho Nelson	Nelson Strait	Détroit Nelson	Пролив Нельсон
Isla Robert	Robert Island	Île Robert	Остров Роберт
Península Coppermine, ZAEP 112	Coppermine Peninsula, ASPA 112	PéninsuleCoppermine, ZSPA 112	Полуостров Коппермайн, ООРА 112
Estrecho Inglés	English Strait	Détroit anglais	Английский пролив
Bahía Chile, ZAEP 144	Chile Bay, ASPA 144	Baie Chile, ZSPA 144	Залив Чили, ООРА 144
Isla Greenwich	Greennwich Island	Île Greennwich	Остров Гринвич
Estrecho McFarlane	McFarlane Strait	Détroit McFarlane	Пролив МакФарлейн
Estrecho Bransfield	Bransfield Strait	Détroit Bransfield	Пролив Брансфилд
Curvas de nivel cada 100 m	Level contours each 100 m	Courbes de niveau tous les 100 m	Горизонтали проведены через каждые 100 м.

Map 2: Coppermine Peninsula, Robert Island ASPA No. 112 is shown in grey.
Based on the Chart of the Hydrographical Institute of the Chilean Army. English Strait and Lautaro Channel, scale 1:40,000.

Español	English	Français	Русский
Isla Robert	Robert Island	Île Robert	Остров Роберт
Caleta Carlota	Carlota Cove	Anse Carlota	Бухта Карлота
Caleta Coppermine	Coppermine Cove	Anse Coppermine	Бухта Коппермайн
Catedral de Neptuno	Neptune´s Cathedral	Cathédrale de Neptune	Храм Нептуна
Fort William	Fort William	Fort William	Мыс Форт-Вильям
ZAEP 112	ASPA 112	ZSPA 112	ООРА 112
Risopatrón	Risopatron	Risopatron	Станция «Ризопатрон»
Cerro Triplet	Triplet Hill	Colline Triplet	Тройной холм

Management Plan for Antarctic Specially Protected Area No. 115

LAGOTELLERIE ISLAND, MARGUERITE BAY, GRAHAM LAND

Introduction

The primary reason for the designation of Lagotellerie Island, Marguerite Bay, Graham Land (Latitude 67°53'20" S, Longitude 67°25'30" W; area 1.58 km²) as an Antarctic Specially Protected Area (ASPA) is to protect environmental values, and primarily the terrestrial flora and fauna but also the avifauna within the Area.

Lagotellerie Island is approximately 2 km by 1.3 km, oriented generally in an east-west direction. The Area is 11 km south of Porquois Pas Island and 3.25 km west of the south end of Horseshoe Island. Lagotellerie Island was first mapped by Jean-Baptiste Charcot during the Deuxième Expédition Antarctiques Française in 1908-10. There are no records of further visits until the 1940s, when the island was visited occasionally by American, Argentine and British field parties from nearby scientific stations. The island has not been the subject of any major scientific investigations and is thus largely undisturbed by human activities.

Lagotellerie Island was originally designated as a Specially Protected Area through Recommendation XIII-II (1985, SPA No. 19) after a proposal by the United Kingdom. It was designated on the grounds that the island contains a rich and diverse flora and fauna typical of the southern Antarctic Peninsula region. These values were reiterated in Recommendation XVI-6 (1991) when a management plan for the site was adopted, and are largely reaffirmed again in the present management plan.

Resolution 3 (2008) recommended that the Environmental Domains Analysis for the Antarctic Continent, be used as a dynamic model for the identification of Antarctic Specially Protected Areas within the systematic environmental-geographical framework referred to in Article 3(2) of Annex V of the Protocol (see also Morgan et al., 2007). Using this model, ASPA 115 is contained within Environment Domain B (Antarctic Peninsula mid-northern latitudes geologic). Other protected areas containing Domain B include ASPAs 108, 134, 140 and 153 and ASMAs 4.

The three other ASPAs are present within the Marguerite Bay area (ASPA 107 Emperor Island, Dion Islands, ASPA 117 Avian Island and ASPA 129 Rothera Point). ASPA 107 Emperor Island and ASPA 117 Avian Island were designated to protect predominantly the avifauna of the area, while ASPA 129 Rothera Point was designated to monitor the impact of the nearby station on an Antarctic fellfield ecosystem. Therefore, Lagotellerie Island complements the local network of ASPAs by primarily protecting terrestrial biological communities.

1. Description of values to be protected

Following a visit to the ASPA in February 2011, the values specified in the earlier designation were reaffirmed. These values are set out as follows:

- Lagotellerie Island contains a relatively diverse flora typical of the southern Antarctic Peninsula region. Of particular interest is the abundance of the only two Antarctic flowering plants *Deschampsia antarctica* and *Colobanthus quitensis* which form stands up to 10 m². These are amongst the largest stands known south of the South Shetland Islands, being only 90 km north of their southern limit. Both species flower profusely and the seeds have a greater viability than those produced in the South Orkney or South Shetland Islands.

- Numerous mosses and lichens form well-developed communities on the island. A few of the mosses are fertile, which is a rare phenomenon in most Antarctic localities.

- The island is notable for the occurrence of *Deschampsia antarctica* at the highest recorded altitude south of 56° S, with scattered small plants observed at heights of up to 275 m. The island therefore has a particular future scientific value for study of the influence of altitudinal gradient on biological viability for plant species represented at this site.

- The invertebrate fauna is rich and the island is one of the southernmost sites for the apterous midge *Belgica antarctica*

- The shallow loamy soil developed beneath the vegetation and its associated invertebrate fauna and microbiota are probably unique at this latitude

- There is a colony of c. 1850 Adélie penguins (*Pygoscelis adeliae*) and one of the farthest south colonies of a few dozen blue-eyed cormorants (*Phalacrocorax atriceps*) at the south-east corner of the island. Numerous pairs of brown and south polar skuas (*Catharacta lonnbergii* and *C. maccormicki*) breed on the island.

- The values associated with the penguin and skua colonies are now considered to be their ecological interrelationship with the other biological features of exceptional value noted above.

- Fossiliferous strata present at the eastern end of the island are of particular geological value, as such formations are not commonly exposed in the Antarctic Peninsula Volcanic Group.

- The island has not been subject to frequent visits, scientific research or sampling and therefore may be regarded as one of the most pristine highly vegetated areas in the region.

2. Aims and objectives

Management at Lagotellerie Island aims to:

- avoid degradation of, or substantial risk to, the values of the Area by preventing unnecessary human disturbance to the Area;

- allow scientific research in the Area provided it is for compelling reasons which cannot be served elsewhere which will not jeopardise the natural ecological system in that Area;

- allow visits for management purposes in support of the aims of the management plan;

- prevent or minimise the introduction to the Area of non-native plants, animals and microorganisms;

- minimise the possibility of introduction of pathogens which may cause disease in bird populations within the Area;

- preserve the natural ecosystem of the Area as a reference area for future studies.

3. Management activities

The following management activities are to be undertaken to protect the values of the Area:

- Visits shall be made as necessary to assess whether the ASPA continues to serve the purposes for which it was designated and to ensure management and maintenance measures are adequate.

- The Management Plan shall be reviewed at least every five years and updated as required.

- Markers, signs or other structures erected within the Area for scientific or management purposes shall be secured and maintained in good condition and removed when no longer required.

- In accordance with the requirements of Annex III of the Protocol on Environmental Protection to the Antarctic Treaty, abandoned equipment or materials shall be removed to the maximum extent possible provided doing so does not adversely impact on the environment and the values of the Area.

- A copy of this Management Plan shall be made available at Rothera Research Station (UK; Latitude 67°34' S, Longitude 68°07' W) and General San Martín Station (Argentina; Latitude 68°08' S, Longitude 67°06' W).

- All scientific and management activities undertaken within the Area should be subject to an Environmental Impact Assessment, in accordance with the requirements of Annex I of the Protocol on Environmental Protection to the Antarctic Treaty.

4. Period of designation

The ASPA is designated for an indefinite period.

5. Maps

Map 1. Lagotellerie Island Antarctic Specially Protected Area No. 115, Marguerite Bay, location map, showing the location of General San Martín Station (Arg.), the station Teniente Luis Carvajal (Chile), Adelaide Island, Rothera Research Station (UK) and nearby ASPA 129 at Rothera Point, also on Adelaide Island, and the location of the other protected areas in the region [Emperor Island, Dion Islands (ASPA 107) and Avian Island (ASPA 117)]. 'Base Y' (UK) (Historic Monument No. 63) on Horseshoe Island is shown. Inset: the location of Lagotellerie Island along the Antarctic Peninsula.

Map 2. Lagotellerie Island (ASPA 115) topographic map. Map specifications: Projection: Lambert Conformal Conic. Standard parallels: 1st 63° 20' 00" S; 2nd 76° 40' 00"S. Central Meridian: 65° 00' 00" W. Latitude of Origin: 70° 00' 00" S. Spheroid: WGS84. Datum: Mean Sea Level. Vertical contour interval 20 m. Horizontal and vertical accuracy expected to be better than ±5 m.

Map 3. Lagotellerie Island (ASPA 115) geological sketch map.

6. Description of the Area

6(i) Geographical coordinates and natural features

BOUNDARIES AND CO-ORDINATES
The corner co-ordinates of the Area are shown in Table 1.

Corner	Latitude	Longitude
northwest	67°52'30'' S	67°27'00'' W
northeast	67°52'30'' S	67°22'00'' W
southwest	67°54'00'' S	67°27'00'' W
southeast	67°54'00'' S	67°22'00'' W

The Area includes all of Lagotellerie Island and unnamed adjacent islands and islets. The Area encompasses all of the ice-free ground, permanent ice and semi-permanent ice found within the boundaries, but excludes the marine environment extending greater than 10 m offshore from the low tide water line (Map 2). Boundary markers have not been installed because the coast itself is a clearly defined and visually obvious boundary.

Lagotellerie Island is steep-sided and rocky, with about 13% permanent ice cover, most of which is on the southern slopes. The island rises to twin peaks of 268 m and 288 m separated by a broad saddle at around 200 m, with precipitous cliffs up to this height on the south, west and east sides. The upper northern slopes also have steep cliffs, intersected by gullies, screes and traversed by broad rock terraces. The lower northern slopes are more gentle, particularly on the eastern half of the island, with a broad rocky terrace at an elevation of about 15 m which is formed of frost-shattered raised beach debris.

GEOLOGY

The bulk of Lagotellerie Island is formed of quartz diorite of unknown age, cut by pink, coarse-grained granodiorite and numerous basic and felsic dykes (Map 3). At the eastern end of the island the plutonic rocks are in fault contact with folded, mildly hornfelsed volcanic rocks of Jurassic–Cretaceous age. These consist of agglomerates, andesitic lavas and tuffs of the Antarctic Peninsula Volcanic Group, with plant remains – probably Jurassic – present in shaly beds interbedded with tuff. Such fossiliferous strata are not commonly exposed in the Antarctic Peninsula Volcanic Group, and are therefore of particular geological importance.

Locally extensive areas of coarse sand and gravel derived from weathered quartz-diorite occur on slopes, ledges, gullies and depressions; the most extensive accumulations are on the saddle between the two summits where the soil is sorted into well-developed stone polygons, circles and stripes. On the broad rock terraces closed stands of moss and grass have developed a relatively rich loamy earth up to 25 cm in depth. Glacial erratics are common on the island.

TERRESTRIAL BIOLOGICAL COMMUNITIES

The island has a relatively diverse flora and luxuriant development of plant communities, representative of the southern maritime Antarctic region. The rich terrestrial biology of Lagotellerie Island was first noted by Herwil Bryant, biologist at East Base (US, on Stonington Island; now Historic Monument No. 55), during a visit in 1940-41 when he observed growths of moss, the Antarctic hair grass *Deschampsia antarctica* and "a small flowering plant" (almost certainly the Antarctic pearlwort *Colobanthus quitensis*), in a small gully – believed to be that found at the north-eastern end of the island – which he considered of such unusual richness for the region that he unofficially referred to it as "Shangri-la Valley". He did not describe the less luxuriant but more extensive communities of *Deschampsia antarctica* and *Colobanthus quitensis* found on the higher north-facing slopes of the island. These slopes and terraces also provide favourable microclimatic conditions for growth, with a relatively long snow-free growing season, and support an abundance of *Deschampsia antarctica* and *Colobanthus quitensis*, the grass forming closed swards of up to 10 m² on some of the terraces. These are among the largest stands of these plants known south of the South Shetland Islands. Both species flower abundantly and the seeds have a greater viability than those produced in the South Orkney or South Shetland Islands, yet they are close to the southern limit of their range. Lagotellerie Island, however, is notable for the growth of *Deschampsia antarctica* at the highest altitude recorded south of 56° S, with scattered small plants observed at heights of up to 275 m. *Colobanthus quitensis* has been observed growing up to 120 m on the island.

Lagotellerie Island also has a rich cryptogamic flora, with small stands of well-developed communities containing several mosses and lichens which are rare at this latitude (notably the mosses *Platydictya jungermannioides* and *Polytrichastrum alpinum*, and lichens *Caloplaca isidioclada*, *Fuscoparmelia gerlachei* and *Usnea trachycarpa*). The number of bryophyte species thus far identified include 20 mosses and two liverworts (*Barbilophozia hatcheri* and *Cephaloziella varians*), and there are at least 60 lichen species. A comprehensive floristic survey of the island has not yet been undertaken, and numerous species, especially of crustose lichens, remain to be accurately determined.

Vegetation is best developed on a series of rock terraces at around 30-50 m a.s.l. on the northern side of the island. Here, both *Deschampsia* and *Colobanthus* are abundant, and closed grass swards form stands of several square metres. Associated with these, especially on the moister terraces, are usually the mosses *Brachythecium austro-salebrosum*, *Bryum* spp., *Pohlia nutans*, *Polytrichastrum alpinum* and *Sanionia uncinata*, and liverworts *Barbilophozia hatcheri* and *Cephaloziella varians*. Many of these grass swards are used as nest sites by skuas.

In drier habitats, especially on scree and rock faces, there are locally dense stands dominated by the macrolichens *Usnea sphacelata* and *U. subantarctica*, with *Pseudephebe minuscula*, *Umbilicaria decussata*, and a large number of crustose taxa. Several lichens are associated with the grass and moss communities (e.g. *Cladonia* spp., *Leproloma* spp., *Leptogium puberulum*, *Ochrolechia frigida*, *Psoroma* spp.). Near the penguin and cormorant colonies several colourful nitrophilous lichens are abundant (e.g. *Buellia* spp., *Caloplaca* spp., *Fuscoparmelia gerlachei*, *Xanthoria* spp.).

Numerous lichens (notably *Caloplaca isidioclada*, *Pseudephebe minuscula*, *Usnea sphacelata*, *Umbilicaria decussata* and many crustose taxa) and a few mosses (notably *Grimmia refelxidens*) occur close to the summit of the island, as do scattered individual plants of *Deschampsia*. Few bryophytes produce sporophytes at far southern latitudes, but several mosses are fertile on Lagotellerie Island (e.g. *Andreaea regularis*, *Bartramia patens*, *Bryum amblyodon*, *B. pseudotriquetrum*, *Grimmia reflexidens*, *Hennediella heimii*, *Pohlia nutans*, *Schistidium antarctici*, *Syntrichia princeps*).

Specific studies of the invertebrate fauna have not been conducted on Lagotellerie Island. However, at least six species of arthropod have been recorded: *Alaskozetes antarcticus*, *Gamasellus racovitzai*, *Globoppia loxolineata* (Acari), *Cryptopygus antarcticus*, *Friesea grisea* (Collembola), and *Belgica antarctica* (Diptera, Chironomidae). Several species of nematophagous fungi have been isolated from the soils associated with mosses and *Deschampsia* on Lagotellerie Island (*Cephalosporium balanoides*, *Dactylaria gracilis*, *Dactylella ellipsospora*), species widely distributed in similar habitats throughout the Antarctic and also commonly found in temperate soils.

Bryant reported several small pools present on the island in the early 1940s, which presumably are the same as, or close to, those observed more recently on the extensive flat low-lying ground on the northern side of the island. He recorded the pools contained many phyllopod crustaceans identified as *Branchinecta granulosa*. Rocks in one of the pools were coated in a bright green filamentous alga, on which the mites *Alaskozetes antarcticus* were observed. *A. antarcticus* was also common under pebbles on the pool floor. Other microorganisms of the trochelminth type were observed living in the algae, with a pink rotifer identified as *Philodina gregaria* being especially numerous. Small tufts of a grey-green alga were observed on large pebbles close to the pool bottom. The algae have not been described in more detail, although the presence of *Prasiola crispa* has been noted. More recent observations in the early 1980s suggested there were no permanent freshwater bodies on the island, but temporary runnels in summer were found, with some brackish pools in rock depressions near the northern coast. Inspection visit January 1989 and February 2011 noted the presence of several small melt pools of around 5-10 m^2, some with fringing wet moss carpets, and suggested these were probably the habitat of *Belgica antarctica*.

VERTEBRATE FAUNA

A small Adélie penguin (*Pygoscelis adeliae*) colony occupies the eastern promontory of the island (Map 2). Numbers have varied from a low of perhaps 350-400 pairs based on an estimate made in December 1936 to a high of 2402 pairs recorded in an accurate nest count in November 1955. A count of the colony made on 19 February 2011 noted approximately 1850 adult and juvenile birds (accurate to within 10%). The colony was regularly used as a source of eggs for personnel stationed at the nearby British Base Y on Horseshoe Island between 1955-60. It was reported that some 800 eggs were taken during 1955. The number of breeding pairs dropped to around 1000 in 1959 and 1960. Adélie penguin colonies are known to exhibit high interannual change in numbers as a result of a variety of natural factors, and in March 1981 it was observed that all of the approximately 1000 chicks in the colony had died. A chick count made in February 1983 suggested the colony consisted of approximately 1700 pairs, which is considered accurate to within 15-25%.

A small colony of blue-eyed cormorants (*Phalacrocorax atriceps*) has been observed on the eastern promontory of the island, which is one of the most southerly breeding sites reported for the species. Some 200 immature birds were observed close to the island, within view of the colony, on 16 January 1956. The colony was reported to consist of 10 nests on 17 February 1983. The colony was not seen in the January 1989 inspection on Lagotellerie Island; however, in February 2011, c. 250 adults and chicks were observed and with many nest containing two large chicks.

Brown and south polar skuas (*Catharacta loenbergi* and *C. maccormicki*) are also present, with 12 nests reported in 1956, when it was noted that many of the chicks were definitely south polar skua (*C. maccormicki*). It was estimated in 1958 that five pairs nested around the penguin colony and that both species occurred. A group of 59 non-breeding birds of both species was recorded on 12 January 1989 mid-way along the northern side of the island. Two Wilson's storm petrel (*Oceanites oceanicus*) nests were recorded on 14 January 1956. A kelp gull (*Larus dominicanus*) nest, with eggs, was recorded in the 'Shangri-La Valley' by Bryant in December 1940.

The inspection visit in January 1989 reported 12 Weddell seals (*Leptonychotes weddellii*) hauled out on a small shingle beach at the base of a rocky spit on the north coast, but no other seals were seen. In contrast, the inspection visit of February 2011 noted c. 200 fur seals on northern side of the island and within the Adélie penguins colony (particular to the south of the colony above the pebble beaches). Twenty Weddell seals were also observed.

HUMAN IMPACT

The most significant environmental impact at Lagotellerie Island appears to have been from the practice of egg harvesting to feed personnel at bases operating nearby in the period 1955-60. The inspection visit of February 2011 reported there was no evidence of any recent physical or biological change on the island and it was concluded that the Area was continuing to serve the purpose for which it was designated.

6(ii) Access to the Area

- Access to the Area shall be by boat. Access from the sea should be to the northern coast of the island (Map 2), unless specifically authorised by Permit to land elsewhere or when landing along this coast is impractical because of adverse conditions. The coastline is generally rocky and recommended landing sites are located on the north coast at Lat. 67°52'57'' Long. 067°24'03'' and Lat. 67°53'04'' Long. 067°23'30'' (see Map 2).

- Access to the Area is not permitted 100 m either side of the gulley on the northeast coast at Lat. 67°53'10'' Long. 067°23'13'' (i.e. the coast below the valley unofficially referred to as "Shangri-la Valley" by Bryant; see Map 2). The valley inland of this coastline contains the richest vegetation growth on the island, and to reduce trampling impacts, non-essential activity within this area is discouraged (Map 2). These restrictions apply equally to persons wishing to access the Area via sea ice in the winter.

- Under exceptional circumstances necessary for purposes consistent with the objectives of the Management Plan helicopters may be permitted to land at the designated landing site located beside the recommended field camp on the broad rock/permanent snow platform about half-way along the northwest coast at about 15 m altitude, and 200 m inland from the sea (Lat. 67°53'04'' Long. 067°23'43''). Helicopters shall not land elsewhere within the Area unless specifically authorized by Permit.

- Within the Area the operation of aircraft should be carried out, as a minimum requirement, in compliance with the 'Guidelines for the Operation of Aircraft near Concentrations of Birds' contained in Resolution 2 (2004). When conditions require aircraft to fly at lower elevations than recommended in the guidelines, aircraft should maintain the maximum elevation possible and minimise the time taken to transit.
- Overflight of the eastern end of the island over the penguin/cormorant colony is prohibited below 610 m (2000 feet) (Map 2).
- Use of helicopter smoke grenades is prohibited within the Area unless absolutely necessary for safety. If used all smoke grenades should be retrieved.

6(iii) Location of structures within and adjacent to the Area

A cairn and the remains of a mast erected for survey purposes in the 1960s are present on the summit of the island. During the inspection visit in February 2011, some of the cabling and the remains of black survey flag associated with the mast were removed. The five 8-10 m long bamboo posts, from which the original mast was constructed, were collected together and secured along with six metal stakes near the eastern summit of the island (288 m).

A cairn (c. 1 m high) is present on the north coast of the island (Lat. 67°53'16'' Long. 067°22'51'') and a 30 cm high pile of stones containing a short wooden post with a 2.5 cm diameter metal disc at one end inscribed with the number '10' is present on cliffs west of the penguin colony (Lat. 67°53'17'' Long. 067°22'46''). No other structures are known to exist on the island.

Two year-round scientific research stations operate in the vicinity: General San Martín (Argentina; Lat. 68°08' S, Long. 67°06' W) which is 29.5 km south-southeast, and Rothera Research Station (UK; Lat. 67°34' S, Long. 68°07' W) which is 46 km to the northwest. A summer-only station, Teniente Luis Carvajal (Lat. 67°46' S, Long. 68°55' W), has been operated by Chile at the southern end of Adelaide Island since 1985.

6(iv) Location of other protected areas in the vicinity

The nearest protected areas to Lagotellerie Island are Emperor Island, Dion Islands (ASPA 107) about 55 km west, Avian Island (ASPA 117) 65 km west and Rothera Point (ASPA 129) 46 km to the northwest (Map 1). Several Historic Sites and Monuments are located in the vicinity: 'Base Y' (UK) on Horseshoe Island (HSM No. 63); 'Base E' (UK) (HSM No. 64) and buildings and artefacts at and near East Base (US) (HSM No. 55), both on Stonington Island; and installations of San Martín Station (Argentina) at Barry Island (HSM No. 26).

6(v) Special zone within the Area
None.

7. Permit conditions

7(i) General permit conditions

Entry into the Area is prohibited except in accordance with a Permit issued by an appropriate national authority as designated under Article 7 of Annex V of the Protocol on Environmental Protection to the Antarctic Treaty.

Conditions for issuing a Permit to enter the Area are that:

- it is issued for a compelling scientific purpose which cannot be served elsewhere;
- it is issued for essential management purposes such as inspection, maintenance or review;
- the actions permitted will not jeopardise the natural ecological system in the Area;
- any management activities are in support of the objectives of this Management Plan;
- the actions permitted are in accordance with this Management Plan;
- the Permit must be carried within the Area;
- permits shall be issued for a stated period;
- a report or reports are supplied to the authority or authorities named in the Permit;
- the appropriate authority should be notified of any activities/measures undertaken that were not included in the authorised Permit.

7(ii) Access to and movement within over the Area

- Vehicles are prohibited within the Area

- Movement within the Area shall be on foot.

- Pilots, helicopter or boat crew, or other people on helicopters or boats, are prohibited from moving on foot beyond the immediate vicinity of their landing site unless specifically authorised by Permit.

- Pedestrian traffic should be kept to the minimum consistent with the objectives of any permitted activities and every reasonable effort should be made to minimise trampling effects, i.e. all movement should be undertaken carefully so as to minimise disturbance to the soil and vegetated surfaces, walking on rocky terrain if practical.

7(iii) Activities which may be conducted in the Area

- Scientific research that will not jeopardise the ecosystem or scientific values of the Area and which cannot be served elsewhere;

- Essential management activities, including monitoring.

7(iv) Installation, modification or removal of structures

No new structures are to be erected within the Area, or scientific equipment installed, except for compelling scientific or management reasons and for a pre-established period, as specified in a permit. Installation (including site selection), maintenance, modification or removal of structures and equipment shall be undertaken in a manner that minimises disturbance to the values of the Area. All structures or scientific equipment installed in the Area shall be clearly identified by country, name of the principal investigator and year of installation. All such items should be free of organisms, propagules (e.g. seeds, eggs) and non-sterile soil, and be made of materials that can withstand the environmental conditions and pose minimal risk of contamination of the Area (see Section *7(vi)*). Removal of specific structures or equipment for which the Permit has expired shall be a condition of the Permit. Permanent structures or installations are prohibited.

7(v) Location of field camps

When necessary for purposes specified in the Permit, temporary camping is allowed at the designated site on the broad rock/permanent snow platform about half-way along the northwest coast at about 15 m altitude, and 200 m inland from the sea (Lat. 67°53'04'' Long. 067°23'43'';
Map 2).

7(vi) Restrictions on materials and organisms which can be brought into the Area

No living animals, plant material or microorganisms shall be deliberately introduced into the Area. To ensure that the floristic and ecological values of the Area are maintained, special precautions shall be taken against accidentally introducing microbes, invertebrates or plants from other Antarctic sites, including stations, or from regions outside Antarctica. All sampling equipment or markers brought into the Area shall be cleaned or sterilized. To the maximum extent practicable, footwear and other equipment used or brought into the Area (including bags or backpacks) shall be thoroughly cleaned before entering the Area. Further guidance can be found in the CEP Non-native Species Manual (Edition 2011) and COMNAP/SCAR Checklists for supply chain managers of National Antarctic Programmes for the reduction in risk of transfer of non-native species. In view of the presence of breeding bird colonies within the Area, no poultry products, including wastes from such products and products containing uncooked dried eggs, shall be released into the Area or into the adjacent sea.

No herbicides or pesticides shall be brought into the Area. Any other chemicals, including radio-nuclides or stable isotopes, which may be introduced for scientific or management purposes specified in the Permit, shall be removed from the Area at or before the conclusion of the activity for which the Permit was granted. Release of radio-nuclides or stable isotopes directly into the environment in a way that renders them unrecoverable should be avoided. Fuel or other chemicals shall not be stored in the Area unless specifically authorised by Permit condition. They shall be stored and handled in a way that minimises the risk of their accidental introduction into the environment. Materials introduced into the Area shall be for a stated period only and shall be removed by the end of that stated period. If release occurs which is likely to compromise the values of the Area, removal is encouraged only where the impact of removal is not likely to be greater than that of leaving the material in situ. The appropriate authority should be notified of anything released and not removed that was not included in the authorised Permit.

7(vii) Taking or harmful interference with native flora or fauna

Taking or harmful interference with native flora or fauna is prohibited, except by Permit issued in accordance with Annex II to the Protocol on Environmental Protection to the Antarctic Treaty. Where taking or harmful interference with animals is involved, the *SCAR Code of Conduct for the Use of Animals for Scientific Purposes in Antarctica* should be used as a minimum standard.

To prevent human disturbance of the breeding cormorant colony and in particular the premature fledging of juvenile cormorants, visitors shall not approach within 10 m of the cormorant colony on the eastern tip of the island between 15 October and 28 February, unless authorised by Permit for specific scientific or management purposes.

7(viii) Collection and removal of materials not brought into the Area by the Permit holder

Collection or removal of anything not brought into the Area by the Permit holder shall only be in accordance with a Permit and should be limited to the minimum necessary to meet scientific or management needs. Permits shall not be granted in instances where it is proposed to take, remove or damage such quantities of soil, native flora or fauna that their distribution or abundance on Lagotellerie Island would be significantly affected. Anything of human origin likely to compromise the values of the Area, which was not brought into the Area by the Permit Holder or otherwise authorised, may be removed unless the impact of removal is likely to be greater than leaving the material *in situ*: if this is the case the appropriate authority should be notified.

7(ix) Disposal of waste

As a minimum standard, all waste shall be disposed of in accordance with Annex III to the Protocol on Environmental Protection to the Antarctic Treaty. In addition, all wastes shall be removed from the Area. Liquid human wastes may be disposed of into the sea. Solid human waste should not be disposed of to the sea, but shall be removed from the Area. No solid or liquid human waste shall be disposed of inland.

7(x) Measures that may be necessary to ensure that the aims and objectives of the Management Plan continue to be met

- Permits may be granted to enter the Area to carry out scientific research, monitoring and site inspection activities, which may involve the collection of a small number of samples for analysis, to erect or maintain signboards, or to carry out protective measures.

- Any long-term monitoring sites shall be appropriately marked and the markers or signs maintained.

- Scientific activities shall be performed in accordance with *SCAR's environmental code of conduct for terrestrial scientific field research in Antarctica.*

7(xi) Requirements for reports

The principal permit holder for each visit to the Area shall submit a report to the appropriate national authority as soon as practicable, and no later than six months after the visit has been completed. Such reports should include, as appropriate, the information identified in the visit report form contained in the Guide to the Preparation of Management Plans for Antarctic Specially Protected Areas. If appropriate, the national authority should also forward a copy of the visit report to the Party that proposed the Management Plan, to assist in managing the Area and reviewing the Management Plan. Wherever possible, Parties should deposit the original or copies of the original visit reports, in a publicly accessible archive to maintain a record of usage, for the purpose of any review of the Management Plan and in organising the scientific use of the Area.

8. Supporting documentation

Bryant, H.M. 1945. Biology at East Base, Palmer Peninsula, Antarctica. Reports on scientific results of the United States Antarctic Service Expedition 1939-1941. In *Proceedings of the American Philosophical Society* **89**(1): 256-69.

Block, W. and Star, J. 1996. Oribatid mites (Acari: Oribatida) of the maritime Antarctic and Antarctic Peninsula. *Journal of Natural History* **30**: 1059-67.

Convey, P. and Smith, R.I. Lewis 1997. The terrestrial arthropod fauna and its habitats in northern Marguerite Bay and Alexander Island, maritime Antarctic. *Antarctic Science* **9**(1):12-26.

Croxall, J.P. and Kirkwood, E.D. 1979. The distribution of penguins on the Antarctic Peninsula and the islands of the Scotia Sea. British Antarctic Survey, Cambridge.

Farquharson, G.W and Smellie, J.L. 1993. Sedimentary section, Lagotellerie Island. Unpublished document, British Antarctic Survey Archives Ref 1993/161.

Gray, N.F. and Smith, R.I. Lewis. 1984. The distribution of nematophagous fungi in the maritime Antarctic. *Mycopathologia* **85**: 81-92.

Lamb, I.M. 1964. Antarctic lichens: the genera *Usnea, Ramalina, Himantormia, Alectoria, Cornicularia. BAS Scientific Report* **38**, British Antarctic Survey, Cambridge.

Matthews D.W. 1983. The geology of Horseshoe and Lagotellerie Islands, Marguerite Bay, Graham Land. *British Antarctic Survey Bulletin* **52**: 125-154.

McGowan, E.R. 1958. Base Y Ornithological report 1958-59. Unpublished BAS internal report AD6/2Y/1958/Q.

Morgan, F., Barker, G., Briggs, C., Price, R. and Keys, H. 2007. Environmental Domains of Antarctica Version 2.0 Final Report, Manaaki Whenua Landcare Research New Zealand Ltd, 89 pp.

Poncet, S. and Poncet, J. 1987. Censuses of penguin populations of the Antarctic Peninsula, 1983-87. *British Antarctic Survey Bulletin* **77**: 109-129.

Smith, H.G. 1978. The distribution and ecology of terrestrial protozoa of sub-Antarctic and maritime Antarctic islands. *BAS Scientific Report* **95**, British Antarctic Survey, Cambridge.

Smith, R.I. Lewis, 1982. Farthest south and highest occurrences of vascular plants in the Antarctic. *Polar Record* **21**: 170-73.

Smith, R.I. Lewis, 1996. Terrestrial and freshwater biotic components of the western Antarctic Peninsula. In Ross, R.M., Hofmann, E.E. and Quetin, L.B. *Foundations for ecological research west of the Antarctic Peninsula*. Antarctic Research Series **70**: American Geophysical Union, Washington D.C.: 15-59.

Star, J. and Block, W. 1998. Distribution and biogeography of oribatid mites (Acari: Oribatida) in Antarctica, the sub-Antarctic and nearby land areas. *Journal of Natural History* **32**: 861-94.

United Kingdom. 1997. *List of protected areas in Antarctica*. Foreign and Commonwealth Office, London.

Usher, M.B. 1986. Further conserved areas in the maritime Antarctic. *Environmental Conservation* 13: 265-66.

Vaughan, A. 1994. A geological field report on N and E Horseshoe Island and SE Lagotellerie Island, Marguerite Bay, and some adjoining areas of S. Graham Land. 1993/94 Field Season. Unpublished report, BAS Archives Ref R/1993/GL5.

Woehler, E.J. (ed) 1993. The distribution and abundance of Antarctic and sub-Antarctic penguins. SCAR, Cambridge

Map 1. Lagotellerie Island Antarctic Specially Protected Area No. 115, Marguerite Bay, location map, showing the location of General San Martin Station (Arg.), the station Teniente Luis Carvajal (Chile), Adelaide Island, Rothera Research Station (UK) and nearby ASPA 129 at Rothera Point, also on Adelaide Island, and the location of the other protected areas in the region [Emperor Island, Dion Islands (ASPA 107) and Avian Island (ASPA 117)]. 'Base Y' (UK) (Historic Monument No. 63) on Horseshoe Island is shown. Inset: the location of Lagotellerie Island along the Antarctic Peninsula.

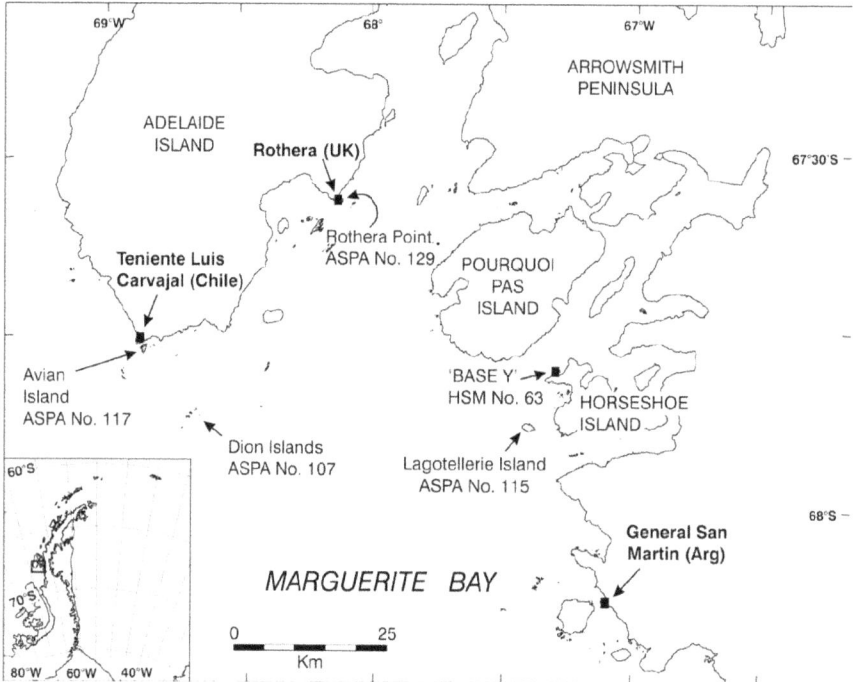

Map 2. Lagotellerie Island (ASPA 115) topographic map.

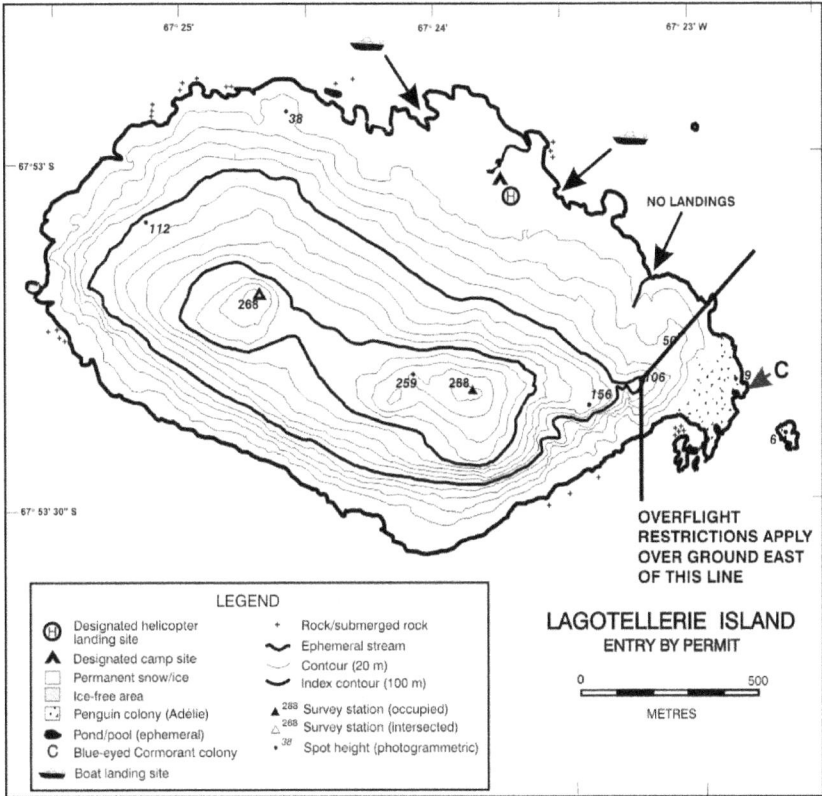

Map 3. Lagotellerie Island (ASPA 115) geological sketch map.

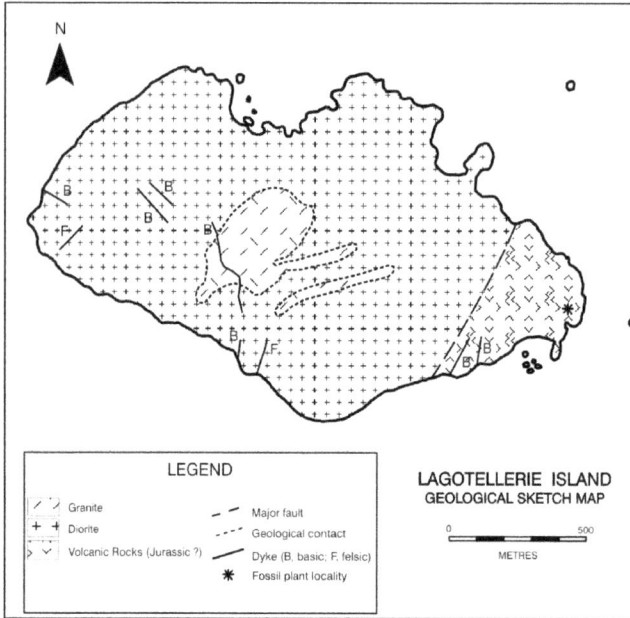

Management Plan for Antarctic Specially Protected Area (ASPA) No. 129

ROTHERA POINT, ADELAIDE ISLAND

Introduction

The primary reason for the designation of Rothera Point, Adelaide Island (Lat. 68°07'S, Long. 67°34'W), South Shetland Islands, as an Antarctic Specially Protected Area (ASPA) is to protect scientific values, primarily that the Area would serve as a control area, against which the effects of human impact associated with the adjacent Rothera Research Station (UK) could be monitored in an Antarctic fellfield ecosystem. Rothera Point was originally designated in Recommendation XIII-8 (1985, SSSI No. 9) after a proposal by the United Kingdom. The Area itself has little intrinsic nature conservation value.

The Area is unique in Antarctica as it is the only protected area currently designated solely for its value in the monitoring of human impact. The objective is to use the Area as a control area which has been relatively unaffected by direct human impact, in assessing the impact of activities undertaken at Rothera Research Station on the Antarctic environment. Monitoring studies undertaken by the British Antarctic Survey (BAS) began at Rothera Point in 1976, before the establishment of the station later that year. On-going environmental monitoring activities within the Area and Rothera Point include: (i) assessment of heavy metal concentrations in lichens; (ii) measurement of hydrocarbon and heavy metal concentrations in gravel and soils and (iii) survey of the breeding bird populations.

Resolution 3 (2008) recommended that the "Environmental Domains Analysis for the Antarctic Continent", be used as a dynamic model for the identification of Antarctic Specially Protected Areas within the systematic environmental-geographical framework referred to in Article 3(2) of Annex V of the Protocol (see also Morgan et al., 2007). Using this model, Rothera Point is predominantly Environment Domain E (Antarctic Peninsula and Alexander Island main ice fields) which is also found in ASPAs 113, 114, 117, 126, 128, 129, 133, 134, 139, 147, 149, 152 and ASMAs 1 and 4. However, given that Rothera Point is predominantly ice-free this domain may not be full representative of the environment encompassed within the Area. Although not specifically described as such, Rothera Point may also contain Environment Domain B (Antarctic Peninsula mid-northern latitudes geologic). Other protected areas containing Environment Domain B include ASPAs 108, 115, 134, 140 and 153 and ASMA 4.

1. Description of values to be protected

- The Area itself has little intrinsic nature conservation value. However, it has scientific value as a control area, against which the effects of human impact associated with the adjacent Rothera Research Station (UK) could be monitored in an Antarctic fellfield ecosystem.
- The Area also has value as a biological research site, particularly for scientists working in the Bonner Laboratory (Rothera Research Station).

2. Aims and objectives

Management of the Area aims to:

- avoid degradation of, or substantial risk to, the values of the Area by preventing unnecessary human disturbance to the Area;

- avoid major changes to the structure and composition of the terrestrial ecosystems, in particular to the fellfield ecosystem and breeding birds, by (i) preventing physical development within the site, and (ii) limiting human access to the Area to maintain its value as a control area for environmental monitoring studies;

- allow scientific research and monitoring studies in the Area provided it is for compelling reasons which cannot be served elsewhere and which will not jeopardise the natural ecological system in that Area;

- minimize to the maximum extent practicable, the introduction of non-native species, which could compromise the scientific values of the Area;

- preserve the natural ecosystem of the Area as a reference area for future comparative studies

- allow regular visits for management purposes in support of the objectives of the management plan.

3. Management activities

The following management activities are to be undertaken to protect the values of the Area:

- Signboards illustrating the location and boundary of the Area and stating entry restrictions shall be erected at the major access points and serviced on a regular basis;

- A map showing the location and boundaries of the Area and stating entry requirements shall be displayed in a prominent position at Rothera Research Station;

- Visits shall be made as necessary to assess whether the Area continues to serve the purposes for which it was designated and to ensure management and maintenance measures are adequate.

- Abandoned equipment or materials shall be removed to the maximum extent possible provided doing so does not adversely impact on the environment and the values of the Area.

4. Period of designation

Designated for an indefinite period.

5. Maps

Map 1. ASPA No. 129 Rothera Point, location map.
Map specifications: Projection: WGS84 Antarctic Polar Stereographic. Standard parallel: 71°S. Central meridian 67°45'W.

Map 2. ASPA No. 129 Rothera Point, topographic map.
Map specifications: Projection: WGS84 Antarctic Polar Stereographic. Standard parallel: 71°S. Central meridian 67°45'W.

6. Description of the Area

6 (i) Geographical coordinates, boundary markers and natural features

BOUNDARIES AND CO-ORDINATES

Rothera Point (67° 34'S, 68° 08'W) is situated in Ryder Bay, at the south-east corner of Wright Peninsula on the east side of Adelaide Island, south-west Antarctic Peninsula (Map 1). The Area is the north-eastern one-third of Rothera Point (Map 2), and is representative of the area as a whole. It is extends about 280 m from west to east and 230 m from north to south, and rises to a maximum altitude of 36 m. At the coast, the Area boundary is the 5 m contour. No upper shore, littoral or sublittoral areas of Rothera Point are therefore included within the ASPA. The southern boundary of the Area, running across Rothera Point, is partially marked by rock filled gabions, in which are placed ASPA boundary signs. The remaining boundary is unmarked. There are two signboards just outside the perimeter of the Area located at the starting points of the pedestrian access route around Rothera Point (see Map 2). The boundary is broadly represented by the following co-ordinates, listed in a clockwise direction, starting with the most northerly point:

Area	Number	Latitude	Longitude
ASPA 129 Rothera Point	1	67°33'59'' S	068°06'47'' W
	2	67°34'06'' S	068°06'48'' W
	3	67°34'06'' S	068°07'00'' W
	4	67°34'02'' S	068°07'08'' W

Rothera Research Station (UK) lies about 250 m west of the western boundary of the Area (see inset on Map 2).

GENERAL DESCRIPTION

Small areas of permanent ice occur to the north and south of the summit of the ASPA. There are no permanent streams or pools. The rocks are predominantly heterogeneous intrusions of diorite, granodiorite and adamellite of the mid-Cretaceous-Lower Tertiary Andean Intrusive Suite. Veins of copper ore are prominent bright green stains on the rock. Soil is restricted to small pockets of glacial till and sand on the rock bluffs. Local deeper deposits produce scattered small circles and polygons of frost sorted material. There are no extensive areas of patterned ground. Accumulations of recent and decaying limpet (*Nacella concinna*) shells forming patches of calcareous soil around prominent rock outcrops used as bird perches by Dominican gulls (*Larus dominicanus*). There are no accumulations of organic matter. There are no special or rare geological or geomorphological features in the Area.

The limited terrestrial biological interest within the Area is confined to the rock bluffs where there is a locally abundant growth of lichens. The vegetation is representative of the southern "maritime" Antarctic fellfield ecosystem and is dominated by the fruticose lichens *Usnea antarctica*, *Usnea sphacelala*, and *Pseudephebe minuscula*, and the foliose lichen *Umbilicaria decussata*. Numerous crustose lichens are found, but bryophytes (mainly *Andreaea* spp.) are sparse. A single very small population of Antarctic pearlwort (*Colobanthus quitensis*) occurs below the northern cliff of the Area. The invertebrate fauna is impoverished and consists only of a few species of mites and springtails, of which *Halozetes belgicae* and *Cryptopygus antarcticus* are the most common. There are no special or rare terrestrial flora or fauna in the Area.

Brown and south polar skuas (*Catharacta lonnbergii* and *C. maccormicki*) are the most abundant breeding birds found in the Area, with up to five pairs of skuas recorded nesting. A pair of Dominican gulls (*Larus dominicanus*) nest in the Area and one Wilson's storm petrels (*Oceanites oceanicus*) nest has been found.

6(ii) Access to the Area

- Access to the Area shall be by foot.

- Helicopter landings are prohibited within the Area.

- The operation of aircraft should be carried out, to the maximum extent possible, in compliance with the 'Guidelines for the Operation of Aircraft near Concentrations of Birds' contained in Resolution 2 (2004). However, the Area is only c. 250 m from the Rothera Research Station runway and for reasons of safety it is recognized that full compliance may not always be possible.

- The Area boundary extends to the 5 m contour at the coast. There is unrestricted pedestrian access below this contour height around the boundary of the Area. The recommended pedestrian access route follows the Mean High Water Mark (MHWM) and is shown on Map 2. During periods when the ground is snow-covered and seaice has formed, pedestrians should ensure that they are at a safe distance from the shoreline and are not in danger of straying onto unreliable seaice or into tide cracks.

6 (iii) Location of structures within and adjacent to the Area

A rock cairn marks the summit of the Area (36 m; Lat. 68°34'01.5'' S, Long. 068°06'58'' W) and 35 m to the east south east of it there is another cairn marking a survey station (35.4 m; Lat. 68°34'02'' S, Long. 068°06'55'' W).

Rothera Research Station (UK) lies about 250 m west of the western boundary of the Area (see inset on Map 2). A number of masts and aerials exist on the raised beach that is adjacent to the southern boundary of the Area.

6 (iv) Location of other protected areas in the vicinity

ASPA No. 107, Emperor Island, Dion Islands, Marguerite Bay, lies about 15 km south of Adelaide Island. ASPA No. 115, Lagotellerie Island, Marguerite Bay, lies about 11 km south of Pourquoi Pas Island. ASPA No. 117, Avian Island, Marguerite Bay, lies about 0.25 km south of the south-west tip of Adelaide Island. The locations of these ASPAs are shown on Map 1.

6 (v) Special zones within the Area

None.

7. Permit Conditions

7(i) General permit conditions

Entry into the Area is prohibited except in accordance with a Permit issued by an appropriate national authority. Conditions for issuing a Permit to enter the Area are that:

- it is issued only for compelling scientific reasons which cannot be served elsewhere; or

- it is issued for essential management purposes such as inspection, maintenance or review;

- the actions permitted will not jeopardise the environmental or scientific values of the Area;

- any management activities are in support of the objectives of the Management Plan;

- the actions permitted are in accordance with this Management Plan;

- the Permit, or an authorised copy, must be carried within the Area;

- permits shall be issued for a stated period;

- the appropriate authority should be notified of any activities/measures undertaken that were not included in the authorised Permit.

7(i) Access to, and movement within or over, the Area

- Access to, and movement within, the Area shall be on foot.
- Land vehicles are prohibited in the Area.
- Landing of helicopters within the Area is prohibited.
- All movement shall be undertaken carefully so as to minimize disturbance to soil and vegetation.

7(iii) Activities which may be conducted in the Area

Activities which are or may be conducted within the Area are:

- scientific research or monitoring which will not jeopardise the ecosystems of the Area;
- essential management activities.

7(iv) Installation, modification or removal of structures

No new structures are to be erected within the Area, or scientific equipment installed, except for compelling scientific or management reasons and for a pre-established period, as specified in a permit. Installation (including site selection), maintenance, modification or removal of structures and equipment shall be undertaken in a manner that minimises disturbance to the values of the Area. All structures or scientific equipment installed in the Area shall be clearly identified by country, name of the principal investigator and year of installation. All such items should be free of organisms, propagules (e.g. seeds, eggs) and non-sterile soil, and be made of materials that can withstand the environmental conditions and pose minimal risk of contamination of the Area. Removal of specific structures or equipment for which the Permit has expired shall be a condition of the Permit. Permanent structures or installations are prohibited.

7(v) Location of field camps
Camping in the Area is prohibited. Accommodation may be available at Rothera Research Station.

7(vi) Restrictions on materials and organisms that may be brought into the Area

No living animals, plant material or microorganisms shall be deliberately introduced into the Area. To ensure that the values of the Area are maintained, special precautions shall be taken against accidentally introducing microbes, invertebrates or plants from other Antarctic sites, including stations, or from regions outside Antarctica. All sampling equipment or markers brought into the Area shall be cleaned or sterilized. To the maximum extent practicable, footwear and other equipment used or brought into the Area (including bags or backpacks) shall be thoroughly cleaned before entering the Area. No poultry or egg products shall be taken into the Area. Further guidance can be found in the CEP *Non-native Species Manual* and COMNAP/SCAR *Checklists for supply chain managers of National Antarctic Programmes for the reduction in risk of transfer of non-native species.*

No herbicides or pesticides shall be brought into the Area. Any other chemicals, including radio-nuclides or stable isotopes, which may be introduced for scientific or management purposes specified in the permit, shall be removed from the Area at or before the conclusion of the activity for which the permit was granted. Release of radio-nuclides or stable isotopes directly into the environment in a way that renders them unrecoverable shall not be permitted.

Fuel, food and other materials are not to be deposited within the Area, unless authorized by Permit for specific scientific or management purposes. Permanent depots are not permitted. All materials introduced shall be for a stated period only, shall be removed at or before the conclusion of the stated period, and shall be stored and handled so that risk of their introduction into the environment is minimised. If release occurs which is likely to compromise the values of the Area, removal is encouraged only where the impact of removal is not likely to be greater than that of leaving the material *in situ*. The appropriate authority shall be notified of any materials released and not removed that were not included in the authorised Permit.

7(vii) Taking of, or harmful interference with, native flora and fauna

Taking of or harmful interference with native flora and fauna is prohibited, except in accordance with a Permit issued in accordance with Annex II to the *Protocol on Environmental Protection to the Antarctic Treaty.* Where taking of, or harmful interference with, animals is involved this should in accordance with the *SCAR Code of Conduct for the use of Animals for Scientific Purposes in Antarctica,* as a minimum standard.

7 (viii) The collection or removal of materials not brought into the Area by the Permit holder

Material of a biological or geological nature may be collected and/or removed from the Area only in accordance with a Permit and should be limited to the minimum necessary to meet scientific or management needs. Permits shall not be granted if there is reasonable concern that the sampling proposed would take, remove or damage such quantities of soil, sediment, flora or fauna that their distribution or abundance within the Area would be significantly affected. Material of human origin not brought into the site by the Permit holder, or otherwise authorised, which is likely to compromise the values of the Area shall be removed unless the impact of removal is likely to be greater than leaving the material *in situ*. In the latter case the appropriate authority shall be notified.

7 (ix) Disposal of wastes

All wastes shall be removed from the Area in accordance with Annex III (Waste disposal and waste management) of the Protocol on Environmental Protection to the Antarctic Treaty (1998). All solid and/or liquid human waste shall be removed from the Area.

7 (x) Measures that may be necessary to continue to meet the aims of the Management Plan

- Permits may be granted to enter the Area to carry out scientific research, monitoring and site inspection activities, which may involve the collection of a small number of samples for analysis, to erect or maintain signboards, or to carry out protective measures.

- Any long-term monitoring sites shall be appropriately marked and the markers or signs maintained.

- Scientific activities shall be performed in accordance with *SCAR's environmental code of conduct for terrestrial scientific field research in Antarctica.*

7 (xi) Requirements for reports

The principal permit holder for each visit to the Area shall submit a report to the appropriate national authority as soon as practicable, and no later than six months after the visit has been completed. Such visit reports should include, as applicable, the information identified in the recommended visit report form (contained as an Appendix in the *Guide to the Preparation of Management Plans for Antarctic Specially Protected Areas* (available from the website of the Secretariat of the Antarctic Treaty; www.ats.aq)). If appropriate, the national authority should also forward a copy of the visit report to the Party that proposed the Management Plan, to assist in managing the Area and reviewing the Management Plan. Wherever possible, Parties should deposit the original or copies of the original visit reports, in a publicly accessible archive to maintain a record of usage, for the purpose of any review of the management plan.

8. Supporting documentation

Block, W., and Star, J. 1996. Oribatid mites (Acari: Oribatida) of the maritime Antarctic and Antarctic Peninsula. Journal of Natural History 30: 1059-67.

Bonner, W. N. 1989. Proposed construction of a crushed rock airstrip at Rothera Point, Adelaide Island - final Comprehensive Environmental Evaluation. NERC, Swindon. 56 pp.

Convey, P., and Smith, R.I.L. 1997. The terrestrial arthropod fauna and its habitats in northern Marguerite Bay and Alexander Island, maritime Antarctic. Antarctic Science 9:12-26.
Downie, R., Ingham, D., Hughes, K. A., and Fretwell, P. 2005. Initial Environmental Evaluation: proposed redevelopment of Rothera Research Station, Rothera Point, Adelaide Island, Antarctica. British Antarctic Survey, Cambridge, 29 pp.

Milius, N. 2000. The birds of Rothera, Adelaide Island, Antarctic Peninsula. Marine Ornithology 28: 63-67.

Morgan, F., Barker, G., Briggs, C., Price, R., and Keys, H. 2007. *Environmental Domains of Antarctica Version 2.0 Final Report.* Manaaki Whenua Landcare Research New Zealand Ltd, 89 pp.

Øvstedal, D.O. and Smith, R.I.L. 2001. *Lichens of Antarctica and South Georgia. A Guide to their Identification and Ecology.* Cambridge University Press, Cambridge, 411 pp.

Ochyra, R., Bednarek-Ochyra, H. and Smith, R. I. L. 2008. *The Moss Flora of Antarctica.* Cambridge University Press, Cambridge. pp 704.

Peat, H., Clarke, A., and Convey, P. 2007. Diversity and biogeography of the Antarctic flora. *Journal of Biogeography,* **34**: 132-146.

Riley. T. R., Flowerdew, M. J. and Whitehouse, M. J. 2011. Chrono- and lithostratigraphy of a Mesozoic–Tertiary fore- to intra-arc basin: Adelaide Island, Antarctic Peninsula. *Geologocial Magazine,* doi:10.1017/S0016756811001002

Shears, J. R. 1995. Initial Environmental Evaluation – expansion of Rothera Research Station, Rothera Point, Adelaide Island, Antarctica. British Antarctic Survey, Cambridge, 80 pp.

Shears, J. R., and Downie, R. 1999. Initial Environmental Evaluation for the proposed construction of an accommodation building and operations tower at Rothera Research Station, Rothera Point, Adelaide Island, Antarctica. British Antarctic Survey, Cambridge, 22 pp.

Map 1. ASPA No. 129 Rothera Point, location map.
Map specifications: Projection: WGS84 Antarctic Polar Stereographic. Standard parallel: 71°S.
Central meridian 67°45'W.

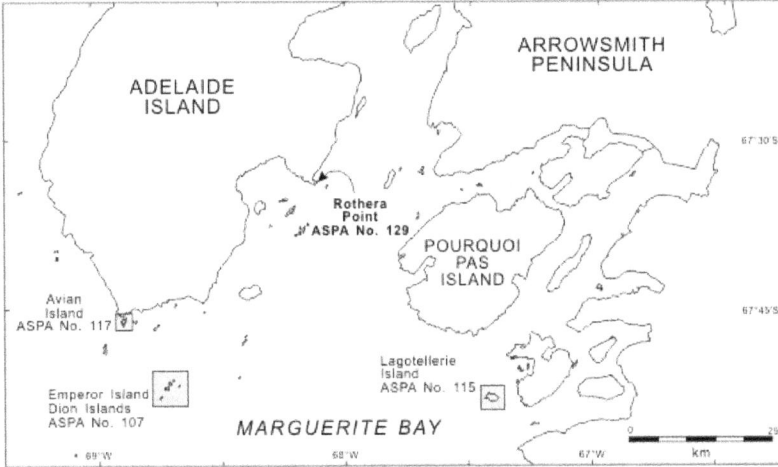

Map 2. ASPA No. 129 Rothera Point, topographic map.
Map specifications: Projection: WGS84 Antarctic Polar Stereographic. Standard parallel: 71°S.
Central meridian 67°45'W.

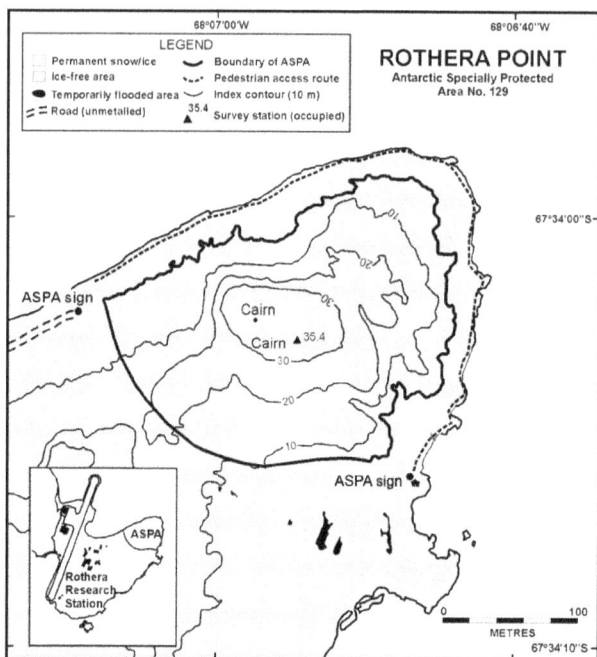

Management Plan for
Antarctic Specially Protected Area No. 133

HARMONY POINT, NELSON ISLAND, SOUTH SHETLAND ISLANDS

Introduction

This Area was originally designated as Site of Special Scientific Interest No. 14 under Antarctic ATCM Recommendation XIII-8 (1985), after a proposal by Argentina, because the Area is an excellent example of the maritime Antarctic communities of birds and land ecosystems present in the South Shetland Islands, making it possible to carry out long-term research programs without damage or harmful interference.

In 1997, the Management Plan was adapted to the requirements of Annex V of the Protocol on Environmental Protection to the Antarctic Treaty, and approved through Measure 3 (1997). This version consists of the revision to the Management Plan approved pursuant to Measure 2 (2005), and it is the second revision since entry into force of Annex V.

The original goals for designating this Area are still relevant, and are specified on point 2. The anthropic disturbance could jeopardize the long term studies carried out there, especially during the breeding season.

1. Description of values to be protected

The values to be protected in the Area still relate to the composition and biological diversity of the site.

Ice-free land supports large breeding colonies of 12 seabird species, among which we find one of the largest single colonies of chinstrap penguin *(Pygoscelis antarctica)* of Antarctica. In the Area, there is also a large giant petrel colony (*Macronectes gianteus),* a species which is highly sensitive to human disturbance, and a large colony of gentoo penguin (*Pygoscelis papua).*

The Area has profuse vegetation, developed on various types of soils, particularly characterized by the presence of vast moss carpets, as well as lichens and fungi. It is also possible to find two species of vascular plants in the Area. As vegetation is one of the factors responsible for soil formation, the protection of the Area ensures the development of research linked to the soils and the flora present in the Area.

2. Aims and objectives

- Preventing unnecessary human disturbance;
- Permitting the development of any scientific research provided it does not compromise the values for which the Area is being protected;

- Avoiding major changes in the structure and composition of the flora and fauna communities;

- Preventing or minimising the introduction to the Area of non-native plants, animals and microbes;

- Minimising the possibility of the introduction of pathogens which may cause disease in flora or fauna populations within the Area;

3. Management activities

The staff authorised to access the ASPA shall be specifically instructed on the conditions of the Management Plan.

Approach distances to fauna must be respected, except when the scientific projects may require otherwise and this is specified in the relevant permits.

Collection of samples will be limited to the minimum required for the authorised scientific research plans.

All signs and structures erected within the Area for scientific or management purposes will be properly secured and maintained in good condition.

Due to the vast moss carpets developed in the Area, and the presence of large seabird colonies adjacent to the areas where scientists and the support staff circulate, tracks towards research sites can be marked, preferably using those previously marked or used.

4. Period of designation

The Area is designated for an indefinite period.

5. Maps

Map 1, attached to this Management Plan as an Annex at the end of the document, shows the location of ASPA No. 133, Harmony Point (Nelson Island).

6. Description of the Area

6(i) Geographical coordinates and boundaries

The Area is located in the west coast of Nelson Island (62° 18'S; 59° 14'W), between the King George (25 de Mayo) Island, to the northeast, and the Robert Island, to the southwest, and includes Harmony Point and the Toe, the sector covered by ice and the adjacent marine area, as shown in Map 1.

6(ii) Natural features

Geomorphologically, Harmony Point presents three well defined units: an andesitic plateau, coastal and shelf outcrops and ancient sea levels.

The plateau reaches 40 meters above sea level and its area is covered by detritus resulting from the action of erosion agents on andesitic rocks, with a well-developed vegetation of mosses and lichens. There are three successive raised paleobeaches, between the coast and the glacier. The paleobeaches are defined by pebble accumulations of variable heights in some instances and the development of soil in others. Lakes and streams with a limited flow appear on the undulations. Some isolated andesitic rocks and ancient nunataks can be seen outside the limits of the glacier, evidencing that the past extension of the glacier covered Harmony Point.

The Area holds breeding colonies of 12 species: 3,347 pairs of gentoo penguins *(Pygoscelis papua)*, 89,685 pairs of chinstrap penguins *(Pygoscelis antarctica)*, 479 pairs of cape petrel *(Daption capense)*, 45 pairs of blue eyed shag *(Phalacrocorax atriceps)*, 144 pairs of snowy sheathbill *(Chionis alba)*, 71 pairs of skuas (61 pairs of Antarctic skuas *(Catharacta antarctica)* and 11 of *C. maccormicki* skuas), 128 pairs of Dominican gulls *(Larus dominicanus)* and 746 pairs of giant petrels *(Macronectes gianteus)*.

Other seabirds nesting in the Area are the Wilson's storm petrel (*Oceanites oceanicus*) and the black-bellied storm petrel (*Fregetta tropica*) which, together, represent around 1000 pairs, and the Antarctic tern (*Sterna vittata*), with an estimated population of between 100 and 150 individuals (57-76 nests).

Most bird colonies are distributed over the north-western and south coast of Harmony Point. Giant petrel colonies are located around Gurruchaga shelter.

There are usually three species of mammals in the Area: the Weddell seal *(Leptonychotes weddelli)*, the elephant seal *(Mirounga leonina)* and the Antarctic fur seal *(Arctocephalus gazella)*. Occasionally some individual crabeater seals *(Lobodon carcinophagus)* have also been seen. The number of mammals in the area varies. The maximum numbers of sighted Antarctic fur seals, Weddell seals and elephant seals are 320, 550 and 100 respectively. The Weddell seals usually breed in the Area in high figures, reaching up to 60 females with their pups in a single season. Births of fur and elephant seals have also been recorded, although the numbers there are much lower.

There are some extensive areas covered by a very rich and diverse development of bryophytes and lichen-dominated plant communities (presently being classified), mainly dominated by *Usnea fasciata* and by *Himantormia luburis,* including, although to a lesser degree, two vascular plant species *(Deschampsia antarctica and Colobanthus quitensis)* present in Antarctica, especially in the areas less affected by recent anthropic perturbation or breeding activities. Moss turf subformations are located in wind protected and moist places, whilst lichen-dominated subformations occur in places with a high wind exposure.

Five soil orders have been identified so far in the Area, according to the taxonomic system: Soil Taxonomy (1999): Histosols *(Hydric Cryfibrists)*, Entisols *(Lithic Criorthents)*, Spodosols *(Oxiaquic Humicryods)*, Mollisols *(Lithic Haplocryolls)* and Inceptisols *(Lithic Eutrocryepts* e *Histic Cryaquepts)*.

6(iii) Access to the Area

The Area can be accessed by air or by sea. To access by sea, the landing site is located about 200 meters to the right of the shelter, at the bottom of the cove, over a protected gravel beach and with no significant presence of fauna.

The navigation beacon located in the westernmost tip of Harmony Point is accessed by landing south of the beacon. Both the navigation beacon and the Toe are only accessed by sea.

Access by air is only permitted when there are no means for access by sea. To avoid interfering with the bird breeding settlements near the shelter, especially the giant petrel, access by air is permitted for small aircrafts landing over the Nelson Island glacier. During landing manoeuvres, the aircrafts may not fly over the ice-free zone of the Area, in order to avoid causing any disturbance to bird colonies. Where absolutely necessary, helicopters may be permitted to land in ice-free areas. In this regards, the provisions of the "Guidelines for operation of aircrafts over bird colonies" (Resolution 2, 2004) shall be observed as a minimum standard, except in cases of emergency or for air safety purposes.

6(iv) Location of structures within and adjacent to the Area

There are permanent year-round structures within the Area.

Shelters: The "Gurruchaga" shelter (ARG, c. 30 m^2) is used to provide accommodation to the research teams visiting the Area. There is also a storage building of 12 m^2. These facilities are only used during spring and summer, and have a maximum capacity of 3 people (See section 7 (ix) Disposal of wastes*)*.

Beacons: There is a Chilean navigation radio beacon at the westernmost tip of Harmony Point, and an Argentine one at the Toe.

Signposts: A sign indicating where the protected Area starts on the sand beach in front of the shelter. Another sign inside the shelter displays the shelter name and owner.

6 (v) Location of other Protected Areas within close proximity

- ASPA No. 112, Coppermine Peninsula, Robert Island, South Shetland Islands lies about 30 km south west.

- ASPA No. 125, Fildes Peninsula, King George / 25 de Mayo Island, South Shetland Islands lies about 23 km north-north east.

- ASPA No. 150, Ardley Island, King George / 25 de Mayo Island, South Shetland Islands lies about 19 km north east.

- ASPA No. 128, Western Shore of Admiralty Bay, King George Island (25 de Mayo), South Shetland Islands lies about 45 km east-northeast.

- ASPA No. 132, Potter Peninsula, King George / 25 de Mayo Island, South Shetland Islands lies about 30 km east-north east.

- ASPA No. 171, Narebski Point (south-eastern coast of Barton Peninsula, 25 de Mayo/King George Island, about 25 km northeast of Harmony Point.

6(vi) Restricted zones within the Area

There are no restricted zones within the protected Area.

7. Permit conditions

7(i) General conditions

Access to the Area is prohibited except in accordance with a Permit issued by appropriate national authorities.

Conditions for the issuance of a Permit to access the Area:

- The activity serves a scientific, ASPA management or outreach purpose, in accordance with the objectives of the Management Plan, which cannot be served elsewhere; and any management activity (inspection, maintenance or review), is in support of the objectives of this Management Plan;

- the Permit is carried by staff authorised to access the Area;

- a post-visit report is supplied to the appropriate national authority mentioned in the Permit upon completion of the activity, within the terms established by national authorities issuing the Permit.

- Neither tourism nor any other recreational activities are permitted.

7(ii) Access to, and movement within or over, the Area

All movement within the ASPA shall be exclusively on foot.

7(iii) Activities which may be conducted in the Area

- Scientific research which cannot be conducted elsewhere and which will not jeopardise the natural ecosystem of the Area;

- Essential management activities;

- Activities contributing to raise awareness of scientific activities, under National Antarctic Programs.

7(iv) Installation, modification or removal of structures

No new structures are to be erected within the Area, or scientific equipment installed, except for compelling scientific or management reasons and subject to the relevant Permit.

Any scientific equipment to be installed in the Area, as well as any research marker, shall be approved by a Permit and be clearly labelled, indicating the country, name of principal investigator and year of installation. All such materials should be of such nature as to pose minimal risks of contamination to the Area, or the risk of interfering with the fauna or damaging the vegetation.

No research traces are to remain once the Permit has expired. If a specific project cannot be finished within the timeframe specified in the Permit, such circumstance shall be informed in the post-visit report, and an extension of the validity of the Permit authorising any materials to remain in the Area shall be requested.

7(v) Location of field camps

95

The Gurruchaga shelter will usually be available for the Parties using the Area. The use of the shelter for scientific purposes, by staff other than Argentine Antarctic Program staff shall be arranged in advance with such Program. If it is necessary to install tents they will have to be located in the immediate vicinity of the shelter. No other locations shall be used for this purpose, in order to restrict the human impact.

Such exclusion is not valid for installing tents with scientific instruments or materials, or those that are used as an observation base, which shall be removed upon conclusion of the activity.

7(vi) Restrictions on materials and organisms that may be brought into the Area

No living animals or plant material shall be deliberately introduced into the Area.

All reasonable precautions against the unintentional introduction of alien species to the Area shall be adopted. It should be taken into account than alien species are most frequently and effectively introduced by humans. Clothes (pockets, boots, velcro fasteners on garments) and personal equipment (bags, backpacks, camera bags, tripods), as well as scientific instruments and work tools may carry insect larvae, seeds or propagules. For more information, refer to the "Non-Native Species Manual – CEP 2011"

No herbicides or pesticides shall be brought into the Area. Any other chemical, which shall be introduced under the relevant Permit, shall be removed of the Area upon conclusion of the activity. The purpose and type of chemicals shall be documented in as much detail as possible for other scientists´ future information.

Fuel, food and other material are not to be stored in the Area, unless required for essential purposes connected with the activity for which the Permit has been granted, provided it is stored inside the shelter or close to it. Any fuel used at the Gurruchaga shelter shall be handled pursuant to procedures established by the Argentine Antarctic Program involved in the activity.

7(vii) Taking of, or harmful interference with, native flora and fauna

All forms of taking or harmful interference are prohibited, except in accordance with a permit. Where an activity involves taking or harmful interference, it should be carried out in accordance with the SCAR *Code of Conduct for Use of Animals for Scientific Purposes in Antarctica,* as a minimum standard.

Information on taking and harmful interference will be duly exchanged through the Antarctic Treaty Information Exchange system, as established by Art. 10.1 of Annex V to the Madrid Protocol.

Scientists taking samples of any kind in the Area will ensure that they are familiar with samples previously taken, in order to minimise the risk of a potential duplication. For that purpose, they must refer to the Antarctic Treaty Electronic Information Exchange System (available at http://www.ats.aq/s/ie.htm) and/or contact the relevant National Antarctic Programs.

7(viii) Collection or removal of materials not brought into the Area by the Permit holder

Material may be collected or removed from the Area only in accordance with a Permit. Removal of dead biological specimens for scientific purposes must not exceed levels that deteriorate the nutritional base of local scavengers and with the sole purpose of performing pathological analyses.

7 (ix) Disposal of waste

All non-physiological waste shall be removed from the Area. Wastewater and liquid domestic waste may be dumped into the sea, in accordance with Article 5 of Annex III to the Madrid Protocol.

Waste generated as a consequence of research activities carried out in the Area may be temporarily stored next to the Gurruchaga shelter awaiting removal. Such waste must be disposed of pursuant to Annex III to the Madrid Protocol, labelled as trash and duly sealed to prevent accidental leaks.

7(x) Measures that may be necessary to continue to meet the aims of the Management Plan

Access Permits to the Area may be granted in order to conduct biological monitoring and site inspection activities, including the collection of plant material and animal samples for scientific purposes, the erection or maintenance of signposts, and any other management measures. All structures and markers installed in the Area must be authorised by a Permit and clearly identified by country, name of principal researcher and year of installation. Research markers and structures must be removed on or before the expiry of the Permit. If specific projects cannot be concluded within the permitted time, an application must be made for an extension to leave the items in the Area.

7(xi) Requirements for reports

Parties granting permits to access ASPA 133 should ensure that the principal holder for each permit issued submits to the appropriate authority a report describing the activities undertaken. Such reports must be submitted as soon as possible, within the terms established by the relevant competent authorities. The reports must include the information outlined in the Visit Report form, in accordance with Resolution 2 (2011).

Parties granting permits to Access ASPA 133 should maintain e record of such activities and, in the Annual Exchange of Information, should provide summary descriptions of the activities conducted by persons subject to their jurisdiction. Wherever possible, Parties should deposit originals or copies of such original reports in an archive, to be used both for review of the Management Plan and in organising the scientific use of the Area.

8. Supporting documentation.

Non-Native Species Manual. Resolution 6 (2011) – ATCM XXXIV – CEP XIV, Buenos   Aires   (available   at *http://www.ats.aq/documents/atcm34/ww/atcm34_ww004_e.pdf*)

Guidelines for the Operation of Aircrafts. Resolution 2 (2004) – ATCM XXVII - CEP VII, Cape Town (available at *http://www.ats.aq/documents/recatt/Att224_e.pdf*)

SCAR Code of Conduct for the Use of Animals for Scientific Purposes (available at http://www.scar.org/treaty/atcmxxxiv/ATCM34_ip053_e.pdf)

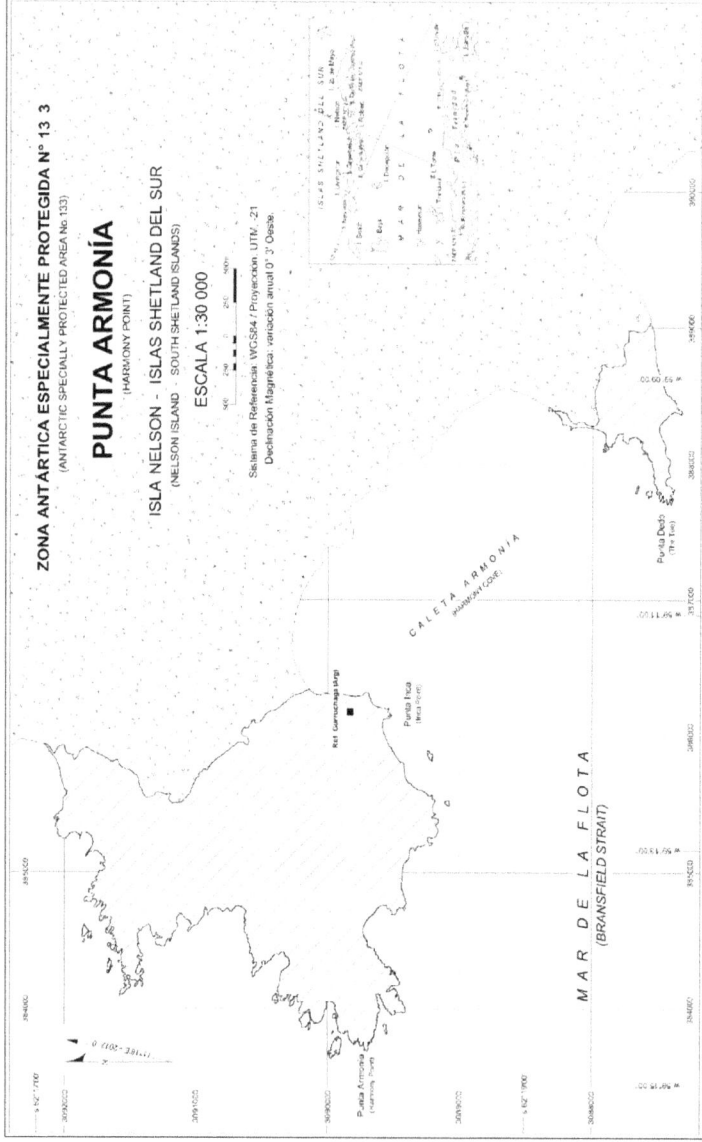

REPÚBLICA ARGENTINA

DIRECCIÓN NACIONAL DEL ANTÁRTICO · INSTITUTO ANTÁRTICO ARGENTINO

ZONA ANTÁRTICA ESPECIALMENTE PROTEGIDA N° 13 3

(ANTARCTIC SPECIALLY PROTECTED AREA No 133)

PUNTA ARMONÍA

(HARMONY POINT)

ISLA NELSON - ISLAS SHETLAND DEL SUR

(NELSON ISLAND · SOUTH SHETLAND ISLANDS)

ESCALA 1:30 000

Sistema de Referencia: WGS84 / Proyección UTM - 21
Declinación Magnética: variación anual 0° 3' Oeste

Map 1: Location of Antarctic Specially Protected Area No. 133. In continuous diagonal lines, ice-free areas. In dotted pattern, areas covered in ice.

Management Plan for Antarctic Specially Protected Area No 140

PARTS OF DECEPTION ISLAND, SOUTH SHETLAND ISLANDS

Introduction

The primary reason for the designation of Parts of Deception Island, (Lat. 62°57'S, Long. 60°38'W), South Shetland Islands, as an Antarctic Specially Protected Area (ASPA) is to protect environmental values, predominantly the terrestrial flora within the Area. The flora of the island is unique in Antarctic terms, particularly where associated with these geothermal areas, but also because of the recently formed surfaces that provide known-age habitats for the study of colonisation and other dynamic ecological processes by terrestrial organisms (Smith 1988).

Deception Island is an active volcano. Recent eruptions occurring in 1967, 1969 and 1970 (Baker *et al.* 1975) altered many of the topographical features of the island and created new, and locally transient, surfaces for the colonisation of plants and other terrestrial biota (Collins 1969; Cameron & Benoit 1970; Smith 1984b; c). There are a number of sites of geothermal activity, some with fumaroles (Smellie *et al.* 2002).

Five small Sites around the coast of Port Foster were adopted under Recommendation XIII–8 (ATCM XIII, Brussels, 1985) as Site of Special Scientific Interest No 21 on the grounds that '*Deception Island is exceptional because of its volcanic activity, having had major eruptions in 1967, 1969 and 1970. Parts of the island were completely destroyed, new areas were created, and others were covered by varying depths of ash. Few areas of the interior were unaffected. The island offers unique opportunities to study colonization processes in an Antarctic environment*'. Following an extensive scientific survey, protection of the island's botanical values was enhanced through Measure 3 (2005) when the number of Sites of botanical interest included within the ASPA was increased to 11.

ASPA 140 makes a substantial contribution to the Antarctic protected areas system as it (a) contains a particularly wide diversity of species, (b) is distinct from other areas due to the geothermally-heated ground in some parts of the island which create habitats of great ecological importance unique to the Antarctic Peninsula region and (c) is vulnerable to human interference, in particular, due to highly restricted spatial distribution of many plant species, particularly those associated with heated ground. While ASPA 140 is protected primarily for its outstanding environmental values (specifically its biological diversity) it is also protected for its scientific values (ie, for terrestrial biology, zoology, geomorphology and geology). In particular, scientific research includes long-term colonisation studies and ground temperature measurements.

The 11 Sites within the Area (c. 2.4km^2) encompass terrestrial and lagoon habitats around geo-thermally heated ground, areas of rich flora and known-age surfaces created following eruptions of 1967, 1969 and 1970 which are potentially useful for recolonisation studies. The Area is considered to be of sufficient size to provide adequate protection of the values identified, which may be highly susceptible to direct physical disturbance, due to activities of national and non-governmental visitors, and the identified boundaries provide an adequate buffer around sensitive features.

1. Description of values to be protected

Following a detailed botanical survey of the island in 2002 (reviewed in 2010), 11 Sites of unique botanical interest were identified. Consequently, the values specified in the original designation were reaffirmed and considerably augmented.

These values are set out as follows:

- The island has the greatest number of rare (ie, known to grow at a few localities in the Antarctic and often in small quantity) and extremely rare (ie, known to grow at only one or two localities in the Antarctic) plant species of any site in the Antarctic. Twenty eight of the 54 mosses recorded on the island, four of the eight liverworts and 14 of the *c.* 75 lichens are considered to be rare or extremely rare. Annex 1 lists the plant species classed as rare or extremely rare in the Antarctic Treaty area, which occur on Deception Island. These represent 25%, 17% and *c.* 4% of the total number of mosses, liverworts and lichens, respectively, known from the Antarctic (Aptroot & van der Knaap 1993; Bednarek-Ochyra *et al.* 2000; Ochyra *et al.* 2008; Øvstedal & Lewis Smith 2001). Thirteen species of moss (including two endemics), two species of liverwort and three species of lichen growing on Deception Island have not been recorded elsewhere in the Antarctic. No other site in the Antarctic is comparable. This suggests that there is a significant deposition of immigrant propagules (by wind and seabirds), particularly of southern South American provenance, over the Antarctic, which become established only where favourable germinating conditions prevail (eg, the heat and moisture provided around fumaroles) (Smith 1984b; c). Such sites are unique in the Antarctic Treaty area.

- The more stable geothermal areas, some of which have fumaroles issuing steam and sulphurous gas, have developed bryophyte communities of varying complexity and density, each with a distinct and unique flora. Most of these areas were created during the 1967-70 series of eruptions, but at least one (Mt. Pond) predates that period. Species growing close to active vents are continuously subjected to temperatures between 30 to 50°C, thereby posing important questions regarding their physiological tolerance.

- Areas of volcanic ash, mudflows, scoria and lapilli deposited between 1967 and 1970 provide unique known-age surfaces. These are currently being colonised by vegetation and other terrestrial biota, allowing the dynamics of immigration and colonisation to be monitored. These areas are unstable and subject to wind and water erosion, so exposing some areas to continual surface change and a cycle of recolonisation.

- Kroner Lake, the only intertidal lagoon with hot springs in Antarctica, supports a unique community of brackish-water algae.

- Several Sites within the Area, unaffected by ash deposits during the 1967-70 eruptions, support long-established mature communities with diverse vegetation and are typical of the older stable ecosystems on the island.

- The largest known stand of Antarctic pearlwort (*Colobanthus quitensis*), one of only two flowering plants in the Antarctic, is located within the Area. After being virtually eradicated by burial in ash during the 1967 eruption, it has recovered and is now spreading at an unprecedented rate. This correlates with the current trend in regional climate change, particularly increasing temperature.

- The Area contains some Sites where on-going scientific research is performed including long-term colonization experiments (Collins Point) and long-term ground temperature variation measurements (Caliente Hill).

- The Area also contains some Sites with surfaces that date from the eruption in 1967, which allowing accurate monitoring of colonisation by plants and other biota and are of important scientific value.

2. Aims and objectives

Management of the Area aims to:

- avoid degradation of, or substantial risk to, the values of the Area by preventing unnecessary human disturbance to the Area;
- allow scientific research in the Area provided it is for compelling reasons which cannot be served elsewhere and which will not jeopardise the natural ecological system in that Area;
- prevent or minimise the introduction to the Area of alien plants, animals and microorganisms;
- ensure that the flora is not adversely affected by excessive sampling within the Area;
- preserve the natural ecosystem of the Area as a reference area for future comparative studies and for monitoring floristic and ecological change, colonisation processes and community development;

3. Management activities

The following management activities shall be undertaken to protect the values of the Area:

- Visits shall be made as necessary to assess whether the individual Sites continue to serve the purposes for which they were designated and to ensure management and maintenance measures are adequate.
- Markers, signs or other structures (eg, fences, cairns) erected within the Area for scientific or management purposes shall be secured and maintained in good condition and removed when no longer required.
- In accordance with the requirements of Annex III of the Protocol on Environmental Protection to the Antarctic Treaty, abandoned equipment or materials shall be removed to the maximum extent possible provided doing so does not adversely impact on the environment and the values of the Area.
- A map showing the location of each Site on Deception Island (stating any special restrictions that apply) shall be displayed prominently and a copy of this Management Plan shall be made available at Gabriel de Castilla Station (Spain) and Decepción Station (Argentina). Copies of the Management Plan shall be freely available and carried aboard all vessels planning visits to the island.
- Where appropriate, National Antarctic Programmes are encouraged to liaise closely to ensure management activities are implemented (including through the Deception Island Antarctic Specially Managed Area Management Group). In particular, National Antarctic Programmes are encouraged to consult with one another to prevent excessive sampling of biological material within the Area, particularly given the often slow rate of re-growth and limited quantity and distribution of some flora. Also, National Antarctic Programmes are encouraged to consider joint implementation of guidelines intended to minimize the introduction and dispersal of non-native species within the Area.
- At Site K Ronald Hill to Kroner Lake, any wind-blown debris from HSM No 71 shall be removed. At Site G Pendulum Cove, any wind-blown debris from HSM No 76 shall be removed (see Section *7(viii)*).
- At Site A Collins Point, the existing staked plots should be maintained to allow continued monitoring of vegetation change since 1969.

4. Period of designation

Designated for an indefinite period.

5. Maps

Figure 1: Antarctic Specially Protected Area No 140, Deception Island, showing the location of Sites A – L (Scale 1:100 000).

Figures 1a–d: Topographic Maps of Antarctic Specially Protected Area No 140 showing Sites A – L (Scale 1: 25 000). The 'hill shade' effect has been added to highlight the topography of the areas.

6. Description of the Area

6 (i) Geographical co-ordinates, boundary markers and natural features

GENERAL DESCRIPTION

Research by Smith (1984) and Peat *et al.* (2007) described the recognised biogeographical regions present within the Antarctic Peninsula. Antarctica can be divided into three major biological provinces: northern maritime, southern maritime and continental. Deception Island lies within the northern maritime zone (Smith 1984).

Resolution 3 (2008) recommended that the "Environmental Domains Analysis for the Antarctic Continent", be used as a dynamic model for the identification of Antarctic Specially Protected Areas within the systematic environmental-geographical framework referred to in Article 3(2) of Annex V of the Protocol (see also Morgan et al. 2007). Using this model, Deception Island is predominantly Environment Domain G (Antarctic Peninsula off-shore islands geologic). The scarcity of Environment Domain G, relative to the other environmental domain areas, means that substantial efforts have been made to conserve the values found within this environment type elsewhere: other protected areas containing Domain G include ASPAs 109, 111, 112, 114, 125, 126, 128, 145, 149, 150, and 152 and ASMAs 1 and 4. Environment Domain B (Antarctic Peninsula mid-northern latitudes geologic) is also present. Other protected areas containing Environment Domain B include ASPAs 108, 115, 134 and 153 and ASMA 4.

NATURAL FEATURES, BOUNDARIES, AND SCIENTIFIC VALUES

ASPA 140 comprises 11 Sites, shown in Figures 1 and 1a-1d. Annotated photographs of each Site are shown in Annex 2. This fragmented distribution is characteristic of the vegetation cover of Deception Island. Because of the patchy nature of stable and moist substrata not subjected to erosion, the vegetation has a disjunct distribution and is consequently restricted to widely scattered, and often very small, habitats.

The Sites are lettered A to L (but excluding I), in a clockwise direction from the south-west of the caldera and referred to by the most prominent named geographical feature associated with each Site. Photographs of each Site are shown in Annex 2. Boundary co-ordinates are listed in Annex 3, but as many of the boundaries follow natural features, the boundary description outlines below should also be consulted.

Site A - Collins Point

Area encompassed. The north-facing slopes between Collins Point and the unnamed point 1.15 km to the east (0.6km west of Entrance Point), directly opposite Fildes Point, and extending from the back of the beach to a ridge extending up to *c.* 1km inland from the shoreline.

Boundaries. The eastern boundary of Site A runs south from the shore at the unnamed point 0.6 km west of Entrance Point, following the outline of a ridge to an elevation of 184m. The western boundary extends from Collins Point, following a ridge south to an elevation of 145m. The southern boundary is delimited by the arcuate ridge crest (following a line of summits east to west at 172, 223 and 214m) joining points 184 and 145m. The beach area, including the Collins Point light beacon (maintained by the Chilean Navy), to the 10m contour is excluded from the Site.

Scientific value. No geothermally-heated ground is known within the Site boundary. The Site contains some of the best examples of the island's longest established vegetation, largely unaffected by the recent eruptions, with high species diversity and several Antarctic rarities, some in considerable abundance. A few small plants of *Colobanthus quitensis* have recently become established, while the large liverwort (*Marchantii berteroana*) is a fairly recent and spreading colonist. Research on seals is undertaken on the beach to the north of the Site, and the Site also contains a colony of kelp gulls in the low cliffs above the beach. Six 50 × 50cm plots marked with wooden corner stakes (Lat. 62°60'00''S, Long. 060°34'48''W) were established by the British Antarctic Survey in 1969 to monitor changes in the vegetation in subsequent years (Collins 1969).

Site B - Crater Lake

Area encompassed. Crater Lake and its shoreline, the flat ground to its north and the scoria-covered lava tongue to the south.

Boundaries. The northern boundary extends along the foot of the slope to the north of the broad valley *c.* 300m north of Crater Lake (at *c.* 30m altitude). The western boundary follows the ridgeline immediately west of the lake, and to the east of the small unnamed lake at Lat. 62°59'00''S, Long. 060°40'30''W. The southwestern and southern boundaries follow the top of the slope (at altitude *c.* 80m) that extend to the southwest and south of the lake. The eastern boundary passes to the east of the lava tongue south of Crater Lake, around the eastern rim of the lake and *c.* 300m across the flat plain to the north of the Crater Lake.

Scientific value. No geothermally-heated ground is known within the Site boundary. The principal area of botanical interest lies on a scoria-covered lava tongue south of the lake. The Site was unaffected by the recent eruptions. The vegetation on the scoria tongue has a diverse cryptogamic flora, including several Antarctic rarities, and exceptional development of turf-forming moss, dominated by one relatively common species (*Polytrichastrum alpinum*). Of particular interest is that it reproduces sexually in great abundance here. Sporophytes of this species are not known in such profusion in this, or any other moss, anywhere else in the Antarctic. The extensive, virtually monospecific, moss carpet (*Sanionia uncinata*), on the flat ground to the north of Crater Lake, is one of the largest continuously vegetated stands on the island.

Site C – Caliente Hill, southern end of Fumarole Bay

Area encompassed. A narrow line of fumaroles extending c. 40 × 3m along the gently sloping summit ridge at *c.* 95 to 107m elevation on Caliente Hill above the north-west side of Albufera Lagoon northwest of Decepción Station (Argentina) at the southern end of Fumarole Bay.

Boundaries. The area includes all the ground above the 90m contour on the hill, with the exception of the ground south east of a point 10m north west of the cairn (Lat. 62°58'27''S, Long. 060°42'31''W) at the southeast end of the ridge. Access to the cairn at the southeast end of the ridge is not restricted.

Scientific value. Geothermally-heated ground is included within the Site. Several rare species of moss, some unique to the island, colonise the heated soil crust close to the vents, of which only two or three are visible. The vegetation is extremely sparse and not obvious, in total encompassing less than *c.* 1m^2 in area, and is therefore particularly vulnerable to trampling and over-sampling. Structures within the Site include experimental apparatus monitoring long-term ground temperature variations (operated by the Spanish Antarctic programme) and several short metal stakes arranged along the ridgeline near the highest point of the ridge.

Site D - Fumarole Bay

Area encompassed. The unstable moist scree slopes below the precipitous lava cliffs on the east side of the southern end of Stonethrow Ridge to the break of slope beyond the beach west of mid-Fumarole Bay. No structures are located within the Site, although much timber debris is found at the back of the beach several metres above the high tide mark. The timber may have been deposited at this location by a tsunami generated by earlier vulcanological activity.

Boundaries. The southern end of the cliffs terminate in a prominent ridge sloping southeastward down to the beach. The southern boundary of the Site extends from the base of this ridge (at altitude *c.* 10m) along the ridge line to the base of the cliffs at an altitude of *c.* 50m. The western boundary follows the limit of the scree at the base of the cliffs roughly northwards for 800m at altitude of approximately 50m. The eastern boundary extends northwards along the break-of-slope at the back of the beach for 800m including all the large boulders. The northern boundary (*c.* 100m in length) joins the break of slope at the back of the beach to the scree at the base of the lava flow cliffs. The flat beach area from the shore, including two prominent inter-tidal fumaroles to the south of Fumarole Bay, to the break-of-slope is excluded from the Site.

Scientific value. No geothermally-heated ground is known within the Site, although fumarole activity is present in the inter-tidal zone east of the Site. The Site has a complex geology and contains the most diverse flora on the island, including several Antarctic rarities. It was unaffected by the recent eruptions.

Site E – west of Stonethrow Ridge

Area encompassed. The Site encompasses an area of fumarole activity and includes a red scoria cone at *c.* 270m altitude, on the northern side of the east-west trending ridge, *c.* 600m south-southwest of the highest point on Stonethrow Ridge (330m), west of central Fumarole Bay. It comprises two fumaroles about 20m apart, the more easterly fumarole being more highly vegetated with lichens, mosses and liverworts covering an area of *c.* 15 × 5m.

Boundaries. The boundary extends to 10m beyond all evidence of geothermal activity and the non-heated ground linking the two fumaroles.

Scientific value. Areas of geothermally-heated ground are present within the Site. The Site possesses several very rare mosses, liverworts and lichens, two of the dominant species being a liverwort (*Clasmatocolea grandiflora*) and lichen (*Stereocaulon condensatum*), neither of which is known elsewhere in Antarctica. Photographs taken in the mid-1980s indicate that the development and diversity of this vegetation has advanced considerably. A skua nest (noted in 1993 and 2002 and occupied in 2010) is present within the vegetation. These birds may be responsible for introducing some of the plants from Tierra del Fuego, notably the dominant liverwort.

Site F - Telefon Bay

Area encompassed. The Site incorporates several features created during the 1967 eruption in Telefon Bay: Pisagua Hill on the south side of the Site, the small shallow Ajmonecat Lake on the ash plain north of Stancomb Cove and the low flat ash plain extending from the shoreline of Telefon Bay to the steep slopes and lava outcrops *c.* 0.5km inland. Pisagua Hill was created as a new island in 1967, but is now joined to the main island by the aforementioned ash plain. At the northern end of the plain is Extremadura Cove, which was a lake until the narrow isthmus (*c.* 2m wide and 50m long) separating it from Port Foster was breached sometime around 2006. Extremadura Cove is excluded from the Site.

Boundaries. The north shoreline of the lagoon (Stancomb Cove) at the south-west of Telefon Bay marks the southern boundary of the Site, while the southwest shore of the Extremadura Cove to the north of Telefon Bay marks the northeastern boundary of the Site. The southeast boundary extends along the shore south of Pisagua Hill, northwards to the shoreline of the Extremadura Cove at the northern end of Telefon Bay. The northwest boundary is roughly delineated by the 10m contour of Telefon Ridge that links Stancomb Cove to Extremadura Cove. Ajmonecat Lake (Lat. 62°55'23''S, Long. 060°40'45''W), including its shoreline, is included in the Site. The shoreline of Telefon Bay is excluded from the Site to allow access past the Site.

Scientific value. No geothermally-heated ground is known within the Site. The main point of botanical interest is that all surfaces within the Site date from 1967, thereby allowing accurate monitoring of colonisation by plants and other biota. The Site has a generally barren appearance, but close inspection reveals an abundance of inconspicuous mosses and lichens. In the absence of geothermal activity here, colonisation processes may be related to aspects of the current trend in climate change. Although species diversity is low, the developing communities are typical of non-heated habitats throughout the island.

Site G - Pendulum Cove

Area encompassed. The Site comprises the uneven gentle slope of coarse grey, crimson, and red scoria and occasional disintegrating blocks of yellowish tuff, east-northeast of Crimson Hill and *c.* 0.4 – 0.8km east of Pendulum Cove. It extends *c.* 500m from west to east and is up to *c.* 400m wide from north to south. It was created largely by the 1969 eruption which destroyed the nearby abandoned Chilean Base (Historic Site and Monument No 76). The Site includes the slope and undulating "plateau" behind Pendulum Cove.

Boundaries. The western boundary follows the 40m contour line and the eastern boundary follows the 140m contour line east-southeast of Pendulum Cove. The northern and southern boundaries follow the edge of the volcanic debris-covered permanent ice that borders the Site.

Scientific value. Geothermal activity was recorded during a survey in 1987, with substantial heat being emitted from crevices amongst scoria. There was no such evidence in 2002. Although vegetation is very sparse, this known-age site is being colonised by numerous moss and lichen species. Two of the mosses (*Racomitrium lanuginosum* and *R. heterostichoides*) are unique both on the island and in the Antarctic, and both are very rare here. Several other mosses are Antarctic rarities.

Site H - Mt. Pond

Area encompassed. The Site is situated *c.* 1.4 to 2km north-north-west of Mount Pond summit. The extensive area of geothermally-heated ground includes an area (c. 150 × 500m) on the north eastern side of the gently sloping upper part of a broad ridge at *c.* 385 to 500m elevation (Smith 1988). At the northern end of the Site there are numerous inconspicuous fumarole vents in low mounds of very fine, compacted baked soil. The higher, southern, part of the Site is close to a large rime dome at 512m, in the lee of which (at c. 500 to 505m) are numerous active fumaroles, also surrounded by fine, compacted baked soil, on a steep, moist, sheltered slope. The extensive areas of heated ground surrounding the fumaroles comprise a fine soil with a soft crust that is extremely vulnerable to trampling. There are several stands of dense, thick (up to 10cm) bryophyte vegetation associated with these areas. The adjacent yellowish tuff outcrops support a different community of mosses and lichens.

Boundaries. The northern boundary is marked by Lat. 62°55'51''S, the southern boundary by Lat. 62°56'12''S and the eastern boundary is marked by Long. 060°33'30''W. The western boundary follows the ridgeline of the broad ridge that slopes north northwest from the summit of Mt. Pond between Long. 060°33'48''W and Long. 060°34'51''W.

Scientific value. This is an outstanding site of botanical interest, unique in the Antarctic. It possesses several moss species which are either unique to the Antarctic or are extremely rare in Antarctica. The development of the moss turf (*Dicranella hookeri* and *Philonotis polymorpha*) in the main upper part of the Site is exceptional, and two or more species have colonised profusely since last inspected in 1994. The large liverwort (*Marchantii berteroana*) is rapidly colonising the warm moist soil crust at the periphery of the moss stands. At least one species of toadstool fungus also occurs amongst the moss, the highest known record for these organisms in Antarctica. A totally different community of mosses and lichens occurs on the rock outcrops, and also includes several extremely rare species (notably *Schistidium andinum* and *S. praemorsum*).

Site J - Perchué Cone

Area encompassed. This ash cone lies *c.* 750m northeast of Ronald Hill and comprises a very narrow line of fumaroles and adjacent heated ground on the west-facing slope at *c.* 160-170m elevation. The geothermal area covers *c.* 25 × 10m, and the fine ash and lapilli surface of the entire slope is very vulnerable to pedestrian damage.

Boundaries. The boundary encompasses all of the ash and cinder cone referred to as Perchué Cone.

Scientific value. The Site contains several mosses that are extremely rare in Antarctica. Photographic evidence suggests that the extent of moss colonisation has decreased since the mid-1980s.

Site K – Ronald Hill to Kroner Lake

Area encompassed. This Site includes the circular flat plain of the crater immediately to the south of Ronald Hill, and extends along the prominent broad shallow outwash gulley with a low bank on either side, leading southwards from here to Kroner Lake. The substratum throughout the area is consolidated mud, fine ash and lapilli deposited by the lahar during the 1969 eruption. Part of the Site, notably the gulley, remains geothermally active. The Site also includes the intertidal geothermal lagoon (Kroner Lake) as it is part of the same volcanological feature. This small, shallow, circular, brackish crater lake was broached by the sea during the 1980's, and is now the only geothermally heated lagoon in the Antarctic.

Boundaries. The boundary surrounds the crater basin, gulley, Kroner Lake and an area between *c.* 100 – 150m wide around the lake. A corridor below Ronald Hill, from the break-of-slope to the lowermost massive boulders about 10 to 20m beyond, remains outside the boundary to allow access past the Area.

Scientific value. The surfaces of this Site are of a known age and are being colonised by numerous moss, liverwort and lichen species, several of which are extremely rare in the Antarctic (eg, the mosses *Notoligotrichum trichodon* and *Polytrichastrum longisetum*, and a rare lichen, *Peltigera didactyla*, is colonising >1ha of the crater floor). The geothermal northern intertidal shore of Kroner Lake possesses a unique community of algae.

Site L - South East Point

Area encompassed. An east-west trending rocky ridge *c.* 0.7km north of South East Point, extending from the top of the sea cliff (*c.* 20m altitude) westwards for *c.* 250m, to a point about 80m altitude. The north edge of the ridge is a low vertical lava outcrop, giving way to a steep unstable slope leading to the floor of a gully parallel to the ridge. The south side of the Site is the gently sloping ridge crest covered with ash and lapilli.

Boundaries. The Site extends 50m north and south of the lava outcrop.

Scientific value. This Site has the most extensive population of Antarctic pearlwort (*Colobanthus quitensis*) known in the Antarctic. It was the largest population before the 1967 eruption (Longton 1967), covering *c.* 300m^2, but was almost completely destroyed by ash burial. It gradually recovered, but since about 1985-1990 there has been a massive increase in seedling establishment and the population has expanded downwind (westwards, uphill). It is now very abundant in an area of *c.* 2ha. It is also remarkable for the absence of the other native vascular plant, Antarctic hairgrass (*Deschampsia antarctica*), almost always associated with this plant. Photographs of the Site immediately after the eruption revealed almost total loss of lichens, but these too have recolonised rapidly and extensively, the large bushy *Usnea antarctica* being particularly abundant and attaining a considerable size after the relatively short period since recolonisation. The cryptogamic flora of the Site is generally sparse and typical of most of the island. The Site is particularly important for monitoring the reproduction and spread of the pearlwort in a known-age site.

6(ii) Access to the Area

- Access to the Sites shall be by foot or small boat.
- Helicopter landings are prohibited within the Area. The Management Plan for Deception Island ASMA 4 shows recommended helicopter landing sites on Deception Island, which are also shown in Figure 1. Helicopter landings sites which may be useful for accessing Sites are located at: Decepción Station (Argentina; Lat. 62°58'30''S, Long. 060°42'00''W), northern Fumarole Bay (Lat. 62°57'18''S, Long. 060°42'48''W), the south of Cross Hill (Lat. 62°56'39''S, Long. 060°41'36''W), eastern Telefon Bay (Lat. 62°55'18''S, Long. 060°38'18''W), Pendulum Cove (Lat. 62°56'12''S, Long. 060°35'45''W) and Whalers Bay (Lat. 62°58'48''S, Long. 060°33'12''W).
- All travel to the Sites shall be undertaken carefully so as to minimize disturbance to soil and vegetation en route.
- The operation of aircraft should be carried out, as a minimum requirement, in compliance with the 'Guidelines for the Operation of Aircraft near Concentrations of Birds' contained in Resolution 2 (2004). Particular care should be taken when overflying Site A Collins Point, which contains a colony of kelp gulls in the low cliffs above the beach.

6(iii) Location of structures within and adjacent to the Area

Two research stations are found close to the ASPA sites: Decepción Station (Argentina; Lat. 62°58'30''S, Long. 060°41'54''W) and Gabriel de Castilla Station (Spain; Lat. 62°58'36''S, Long. 060°40'30''W). Two Historic Sites or Monuments are found close to the ASPA sites: Whalers Bay (HSM 71; Lat. 62°58'42''S, Long. 060°33'36''W) and the ruins of the Base Pedro Aguirre Cerda Station (HSM 76; Lat. 62°56'12''S, Long. 060°35'36''W). Collins Point navigation beacon is situated at Lat. 62°59'42''S, Long. 060°35'12''W. At Site A, Collins Point, there are six 50 × 50cm plots marked with wooden corner stakes, although not all of the four stakes per plot remain (Lat. 63°00'00''S, Long. 060°34'48''W). These were established by the British Antarctic Survey in 1969 to monitor changes in the vegetation in subsequent years (Collins 1969); data were obtained in 1969 and 2002. These markers should be maintained.

Structures within the Site C, Caliente Hill, include some experimental apparatus monitoring long-term ground temperature variations (operated by the Spanish National Antarctic Programme) and several short metal stakes arranged along the ridgeline near the summit.

Other structures near to the Area are listed in the ASMA Management Plan for Deception Island.

6(iv) Location of other protected areas in the vicinity

ASPA 145 comprises two Sites of benthic importance within Port Foster. Deception Island and Port Foster are managed within ASMA 4 Deception Island.

6(v) Special zones within the Area

None

7. Permit conditions

7(i) General permit conditions

Entry into the Area is prohibited except in accordance with a Permit issued by an appropriate national authority. Conditions for issuing a Permit to enter the Area are that:

- it is issued only for compelling scientific reasons which cannot be served elsewhere; or
- it is issued for essential management purposes such as inspection, maintenance or review;
- the actions permitted will not jeopardise the floristic, ecological or scientific values of the Area;
- any management activities are in support of the objectives of the Management Plan;
- the actions permitted are in accordance with this Management Plan;
- the Permit, or an authorised copy, must be carried within the Area;
- permits shall be issued for a stated period;
- the appropriate authority should be notified of any activities/measures undertaken that were not included in the authorised Permit.

7(ii) Access to, and movement within or over, the Area

- Land vehicles are prohibited in the Area.
- Helicopter landings are prohibited within the Area. The Management Plan for Deception Island ASMA 4 shows recommended helicopter landing sites on Deception Island (see also Figure 1).
- Movement within the Area Sites shall be on foot.
- Rowing boats are permitted for sampling purposes in the lakes in Site B - Crater Lake and Site F - Telefon Bay, and the lagoon in Site K - Ronald Hill to Kroner Lake. Prior to use at each Site, boats shall be cleaned to reduce the risk of introductions of non-native species from outside the Treaty area and other Antarctic locations, including other Sites within ASPA 140.
- All movement shall be undertaken carefully so as to minimize disturbance to soil and vegetation. In particular, the vegetation on Site C - Caliente Hill is sparse and not obvious and is therefore particularly vulnerable to trampling.

7(iii) Activities which may be conducted in the Area

Activities include:

- compelling scientific research which cannot be undertaken elsewhere and which will not jeopardize the flora and ecology of the Area;
- essential management activities, including monitoring.
- surveys, to be undertaken as necessary, to determine the state of the botanical values for which each Site has been designated, in support of the aims of this Management Plan.

7(iv) Installation, modification or removal of structures

Structures shall not be erected within the Area except as specified in a Permit. All scientific equipment, botanical quadrats or other markers installed in the Area must be approved by Permit and clearly identified by country, name of the principal investigator and year of installation. All such items should be made of materials that pose minimal risk of contamination of the Area (see Section *7(vi)*).

7(v) Location of field camps

Camping is not permitted within the Area. The ASMA Management Plan for Deception Island shows recommended sites for field camps on the island, but outside ASPA 140. Campsites which may be useful for accessing Sites are located at: northern Fumarole Bay (Lat. 62°57'18''S, Long. 060°42'42''W), the south of Cross Hill (Lat. 62°56'36''S, Long. 060°41'30''W), eastern Telefon Bay (Lat. 62°55'18''S, Long. 060°38'12''W), Pendulum Cove (Lat. 62°56'12''S, Long. 060°35'42''W) and Whalers Bay (Lat. 62°58'54''S, Long. 060°33'0''W) (see Figure 1).

7(vi) Restrictions on materials and organisms which may be brought into the Area

No living animals, plant material or microorganisms shall be deliberately introduced into the Area. To ensure that the floristic and ecological values of the Area are maintained, special precautions shall be taken against accidentally introducing microbes, invertebrates or plants from other Antarctic sites, including stations, or from regions outside Antarctica. All sampling equipment or markers brought into the Area shall be cleaned or sterilized. To the maximum extent practicable, footwear and other equipment used or brought into the Area (including bags or backpacks) shall be thoroughly cleaned before entering the Area. No poultry or egg products shall be taken into the Area. Further guidance can be found in the CEP Non-native Species Manual (Edition 2011) and COMNAP/SCAR Checklists for supply chain managers of National Antarctic Programmes for the reduction in risk of transfer of non-native species.

No herbicides or pesticides shall be brought into the Area. Any other chemicals, including radio-nuclides or stable isotopes, which may be introduced for scientific or management purposes specified in the permit, shall be removed from the Area at or before the conclusion of the activity for which the permit was granted. Release of radio-nuclides or stable isotopes directly into the environment in a way that renders them unrecoverable shall not be permitted.

Fuel, food and other materials are not to be deposited within the Area, unless authorized by Permit for specific scientific or management purposes. Permanent depots are not permitted. All materials introduced shall be for a stated period only, shall be removed at or before the conclusion of the stated period, and shall be stored and handled so that risk of their introduction into the environment is minimised. If release occurs which is likely to compromise the values of the Area, removal is encouraged only where the impact of removal is not likely to be greater than that of leaving the material *in situ*. The appropriate authority shall be notified of any materials released and not removed that were not included in the authorised Permit.

7(vii) Taking of, or harmful interference with, native flora and fauna

Taking or harmful interference with native flora or fauna is prohibited, except by Permit issued in accordance with Annex II to the Protocol on Environmental Protection to the Antarctic Treaty. Where taking of or harmful interference with animals is involved, the *SCAR Code of Conduct for the Use of Animals for Scientific Purposes in Antarctica* should be used as a minimum standard.

7(viii) The collection or removal of materials not brought into the Area by the Permit holder

Material of a biological, geological (including soil and lake sediment), or hydrological nature may be collected or removed from the Area only in accordance with a Permit and should be limited to the minimum necessary to meet scientific or management needs. Permits shall not be granted if there is reasonable concern that the sampling proposed would take, remove or damage such quantities of soil, sediment, flora or fauna that their distribution or abundance within the Area would be significantly affected. Material of human origin likely to compromise the values of the Area, which was not brought into the Area by the Permit Holder or otherwise authorised, may be removed unless the impact of removal is likely to be greater than leaving the material *in situ*; if this is the case the appropriate authority should be notified. If wind-blown debris is found in the Area it should be removed. Plastic debris should be disposed of in accordance with Annex III (Waste disposal and waste management) of the Protocol on Environmental Protection to the Antarctic Treaty (1998). Other wind-blown material should be returned to the Historic Site or Monument from which it originated and secured to prevent further dispersal by wind. A report describing the nature of the material removed from the ASPA and the location within the Historic Site and Monument where it has been secured and stored, should be submitted to the Deception Island Antarctic Specially Managed Area (ASMA) Management Group, via the Chair, to establish the most appropriate way to deal with the debris (ie, conservation to preserve any historic value or appropriate disposal) (see Deception Island ASMA website: *http://www.deceptionisland.aq/contact.php*).

7(ix) Disposal of waste

All wastes shall be removed from the Area in accordance with Annex III (Waste disposal and waste management) of the Protocol on Environmental Protection to the Antarctic Treaty (1998). In order to avoid anthropogenic microbial and nutrient enrichment of soils, no solid or liquid human waste should be deposited within the Area. Human wastes may be disposed of within Port Foster, but avoiding ASPA 145.

7(x) Measures that may be necessary to continue to meet the aims of the Management Plan

- Permits may be granted to enter the Area to carry out biological, vulcanological or seismic monitoring and site inspection activities.
- Any long-term monitoring sites shall be appropriately marked and the markers or signs maintained.
- Permits may be granted to allow for monitoring of the Area, or to allow for some active management as set out in Section 3.

7(xi) Requirements for reports

The principal permit holder for each visit to the Area shall submit a report to the appropriate national authority as soon as practicable, and no later than six months after the visit has been completed. Such visit reports should include, as applicable, the information identified in the recommended visit report form (contained as an Appendix in the Guide to the Preparation of Management Plans for Antarctic Specially Protected Areas (available from the website of the Secretariat of the Antarctic Treaty; *www.ats.aq*)). If appropriate, the national authority should also forward a copy of the visit report to the Party that proposed the Management Plan, to assist in managing the Area and reviewing the Management Plan. Wherever possible, Parties should deposit the original or copies of the original visit reports, in a publicly accessible archive to maintain a record of usage, for the purpose of any review of the Management Plan and in organising the scientific use of the Area.

8. Supporting documentation

Aptroot, A. and van der Knaap, W.O. 1993. The lichen flora of Deception Island, South Shetland Islands. *Nova Hedwigia*, **56**, 183-192.

Baker, P.E., McReath, I., Harvey, M.R., Roobol, M., & Davies, T.G. 1975. The geology of the South Shetland Islands: V. Volcanic evolution of Deception Island. *British Antarctic Survey Scientific Reports,* No. 78, 81 pp.

Bednarek-Ochyra, H., Váňa, J., Ochyra, R. and Lewis Smith, R.I. 2000. *The Liverwort Flora of Antarctica*. Polish Academy of Sciences, Krakow, 236 pp.

Cameron, R.E. and Benoit, R.E. 1970. Microbial and ecological investigations of recent cinder cones, Deception Island, Antarctica – a preliminary report. *Ecology*, **51**, 802-809.

Collins, N.J. 1969. The effects of volcanic activity on the vegetation of Deception Island. *British Antarctic Survey Bulletin*, **21**, 79-94.

Peat, H., Clarke, A., and Convey, P. 2007. Diversity and biogeography of the Antarctic flora. *Journal of Biogeography*, **34**, 132-146.

Longton, R.E. 1967. Vegetation in the maritime Antarctic. In Smith, J.E., *Editor*, A discussion of the terrestrial Antarctic ecosystem. *Philosophical Transactions of the Royal Society of London*, B, **252**, 213-235.

Morgan F, Barker G, Briggs C, Price R and Keys H. 2007. Environmental Domains of Antarctica Version 2.0 Final Report, Manaaki Whenua Landcare Research New Zealand Ltd, 89 pages.

Ochyra, R., Bednarek-Ochyra, H. and Smith, R.I.L. *The Moss Flora of Antarctica*. 2008. Cambridge University Press, Cambridge. pp 704.

Øvstedal, D.O. and Smith, R.I.L. 2001. *Lichens of Antarctica and South Georgia. A Guide to their Identification and Ecology*. Cambridge University Press, Cambridge, 411 pp.

Smellie, J.L., López-Martínez, J., Headland, R.K., Hernández-Cifuentes, Maestro, A., Miller, I.L., Rey, J., Serrano, E., Somoza, L. and Thomson, J.W. 2002. *Geology and geomorphology of Deception Island*, 78 pp. BAS GEOMAP Series, Sheets 6-A and 6-B, 1:25,000, British Antarctic Survey, Cambridge.

Smith, R. I. L. 1984a. Terrestrial plant biology of the sub-Antarctic and Antarctic. In: Antarctic Ecolgy, Vol. 1. Editor: R. M. Laws. London, Academic Press.

Smith, R.I.L. 1984b. Colonization and recovery by cryptogams following recent volcanic activity on Deception Island, South Shetland Islands. *British Antarctic Survey Bulletin*, **62**, 25-51.

Smith, R.I.L. 1984c. Colonization by bryophytes following recent volcanic activity on an Antarctic island. *Journal of the Hattori Botanical Laboratory*, **56**, 53-63.

Smith, R.I.L. 1988. Botanical survey of Deception Island. *British Antarctic Survey Bulletin*, **80**, 129-136.

Figure 1. Map of Deception Island showing the 11 sites that make up ASPA 140 Parts of Deception Island, South Shetland Islands.

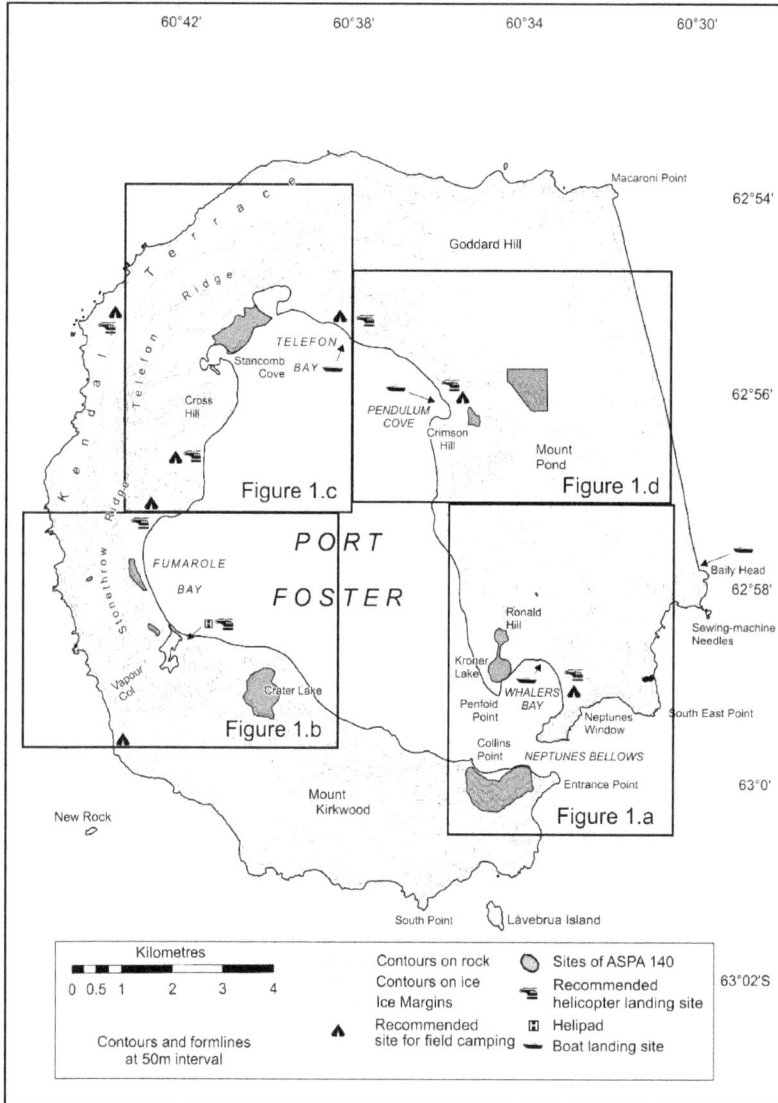

Figure 1a. Map showing the location of ASPA No. 140 Sites A, J, K and L.

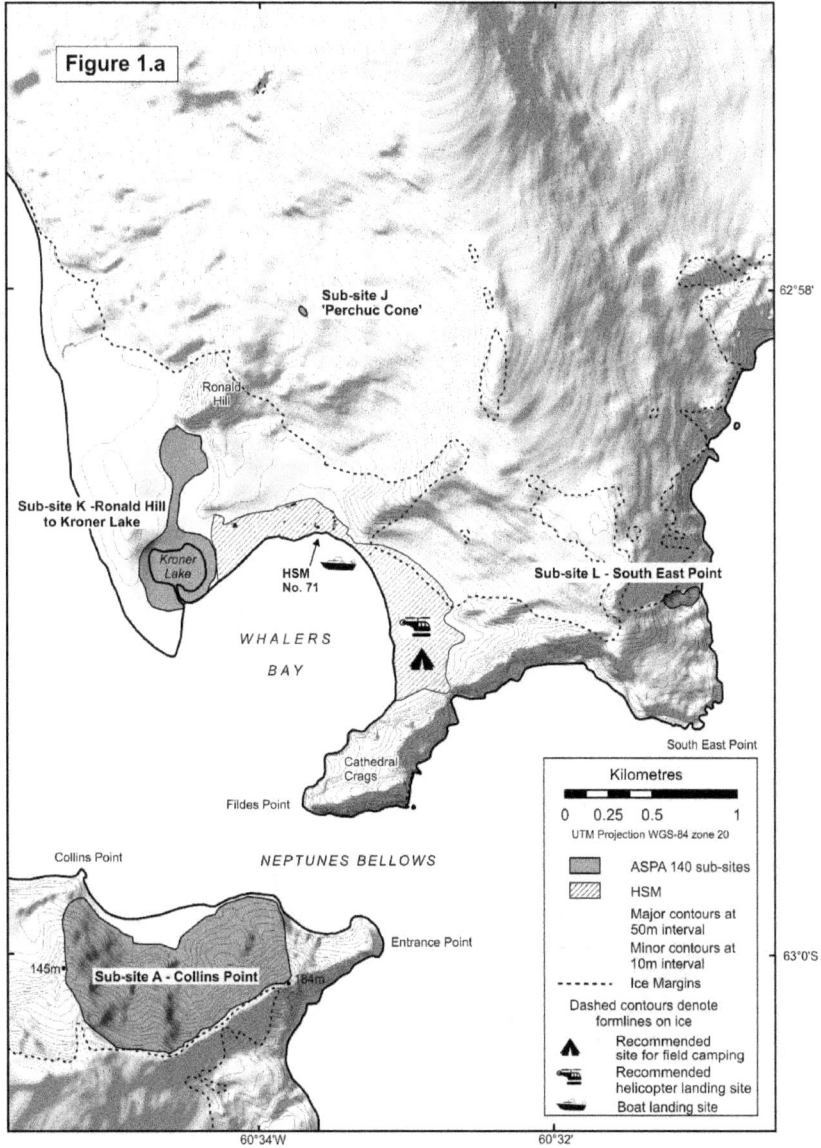

Figure 1b. Map showing the location of ASPA No. 140 Sites B, C, D and E.

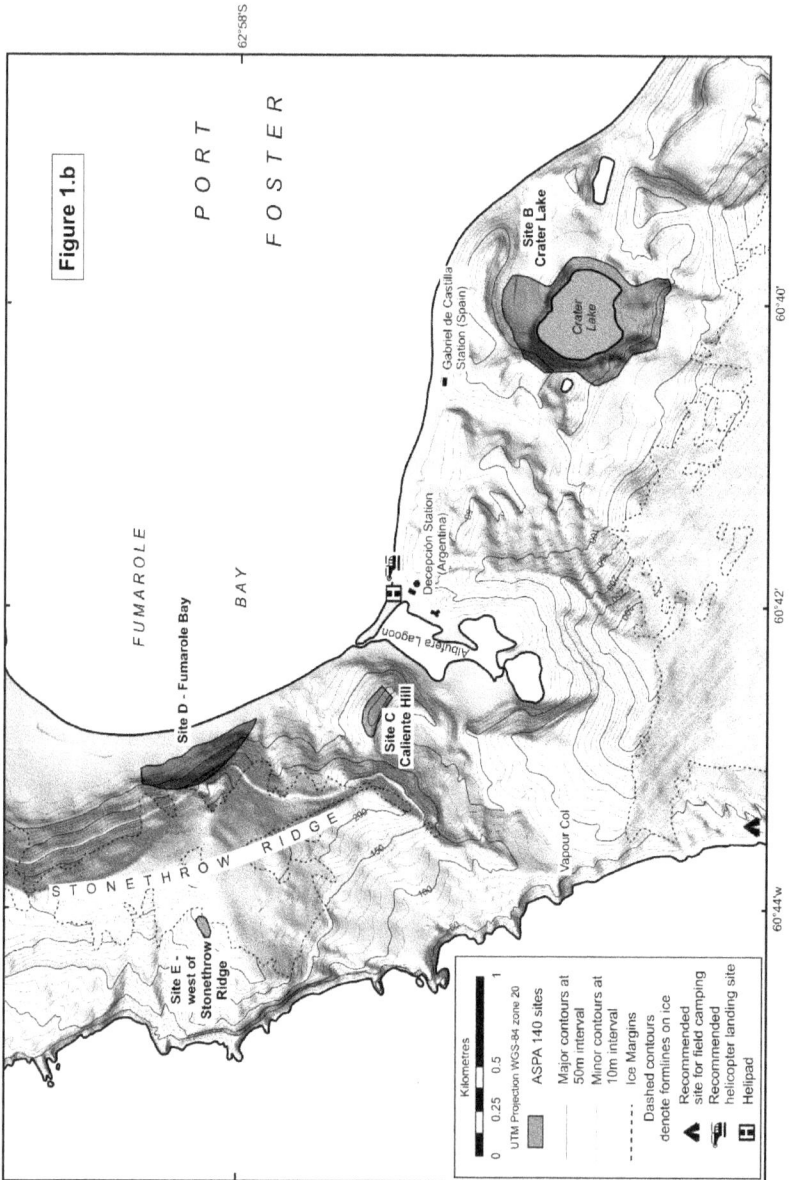

Figure 1c. Map showing the location of ASPA No. 140 Site F.

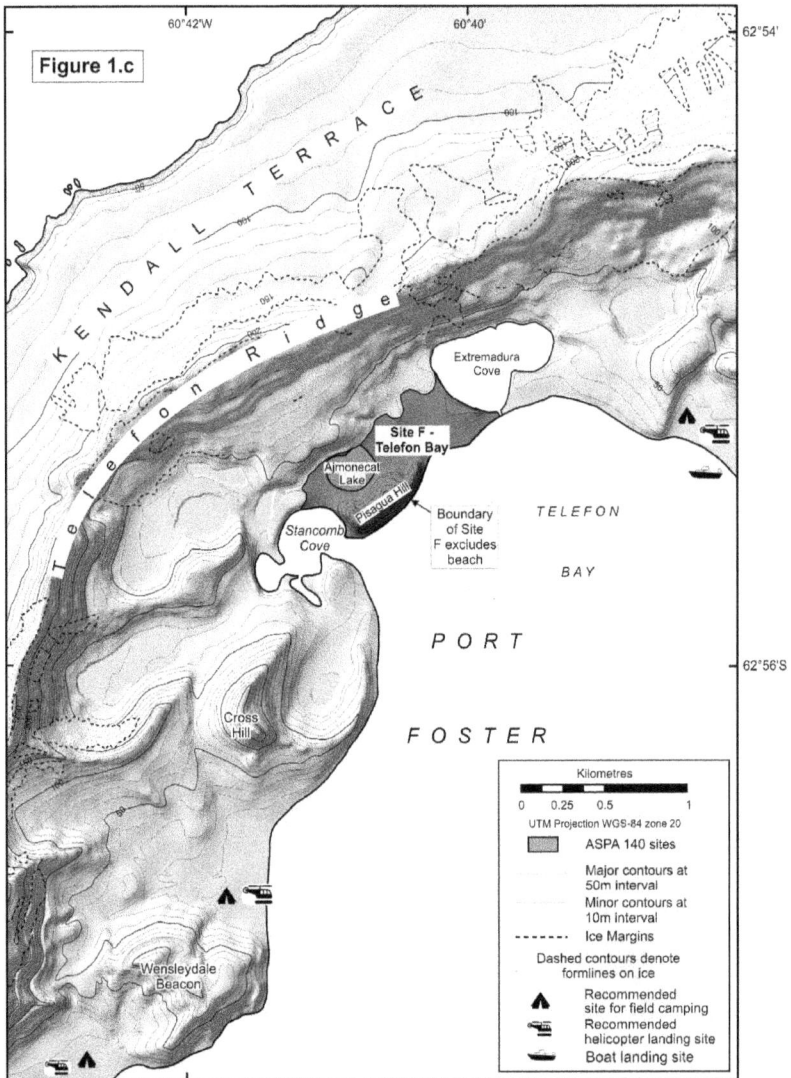

Figure 1d. Map showing the location of ASPA No. 140 Sites G and H.

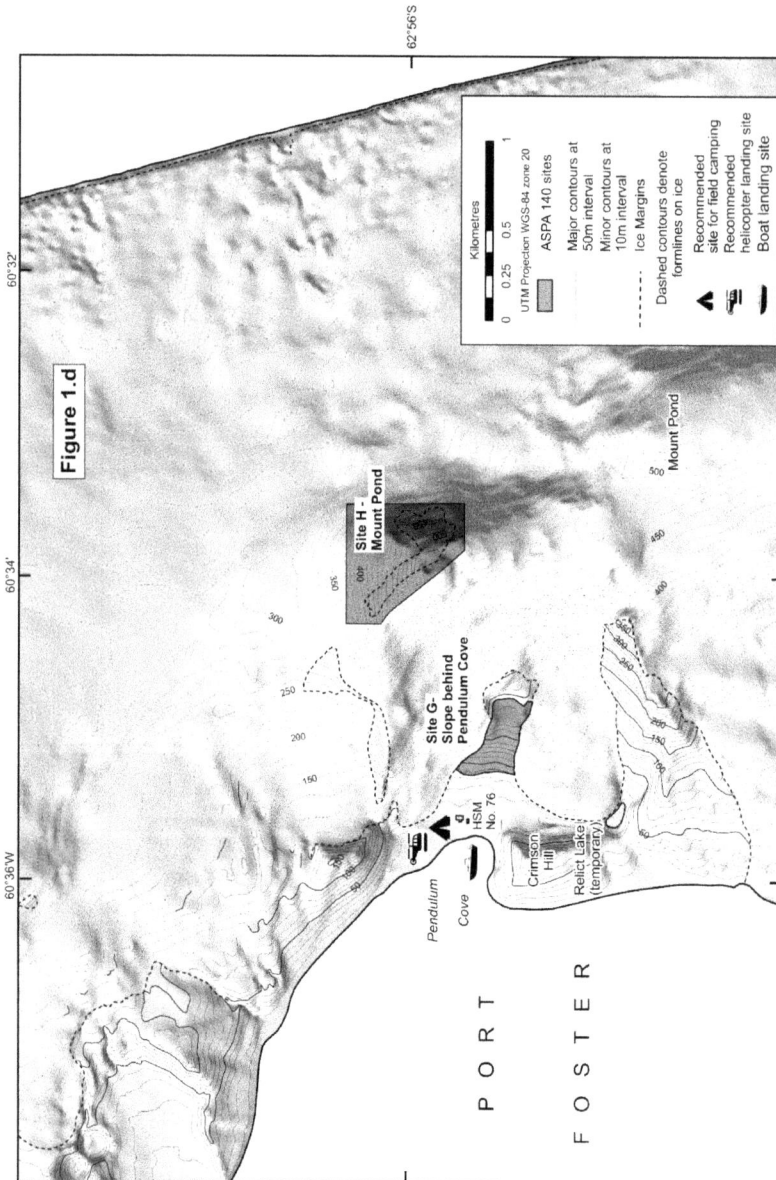

Annex 1. List of plant species, classed as rare or very rare in the Antarctic Treaty Area, occurring on Deception Island.

A. Bryophytes (L = Liverwort)

Species	Sites where species occurs	Notes
Brachythecium austroglareosum	D	Few other known Antarctic sites
B. fuegianum	G	Only known Antarctic site
Bryum amblyodon	C, D, G, K	Few other known Antarctic sites
B. dichotomum	C, E, H, J	Only known Antarctic site
B. orbiculatifolium	H, K	One other known Antarctic site
B. pallescens	D	Few other known Antarctic sites
Cryptochila grandiflora (L)	E	Only known Antarctic site
Dicranella hookeri	C, E, H	Only known Antarctic site
Didymodon brachyphillus	A, D, G, H	Locally more abundant than any other known Antarctic site
Ditrichum conicum	E	Only known Antarctic site
D. ditrichoideum	C, G, J	Only known Antarctic site
D. heteromallum	C, H	Only known Antarctic site
D. hyalinum	G	Few other known Antarctic sites
D. hyalinocuspidatum	G	Few other known Antarctic sites
Grimmia plagiopodia	A, D, G	A continental Antarctic species
Hymenoloma antarcticum	B, C, D, E, G, K	Few other known Antarctic sites
H. crispulum	G	Few other known Antarctic sites
Notoligotrichum trichodon	K	One other known Antarctic site
Philonotis polymorpha	E, H	Only known Antarctic site
Platyneurum jungermannioides	D	Few other known Antarctic sites
Polytrichastrum longisetum (L)	K	One other known Antarctic site
Pohlia wahlenbergii	C, E, H	One other known Antarctic site
Racomitrium heterostichoides	G	Only known Antarctic site
R. lanuginosum	G	Only known Antarctic site
R. subsecundum	C	Only known Antarctic site
S. amblyophyllum	C, D, G, H	Few other known Antarctic sites
S. andinum	H	Few other known Antarctic sites
S. deceptionensis sp. nov.	C	Deception endemic
S. leptoneurum sp. nov.	D	Deception endemic
Schistidium praemorsum	H	One other known Antarctic site
Syntrichia andersonii	D, L	Only known Antarctic site

B. Lichens

Species	Sites where species occurs	Notes
Acarospora austroshetlandica	A	One other known Antarctic site
Caloplaca johnstonii	B, D, F, L	Few other known Antarctic sites
Catapyrenium lachneoides	?	Few other known Antarctic sites
Cladonia galindezii	A, B, D	More abundant than any other known site
Degelia sp.	K	Only known Antarctic site
Ochrolechia parella	A, B, D	More abundant than any other known site
Peltigera didactyla	B, K	Very rare in B; very small colonising form abundant in K
Pertusaria excludens	D	Few other known Antarctic sites
P. oculae-ranae	G	Only known Antarctic site
Placopsis parellina	A, B, D, G, H	More abundant than any other known site
Protoparmelia loricata	B	Few other known Antarctic sites
Psoroma saccharatum	D	Only known Antarctic site
Stereocaulon condensatum	E	Only known Antarctic site
S. vesuvianum	B, G	Few other known Antarctic sites

Annex 2. Photographs of the Sites comprising ASPA 140. Photographs were taken between 19-26 Jan 2010 (K. Hughes: A, B, C, E, F, G, J, K, L; P. Convey: D, H).

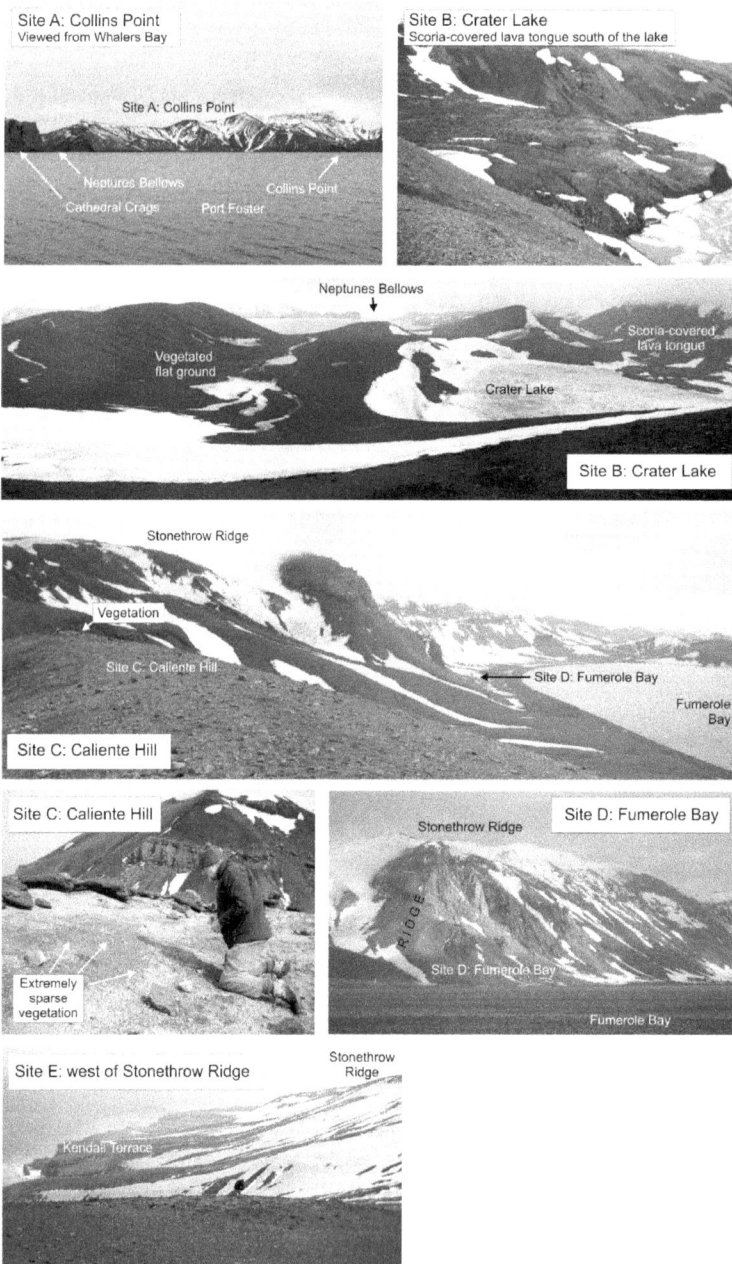

Site A: Collins Point
Viewed from Whalers Bay

Site B: Crater Lake
Scoria-covered lava tongue south of the lake

Site A: Collins Point

Neptures Bellows

Collins Point

Cathedral Crags   Port Foster

Neptunes Bellows

Vegetated
flat ground

Scoria-covered
lava tongue

Crater Lake

Site B: Crater Lake

Stonethrow Ridge

Vegetation

Site C: Caliente Hill

Site D: Fumerole Bay

Fumerole
Bay

Site C: Caliente Hill

Site C: Caliente Hill

Site D: Fumerole Bay

Stonethrow Ridge

RIDGE

Site D: Fumerole Bay

Extremely
sparse
vegetation

Fumerole Bay

Site E: west of Stonethrow Ridge

Stonethrow
Ridge

Kendall Terrace

Site F: Telefon Bay

Telefon Ridge

Pisagua Hill — Site F: Telefon Bay

Stancomb Cove — Entrance to Extremadura Cove —

Telefon Bay

Site G: Pendulum Cove

Mount Pond

Site G: Pendulum Cove

Crimson Hill

HSM No. 76 — Pendulum Cove

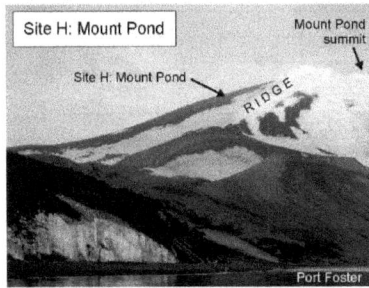

Site H: Mount Pond

Mount Pond summit

Site H: Mount Pond

RIDGE

Port Foster

Site J: Perchuć Cone

Site J: Perchuć Cone

Ronald Hill

Hangar HSM No. 71

Port Foster

Site K: Ronald Hill to Kroner Lake

Ronald Hill

Penfold Point — Kroner Lake — Whalers Bay — Hangar HSM No. 71

Port Foster

Site L: South East Point

Cathedral Crags

Site L: South East Point

South East Point

Bransfield Strait

121

Annex 3. Boundary coordinates for the Sites that comprise ASPA 140 Parts of Deception Island. Many of the boundaries follow natural features and detailed descriptions of the boundaries are found in Section 6. The boundary coordinates are numbered, with number 1 the most northerly co-ordinate and further coordinates numbered sequentially in a clockwise direction around each Site.

Site	Number	Latitude	Longitude
A: Collins Point	1	62°59'50'' S	060°33'55'' W
	2	63°00'06'' S	060°33'51'' W
	3	63°00'16'' S	060°34'27'' W
	4	63°00'15'' S	060°34'53'' W
	5	63°00'06'' S	060°35'15'' W
	6	62°59'47'' S	060°35'19'' W
	7	62°59'59'' S	060°34'48'' W
	8	62°59'49'' S	060°34'07'' W
B: Crater Lake	1	62°58'48'' S	060°40'02'' W
	2	62°58'50'' S	060°39'45'' W
	3	62°58'56'' S	060°39'52'' W
	4	62°59'01'' S	060°39'37'' W
	5	62°59'11'' S	060°39'47'' W
	6	62°59'18'' S	060°39'45'' W
	7	62°59'16'' S	060°40'15'' W
	8	62°59'04'' S	060°40'31'' W
	9	62°58'56'' S	060°40'25'' W
C: Caliente Hill	1	62°58'33'' S	060°42'12'' W
	2	62°58'27'' S	060°42'28'' W
	3	62°58'29'' S	060°42'33'' W
	4	62°58'25'' S	060°42'51'' W
D: Fumarole Bay	1	62°57'42'' S	060°43'05'' W
	2	62°58'04'' S	060°42'42'' W
	3	62°57'53'' S	060°43'08'' W
	4	62°57'43'' S	060°43'13'' W
E: west of Stonethrow Ridge	1	62°57'51'' S	060°44'00'' W
	2	62°57'54'' S	060°44'00'' W
	3	62°57'54'' S	060°44'10'' W
	4	62°57'51'' S	060°44'10'' W
F: Telefon Bay	1	62°55'02'' S	060°40'17'' W
	2	62°55'11'' S	060°39'45'' W
	3	62°55'35'' S	060°40'43'' W
	4	62°55'30'' S	060°41'13'' W
	5	62°55'21'' S	060°41'07'' W
G: Pendulum Cove	1	62°56'10'' S	060°35'15'' W
	2	62°56'20'' S	060°34'41'' W
	3	62°56'28'' S	060°34'44'' W

	4	62°56'21'' S	060°35'16'' W
H: Mt. Pond	1	62°55'51'' S	060°33'30'' W
	2	62°56'12'' S	060°33'30'' W
	3	62°56'12'' S	060°33'48'' W
	4	62°55'57'' S	060°34'42'' W
	5	62°55'51'' S	060°34'42'' W
J: Perchuć Cone	Point location	62°58'02'' S	060°33'39'' W
K: Ronald Hill to Kroner Lake	1	62°58'25'' S	060°34'22'' W
	2	62°58'32'' S	060°34'20'' W
	3	62°58'34'' S	060°34'27'' W
	4	62°58'41'' S	060°34'30'' W
	5	62°58'44'' S	060°34'18'' W
	6	62°58'50'' S	060°34'18'' W
	7	62°58'58'' S	060°34'38'' W
	8	62°58'49'' S	060°34'53'' W
	9	62°58'41'' S	060°34'40'' W
	10	62°58'24'' S	060°34'44'' W
L: South-east Point	1	62°58'53'' S	060°31'01'' W
	2	62°58'56'' S	060°30'59'' W
	3	62°58'57'' S	060°31'13'' W
	4	62°58'55'' S	060°31'14'' W

Annex 4. Recommended access to the Sites that comprise ASPA 140.

Site	Name	Recommended access route
A	Collins Point	By boat: land at the coast to the north of the site (Port Foster)
B	Crater Lake	Overland: traverse the west side of the ridge that rises to the south of Gabriel de Castilla Station for 500m, then travel east for 200 m until the western boundary of the Areas is reached.
C	Caliente Hill	Overland: access the site from Fumarole Bay to the north of the site, or along the prominent ridge that lies to the south west of the summit of Caliente Hill.
D	Fumarole Bay	By boat: access anywhere along the coast of Fumarole Bay.
E	west of Stonethrow Ridge	Overland: from Fumarole Bay, head southwest pass Albufera Lagoon then head north, traversing the west slope of Stonethrow Ridge. The Site lies on the north side of the east-west trending ridge that lies *c.* 600m south-southwest of the highest point on Stonethrow Ridge.
F	Telefon Bay	By boat: access the Site from either Telefon Bay or Stancomb Cove.
G	Pendulum Cove	By boat: access the site from Pendulum Cove, Port Foster, then overland past HSM No 76.
H	Mt. Pont	Overland: access with caution from Pendulum Cove via the prominent ice-free ridge to the west of the Site.
J	Perchuć Cone	Overland: access from Whalers Bay via Ronald Hill.
K	Ronald Hill to Kroner Lake	By boat: land in Whalers Bay, south of the Site - do not take boats into Kroner Lake to access the site (see Section *7(ii)* for details) Over land: access from Whalers Bay to the east of the Site.
L	South-east Point	On foot: Access overland, with caution, from either Whalers Bay (to the west of the Site) or Bailey Head (to the north of the Site)

Management Plan for
Antarctic Specially Protected Area No 172

Lower Taylor Glacier and Blood Falls,
McMurdo Dry Valleys, Victoria Land

Introduction

Blood Falls is an iron-rich saline discharge located at the terminus of the Taylor Glacier, Taylor Valley, McMurdo Dry Valleys. The source of the discharge is believed to be a subglacial marine salt deposit and brine reservoir located beneath the ablation zone of the Taylor Glacier, estimated to be located between one to six kilometres above Blood Falls. Approximate area and coordinates: sub-surface area 436km^2 (centered at 161°40.230'E, 77°50.220'S); sub-aerial area 0.11km^2 (centered at the Blood Falls discharge at 162°15.809'E, 77°43.365'). The primary reasons for designation of the Area are its unique physical properties, and the unusual microbial ecology and geochemistry. The Area is an important site for exobiological studies and provides a unique opportunity to sample the subglacial environment without direct contact. The influence of Blood Falls on adjacent Lake Bonney is also of significant scientific interest. Furthermore, the ablation zone of the Taylor Glacier is an important site for paleoclimatic and glaciological research. The lower Taylor Glacier subglacial brine reservoir and Blood Falls are globally unique and a site of outstanding scientific importance. Based on the Environmental Domains Analysis for Antarctica (Resolution 3 (2008)) the Area lies within Environment S – McMurdo – South Victoria Land geologic. Designation of the Area allows for scientific access to ice deep within Taylor Glacier, provided measures are in place to ensure this does not compromise the Blood Falls reservoir and hydrological system.

1. Description of values to be protected

Blood Falls is a distinctive glacial feature located at 162°16.288'E, 77°43.329'S, at the terminus of the Taylor Glacier in the Taylor Valley, McMurdo Dry Valleys, southern Victoria Land (Map 1). The feature forms where an iron-rich, saline liquid discharge of subglacial origin emerges at the surface and then rapidly oxidizes to give it a distinctive red coloration (Figure 1). Available evidence suggests the source of the discharge is a subglacial marine salt deposit and brine reservoir located beneath the Taylor Glacier (Keys 1980; Hubbard *et al.* 2004) (Map 1). The feature is unique in its physical configuration, microbial biology and geochemistry and has an important influence on the local ecosystem of Lake Bonney. Furthermore, the episodic discharge events at Blood Falls provide a unique opportunity to sample the properties of the subglacial reservoir and its ecosystem.

Blood Falls was first observed by Griffith Taylor, Robert F. Scott's Senior Geologist, in 1911. However, scientific research into its unusual morphological and geochemical characteristics did not commence until the late 1950s (Hamilton *et al.* 1962; Angino *et al.* 1964; Black *et al.* 1965). The feature named as Blood Falls is the primary discharge site at the terminus of the Taylor Glacier (Map 2). A secondary lateral saline discharge has been observed to emerge at the surface from under sediments ~40 m north from the Taylor Glacier at the margin of the Santa Fe Stream delta (162°16.042'E, 77°43.297'S, Map 2). The exact location and form of the subglacial reservoir source feeding Blood Falls is currently uncertain, although geological, glacio-chemical and geophysical mapping results suggest that the reservoir is located between one to six kilometres from the terminus (Keys 1980; Hubbard *et al.* 2004). It has been estimated that the brine reservoir became encased by ice approximately 3 to 5 Ma BP (Mikucki *et al.* 2004) and may represent the oldest liquid feature in the Taylor Valley (Lyons *et al.* 2005).

The Blood Falls outflow contains a unique microbial community of apparently marine origin. The microbes may survive in the subglacial environment for millions of years without external carbon input. On account of its high iron and salt content, the microbial ecosystem at Blood Falls is an important site for exobiological studies and may provide an analogue for the conditions found beneath the polar ice caps on Mars. It is therefore important to ensure that the Blood Falls microbial community, the brine reservoir and associated subglacial hydrological system are protected.

The discharge episodically released from Blood Falls into adjacent Lake Bonney alters the geochemical composition of the lake and provides nutrients that are otherwise limited, making the site valuable for investigation of the impacts of subglacial outflow on lake ecosystems.

The Taylor Glacier is an important site for Antarctic glaciological and paleoclimatic studies. It provides a unique opportunity to study Antarctic outlet glacier behaviour in relation to environmental change, using ice core paleoclimatic data from Taylor Dome, geologic evidence from the Taylor Valley and climatic data from nearby US Long Term Ecological Research (LTER) sites (Kavanaugh *et al.* 2009a; Bliss *et al.* 2011). The lower ablation zone of the Taylor Glacier has been identified as a potentially valuable site for paleoclimatic studies, as it exposes ice from the last glacial period and allows past concentrations of trace gases to be measured at a high temporal resolution (Aciego *et al.* 2007). In addition, the Taylor Glacier is of scientific value for glaciological studies, in particular glacier dynamics and the relationships between stresses and glacier flow, and for other glaciological research (Kavanaugh & Cuffey 2009).

The Blood Falls system is a valuable site for study of microbiology, water chemistry, glaciology, and paleoclimatology. The most unusual aspects of the Blood Falls system are its physical configuration, brine chemistry and microbial ecosystem. Blood Falls also exerts considerable influence over the geochemistry and microbiology of Lake Bonney. The Area possesses outstanding aesthetic values and significant educational value, as the site has been the subject of a range of scientific and media articles in recent years. Blood Falls and the Taylor Glacier brine reservoir merit special protection due to their outstanding scientific values, unique configuration, ancient origin, importance to ecosystems in the local area, and their vulnerability to disturbance by human activities.

On the basis of presently available knowledge, the input of contaminants directly into the subglacial reservoir or into areas of the bed from which subglacial fluids could flow towards the reservoir has been identified as the most likely potential mechanism for contamination of the Taylor Glacier brine reservoir. However, the uncertainties surrounding the location of the subglacial reservoir and its connectivity with the subglacial hydrological system make it difficult to assess the likelihood of this occurring and for this reason a precautionary approach has been adopted when defining the boundaries of the sub-surface component of the Area.

2. Aims and objectives

Management at the lower Taylor Glacier and Blood Falls aims to:

- avoid degradation of, or substantial risk to, the values of the Area by preventing unnecessary human disturbance and sampling in the Area;
- allow scientific research, in particular on the microbial community, water chemistry and physical configuration of the lower Taylor Glacier and Blood Falls;
- allow other scientific research and visits for education / outreach provided they will not jeopardize the values of the Area;
- minimize the possibility of introduction of alien plants, animals and microbes into the Area;
- allow visits for management purposes in support of the aims of the Management Plan.

3. Management activities

The following management activities shall be undertaken to protect the values of the Area:

- Markers or signs illustrating the location and boundaries, with clear statements of entry restrictions, shall be placed at appropriate locations on the boundary of the Area to help avoid inadvertent entry;
- Markers, signs or structures erected within the Area for scientific or management purposes shall be secured and maintained in good condition, and removed when no longer necessary;
- Visits shall be made as necessary (no less than once every five years) to assess whether the Area continues to serve the purposes for which it was designated and to ensure management and maintenance measures are adequate;
- A copy of this Management Plan shall be kept available in the principal research hut facilities proximal to the Area, in particular the Lake Bonney, Lake Hoare, Lake Fryxell, F6, and New Harbor camps, and at McMurdo Station and Scott Base;
- National Antarctic programmes operating in the region shall consult together for the purpose of ensuring that the above provisions are implemented.

4. Period of designation

Designated for an indefinite period.

5. Maps and photographs

Map 1: ASPA 172: Lower Taylor Glacier and Blood Falls sub-surface protected area boundary. Projection: Lambert Conformal Conic; Standard parallels: 1st 77°35'S; 2nd 77°50'S; Central Meridian: 161°30'E; Latitude of Origin: 78°00'S; Spheroid and horizontal datum: WGS84; Contour interval 200m.

Inset 1: Location of ASMA 2 McMurdo Dry Valleys in the Ross Sea region.

Inset 2: Location of the Taylor Glacier in ASMA 2 McMurdo Dry Valleys.

Map 2: ASPA 172: Blood Falls sub-surface and sub-aerial protected area boundary and designated camp site. Projection: Lambert Conformal Conic; Standard parallels: 1st 77°43'S; 2nd 77°44'S; Central Meridian: 162°16'E; Latitude of Origin: 78°00'S; Spheroid and horizontal datum: WGS84; Contour interval 20m.

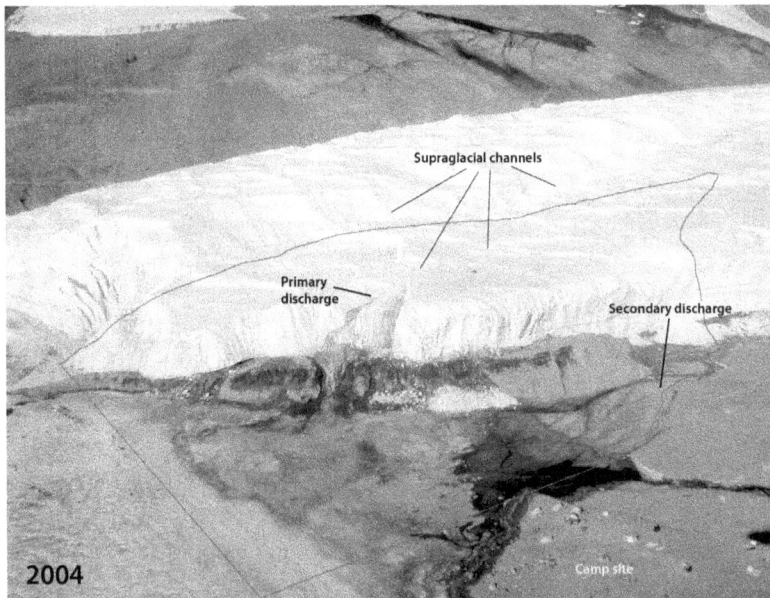

Figure 1. Aerial view of the terminus of the Taylor Glacier in 2004, with Blood Falls at center and Lake Bonney at lower left (Photographer unknown: 18 Nov 2004).

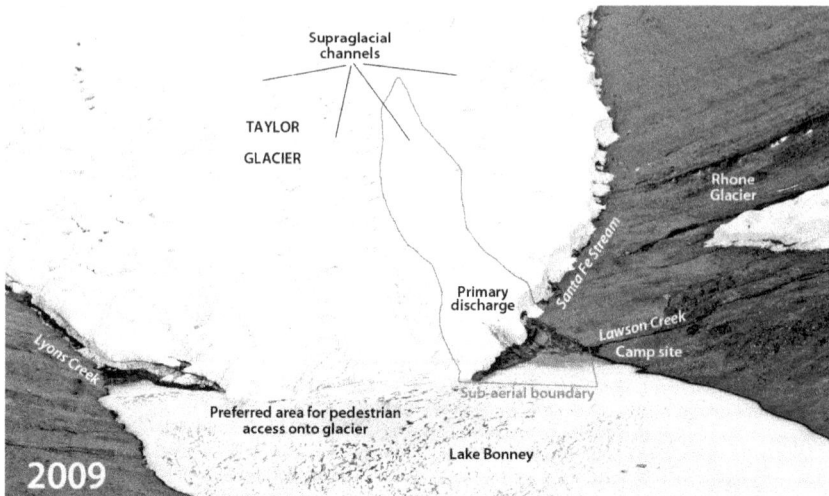

Figure 2. Aerial view of the terminus of the Taylor Glacier in 2009, showing the extent of the sub-aerial component of the Area. A comparison with Figure 1 highlights the extent to which the size of the discharge varies over time (C. Harris, ERA / USAP: 10 Dec 2009).

6. Description of the Area

6(i) Geographical co-ordinates, boundary markers and natural features

Overview

Blood Falls (located at 162°16.288'E, 77°43.329'S) is an iron-rich, hypersaline discharge that emerges from a crevasse near the terminus of Taylor Glacier, in the McMurdo Dry Valleys, southern Victoria Land. The brine initially lacks color, but freezes to a bubbly white icing as it flows off the glacier and then oxidises to produce its distinctive red-orange colour. Many traces of iron coloured material remain encapsulated in former crevasses and cracks in the glacier especially near the primary discharge point. A secondary, much smaller and less distinct, surface discharge has been observed twice (1958, 1976) ~40m north of Taylor Glacier at the margin of the Santa Fe stream delta (162°16.042'E, 77°43.297'S, Map 2). The secondary discharge has a similar physical and chemical composition to the primary outlet at Blood Falls (Keys 1980).

The volume and physical extent of the primary Blood Falls surface outflow and icing accumulation varies over time, ranging from a few hundred to several thousand cubic metres of saline icing, and the discharge events occur at intervals of one to three years or more (Keys 1980). An unknown proportion of brine sometimes drains, before it freezes (e.g. 1972, 1978) into Lake Bonney. At its minimum extent, the discharge appears as a small area of discoloration at the Taylor Glacier terminus, but can extend tens of metres across Lake Bonney at its maximum (see eg, Figures 1 & 2).

The source of the brine discharges is subglacial, and the water in the discharge brine is melted glacial ice but the nature of the source is unclear (Keys pers. comm. 2012). Chemical and isotopic analyses indicate that a marine salt deposit or deposits are melting and / or have melted ice of Taylor Glacier (Keys 1980). Deepened subglacial topography beneath the Taylor Glacier between one to six kilometres from the terminus suggests the salt body is likely to be located there but there could be other locations further up glacier. The thickness and extent of the resulting subglacial brine, or the exact location and nature of the resulting reservoir(s) and brine drainage paths have yet to be firmly established (Keys 1980; Hubbard *et al.* 2004).

Boundaries and coordinates

The boundaries of the Area are designed to protect the values of the subglacial brine reservoir and the Blood Falls surface discharge, taking into account the size of the catchment, likely hydrological connections and practicality. Because there is evidence that hydrological connections and interactions between the surface and bed of the Taylor Glacier are likely to be minimal, restricting access on and / or over the majority of the surface of the catchment is not considered necessary. However, a small area encompassing the confirmed primary and secondary Blood Falls discharges, including a part of the Taylor Glacier surface that drains directly into the primary discharge, is included within the boundary at the surface to provide adequate protection for the confirmed outflow areas (Map 2). The 'possible discharge' location examples shown on Map 1 are not currently included within the Area because they remain unconfirmed. They may represent exposures that indicate basal processes that may at one time have involved the reservoir or related features rather than be points of contemporary discharge. Moreover these features do not feed into the reservoir or primary outflow site at Blood Falls.

Subglacial interconnections, on the other hand, could be extensive, so a relatively large sub-surface component extending ~50km up-glacier aims to protect the main part of the subglacial catchment of the lower Taylor Glacier that could be interconnected with the brine reservoir (Map 1). This extent is currently considered sufficient to protect the values of the reservoir, although it is recognized that some interconnections may extend further since technically the catchment extends far onto the polar plateau; the western boundary was therefore selected in part as a practical limit beyond which the risks to the Area are considered minimal.

In summary, the vertical and lateral extents of the Area were defined on the grounds that the boundary:

- protects the integrity of the subglacial reservoir and the confirmed primary and secondary Blood Falls discharge areas;

- allows for uncertainties in the location of the reservoir and in the connectivity within the subglacial hydrological system;

- provides a practical boundary based on catchments that is straightforward to map and identify in the field; and

- does not unnecessarily restrict activities on and / or over the surface of the Taylor Glacier.

Key boundary coordinates are summarized in Table 1.

Table 1: Summary list of key protected area boundary coordinates (see Maps 1 & 2)

Location	Label	Longitude (E)	Latitude (S)
Sub-surface boundary			
Blood Falls primary discharge	A	162° 16.305'	77° 43.325'
Taylor / Ferrar glaciers ice divide, southern margin of Kukri Hills	B	161° 57.300'	77° 49.100'
Knobhead, foot of NE ridge	C	161° 44.383'	77° 52.257'
Kennar Valley, center at Taylor Glacier margin	D	160° 25.998'	77° 44.547'
Beehive Mountain, foot of SW ridge	E	160° 33.328'	77° 39.670'
Mudrey Cirque SW extent	F	160° 42.988'	77° 39.205'
Mudrey Cirque SE extent	G	160° 48.710'	77° 39.525'
Sub-aerial boundary			
Taylor Glacier terminus, prominent ice / moraine outcrop	*a*	162° 16.639'	77° 43.356'
Supraglacial catchment feeding Blood Falls, western extent	*b*	162° 14.508'	77° 43.482'
Taylor Glacier, northern margin	*c*	162° 15.758'	77° 43.320'
Santa Fe Stream delta, western margin	*d*	162° 15.792'	77° 43.315'
Lawson Creek, boulder on west bank	*e*	162° 16.178'	77° 43.268'
Lake Bonney, ~80m east from shore at Santa Fe Stream delta	*f*	162° 16.639'	77° 43.268'

Sub-surface

The sub-surface boundary encompasses the entire ablation zone of the Taylor Glacier, from a depth of 100m below the surface to the glacier bed. In order to aid identification of the boundary at the surface, and because of practical constraints over the availability of data on the configuration of the 100m depth within the glacier, the surface margin of the Taylor Glacier is used as a surrogate for the 100m depth line and thus is used to define the lateral extent of the sub-surface component of the Area. The following description first defines the lateral extent of the sub-surface component of the Area and subsequently defines the vertical extent.

The sub-surface component of the protected area boundary extends from the primary Blood Falls discharge site (162°16.288'E 77°43.329'S) (labelled 'A' in Table 1 and on Maps 1 & 2) and follows the Taylor Glacier terminus southward 0.8km to the southern margin of the glacier at Lyons Creek. The boundary of the Area thence extends 19.3km SW (Map 1), following the southern margin of the Taylor Glacier to the western extremity of the Kukri Hills. The boundary thence extends 7.8km east to an approximate position where the ice divides between the Taylor and Ferrar glaciers along the southern margin of the Kukri Hills, located at 161°57.30'E, 77°49.10'S ('B', Table 1, Map 1). The boundary thence extends 7.9km SW, following the approximate divide between the Taylor and Ferrar glaciers to the eastern extremity of Knobhead at 161°44.383'E, 77°52.257'S ('C', Table 1, Map 1). The boundary thence follows the southern margin of the Taylor Glacier westward 11.8km to Windy Gully, crosses Windy Gully and thence extends 45.2km NW, following the margins of the Taylor, Beacon and Turnabout glaciers to the Kennar Valley, located at 160°25.998'E, 77°44.547'S ('D', Table 1, Map 1). The boundary thence extends NE across the Taylor Glacier 9.5km to the foot of Beehive Mountain at 160°33.328'E, 77°39.670'S ('E', Table 1, Map 1). As a visual reference, the protected area boundary runs parallel to a distinct ridge evident in the surface of the Taylor Glacier immediately downstream from an area of heavy crevassing.

From Beehive Mountain, the boundary extends 5km east to the boundary between Mudrey Cirque and the Taylor Glacier at 160°42.988'E, 77°39.205'S ('F', Table 1, Map 1). The boundary thence follows the margin of Mudrey Cirque for 9.6km to rejoin the Taylor Glacier at 160°48.710'E, 77°39.525'S ('G', Table 1, Map 1) and thence extends 59.6km SE to the foot of the Cavendish Icefalls, following the northern margin of the Taylor Glacier. The boundary thence extends north and east along the Taylor Glacier margin for 16.9km, excluding Simmons Lake and Lake Joyce, and extends a further 15.4km east to the primary Blood Falls discharge site ('A', Table 1, Map 2).

The vertical extent of the sub-surface component of the Area is defined in terms of depth below the surface of the Taylor Glacier (Figure 3). The sub-surface boundary extends from a depth of 100m below the Taylor Glacier surface to the glacier bed, which is defined as the underlying bedrock surface below the glacier. The subglacial hydrological system, the Blood Falls brine reservoir, and any layers of mixed ice / sediment and / or unconsolidated sediments are included within the boundary. The sub-surface component of the Area does not impose additional constraints on activities conducted at the surface or within the upper 100m depth within the body of the Taylor Glacier.

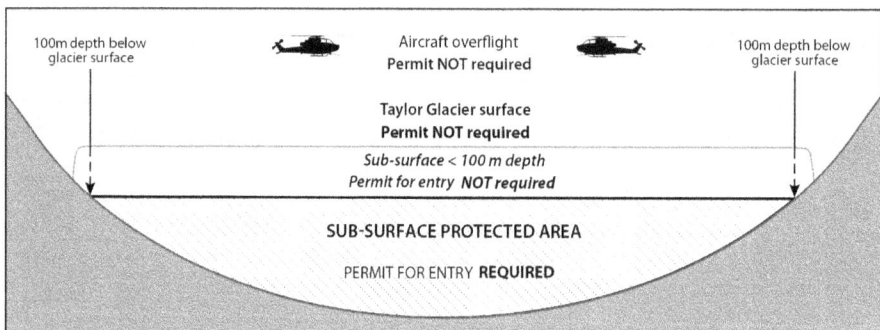

Figure 3: Depth-based definition of the vertical extent of the sub-surface component of the lower Taylor Glacier and Blood Falls protected area

Sub-aerial

This sub-aerial component of the Area comprises the delta of Santa Fe Stream, part of the western extremity of Lake Bonney, and a small supraglacial catchment surrounding Blood Falls that is defined by a system of ice ridges that persist in the local glacier morphology over at least decadal time-scales. The SE boundary of the sub-aerial component of the Area is indicated by a prominent ice and moraine outcrop extending from the Taylor Glacier terminus at 162°16.639'E, 77°43.356'S (labelled '*a*' in Table 1 and on Map 2). The boundary thence extends SW and up-glacier for 900.8m, following the southern margin of the supraglacial catchment surrounding Blood Falls to the most westerly extent of the supraglacial catchment, located at 162°14.508'E, 77°43.482'S ('*b*', Table 1, Map 2). The boundary thence extends NE by 594.5m to the Taylor Glacier margin at 162°15.758'E, 77°43.320'S ('*c*', Table 1, Map 2), following the northern margin of the supraglacial catchment. The boundary of the Area thence extends 16.8m NE in a straight line, to the top of the river bank above the Santa Fe Stream delta at 162°15.792'E, 77°43.315'S ('*d*', Table 1, Map 2). The boundary thence extends NE for 198.7m, following the top of the bank to the point at which it meets Lawson Creek, at 162°16.178'E, 77°43.268'S ('*e*', Table 1, Map 2). The boundary thence extends due east in a straight line for 180.5m to a point on Lake Bonney at 162°16.639'E , 77°43.268'S ('*f*', Table 1, Map 2) and thence due south in a straight line for 166.5m to the prominent ice and moraine outcrop.

Climate

Two meteorological stations operated by the McMurdo Dry Valleys Long Term Ecological Research (LTER) programme are located close to Blood Falls (*http://www.mcmlter.org/queries/avg_met_queries.jsp*): 'Lake Bonney' (Point '*a* ', 162°27.881'E, 77°42.881'S) located ~4.5km to the east, and 'Taylor Glacier' (162°07.881'E, 77°44.401'S), located ~ 4km up-glacier. The mean annual air temperature at both stations was approximately –17°C during the period 1995 – 2009. The lowest temperature at these stations during this period was –48.26°C, recorded at Lake Bonney in August 2008, whilst the maximum of 10.64°C was recorded at Lake Bonney in December 2001. August was the coolest month at both stations, with January and December the warmest at Lake Bonney and Taylor Glacier respectively.

Mean annual wind speeds over the same period (1995 – 2009) ranged from 3.89m/s at Lake Bonney to 5.16m/s at the Taylor Glacier, with the maximum of 30.8m/s recorded at Taylor Glacier in August 2004. Taylor Valley topography, in particular Nussbaum Riegel, encourages formation of isolated weather systems within the Lake Bonney basin and limits the flow of coastal winds into the area (Fountain *et al.* 1999).

Average mean annual precipitation at Lake Bonney between 1995 and 2009 was 340mm water equivalent. Ablation rates on the Taylor Glacier are highest in the area surrounding the Cavendish Ice Falls, reaching a maximum at the base of Windy Gully (~ 0.4m a^{-1}), and are lowest up-glacier of Beacon Valley (~0 to 0.125m a^{-1}). Ablation rates on the lower Taylor Glacier generally range from 0.15 to 0.3m a^{-1} (Bliss *et al.* 2011).

Geology and geomorphology

The Taylor Valley is comprised of a mosaic of tills of varying ages and rock types, including: Precambrian metamorphic basement rocks (Ross Supergroup), early Paleozoic intrusives (Granite Harbor formation), a series of sedimentary rocks of Devonian to Jurassic age (Beacon Supergroup) and the Jurassic age Ferrar Dolerite sills (Pugh *et al.* 2003).

The Blood Falls subglacial reservoir is thought to be a marine brine originating from a marine incursion into the McMurdo Dry Valleys during the Pliocene (3 to 5 Ma BP) and may represent the oldest liquid water feature in the Dry Valleys (Lyons *et al.* 2005). It has been proposed that during the subsequent retreat of seawater from the Taylor Valley, the brine was trapped close to the modern-day terminus of the Taylor Glacier and was then 'sealed' beneath the glacier as ice advanced during the late Pliocene or Pleistocene (Marchant *et al.* 1993). The brine deposit is now thought to form a subglacial reservoir, which episodically emerges at the surface at the primary outflow and the secondary lateral discharge site. It has been suggested the brine has been modified since entrapment, partly due to inputs from chemical weathering (Keys 1980; Lyons *et al.* 2005; Mikucki *et al.* 2009).

Soils and sediment

Taylor Valley soils are generally poorly developed and largely composed of sand (95- 99% by weight) (Burkins *et al.* 2000; Barrett *et al.* 2004). Taylor Valley soils have some of the lowest organic matter concentrations on Earth (Campbell & Claridge 1987; Burkins *et al.* 2000) and soils within the Lake Bonney basin are particularly low in organic carbon content (Barrett *et al.* 2004). In the Taylor Valley, soils generally extend to a depth of 10 to 30cm, below which is permafrost (Campbell & Claridge 1987). In addition to glacial till, the Taylor Valley floor is covered by lacustrine sediments, deposited by the formerly extensive glacial Lake Washburn, which extend to a depth of approximately 300m (Hendy *et al.* 1979; Stuiver *et al.* 1981; Hall & Denton 2000).

Moraines at the snout of the Taylor Glacier are composed of reworked lacustrine sediment, which dates from approximately 300 ka BP (Higgins *et al.* 2000). Sediments at the Taylor Glacier margin are also composed of silty and sandy tills, formed by melt-out from debris-rich basal glacier ice and from erosion by ice marginal streams (Higgins *et al.* 2000). A thick basal ice sequence characterised by fine-grained sediments and thought to contain salts originating from the Blood Falls subglacial reservoir was documented in a tunnel excavated on the northern margin of the Taylor Glacier (Samyn *et al.* 2005, 2008; Mager 2006; Mager *et al.* 2007). These observations suggest that the base of the Taylor Glacier is interacting with the underlying sediment and that localised melting and refreezing may be occurring (Souchez *et al.* 2004; Samyn *et al.* 2005; Mager *et al.* 2007).

Glaciology and glacial hydrology

The Taylor Glacier is an outlet glacier of the East Antarctic Ice Sheet and terminates in the western lobe of Lake Bonney. A comprehensive study has recently been undertaken to investigate the dynamics of the Taylor Glacier ablation zone, including its geometry and surface velocity field (Kavanaugh *et al.* 2009a), its force balance (Kavanaugh & Cuffey 2009) and its contemporary mass balance (Fountain *et al.* 2006; Kavanaugh *et al.* 2009b). Results suggest that the glacier primarily flows through deformation of cold ice and that the Taylor Glacier is approximately in mass balance. Ice samples from the lower Taylor Glacier ablation zone have been used in paleoclimatic studies and the ice has been dated to the last glacial period (Aciego *et al.* 2007). Other recent glaciological studies conducted on the Taylor Glacier have investigated the evolution of the dry ice cliffs at the terminus (Pettit *et al.* 2006; Carmichael *et al.* 2007), carried out textural and gas measurements on basal ice within a subglacial tunnel proximal to the primary Blood Falls outlet (Samyn *et al.* 2005, 2008; Mager *et al.* 2007) and assessed the surface energy budget of the glacier (Bliss *et al.* 2011). Studies of the supraglacial hydrology of the Taylor Glacier suggest that meltwater channels cover approximately 40% of the lower ablation zone of the Taylor Glacier and melting within the channels contributes significantly to total runoff into Lake Bonney (Johnston *et al.* 2005). Two large channels drain across the primary Blood Falls outlet, but it is considered highly unlikely that direct connections exist between surface meltwater channels and the Blood Falls subglacial reservoir due to the cold temperatures of the near-surface ice and the lack of crevasse penetration beyond 100m depth (Cuffey, Fountain, Pettit and Severinghaus, pers. comms. 2010).

The extent of subglacial meltwater beneath the Taylor Glacier and its connectivity with the Blood Falls system is currently uncertain. Inferred basal temperatures suggest that the majority of the Taylor Glacier base is substantially below the pressure melting point (Samyn *et al.* 2005, 2008) and a radar survey conducted by Holt *et al.* (2006) found no evidence of widespread liquid water beneath the Taylor Glacier. Measurements made by Samyn *et al.* (2005) recorded a basal temperature of -17°C at the side of the glacier near Blood Falls. However, ice thickness and plausible gradients of englacial temperature are consistent with temperatures around -5 to -7°C at the base of the glacier within 1–3km of Blood Falls, similar to the measured temperatures of brine discharging at the primary and secondary sites (Keys 1980). Ice-penetrating radar surveys suggest that water, probably hypersaline, may exist within an 80m bedrock depression, located between 4 and 6km from the Taylor Glacier terminus (Hubbard *et al.* 2004).

Saline water is released episodically from the subglacial reservoir of Blood Falls, usually via the primary outlet and on occasions via the secondary lateral discharge site. However, detailed underwater surveys of the Taylor Glacier terminus conducted by the ENDURANCE (Environmentally Non-Disturbing Under-Ice Robotic Antarctic Explorer) AUV (autonomous underwater vehicle) suggest that the subglacial brine may enter Lake Bonney across the majority of the Taylor Glacier terminus (Stone *et al.* 2010; Priscu, pers. comm. 2011). In addition, a number of sites have been identified on both the northern and southern margins of the Taylor Glacier where salts and orange discolouration exist in layers (examples of which are identified on Map 1 as 'Possible discharge'), but the nature of these features has yet to be confirmed (Keys 1980; Nylen, pers. comm. 2010). The trigger for subglacial release events is uncertain, although it has been suggested that after accumulating under pressure beneath the glacier, the brine must travel through a discrete subglacial conduit which controls the location of the primary discharge: this behavior is similar to some aperiodic glacier bursts (jökulhlaups) where basal melting processes and changing stress patterns (such as physical shifts of the Taylor Glacier) may create a passage for the brine through impounding basal ice or force the subglacial liquid out from its bedrock depression (Keys 1980; Higgins *et al.* 2000; Mikucki 2005).

The primary Blood Falls discharge is cold (~ 6°C), high in dissolved organic carbon, iron and sodium chloride, and has a conductivity approximately 2.5 times seawater (Mikucki *et al.* 2004; Mickuki 2005).

A number of lines of geochemical evidence support a marine origin for the Blood Falls outflow, which generally shows very similar characteristics to seawater. Studies have demonstrated that the volume, spatial extent and geochemistry of the Blood Falls discharge varies over time (Black *et al.* 1965; Keys 1979; Lyons *et al.* 2005) and differs between normal flow and rapid discharge events (Mikucki 2005).

Ecology and microbiology

The Blood Falls outflow contains a microbial community, apparently of marine origin (Mikucki & Priscu 2007; Mikucki *et al.* 2009). The bacteria may be capable of metabolising iron and sulphur compounds, allowing the population to survive in the subglacial environment for extended periods of time, possibly millions of years (Mikucki *et al.* 2009). The microbes are also thought to play an important role in carbon cycling, allowing the ecosystem to survive without external carbon input (Mikucki & Priscu 2007). The primary controls on the characteristics of the microbial ecosystem at Blood Falls may provide an analogue for the conditions found beneath the polar ice caps on Mars (Mikucki *et al.* 2004). A living bacterial assemblage has been identified within the basal ice and sediments sampled within the tunnel excavated on the northern margin of Taylor Glacier (Christner *et al.* 2010).

Microbial studies have provided further support for a marine origin of the brine reservoir, as the microbial assemblages recorded at Blood Falls are similar to those found in other marine systems (Mikucki *et al.* 2004; Mikucki & Priscu 2007). The ecosystem has been highlighted as an important site for exobiological studies, particularly as an analogue for Martian ice masses (Mikucki *et al.* 2004; Mikucki 2005). The primary controls on the Blood Falls microbial assemblage are thought to be the pre-glacial history of the ecosystem and the surrounding terrain, the bed lithology and the glacier hydrology, although the extent of contact between the microbial ecosystem and the glacial hydrological system is currently uncertain (Mikucki 2005; Mikucki & Priscu 2007).

The saline subglacial waters of Blood Falls meet the comparatively fresh surface water of western Lake Bonney in the lake perimeter area (often referred to as a 'moat', as this zone is prone to melt in summer). The moat area acts as a transition zone and its geochemical composition becomes less similar to Blood Falls with distance from the primary discharge site (Mikucki 2005). The Blood Falls discharge is also diluted in the moat area by input from Santa Fe Stream, which is primarily fed by surface melt from the Taylor Glacier and flows along its northern margin (Mikucki 2005). Lawson Creek also flows into the Area and drains into Lake Bonney approximately 100m north of the primary Blood Falls outflow.

Saline discharge, organic carbon and viable microbes from Blood Falls are episodically released into the western lobe of Lake Bonney, altering the geochemistry and biology of the lake and providing nutrients that are otherwise limited (Lyons *et al.* 1998, 2002, 2005; Mikucki *et al.* 2004). Discharges into Lake Bonney have been observed at a depth of 20 to 25m, and below this depth Lake Bonney exhibits a very similar geochemistry to Blood Falls, including high iron levels and a similar ion chemistry to seawater (Black & Bowser 1967; Lyons *et al.* 1998, 2005; Mikucki *et al.* 2004). Studies have shown that bacteria in the deep areas of western Lake Bonney are similar in size to those from Blood Falls, but much smaller than other those found in the deep waters of other lakes in the Dry Valleys (Takacs 1999).

Terrestrial ecology

Invertebrate communities in the Blood Falls area have not been extensively studied. However, soil samples from the shore of western Lake Bonney identified *Scottnema lindsayae* as the most abundant nematode in the Lake Bonney basin and also recorded *Eudorylaimus antarcticus* and *Plectus antarcticus* (Barrett *et al.* 2004).

Human activities and impact

Local field camps historically have been located in two main areas on the north-western shore of Lake Bonney, close to the moat area and the primary Blood Falls outflow (Map 2). The camp site contains a number of tent sites marked by stone circles. This has resulted in localized soil disturbance, although activities at the camp site are considered unlikely to have had an impact on Blood Falls (Keys, Skidmore, pers. comms. 2010). A helicopter landing site is located approximately 160m north of the primary Blood Falls outflow, although usage is also unlikely to have adverse effects on Blood Falls (Hawes, Skidmore, pers. comms. 2010). A pedestrian trail has formed to the west of Lawson Creek, which extends parallel to and above Santa Fe Stream around 50 – 100m from the northern margin of the Taylor Glacier. The trail has become prominent due to foot traffic and shows signs of minor erosion.

Stream monitoring equipment, including a weir, was installed by the LTER in the Santa Fe Stream delta area (Map 2), which was largely removed in January 2010. Parts of the weir embedded into stream sediments proved difficult to extract and have been left *in situ* because the impact of removal was considered greater than leaving the material in place. A number of items of disused glaciological equipment have been collected from the northern margin of the Taylor Glacier in the Santa Fe Stream delta area, and it is possible some of these items remain either on inaccessible locations on the glacier surface and / or embedded in sediments at the foot of the ice cliffs. Two tunnels cut into the basal ice remain from previous scientific studies, on the northern margin of Taylor Glacier ~ 600m and 1000m from Blood Falls respectively, although in time these will collapse and melt out.

6(ii) Access to the Area

- Access to, movement on, and / or over the surface of the Taylor Glacier within the region covered by the sub-surface component of the Area is not subject to any special restrictions.

- Access to the sub-aerial component of the Area is normally made first by helicopter to the designated landing site on the north-western shore of Lake Bonney (162°16.30'E, 77°43.24'S, Map 2), and from there on foot. Access may also be made on foot from the direction of Lake Bonney or from higher up the Taylor Glacier.

- The preferred route for pedestrian access to the sub-aerial component of the Area from the designated helicopter landing site and camp site is from Lake Bonney, avoiding the coloured saline icing of the discharge and Santa Fe Stream delta when possible, ascending the terminus of the Taylor Glacier from slopes to the south of the sub-aerial component boundary (Map 2). Steep ice cliffs impede foot access to the sub-aerial component of the Area along the northern margins of the Taylor Glacier. Moats and pools forming around the margin of Lake Bonney may impede access later in the season.

- A pedestrian walking route has formed parallel to and ~50 – 100m from the northern margin of the Taylor Glacier, providing access several kilometres up-valley from the designated helicopter landing site and camp site. Steep ice cliffs on the northern margin of the Taylor Glacier impede access onto the surface of the glacier from this route.

6(iii) Structures within and near the Area

No permanent structures exist within the Area. Two permanent survey markers are set in a boulder located approximately 175m north of the Area: NZAP Benchmark TP01 is a tube with female thread (162°16.466'E, 77°43.175'S, elevation 72.7m); UNAVCO benchmark TP02 is a 5/8" threaded bolt (162°16.465'E, 77°43.175'S, elevation 72.8m). The boulder is located on an area of sloping ground on the northern shore of Lake Bonney situated approximately 140m NE of the helicopter landing site. A stream weir and a stream gauge are located approximately 80m NW of the Area at Lawson Creek. Lake Bonney Camp is located approximately 4.3km east of the Area.

6(iv) Location of other protected areas within close proximity of the Area

The Area lies within ASMA 2 McMurdo Dry Valleys. The closest Antarctica Specially Protected Areas (ASPAs) are: Canada Glacier (APSA 131) which is located 22km NE of Blood Falls in the Taylor Valley; Linneaus Terrace (ASPA 138), which lies 31km NW of Blood Falls in the Wright Valley; and Barwick Valley (ASPA 123) situated approximately 43km NW of Blood Falls.

6(v) Special zones within the Area

There are no special zones within the Area.

7. Permit conditions

7(i) General permit conditions

Entry into the sub-aerial or sub-surface component of the Area is prohibited except in accordance with a Permit issued by an appropriate national authority. Conditions for issuing a Permit to enter the Area are that:

- it is issued for compelling scientific, educational or outreach reasons that cannot be served elsewhere, or for reasons essential to the management of the Area;

- the actions permitted are in accordance with this Management Plan;

- the activities permitted will give due consideration via the environmental impact assessment process to continued protection of the environmental, ecological, scientific, or educational values of the Area;

- the Permit shall be issued for a finite period;
- the Permit, or a copy, shall be carried within the Area.

7(ii) Access to, and movement within or over, the Area

- Vehicles are prohibited within the Area;
- Access to, movement on, and / or over the surface of the Taylor Glacier within the region covered by the sub-surface component of the Area is not subject to any special restrictions;
- Access to and movement within the sub-aerial component of the Area shall normally be on foot;
- Helicopters facilitating access to Blood Falls should normally avoid landings within the sub-aerial component of the Area, and instead land at the designated landing site on the NW shore of Lake Bonney (162°16.30'E, 77°43.24'S, Map 2). Helicopters may be used to deliver essential equipment into the sub-aerial component of the Area when necessary for scientific or management purposes for which a Permit has been granted, taking care that to the maximum extent practicable such deliveries avoid supraglacial channels;
- Visitors accessing the sub-aerial component of the Area should avoid the primary and secondary Blood Falls discharge areas unless permitted activities specifically require access to these sites;
- The preferred route for pedestrian access to the sub-aerial component of the Area from the designated helicopter landing site and camp site is from Lake Bonney, ascending the terminus of the Taylor Glacier from slopes to the south of the sub-aerial component boundary (Map 2).
- Movement within the sub-aerial component of the Area should be limited to that which is necessary for the performance of permitted activities.

7(iii) Activities that are or may be conducted in the Area, including restrictions on time or place

- Scientific research that will not jeopardize the ecosystem or scientific values of the Area or compromise the integrity of the Blood Falls system;
- Essential management activities, including monitoring and inspection;
- Activities with educational aims (such as documentary reporting (photographic, audio or written) or the production of educational resources or services) that cannot be served elsewhere;
- Specific conditions apply to activities that are or may be conducted in the sub-surface and sub-aerial components of the Area, which are as follows:

  a) Activities that are or may be conducted in the sub-surface component of the Area

  - All projects proposing to access the sub-surface component of the Area shall consider in advance the uncertainties that exist in the properties of the sub-surface hydrological system, and the risk that such activities could have more than a minor or transitory impact on the values of the Area. As such, prior environmental impact assessment of such activities should include a detailed and robust scientific review with the opportunity for input by relevant experts.
  - Such proposals shall take into account the SCAR Code of Conduct for Subglacial Aquatic Environments, and as appropriate other best-practice protocols and procedures which have been developed for safe and environmentally sound access to the subglacial environment (see eg, Committee on Principles of Environmental Stewardship for the Exploration and Study of Subglacial Environments 2007; Arctic and Antarctic Research Institute 2010; Lake Ellsworth Consortium 2011).
  - Any activities involving entry into the sub-surface component of the Area shall monitor the effectiveness of control measures to minimize / prevent releases to the environment.

  b) Activities that are or may be conducted in sub-aerial component of the Area

  - Meltwater sampling from supraglacial channels draining into the primary Blood Falls outflow is permitted, provided the appropriate measures specified in Section 7(vi) are taken to minimize potential contamination.

7(iv) Installation, modification or removal of structures / equipment

- No structures are to be erected within the Area except as specified in a permit and, with the exception of permanent survey markers and signs, permanent structures or installations are prohibited;

- All structures, scientific equipment or markers installed in the Area shall be authorized by permit and clearly identified by country, name of the principal investigator and year of installation. All such items should be made of materials that pose minimal risk of contamination of the Area;

- Installation (including site selection), maintenance, modification or removal of structures or equipment shall be undertaken in a manner that minimizes disturbance to the environment and to flora and fauna.

- Removal of specific structures / equipment for which the permit has expired shall be the responsibility of the authority which granted the original Permit, and shall be a condition of the Permit.

- If equipment is left *in situ* in the sub-surface component of the Area for extended periods, provisions shall be made to minimize the risk of contamination and / or loss of the equipment.

- Certain equipment and materials may need to be installed into subglacial aquatic environments for scientific and / or monitoring purposes (eg, to measure geophysical or biogeochemical processes, or to monitor impacts of human activities on the subglacial environment). Any such installations shall be specifically covered in the environmental impact assessment for the activity, and include consideration of procedures for removal and the risks and benefits should removal not be practical.

7(v) Location of field camps

- Camping within the sub-aerial component of the Area is prohibited.

- Camping on the surface of the Taylor Glacier within the region covered by the sub-surface component of the Area is not restricted.

- A designated field camp is located at 77°43.24'S, 162°16.29'E, approximately 100m north of the primary Blood Falls outlet and on the northwestern shore of Lake Bonney. The camp site is located on gently sloping ground extending ~100m from the shore of Lake Bonney and ~200m northeast from Lawson Creek to a permanent survey benchmark (TP02), which is located ~20m from the lake shore. Individual tent sites are marked by stone circles. Where practicable, use tent sites located furthest from the shore of Lake Bonney.

7(vi) Restrictions on materials and organisms which may be brought into the Area

- No living animals, plant material, microorganisms or soils shall be deliberately introduced into the Area, and the precautions listed below shall be taken against accidental introductions;

- To help maintain the ecological and scientific values at Blood Falls and to minimize the risk of microbial introductions to the Blood Falls system visitors shall take special precautions against introductions. Of concern are pathogenic, microbial, invertebrate or plant introductions sourced from other Antarctic sites, including stations, or from regions outside Antarctica. Precautions shall be taken within the sub-aerial and sub-surface components of the Area as follows:

    Sub-aerial component

    Visitors shall ensure that sampling equipment or markers are clean. To the maximum extent practicable, footwear and other equipment (including backpacks and carry-bags) shall be thoroughly cleaned prior to entry. To reduce the risk of microbial contamination, the exposed surfaces of footwear, sampling equipment and markers should be sterilized before use within the Area. Sterilization should be by an acceptable method, such as by washing in 70% ethanol solution in water or in a commercially available solution such as 'Virkon'. Sterile protective overclothing shall be worn when undertaking sampling within the sub-aerial component of the Area. The overclothing shall be suitable for working at temperatures of -20°C or below and comprise at a minimum sterile overalls to cover arms, legs and body and sterile gloves suitable for placing over the top of cold-weather gloves. Disposable sterile / protective foot coverings are not suitable for glacier travel and should not be used;

    Sub-surface component

    All equipment that is proposed to enter the sub-surface component of the Area shall be sterilized prior to deployment into the sub-surface component of the Area to prevent microbial introductions to the maximum extent practicable. Sterilization shall be by acceptable methods and specified in the environmental impact assessment for the activity;

- No herbicides or pesticides shall be brought into the Area;

- Any other chemicals, including radio-nuclides or stable isotopes, which may be introduced for scientific or management purposes specified in the permit, shall be removed from the Area at or before the conclusion of the activity for which the permit was granted;
- Chemical tracers shall not be introduced into the sub-surface component of the Area, and use of tracers in the sub-aerial component of the Area shall follow the guidelines for 'Streams' in the Environmental Guidelines for Scientific Research contained in Appendix B of the Management Plan for ASMA 2 McMurdo Dry Valleys;
- Fuel, food, and other materials shall not be stored in the Area, unless required for essential purposes connected with the activity for which the permit has been granted;
- In general, all materials introduced shall be for a stated period only and shall be removed at or before the conclusion of that stated period, unless installed into subglacial aquatic environments for scientific and / or monitoring purposes on a permanent basis in which case the conditions for their deployment shall be justified and specified in the environmental impact assessment for the activity;
- All materials shall be stored and handled so that risk of their introduction into the environment is minimized;
- If release occurs which is likely to compromise the values of the Area, removal should be undertaken only where the impact of removal is not likely to be greater than that of leaving the material *in situ*.

7(vii) Taking of, or harmful interference with, native flora or fauna

Taking of, or harmful interference with, native flora and fauna is prohibited, except in accordance with a permit issued in accordance with Annex II of the Protocol on Environmental Protection to the Antarctic Treaty.

7(viii) Collection or removal of anything not brought into the Area by the Permit holder

- Material may be collected or removed from the Area only in accordance with a permit and should be limited to the minimum necessary to meet scientific or management needs.
- Material of human origin likely to compromise the values of the Area, and which was not brought into the Area by the permit holder or otherwise authorized, may be removed from the Area, unless the impact of removal is likely to be greater than leaving the material *in situ*: if this is the case the appropriate authority should be notified.

7(ix) Disposal of waste

All wastes, including human wastes, shall be removed from the Area.

7(x) Measures that may be necessary to continue to meet the aims of the Management Plan

Permits may be granted to enter the Area to:

- carry out monitoring and Area inspection activities, which may involve the collection of a small number of samples or data for analysis or review;
- install or maintain signposts, markers, structures or scientific equipment; and
- carry out protective measures.

7(xi) Requirements for reports

- The principal permit holder for each visit to the Area shall submit a report to the appropriate national authority as soon as practicable, and no later than six months after the visit has been completed.
- Such reports should include, as appropriate, the information identified in the visit report form contained in the Guide to the Preparation of Management Plans for Antarctic Specially Protected Areas. If appropriate, the national authority should also forward a copy of the visit report to the Party that proposed the Management Plan, to assist in managing the Area and reviewing the Management Plan.
- Parties should, wherever possible, deposit originals or copies of such original visit reports in a publicly accessible archive to maintain a record of usage, for the purpose of any review of the Management Plan and in organising the scientific use of the Area.
- Where access to the sub-surface component of the Area is undertaken, reports shall additionally document the location of drilling sites to an accuracy of ±1m, details of the drilling method and type

of drilling fluid used. Any contamination of the sub-surface environment shall be reported. Reports shall include the results of monitoring carried out to assess the effectiveness of contamination control measures, particularly those relating to microbial control.

- The appropriate authority should be notified of any activities / measures undertaken, and / or of any materials released and not removed, that were not included in the authorized permit.

References

Aciego, S.M., Cuffey, K.M., Kvanaugh, J.L., Morse, D.L. & Severinghaus, J.P. 2007. Pleistocene ice and paleo-strain rates at Taylor Glacier, Antarctica. *Quaternary Research* **68**: 303–13.

Angino, E.E., Armitage, K.B. & Tash, J.C. 1964. Physicochemical limnology of Lake Bonney, Antarctica. *Limnology and Oceanography* **9** (2): 207–17.

Arctic and Antarctic Research Institute 2010. Water sampling of the subglacial Lake Vostok. Final Comprehensive Environmental Evaluation. Russian Antarctic Expedition, Arctic and Antarctic Research Institute. St Petersburg, Russia.

Barrett, J.E., Virginia, R.A., Wall, D.H., Parsons, A.N., Powers, L.E. & Burkins, M.B. 2004. Variation in biogeochemistry and soil biodiversity across spatial scales in a polar desert ecosystem. *Ecology* **85** (11): 3105-18.

Black, R.F. & Bowser, C.J. 1967. Salts and associated phenomena of the termini of the Hobbs and Taylor Glaciers, Victoria Land, Antarctica. *International Union of Geodesy and Geophysics, Commission on Snow and Ice. Publication* **79**: 226-38.

Black, R. F., Jackson, M. L. & Berg, T. E., 1965. Saline discharge from Taylor Glacier, Victoria Land, Antarctica. *Journal of Geology* **74**: 175-81.

Bliss, A.K., Cuffey, K.M. & Kavanaugh, J.L. 2011. Sublimation and surface energy budget of Taylor Glacier, Antarctica. *Journal of Glaciology* **57** (204): 684-96.

Burkins, M.B., Virginia, R.A., Chamberlain, C.P. & Wall, D.H. 2000. Origin and Distribution of Soil Organic Matter in Taylor Valley, Antarctica. *Ecology* **81** (9): 2377-91.

Campbell, I.B. & Claridge, G.G.C. 1987. *Antarctica: soils, weathering processes and environment* (Developments in Soil Science 16). Elsevier, New York.

Carmichael, J.D., Pettit, E.C., Creager, K.C. & Hallet, B. 2007. Calving of Talyor Glacier, Dry Valleys, Antarctica. Eos Transactions AGU **88** (52), Fall Meeting Supplement, Abstract C41A-0037.

Christner, B.C., Doyle, S.M., Montross, S.N., Skidmore, M.L., Samyn, D., Lorrain, R., Tison, J. and Fitzsimons, S. 2010. A subzero microbial habitat in the basal ice of an Antarctic glacier. AGU Fall Meeting 2010, Abstract B21F-04.

Committee on the Principles of Environmental Stewardship for the Exploration and Study of Subglacial Environments, 2007. Exploration of Antarctic Subglacial Aquatic Environments: Environmental and Scientific Stewardship. Polar Research Board, National Research Council, National Academies Press, Washington D.C. (http://www.nap.edu/catalog/11886.html).

Fountain, A.G., Lyons, W.B., Burkins, M.B. Dana, G.L., Doran, P.T., Lewis, K.J., McKnight, D.M., Moorhead, D.L.,Parsons, A.N., Priscu, J.C., Wall, D.H., Wharton, Jr., R.A. & Virginia, R.A. 1999. Physical controls on the Taylor Valley ecosystem, Antarctica. *BioScience* **49** (12): 961-71.

Fountain, A.G., Nylen, T.H., MacClune, K.J., & Dana, G.L. 2006. Glacier mass balances (1993-2001) Taylor Valley, McMurdo Dry Valleys, Antarctica. *Journal of Glaciology* **52** (177): 451-465.

Lake Ellsworth Consortium 2011. Proposed exploration of subglacial Lake Ellsworth, Antarctica: Draft Comprehensive Environmental Evaluation. British Antarctic Survey, Cambridge.

Hall, B.L. & Denton, G.H. 2000. Radiocarbon Chronology of Ross Sea Drift, Eastern Taylor Valley, Antarctica: Evidence for a Grounded Ice Sheet in the Ross Sea at the Last Glacial Maximum. *Geografiska Annaler: Series A, Physical Geography* **82** (2-3): 305-36.

Hamilton, W. L., Frost, I. C. & Hayes P. T. 1962. Saline Features of a Small Ice Platform in Taylor Valley, Antarctica. USGS Professional Paper **450B**. US Geological Survey: B73-76.

Hendy, C.H., Healy, T.R., Rayner, E.M., Shaw, J. & Wilson, A.T. 1979. Late Pleistocene glacial chronology of the Taylor Valley, Antarctica, and the global climate. *Quaternary Research* **11** (2): 172-84.

Higgins, S.M., Denton, G. H. & Hendy, C. H. 2000. Glacial Geomorphology of Bonney Drift, Taylor Valley, Antarctica. *Geografiska Annaler. Series A, Physical Geography* **82** (2-3): 365-89.

Holt, J.W., Peters, M.E., Morse, D.L., Blankenship, D.D., Lindzey, L.E., Kavanaugh, J.L. & Cuffey, K.M. 2006. Identifying and characterising subsurface echoes in airborne radar sounding from a high-clutter environment in the Taylor Valley, Antarctica. 11th International Conference on Ground Penetrating Radar, June 19-22, 2006, Columbus Ohio, USA.

Hubbard, A., Lawson, W., Anderson, B., Hubbard, B. & Blatter, H. 2004. Evidence of subglacial ponding across Taylor Glacier, Dry Valleys, Antarctica. *Annals of Glaciology* **39**: 79–84.

Johnston, R.R., Fountain, A.G. & Nylen, T.H. 2005. The origins of channels on lower Taylor Glacier, McMurdo Dry Valleys, Antarctica, and their implication for water runoff. *Annals of Glaciology* **40**: 1-7.

Kavanaugh. J.L. & Cuffey, K.M. 2009. Dynamics and mass balance of Taylor Glacier, Antarctica: 2. Force balance and longitudinal coupling. *Journal of Geophysical Research* **114**: F04011.

Kavanaugh. J.L., Cuffey, K.M., Morse, D.L., Conway, H. & Rignot, E. 2009a. Dynamics and mass balance of Taylor Glacier, Antarctica: 1. Geometry and surface velocities. *Journal of Geophysical Research* **114**: F04010.

Kavanaugh. J.L., Cuffey, K.M., Morse, D.L., Bliss, A.K. & Aciego, S.M. 2009b. Dynamics and mass balance of Taylor Glacier, Antarctica: 3. State of mass balance. *Journal of Geophysical Research* **114**: F04012.

Keys, J.R. 1979. The saline discharge at the terminus of Taylor Glacier. *Antarctic Journal of the United States* **14**: 82-85.

Keys, J.R 1980. Salts and their distribution in the McMurdo region, Antarctica. Chapter 8 in unpublished PhD thesis held at Victoria University of Wellington NZ, and Byrd Polar Research Center, Columbus, Ohio: 240-82.

Lyons, W.B., Nezat, C.A., Benson, L.V., Bullen, T.D., Graham, E.Y., Kidd, J., Welch, K.A. & Thomas, J.M. 2002. Strontium isotopic signatures of the streams and lakes of Taylor Valley, Southern Victoria Land, Antarctica: chemical weathering in a polar climate. *Aquatic Geochemistry* **8** (2): 75-95.

Lyons, W.B. Tyler, S.W. Wharton Jr R.A., McKnight D.M. and Vaughn B.H. 1998. A Late Holocene desiccation of Lake Hoare and Lake Fryxell, McMurdo Dry Valleys, Antarctica. *Antarctic Science* **10** (3): 247-56.

Lyons, W.B., Welch, K.A., Snyder, G., Olesik, J., Graham, E.Y., Marion, G.M. & Poreda, R.J. 2005. Halogen geochemistry of the McMurdo dry valleys lakes, Antarctica: Clues to the origin of solutes and lake evolution. *Geochimica et Cosmochimica Acta*, **69** (2): 305–23.

Mager, S., Fitzsimons, S., Frew, R. & Samyn, D. 2007. Stable isotope composition of the basal ice from Taylor Glacier, southernVictoria Land, Antarctica. U.S. Geological Survey and The National Academies; USGS OF-2007-1047, Extended Abstract 109.

Mager, S. 2006. A compositional approach to understanding the formation of basal ice in Antarctic glaciers. Unpublished PhD Thesis; University of Otago, Dunedin, New Zealand.

Marchant, D. R., Denton, G. H. & Sugden, D. E. 1993. Miocene glacial stratigraphy and landscape evolution in the western Asgard Range, Antarctica. *Geografiska Annaler* **75**:269-302.

Mikucki, J. A. 2005. *Microbial Ecology of an Antarctic Subglacial Environment*. Unpublished PhD Thesis; Montana State University, Bozeman, Montana.

Mikucki, J.A., Foreman, C.M., Sattler, B., Lyons, W.B. & Priscu, J.C. 2004. Geomicrobiology of Blood Falls: An iron-rich saline discharge at the terminus of the Taylor Glacier, Antarctica. *Aquatic Geochemistry* **10**:199-220.

Mikucki, J.A., Pearson, A., Johnston, D.T. Turchyn, A.V., Farquhar, J., Schrag, D.P., Anbar, A.D., Priscu, J.C. & Lee, P.A. 2009. A contemporary microbially maintained subglacial ferrous 'ocean'. *Science* **324**: 397-400.

Mikucki, J.A. & Priscu, J.C. 2007. Bacterial diversity associated with Blood Falls, a subglacial outflow from the Taylor Glacier, Antarctica. *Applied and Environmental Microbiology* **73** (12): 4029-39.

Pettit, E.C., Nylen, T.H., Fountain, A.G. & Hallet, B. 2006. Ice Cliffs and the Terminus Dynamics of Polar Glaciers. *Eos Transactions AGU* **87** (52) Fall Meeting Supplement, Abstract C41A-0312.

Pugh, H.E., Welch, K.A., Lyons, W.B., Priscu, J.C. & McKnight, D.M. 2003. The biogeochemistry of Si in the McMurdo Dry Valley lakes, Antarctica. *International Journal of Astrobiology* **1** (4): 401–13.

Samyn, D., Fitzsimmons, S.J. & Lorrain, R.D. 2005. Strain-induced phase changes within cold basal ice from Taylor Glacier, Antarctica, indicated by textural and gas analyses. *Journal of Glaciology* **51** (175): 165–69.

Samyn, D., Svensson, A. & Fitzsimons, S. 2008. Discontinuous recrystallization in cold basal ice from an Antarctic glacier: dynamic implications. *Journal of Geophysical Research* **113** F03S90, doi:101029/2006JF000600.

SCAR 2011. SCAR Code of Conduct for the exploration and research of subglacial aquatic environments. Information Paper 33, ATCM XXXIV, Buenos Aires.

Souchez, R., Samyn, D., Lorrain, R., Pattyn, F. & Fitzsimons, S. 2004. An isotopic model for basal freeze-on associated with subglacial upward flow of pore water. *Geophysical Research Letters* **31** L02401.

Stone, W., Hogan, B., Flesher, C., Gulati, S., Richmond, K., Murarka, A., Kuhlman, G., Sridharan, M., Siegel, V., Price, R.M., Doran, P.T. & Priscu, J. 2010. Design and Deployment of a Four-Degrees-of-Freedom Hovering Autonomous Underwater Vehicle for sub-Ice Exploration and Mapping. *Proceedings of the Institution of Mechanical Engineers, Part M: Journal of Engineering for the Maritime Environment* **224**: 341–61.

Stuvier, M., Denton, G. H., Hughes, T. J. & Fastook, J. L. 1981. History of the marine ice sheet in West Antarctica during the last glaciation: a working hypothesis. In Denton, G. H. and Hughes, T. H., Eds. The last great ice sheets. Wiley-Interscience, New York: 319–436.

Takacs, C.D. 1999. Temporal Change in Bacterial Plankton in the McMurdo Dry Valleys. Unpublished Ph.D. Thesis; Montana State University, Bozeman, Montana.

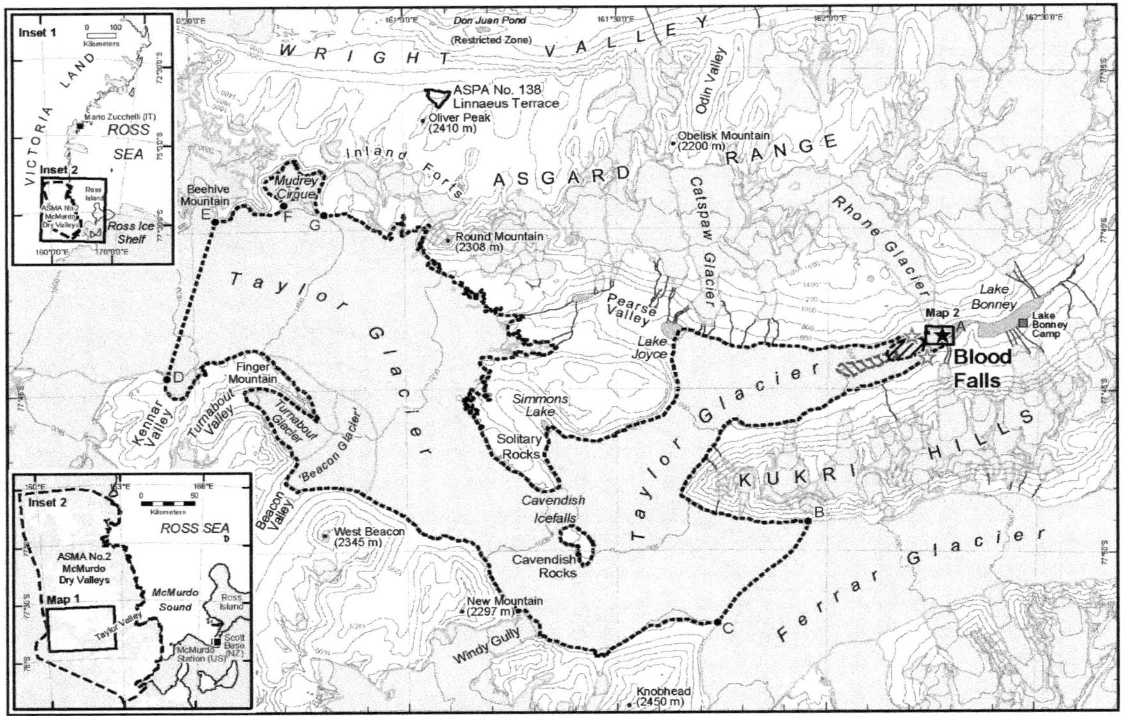

Map 1: Lower Taylor Glacier and Blood Falls sub-surface protected area boundary

v2 Issued 04 Apr 2012 (Map ID: 08.03.06-LN13.06)
Environmental Research & Assessment

Ice free ground; Permanent ice; Lake / pond; Stream; Contour (200m); Mountain peak; Antarctic Specially Managed Area (ASMA) boundary; Antarctic Specially Protected Area (ASPA) boundary (existing); Sub-surface protected area boundary (Extends vertically from bed to 100 m below glacier surface); Boundary point; Facilities Zone

Blood Falls subglacial brine reservoir (estimated): Derived from Hubbard et al 2004; Derived from Keys 1980; Blood Falls primary discharge; Blood Falls possible discharge

Projection: Lambert Conformal Conic
Spheroid & horizontal datum: WGS84
Data source: Glacier & topography: USGS 1:50K map series
Subglacial brine reservoir: Hubbard et al. (2004); Keys (1980)
Discharge sites: GPS survey T.Nylen (Dec 2006)

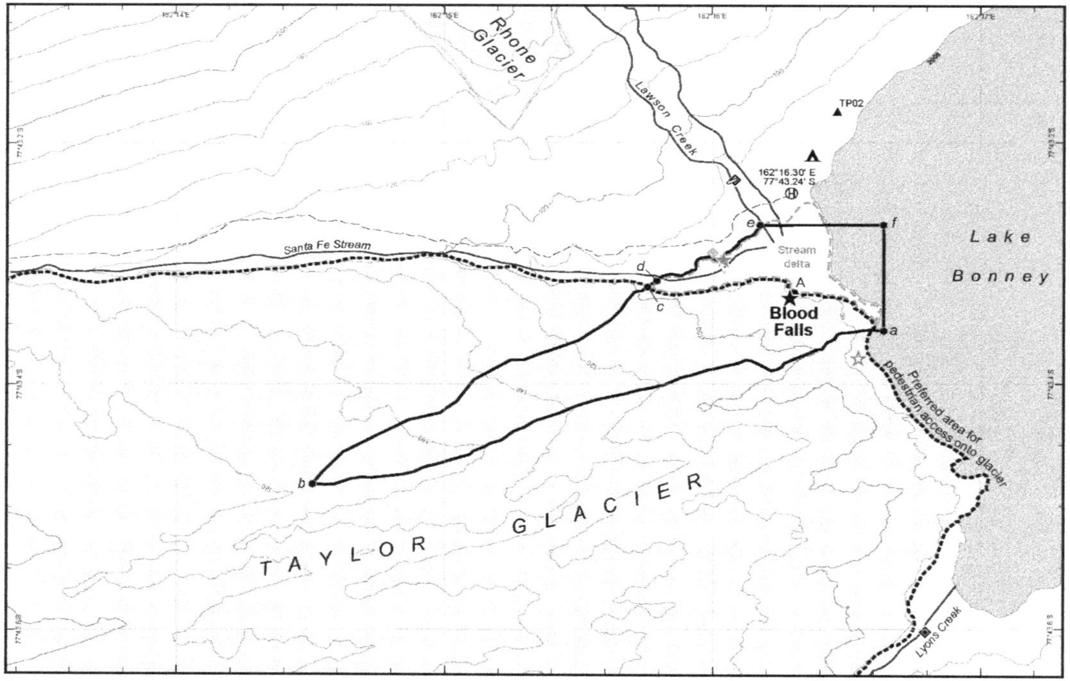

Map 2: Blood Falls sub-surface and sub-aerial protected area boundary

v5 Issued 04 Apr 2012 (Map ID: 06.03.06-LN14.09)
Environmental Research & Assessment

Ice free ground
Glacier
Lake (shoreline year)
Index contour (100 m)
Contour (20 m)
Stream
Stream delta
Sub-surface protected area boundary
Sub-aerial protected area boundary
Boundary point
Blood Falls primary discharge
Blood Falls secondary discharge
Blood Falls possible discharge
Survey mark
Designated campsite
Helicopter landing site
Existing walking track
Stream gauge
Stream gauge (removed Jan 10)
Stream weir
Stream weir (removed Jan 10)

N
0 100 200
Meters

Projection: Lambert Conformal Conic
Spheroid & horizontal datum: WGS84
Data source: Contours: derived from USGS 2m LiDAR DEM
Glacier & stream digitised from aerial imagery (1993)
Lake: digitised from orthorectified Quickbird imagery (Dec 2008)
Campsite, HLS, stream gauges & weirs: ERA field survey (Dec 2009)
Discharge sites: GPS survey T.Nylen (Dec 2006)

Deception Island
Management Package

Introduction

Deception Island is a unique Antarctic island with important natural, scientific, historic, educational and aesthetic values.

Over the years, different parts of the island have been given legal protection under the Antarctic Treaty following piecemeal proposals, but no coherent strategy had been formulated for protecting the whole island. In 2000, an integrated strategy for the management of activities there was agreed by Argentina, Chile, Norway, Spain and the UK.

This strategy recommended an island-wide approach. Deception Island would be proposed as an Antarctic Specially Managed Area (ASMA) comprising a matrix of Antarctic Specially Protected Areas (ASPAs), Historic Sites and Monuments (HSMs), and further zones in which activities would be subject to a code of conduct.

In March 2001, the Instituto Antártico Chileno hosted a workshop in Santiago to progress the Management Plan for Deception Island. The Deception Island working group was widened to include the USA, as well as the Antarctic and Southern Ocean Coalition (ASOC) and the International Association of Antarctica Tour Operators (IAATO) as advisors to the group.

During February 2002, the Dirreción Nacional del Antártico (Argentina) hosted an expedition to the island at Decepción Station. Representatives from the six National Antarctic Programmes, as well as ASOC and IAATO, participated. The overall goal of the expedition was to undertake baseline survey fieldwork to assist with the joint preparation by the six Antarctic Treaty Consultative Parties of a Management Package for Deception Island.

Following further extensive consultation, the first version of the Management Package for Deception Island was produced. Its aim is to conserve and protect the unique environment of Deception Island, whilst managing the variety of competing demands placed upon it, including science, tourism, and the conservation of its natural and historic values. It also aims to safeguard those working on, or visiting, the island. Information Papers submitted to the CEP (XII SATCM/IP8, XXIV ATCM/IP63, XXV ATCM/IP28 and XXVI ATCM/IP48) give further detail of the extensive consultation and site investigations which have resulted in the production of the Management Package for Deception Island.

In accordance with Article 6 (3) of Annex V to the Environmental Protocol, a review process for the management plan was initiated in 2010, and on basis of discussions and new information a revised management plan was produced in 2012 and submitted to the CEP/ATCM for consideration and approval.

Management Plan for Antarctic Specially Managed Area No 4 Deception Island, South Shetland Islands, Antarctica

1.   Values to be protected and activities to be managed

Deception Island (latitude 62°57'S, longitude 60°38'W), South Shetland Islands, is a unique Antarctic island with important natural, scientific, historic, educational and aesthetic values.

i. Natural value

- Deception Island is one of only two volcanoes in the Antarctic where eruptions have been observed. It was responsible for numerous ash layers dispersed across the South Shetland Islands, Bransfield Strait and the Scotia Sea. Ash from the island has even been recorded in an ice core sample from South Pole. The volcano erupted during two short periods in the 20th century, most recently between 1967-1970. It contains a restless caldera that is actively deforming. It is likely, therefore, that Deception Island will witness further eruptions in the future.

- The Area has an exceptionally important floral assemblage, including at least 18 species which have not been recorded elsewhere in the Antarctic. No other Antarctic area is comparable. Of particular importance are the very small, unique biological communities associated with the island's geothermal areas, and the most extensive known community of the flowering plant Antarctic pearlwort (*Colobanthus quitensis*).

- Nine species of seabird breed on the island, including one of the world's largest colonies of chinstrap penguins (*Pygoscelis antarctica*).

- The benthic habitat of Port Foster is of ecological interest due to the natural perturbations caused by volcanic activity.

ii. Scientific value and activities

- The Area is of outstanding scientific interest, in particular for studies in geoscience and biological science. It offers the rare opportunity to study the effects of environmental change on an ecosystem, and the dynamics of the ecosystem as it recovers from natural disturbance.

- Long term geochemical, seismological and biological data-sets have been collected at Decepción Station (Argentina) and Gabriel de Castilla Station (Spain)[1].

iii. Historic value

- The Area has had a long history of human activity since *c.*1820, including exploration, sealing, whaling, aviation and scientific research, and as such has played a significant role in Antarctic affairs.

- At Whalers Bay, the Norwegian Hektor whaling station, the cemetery and other artefacts, some of which pre-date the whaling station, are the most significant whaling remains in the Antarctic. The British 'Base B', which was established in the abandoned whaling station, was the first base of the secret World War II expedition 'Operation Tabarin', the forerunner to the British Antarctic Survey. As such, it was one of the earliest permanent research stations in Antarctica. The whalers' remains and 'Base B' are listed as Historic Site and Monument (HSM) No. 71. Appendix 3 contains the Conservation Strategy for HSM No. 71.

- The remains of the Chilean Presidente Pedro Aguirre Cerda Station at Pendulum Cove are listed as HSM No. 76. Meteorological and volcanological studies were undertaken at the base from 1955 until its destruction by volcanic eruptions in 1967 and 1969.

v. Aesthetic value

- Deception Island's flooded caldera, its 'horse-shoe' shape and linear glaciated eastern coastline, its barren volcanic slopes, steaming beaches and ash-layered glaciers provide a unique Antarctic landscape.

iv. Educational values

- Deception Island is one of the few places in the world where vessels can sail directly into the centre of a restless volcanic caldera, providing the opportunity for visitors to learn about volcanoes and other aspects of the natural world, as well as early Antarctic exploration, whaling and science. Deception Island is also one of the most frequently visited sites in Antarctica by tourists.

2. Aims and objectives

The main aim of this Management Package is to conserve and protect the unique and outstanding environment of Deception Island, whilst managing the variety of competing demands placed upon it, including science, tourism, and the conservation of its natural and historic values. It also aims to protect the safety of those working on, or visiting, the island.

---

[1] Spain has been collecting seismological data since the opening of Gabriel de Castilla station in 1989; the data-sets are available in the National Polar Data Center (NPDC) of Spain. Biological data sets have been collected at irregular intervals from 2001 and are also available in the NPDC.

The objectives of management at Deception Island are to:

- assist in the planning and co-ordination of activities in the Area, encourage co-operation between Antarctic Treaty Parties and other stakeholders, and manage potential or actual conflicts of interest between different activities, including science, logistics and tourism;

- avoid unnecessary degradation, by human disturbance, to the unique natural values of the Area;

- safeguard in particular the scientific and wilderness values of those areas in the Area which thus far have not been significantly modified by human activity (especially the recently created volcanic surfaces);

- minimise the possibility of non-native species being introduced through human activities;

- prevent unnecessary disturbance, destruction or removal of historic buildings, structures and artefacts;

- safeguard those working in or near to, or visiting, the Area from the significant volcanic risk;

- manage visitation to this unique Island, and promote an awareness, through education, of its significance.

3.   Management activities

To achieve the aims and objectives of this Management Plan, the following management activities will be undertaken:

- Parties with an active interest in the Area should establish a Deception Island Management Group to:

  - oversee the co-ordination of activities in the Area;
  - facilitate communication between those working in, or visiting, the Area;
  - maintain a record of activities in the Area;
  - disseminate information and educational material on the significance of Deception Island to those visiting, or working there;
  - monitor the site to investigate cumulative impacts derived from science, permanent facilities, tourism/visitor and management activities;
  - oversee the implementation of this Management Plan, and revise it when necessary.

- a general island-wide Code of Conduct for activities in the Area is included in this ASMA Management Plan (see Section 9). Further site-specific Codes of Conduct are included in the Conservation Strategy for Whalers Bay HSM No.71 (Appendix 3), as well as the Code of Conduct for the Facilities Zone (Appendix

4), the Code of Conduct for Visitors (Appendix 5) and Site Visitor Guidelines for Telefon Bay, Whalers Bay, Pendulum Cove and Baily Head. These Codes of Conduct and Site Visitor Guidelines should be used to guide activities in the Area;

- National Antarctic Programmes operating within the Area should ensure that their personnel are briefed on, and are aware of, the requirements of this Management Plan and supporting documentation;

- tour operators visiting the Area should ensure that their staff, crew and passengers are briefed on, and are aware of, the requirements of this Management Plan and supporting documentation;

- signs and markers will be erected where necessary and appropriate to show the boundaries of ASPAs and other zones, such as the location of scientific activities. Signs and markers will be well designed to be informative and obvious, yet unobtrusive. They will also be secured and maintained in good condition, and removed when no longer necessary;

- the volcanic alert scheme (as at Appendix 6) will be implemented. It, and the emergency evacuation plan, will be kept under review;

- Parties authorizing activities in the South Shetland Island area should ensure that those responsible for the activity are aware of the desirability of avoiding use of Deception Island as an emergency harbour in cases of maritime accidents/incidents due to both the ecological sensitivities and safety issues of the island. Parties should ensure that those responsible for the activity make themselves familiar with alternative emergency harbours in the area and encourage these to be used if the situation at hand deems this possible and appropriate.

- copies of this Management Plan and supporting documentation, in English and Spanish, will be made available at Decepción Station (Argentina), and Gabriel de Castilla Station (Spain). In addition, the Deception Island Management Group should encourage National Antarctic Operators, tour companies and, as far as practicable, yacht operators visiting the Area, to have available copies of this Management Plan when they visit the Area;

- visits should be made to the Area as necessary (no less than once every 5 years) by members of the Deception Island Management Group to ensure that the requirements of the Management Plan are being met.

4.   Period of designation

Designated for an indefinite period of time.

5.   Description of the Area

i. Geographical co-ordinates, boundary markers and natural features

General description

Deception Island (latitude 62°57'S, longitude 60°38'W) is situated in the Bransfield Strait at the southern end of the South Shetland Islands, off the north-west coast of the Antarctic Peninsula (Figures 1 and 2). The boundary of the ASMA is defined as the outer coastline of the island above the low tide water level. It includes the waters and seabed of Port Foster to the north of a line drawn across Neptunes Bellows between Entrance Point and Cathedral Crags (Figure 3). No boundary markers are required for the ASMA, as the coast is clearly defined and visually obvious.

Geology, geomorphology and volcanic activity

Deception Island is an active basaltic volcano. It has a submerged basal diameter of approximately 30 km and rises to 1.5 km above the sea floor. The volcano has a large flooded caldera, giving the island a distinctive horseshoe shape broken only on the south-eastern side by Neptunes Bellows, a narrow shallow passage about 500 m wide.

The eruption which formed the caldera occurred possibly 10,000 years ago. A large scale, violently explosive eruption evacuated about 30 km^3 of molten rock so rapidly that the volcano summit region collapsed to form the Port Foster caldera. Associated ashfalls and tsunamis had a significant environmental impact on the northern Antarctic Peninsula region. The volcano was particularly active during the late 18th and 19th centuries, when numerous eruptions occurred. By contrast, 20th century eruptions were restricted to two short periods, around 1906–1910 and 1967–1970. In 1992, seismic activity on Deception Island was accompanied by ground deformation and increased groundwater temperatures around Decepción Station.

The volcano has since returned to its normal, essentially quiescent state. However, the floor of Port Foster is rising at a geologically rapid rate (approximately 30 cm per annum). Together with the record of historical eruptions and the presence of long lived areas of geothermal activity, it is classified as a restless caldera with a significant volcanic risk.

Approximately 57% of the island is covered by permanent glaciers, many of which are overlain with volcanic ash. Mounds and low ridges of glacially transported debris (moraines) are present around the margins of the glaciers.

An almost complete ring of hills, rising to 539 m at Mount Pond, encircles the sunken interior of Port Foster, and is the principal drainage divide on the island. Ephemeral springs flow toward the outer and inner coasts. Several lakes are located on the inner divide of the watershed.

Climate

The climate of Deception Island is polar maritime. Mean annual air temperature at sea level is –2.9°C. Extreme temperatures range from 11°C at the warmest to – 28 °C at the coldest. Precipitation, which falls on more than 50% of summer days, is high for the region, with a mean annual equivalent of rainfall of approximately 500 mm. Prevailing winds are from the north-east and west.

Marine ecology

The marine ecology of Port Foster has been significantly influenced by volcanic activity and sediment deposition. ASPA No. 145, comprising two sub-sites, is located in the Area. The Management Plan for ASPA 145, contained in Appendix 2, gives further detail of the marine ecology of Port Foster.

Flora

Deception Island is a unique and exceptionally important botanical site. The flora includes at least 18 species of moss, liverwort and lichen which have not been recorded elsewhere in the Antarctic. Small communities, which include rare species and unique associations of taxa, grow at a number of geothermal areas on the island, some of which have fumaroles. Furthermore, the most extensive known concentration of Antarctic pearlwort (*Colobanthus quitensis*) is located between Baily Head and South East Point.

In many areas, ground surfaces created by the 1967-70 eruptions are being colonized rapidly, probably enhanced by the increasing summer temperatures now occurring in the Antarctic Peninsula as a result of regional climate change.

ASPA No. 140, comprising 11 sub-sites, is located in the Area. The Management Plan for ASPA No. 140 is contained in Appendix 1. This gives further details of the flora of Deception Island.

Invertebrates

Recorded terrestrial and freshwater invertebrates on Deception Island include 18 species of Acarina (mite), 1 species of Diptera (fly), 3 species of Tardigrada (tardigrade), 9 species of Collembola (springtail), 3 freshwater Crustacea (crustacean), 14 Nematoda (nematode), 1 Gastrotricha (gastrotrich) and 5 Rotifera (rotifer). Colonies of seabird ticks (*Ixodes uriae*) are frequently found beneath rocks adjacent to penguin rookeries (e.g. at the Vapour Col rookery).

The intertidal zone of the sedimentary shores harbour a number of invertebrate species, mostly in the saturated zone: 3 species of amphipods, 3 species of prosobranchs and a yet unidentified assemblage of oligochaete and polychaete species. Invertebrate abundance and biodiversity is higher in cobble and
boulder beaches than in sandy sediments. Red and green macroalgae are frequently observed in these areas, either stranded or attached to the stones.

Birds

Nine species of bird breed within the Area. The most numerous is the chinstrap penguin (*Pygoscelis antarctica*), with an estimated population of around 70,000 breeding pairs in total on the island. The largest rookery is at Baily Head, with the latest estimates indicating 50,000 breeding pairs[2]. In the last 20 years the chinstrap penguin population has declined in the Area, probably due to the effects of climate change on krill abundance. The most recent studies indicate a 50% decline in breeding pairs at Baily Head since the 1986/87 season census[3].

Although Macaroni penguins (*Eudyptes chrysolophus*) have been observed occasionally nesting in small numbers on the island, no breeding birds have been observed over the last two decades. Brown skuas (*Catharacta antarctica lonnbergi*), south polar skuas (*Catharacta maccormicki*), kelp gulls (*Larus dominicanus*), cape petrels (*Daption capensis*), Wilson's storm-petrels (*Oceanites oceanicus*), Antarctic terns (*Sterna vittata*), Antarctic cormorant (*Phalacrocorax bransfieldensis*) and snowy sheathbills (*Chionis alba*) also breed within the Area.

Mammals

Deception Island has no breeding mammals. Antarctic fur seals (*Arctocephalus gazella*), Weddell seals (*Leptonychotes weddelli*), crabeater seals (*Lobodon carcinophagus*), southern elephant seals (*Mirounga leonina*) and leopard seals (*Hydrurga leptonyx*) haul out on the beaches of the inner and outer coast. At rare intervals whales – mostly humpback whale (*Megaptera novaeangliae*) - can be observed in Port Foster. Humpback whales are also routinely seen feeding in the island's coastal waters from late December onwards. A high number of Antarctic fur seals (around 500) normally can be observed on the beach located between Entrance Point and Collins Point.

ii.   *Structures within the Area*

Decepción Station (Argentina) (latitude 62°58'20" S; longitude 60°41'40" W) is situated on the southern shore of Fumarole Bay. Gabriel de Castilla Station (Spain) (latitude 62°58 ' 40"S, longitude 60°40 ' 30"W) is located approximately 1 km to the south-east. Further details on both stations are contained in the Facilities Zone Code of Conduct (Appendix 4).

The remains of Hektor Whaling Station (Norway) and other remains which pre-date the whaling station, the Whalers Cemetery and the former British 'Base B' (Historic Site and Monument (HSM) No. 71) are located at Whalers Bay (see Appendix 3). A number of steam boilers from the whaling station can be found washed up on the southwest coast of Port Foster. The remains of the Chilean Presidente Pedro Aguirre Cerda Station

---

[2] Estimates are based on surveys conducted by US in the 20111/12 season. The survey findings have been submitted for publication (see footnote 3 for submission details).

[3] Naveen, R., H. J. Lynch, S. Forrest, T. Mueller, and M. Polito. 2012. First direct, site-wide penguin survey at Deception Island, Antarctica suggests significant declines in breeding chinstrap penguins. In review at Polar Biology.

Barbosa, A., Benzal, J., De Leon, A., Moreno, J. Population decline of chinstrap penguins (*Pygoscelis antarctica*) on Deception Island, South Shetlands, Antarctica. In review at Polar Biology (2ª review).

(HSM No. 76) is located at Pendulum Cove. A derelict wooden refuge hut is located approximately 1 km to the south-west of HSM No.76.

A light beacon, maintained by the Chilean Navy, is located on Collins Point. A collapsed light tower, dating from the whaling era, is below it. The remains of a further light tower dating from the whaling era is located at South East Point.

The stern of the *Southern Hunter*, a whale-catcher belonging to the Christian Salvesen Company, which foundered on Ravn Rock, Neptunes Bellows in 1956, remains on the un-named beach to the west of Entrance Point.

A number of beacons and cairns marking sites used for topographical survey are present within the Area.

6.   Protected areas and managed zones within the Area

Figure 3 shows the location of the following ASPAs, HSMs, Facility Zone and other sites with special management provisions within the Area.

- ASPA No. 140, comprising 11 terrestrial sites;

- ASPA No. 145, comprising 2 marine sites within Port Foster;

- HSM No. 71, the remains of Hektor Whaling Station and other remains which pre-date the whaling station, the Whalers Cemetery and 'Base B', Whalers Bay;

- HSM No. 76 , the remains of Pedro Aguirre Cerda Station, Pendulum Cove;

- A Facilities Zone, located on the west side of Port Foster, which includes Decepción Station and Gabriel de Castilla Station;

- Four sites for which Site Visitor Guidelines have been adopted: Pendulum Cove, Baily Head, Whalers Bay and Telefon Bay.

-

7.   Maps

Map 1: The location of Deception Island ASMA No. 4 in relation to the Antarctic Peninsula.

Map 2: Deception Island - topography

Map 3: Deception Island Antarctic Specially Managed Area No 4

8.   Supporting Documents

This Management Plan includes the following supporting documents as appendices:

- Management Plan for Antarctic Specially Protected Area No. 140 (Appendix 1)
- Management Plan for Antarctic Specially Protected Area No. 145 (Appendix 2)

- Conservation Strategy for HSM No. 71, Whalers Bay (Appendix 3)
- Code of Conduct for Facilities Zone (Appendix 4)
- Code of Conduct for visitors at Deception Island (Appendix 5)
- Alert Scheme and Escape Strategy for volcanic eruptions on Deception Island (Appendix 6)
- Site Visitor Guidelines: Telefon Bay (Appendix 7)
- Site Visitor Guidelines: Whalers Bay (Appendix 8)
- Site Visitor Guidelines: Baily Head (Appendix 9)
- Site Visitor Guidelines: Pendulum Cove (Appendix 10)
- Practical biosecurity measures (Appendix 11).

Those appendices containing management plans for ASPAs or Site Visitor Guidelines will be maintained updated with the latest versions of these documents as they have been adopted by the ATCM.

9.   General Code of Conduct

i. Volcanic risk

All activities undertaken within the Area should be planned and conducted taking into account the significant risk to human life posed by the threat of volcanic eruption (see Appendix 6).

ii. Access to and movement within the Area

Access to the Area is generally by ship or yacht, with landings usually taking place by small boat, or less frequently by helicopter.

Vessels arriving in or departing from Port Foster should announce over VHF Marine Channel 16 the intended time and direction of passage through Neptunes Bellows.

Ships may transit ASPA 145, but anchoring within either of the two sub-sites should be avoided except in extreme emergencies.

There are no restrictions on landings on any beaches outside the protected areas covered in Section 6, although recommended landing sites are shown in Figure 3. Boat landings should avoid disturbing birds and seals. Extreme caution should be exercised when attempting landings on the outer coast owing to the significant swell and submerged rocks.

Recommended landing sites for helicopters are shown in Figure 3. Helicopters should avoid overflying areas with high concentrations of birds (i.e. penguin rookeries or other seabird breeding colonies). Aircraft operations over the Area should be carried out, as a minimum requirement, in compliance with ATCM Resolution 4 (2004), "Guidelines for the Operation of Aircraft near Concentrations of birds in Antarctica".

Movement within the area should generally be on foot. All-Terrain Vehicles may also be used with care for scientific support or logistical purposes along the beaches outside of ASPA 140. All movement should be undertaken carefully to minimise disturbance to animals, soil and vegetated areas, and not damage or dislodge flora.

iii. Activities that are or may be conducted within the Area, including restrictions on time or place

- Scientific research, or the logistical support of scientific research, which will not jeopardise the values of the Area;

- Management activities, including the restoration of historic buildings, clean-up of abandoned work-sites, and monitoring the implementation of this Management Plan;

- Tourist or private expedition visits consistent with the Codes of Conduct for Visitors (Appendix 5) and the provisions of this Management Plan;

Overwintering at Deception Island (unless for scientific purposes) is discouraged due to the peculiarities regarding safety (including during rescue operations) with respect to any potential volcanic activity on the island.

Further restrictions apply to activities within ASPA 140 and ASPA 145 (see Appendices 1 and 2).

iv. Installation, modification or removal of structures

Site selection, installation, modification or removal of temporary refuges, hides, or tents should be undertaken in a manner that does not compromise the values of the Area.

Scientific equipment installed in the Area should be clearly identified by country, name of principal investigator, contact details, and date of installation. All such items should be made of materials that pose minimal risk of contamination to the area. All equipment and associated materials should be removed when no longer in use.

v. Location of field camps

Field camps should be located on non-vegetated sites, such as on barren ash plains, slopes or beaches, or on thick snow or ice cover when practicable, and should also avoid concentrations of mammals or breeding birds. Field camps should also avoid areas of geothermally heated ground or fumaroles. Similarly, campsites should avoid dry lake or stream beds. Previously occupied campsites should be re-used where appropriate.

Figure 3 shows the recommended sites for field camps within the Area.

vi. Taking or harmful interference with native flora or fauna

Taking or harmful interference with native flora or fauna is prohibited, except by Permit issued in accordance with Annex II to the *Protocol on Environmental Protection to the Antarctic Treaty* (1998). Where taking or harmful interference with animals for scientific purposes is involved, the *SCAR Code of Conduct for the Use of Animals for Scientific Purposes in Antarctica* should be used as a minimum standard.

vii. Collection or removal of anything not brought into the Area

Material should only be removed from the area for scientific, management, conservation or archeological purposes, and should be limited to the minimum necessary to fulfill those needs.

If objects likely to stem from one of the Historic Sites and Monuments in the Area are found in other areas of the island they should be returned to the Historic Site or Monument from which they originated and secured to prevent further dispersal by wind. A report describing the nature of the material and the location within the Historic Site and Monument where it has been secured and stored, should be submitted to the Chair of the Deception Island Management Group, to establish the most appropriate way to deal with the debris (ie. conservation to preserve any historic value or appropriate disposal).

viii. Restrictions on materials and organisms which may be brought into the Area

The introduction of non-native species is prohibited, except by Permit issued in accordance with Annex II to the Protocol on Environmental Protection to the Antarctic Treaty. Recommended measures aimed at minimising the unintentional introduction of non-native species are put forward in Appendix 11. To minimise the risk of accidental or unintentional introduction of non-native species the 'Non-native species manual' attached to ATCM Resolution 6 (2011) should be consulted.

viii. The disposal of waste

All wastes other than human wastes and domestic liquid waste shall be removed from the Area. Human and domestic liquid wastes from stations or field camps may be disposed of to Port Foster below the low water mark, and not within the boundaries of ASPA No. 145. Freshwater streams or lakes, or vegetated areas, shall not be used to dispose of human wastes.

ix. Requirement for reports

Reports of activities within the Area, which are not already covered under existing reporting requirements should be made available to the Chair of the Deception Island Management Group.

10. Advance exchange of information

- IAATO should, as far as practicable, provide the Chair of the Deception Island Management Group with details of scheduled visits by IAATO-registered vessels. Tour operators not affiliated to IAATO should also inform the Chair of the Deception Island Management Group of planned visits.

- All Parties should, as far as practicable, notify the Chair of the Deception Island Management Group of any governmental and non-governmental expeditions authorized by their national competent authority and which plans to visit or conduct activities in the Area.

- All National Antarctic Programmes should, as far as practicable, notify the Chair of the Deception Island Management Group of the location, expected duration, and any special considerations related to the deployment of field parties, scientific instrumentation or botanical quadrats at the four sites commonly visited by tourists (Whalers Bay, Pendulum Cove, Baily Head or the eastern end of Telefon Bay). This information will be relayed to IAATO (and as far as practicable to non-IAATO members).

Figure 1. The location of Deception Island in relation to the South Shetland Islands and the Antarctic Peninsula

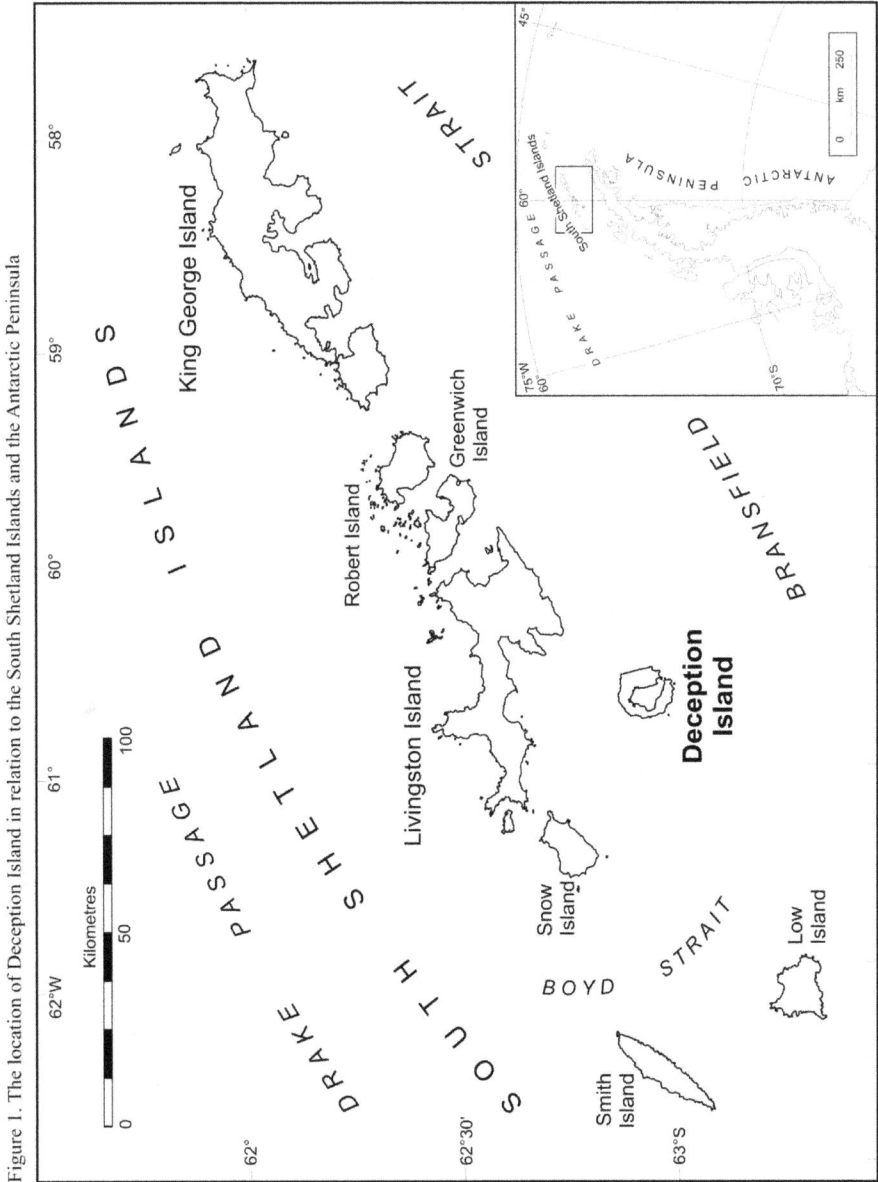

Figure 2. Deception Island - Topography

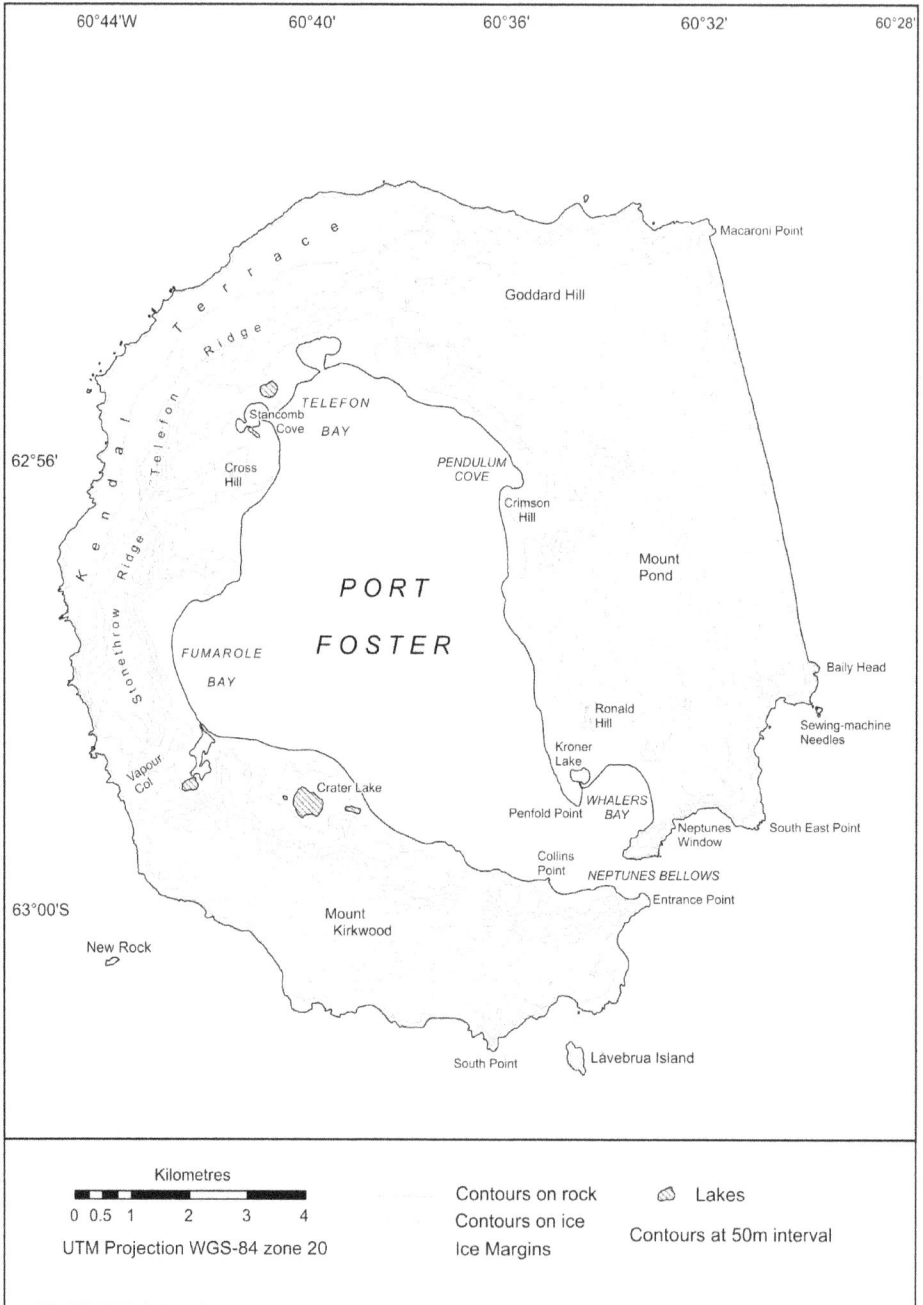

Figure 3. Deception Island Antarctic Specially Managed Area No. 4

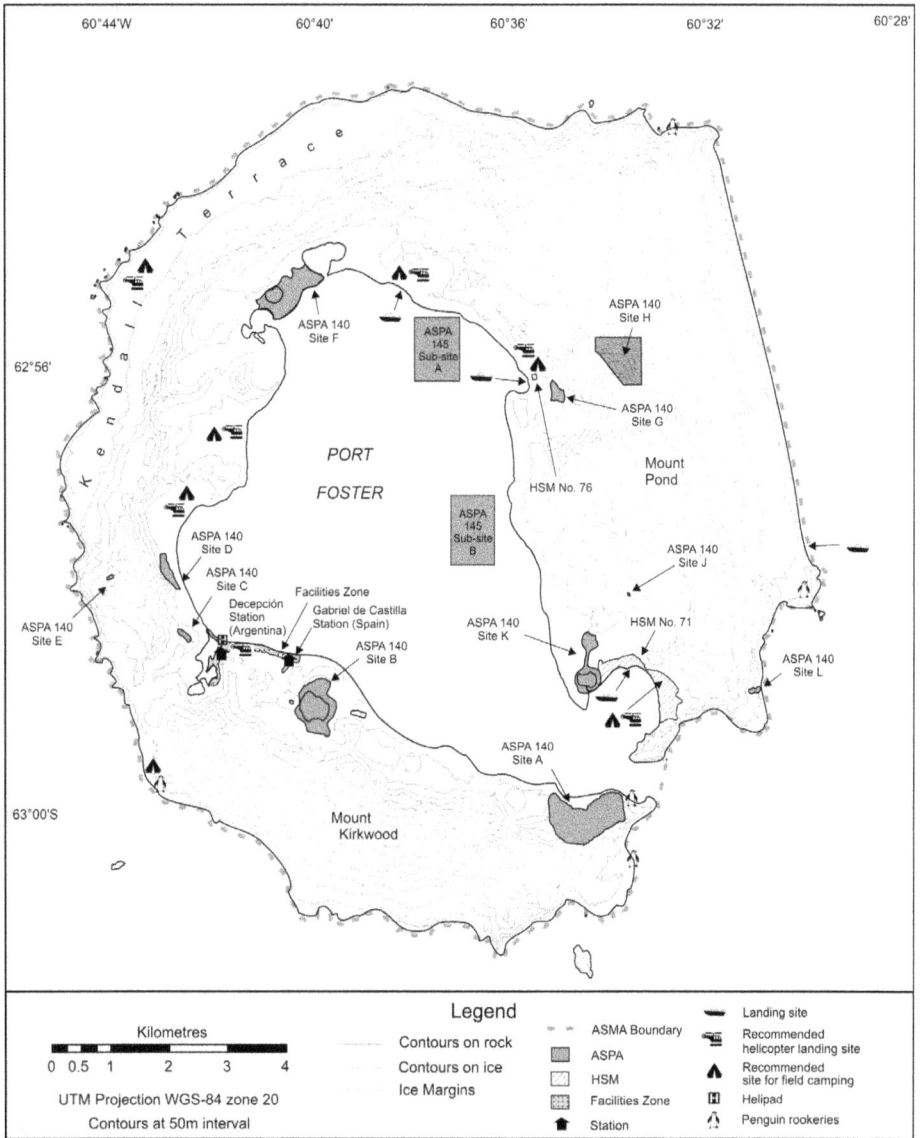

Appendix 1: ASPA 140

Currently valid plan is available at http://www.ats.aq/documents/recatt/Att291_e.pdf.

Appendix 2: ASPA 145

Currently valid plan is available at http://www.ats.aq/documents/recatt/Att284_e.pdf.

Appendix 3: Whalers Bay Conservation Strategy

Conservation Strategy for Historic Site and Monument No. 71, Whalers Bay, Deception Island

1. Introduction

1.1 General background

Historic Site and Monument No 71, Whalers Bay (latitude 62° 59'S, longitude 60° 34'W), is located on Deception Island, South Shetland Islands, Antarctica.

The buildings, structures and other artefacts on the shore of Whalers Bay, which date from the period 1906-1931, represent the most significant whaling remains in the Antarctic. Other buildings, structures and artefacts of the British 'Base B' represent an important aspect of the scientific history of the area (1944-1969).

The remains of the Norwegian Hector whaling station at Whalers Bay were originally listed as Historic Site and Monument No. 71 in ATCM Measure 4 (1995) based on a proposal by Chile and Norway. The extent of the historic site was expanded in 2003 by means of ATCM Measure 3 (2003) (see Section 3).

1.2 Brief historical background (1906-1969)

During the 1906-07 austral summer, the Norwegian Captain Adolfus Andresen, founder of the *Sociedad Ballenera de Magallanes*, Chile, began whaling at Deception Island. Whalers Bay served as a sheltered anchorage for factory ships that processed whale blubber. In 1908 a cemetery was established here. The cemetery was partly buried and partly swept away during a volcanic eruption in 1969, at which time it comprised 35 graves and a memorial to ten men who were lost at sea (only one body was recovered). In 1912, a Norwegian company, *Aktieselskabet Hektor*, established the shore-based whaling station in Whalers Bay. Hektor whaling station operated until 1931.

During the 1943-44 austral summer, the UK established a permanent base (Base B) in part of the abandoned whaling station. Base B was operated as a British scientific station, latterly by the British Antarctic Survey, until 1969, when it was severely damaged by a mud and ash flow caused by a volcanic eruption, and was abandoned.

Attachment A contains further detail on the history of Whalers Bay, including a bibliography.

1.3   Aim and objectives of the conservation strategy

The overall aim of the conservation strategy is to protect the values of Whalers Bay Historic Site. The objectives are to:

- *Maintain and preserve the cultural heritage and the historic values of the site within the constraints of natural processes.* Minor restoration and conservation work will be considered, whilst it is recognised that natural processes will continue to cause the deterioration of buildings, structures and other artefacts over time.

- *Prevent unnecessary human disturbance to the site, its features and artifacts*. Every effort shall be made to ensure that human activity at the site does not diminish its historic values. Any damage, removal or destruction of buildings or structures is prohibited in accordance with Article 8 (4) of Annex V to the Protocol on Environmental Protection to the Antarctic Treaty.

- *Permit ongoing clean up of debris.* Large quantities of waste are present in and around the buildings at Whalers Bay. Wind-scattered debris is present throughout the site. There is also hazardous waste present, including diesel fuel and asbestos. A major clean up of loose debris and waste, identified by conservation and environmental experts as not forming an important part of the historic remains, was undertaken in April 2004. Furthermore, a program of ongoing clean–up of debris resulting from the gradual deterioration of the structures, will be instigated. Any removal of debris must only be undertaken under the advice of a professional heritage expert, and proper documentation must be secured before such debris is removed.

- *Educate visitors to understand, respect and care for the historic values of the site.* Whalers Bay Historic Site is one of the most visited sites in Antarctica. Information on the historic significance of the site, and the need to conserve its values, will be made available to visitors.

- *Protect the natural and cultural environment of the site.* Whalers Bay is an integral part of the unique environment of Deception Island. Activities at the site should be undertaken in such a way that minimizes any impact on the natural and cultural environment.

2.   Parties undertaking management

Chile, Norway and the UK shall consult within the wider Deception Island Management Group to ensure that the provisions of this conservation strategy are implemented and its aim is met.

3. Description of the site

The site comprises all pre-1970 remains on the shore of Whalers Bay, including those from the early whaling period (1906-12) initiated by Captain Adolfus Andresen of the *Sociedad Ballenera de Magallanes*, Chile; the remains of the Norwegian Hektor Whaling Station established in 1912 and all artefacts associated with its operation until 1931; the site of a cemetery with 35 burials and a memorial to ten men lost at sea; and the remains from the period of British scientific and mapping activity (1944-1969). The site also acknowledges and commemorates the historic value of other events that occurred there, from which nothing remains.

3.1 Site boundary

Figure 1 shows the boundary of the Whalers Bay Historic Site. It comprises most of the beach at Whalers Bay from Neptunes Window to the former BAS aircraft hangar. Boundary markers, which would detract from the aesthetic value of the site, have not been erected. Figure 1 also shows the major historic buildings and structures at the site.

3.2 Historic remains

Table 1 summarises the main buildings, facilities and other structures at the site. More detailed information about these historic structures is provided in Attachment B and their location is shown on Figure 1.

Table 1: Historic remains at the Whalers Bay Historic Site

#[4]	Structure	Map 1[5]
Whaling period		
WB1	Various remains from the whaling period at Deception Island (1906-1931), including: - Water boats and rowing boats - Wells and well head houses - Storage building - Wooden and metal barrels - Rampart dams	14
WB2	Cemetery (1 cross and 1 empty coffin currently visible). NB The pile of stones in front of the original cross does NOT indicate a grave, but is a new addition by visitors. One memorial cross has been moved to the site.	Cross
WB3	Magistrate's residence	3
WB4	Hospital/storage building	2
WB5	Boilers	7
WB6	Cookers and associated equipment, including: - cooking grills - driving wheel - steam winch	7
WB7	Foundation of kitchen/mess building (subsequently reused as the foundations for Priestley House) and piggery	4
WB8	Fuel storage tanks	10, 11
WB9	Half floating dock	12
WB10	Whalers Barracks (subsequently renamed Biscoe House)	5
Scientific period		
WB11	'Hunting Lodge' (UK company Hunting Aerosurveys)	9
WB12	Aircraft hangar [6]	1
WB13	Massey Ferguson tractor	6

3.3 Natural environment

The 1967 volcanic eruption on Deception Island resulted in the deposition of a 1-5 cm layer of ash over Whalers Bay, whilst the 1969 eruption caused a lahar (mud slide) which partly buried the site. Fragile fluvial terraces are located to the north of the whaling station which were of geological importance, although have now been naturally eroded by meltwater streams.

The immediate area to the west of the Historic Site, including Kroner Lake, the Ronald Hill crater plain and the valley connecting them, is designated as part of ASPA 140 due to its exceptional botanical and limnological importance.

---

[4] Reference number is cross-referenced with the information in Attachment B.
[5] Reference to map location (Figure 1)
[6] A de Havilland DHC-3 Single Otter was removed from the site in April 2004 by BAS for safe-keeping at the de Havilland Aircraft Heritage Centre, London Colney, UK. The intention is to return it to Whalers Bay once it is safe to do so. This position is due to be reviewed in 2014.

Further areas of botanical importance are located within the Historic Site. These include a geothermally active scoria outcrop to the east of the whaling station, around the 'Hunting Lodge', inside the two accessible whale oil tanks, around the site of the cemetery, and on the cliffs and massive boulders at Cathedral Crags and Neptunes Window. Elsewhere, timber and iron structures, bricks and mortar, are colonised by various crustose lichens, all of which are common on natural substrata on the island.

Kelp gulls (*Larus dominicanus*), Wilson's storm-petrel (*Oceanites oceanicus*) and Antarctic Terns (*Sterna vittata*) breed at Whalers Bay, and Cape petrels (*Daption capensis*) nest in Cathedral Crags, overlooking the site.

4. Management of the site

4.1 Access to, and movement within, the site

All visits at the site should adhere to the adopted visitor site guidelines for Whalers Bay[7]. In addition the following should be used as guidance with respect to access to, and movement within the site:

- Motorized vehicles are only to be used within the HSM for scientific, conservation or clean-up activities (e.g. removal of waste).

- Helicopter landings, where necessary for conservation or management purposes, should only take place in the designated landing site (shown in Figure 1) to avoid dangers associated with loose debris and to prevent damaging structures or causing disturbance to wildlife.

- Field camps for scientific or management purposes should be established in the area to the east of the half floating dock as indicated in the map provided in Attachment B. The use of buildings for camping purposes is prohibited except in an emergency.

4.2 Installation, modification and removal of structures

- In accordance with Article 8 of Annex V to the Protocol on Environmental Protection to the Antarctic Treaty (1998), the historic structures, facilities and artefacts at the site are not to be damaged, removed or destroyed. Graffiti considered to be of historic importance should not be removed. New graffiti should not be added.

- Conservation and/or restoration work agreed by the Parties undertaking management may be carried out. Work on the buildings and structures may be necessary to render them safe or to prevent damage to the environment.

---

[7] The site guidelines are available at the ATS website at www.ats.aq/siteguidelines/documents/Whalers_bay_e.pdf

- No new buildings or other structures (apart from interpretative material agreed by Chile, Norway and the UK, in consultation with the wider Deception Island Management Group) are to be erected at the site.

- Historic remains and artefacts found at other locations on Deception Island, or elsewhere, which originate from Whalers Bay may be returned to the site after due consideration by those Parties undertaking management.

4.3   Visitor guidelines

The Visitor Site Guidelines for Whalers Bay (adopted by ATCM) applies to all visitors, including visits by commercial tour operators (IAATO and non-IAATO affiliated), private expeditions and National Antarctic Programme staff when undertaking recreational visits[8].

4.4   Information

- An informative sign, agreed by the Parties undertaking management, will be located at the recommended landing site. Appropriate and necessary signs advising visitors of any health and safety issues will also be considered.

- Memorial plaques (e.g. listing the names of those buried in the cemetery, or commemorating Captain Adolfus Andresen) may also be located within the site.

- Boundary markers are not considered necessary, as they would detract from the aesthetic value of the site. The boundary generally follows clearly visible natural features.

- The Parties undertaking management will disseminate further information about the significance of the historic site and the need to conserve its values.

4.5   Reporting and Recording

The following records are to be maintained by the Parties undertaking management:

- number of tourists landing at the site;
- number of scientists and associated logistics personnel visiting the site;
- conservation and clean-up work carried out; and
- site inspection reports, including reports and photographs on the condition of the historic remains.

---

[8] The guidelines are available at the ATS website at www.ats.aq/siteguidelines/documents/Whalers_bay_e.pdf

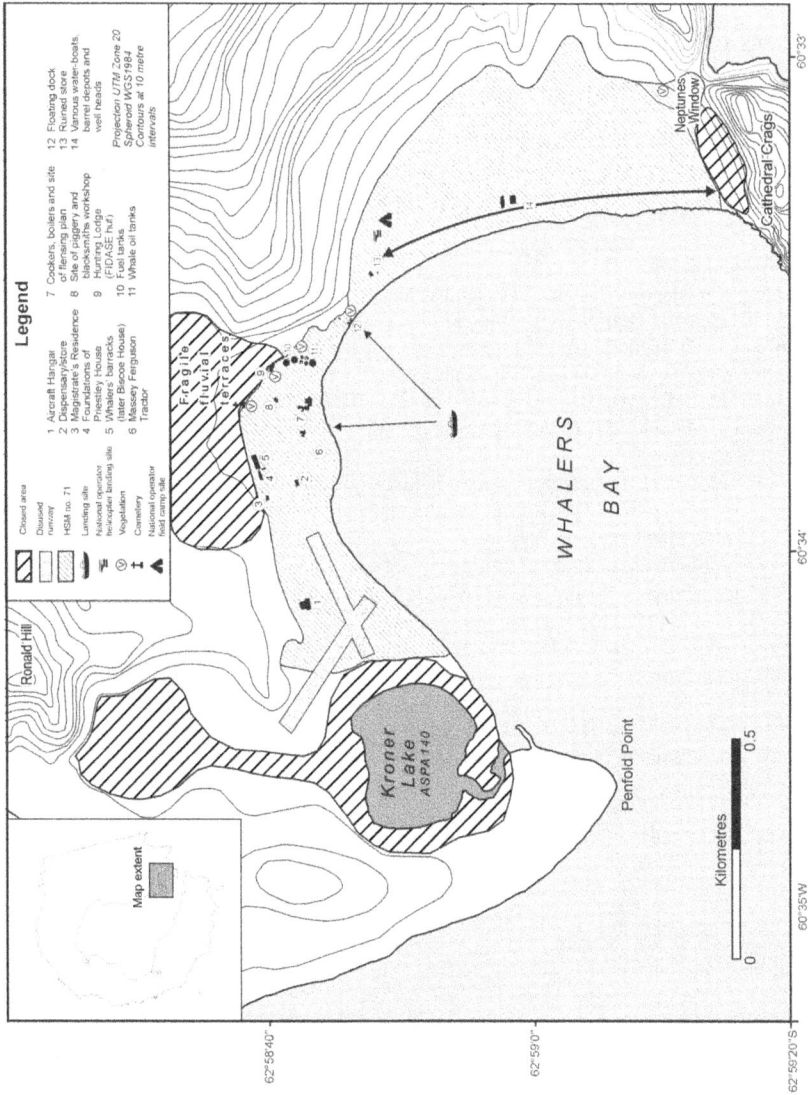

Legend

Ronald Hill

- Closed area
- Disused runway
- HSM no. 71
- Landing site
- National operator helicopter landing site
- Vegetation
- Cemetery
- National operator field camp site

1 Aircraft Hangar
2 Dispensary/store
3 Magistrate's Residence
4 Foundations of Priestley House
5 Whalers' barracks (later Biscoe House)
6 Massey Ferguson Tractor

7 Cookers, boilers and site of flensing plan
8 Site of piggery and blacksmiths workshop
9 Hunting Lodge (FIDASE hut)
10 Fuel tanks
11 Whale oil tanks

12 Floating dock
13 Ruined store
14 Various water-boats, barrel depots and well heads

Projection: UTM Zone 20
Spheroid WGS1984
Contours at 10 metre intervals

WHALERS BAY

Fragile fluvial terraces

Kroner Lake
ASPA 140

Penfold Point

Neptunes Window

Cathedral Crags

Map extent

Kilometres

0   0.5

62°58'40"
62°59'0"
62°59'20"S

60°33'
60°34'
60°35'W

Appendix 4: Facilities Zone Code of Conduct

Code of Conduct for the Deception Island ASMA 4 Facilities Zone, including Decepción Station (Argentina) and Gabriel de Castilla Station (Spain)

1. Introduction

The Deception Island ASMA includes a Facilities Zone (Figure 1) within which is located "Decepción" Station (Argentina, Figure 2) and "Gabriel de Castilla" Station (Spain, Figure 3). Figure 1 shows the extent of the Facilities Zone, which includes the two stations, the surrounding beach area, and a small unnamed lake to the west of Crater Lake from which freshwater is extracted. Activities within this zone are to be undertaken in line with this Code of Conduct, the aims of which are to:

- encourage the pursuit of scientific investigation on Deception Island, including the establishment and maintenance of appropriate supporting infrastructure;
- preserve the natural, scientific and cultural values of the Facilities Zone;
- safeguard the health and safety of station personnel.

This Code of Conduct summarises existing station procedures, a copy of which is available (Spanish language version only) at Decepción and Gabriel de Castilla stations.

Staff and visitors will be made aware of the contents of this Code of Conduct during pre-deployment training programmes and briefing sessions on board ship prior to arrival at the station.

A copy of the complete Deception Island ASMA Management Package will be kept at Decepción Station and Gabriel de Castilla Station, where relevant maps and information posters about the ASMA will also be displayed.

2. Buildings and services

2.1   Buildings

- An Environmental Impact Assessment (EIA) must be undertaken for the construction of any new permanent station buildings in line with Annex I to the Environmental Protocol.
- An EIA must also be undertaken for the quarrying of rock to maintain existing buildings, in line with Annex I to the Environmental Protocol, as well as with the prior approval of the national authorities of Argentina (Decepción Station) or Spain (Gabriel de Castilla Station).
- Consideration will be given to reusing existing sites when practicable, in order to minimise disturbance.

- Buildings are to be maintained in good condition. Buildings not currently in use are to be routinely checked, and assessed for likely removal.
- Work-sites are to be kept as neat as possible.

2.2   Power Generation

- Maintain generators in good condition, and undertake routine inspections, so as to minimise emissions and possible fuel leaks.
- Ensure economy in power consumption and hence fuel usage and emissions.
- The use of renewable energy sources will be encouraged, where appropriate.

2.3   Water Supply

- Handling or disposing of wastes, fuel or other chemicals within the stations' water catchment area is prohibited.
- Use of vehicles within the water catchment area will only be for essential purposes.
- Ensure that regular tests of water quality, as well as routine cleaning of water holding tanks, are conducted.
- Regulate water consumption, so as to avoid unnecessary extraction.

3. Fuel handling

- The integrity of bulk fuel storage facilities, supply lines, pumps, reels and other fuel handling equipment will be regularly inspected.
- At both stations, fuel storage includes secondary containment. Drummed fuel should be stored inside. Storage areas should, as far as practicable, be properly ventilated, and sited away from electrical services. Storage facilities should also be sited away from accommodation facilities for safety reasons.
- All practicable measures will be undertaken to avoid fuel spills, in particular during fuel transfer (e.g. ship to shore transfer by pipeline or zodiac, refuelling day tanks).
- Any fuel, oil or lubricant spills will be reported immediately to the Station Leader, and subsequently to the National Authority.
- Ensure that adequate and sufficient spill response equipment (e.g. absorbents) is kept in a known location and available to deal with any spills.
- Station personnel will be trained in how to use spill response equipment. Training exercises will be undertaken at the beginning of each season.
- In case of fuel spills, response actions will be undertaken in line with the Oil Spill Contingency Plan held at each station.
- Oily wastes will be packaged in appropriate containers and disposed of according to station procedures.

4. Fire prevention and fire-fighting

- Signs indicating no-smoking areas, and flammable substances, will be displayed as appropriate.

- Fire fighting equipment will be available at fuel storage sites and elsewhere. Such equipment will be clearly marked.

5. Waste Management

- Waste management, including waste reduction and the provision of equipment and appropriate packaging material, will be considered in the planning and conducting of all activities at Decepción and Gabriel de Castilla stations.
- All station personnel will be instructed on the provisions of Annex III to the Environmental Protocol.
- A waste management co-ordinator will be appointed at each station.
- Wastes will be segregated at source and stored safely on site prior to removal. After each summer season, wastes generated at Decepción and Gabriel de Castilla stations will be removed from the Antarctic Treaty Area.
- Regular tests of water effluents discharged into Port Foster will be undertaken.
- Any substances that may adversely affect the working of effluent treatment plants will not be disposed of through the drainage system (including toilets and wash basins).
- Cleaning up past waste disposal sites on land and abandoned work sites will be considered a priority, except where removal would result in more adverse environmental impacts than leaving the structure or waste material *in situ*.
- Personnel from both stations should periodically participate in clean-up activities within the facilities area, so as to minimise any scattered wastes around the stations.
- At the end of each summer season, activities connected to clean-up and removal of wastes will be reported to the appropriate national authority.

6.   Other Operational Issues

6.1   Communications

- The installation of permanent or temporary aerials is to be carefully considered through the environmental evaluation procedures in place.
- VHF Marine Channel 16 will be monitored.
- All station personnel leaving the Facilities Zone must be equipped with a VHF radio.

6.2   Use of vehicles and small boats

- Vehicles should only be used around and between the stations when necessary.
- Keep to established tracks within the station area where practicable.
- Refuelling and servicing of vehicles will be carried out at the facilities provided for these purposes. Every effort should be made to avoid spills during refuelling and servicing.
- Do not use vehicles close to sensitive scientific equipment, across flora or near concentrations of fauna, or unnecessarily within the water-catchment area.

- Small boats operating out of Decepción or Gabriel de Castilla Station are only to be used within Port Foster, when weather conditions allow, and principally for scientific and logistic reasons. No small boats will be used outside Port Foster. Avoid the use of small boats close to cliffs and/or glaciers, to avoid rock or ice falls.
- When operating one boat, a second boat will be on stand-by, at the Station, for immediate support in an emergency.
- Small boats will be operated by at least two people. Essential equipment will include boating immersion suits, life jackets and appropriate radio links (for example VHF radios).

6.3 Aircraft Operations

- Helicopters will generally take off from and land at the helipad at Decepción Station. Occasionally, operational reasons may require them to take off from, or land at, other appropriate locations within the Facilities Zone.

6.4 Field travel

- All wastes from field camps, except for human wastes (faeces, urine and grey water) will be returned to the stations for safe disposal. The human and domestic liquid wastes are to be disposed of in Port Foster below the low water mark.
- The Station Leader and/or the Station Environment Officer will brief field parties on environmental management in the field, the location of protected areas, and the provisions of the ASMA Management Plan.
- No uncooked poultry products will be used by field parties.
- All field parties will be equipped with VHF radios.

7. Protected Areas

- Three terrestrial sub-sites of ASPA No. 140 (Site B - Crater Lake, Site C - Unnamed hill, southern end of Fumarole Bay, and Site D - Fumarole Bay), are located close to the Facilities Zone. Station personnel will be made aware of the location of, and restrictions on access to, all protected areas on Deception Island. Information about these protected areas, including a map showing their location, will be prominently displayed at both stations.

8. Flora and fauna

- Any activity involving the taking of, or harmful interference with, native flora or fauna (as defined in Annex II to the Protocol) is prohibited unless authorised by a permit issued by the appropriate authority.
- An appropriate precautionary approach distance, no closer than 10 meters, is to be maintained from birds or seals present in the Facility Zone.
- Staff and visitors are to walk slowly and carefully when near wildlife, in particular avoiding birds which are nesting, moulting, crèching or returning from foraging trips. Give 'right of way' to wildlife at all times.
- Birds are not to be fed on waste food scraps from the stations. Food wastes will be secured to prevent scavenging by birds.

- All reasonable precautions will be taken to avoid the introduction of micro-organisms and any other non-native species, or species from other Antarctic sites. Recommended measures aimed at minimising the unintentional introduction of non-native species are found in Appendix 11 of the Deception Island management plan.
- The introduction of herbicides, pesticides or other harmful substances is prohibited.
- At the end of each summer season, a report on activities involving the taking of, or harmful interference with, native flora and fauna will be forwarded to the appropriate national authorities.

9. Tourist visits to the Facilities Zone

- Any visits to Decepción Station (Argentina) or Gabriel de Castilla Station (Spain) may only be undertaken at the discretion of the respective Station Leader. Contact can be made via VHF Marine Channel 16. Visits will only be allowed if they do not interfere with scientific or logistical work.
- Visits are to be undertaken in line with Recommendation XVIII-1, Measure 15 (2009) "Landing of Persons from Passenger vessels", Resolution 7 (2009) "General Principles of Antarctic Tourism", Resolution 7 (2009) "General Principles of Antarctic Tourism" and Resolution 3 (2011) "General Guidelines for Visitors to Antarctic).
- Station Leaders will co-ordinate visits to stations with Expedition Leaders.
- Visitors will be informed about the principles of this Code of Conduct, as well as the ASMA Management Plan.
- The station leader will appoint a guide (English speaking, when appropriate and possible), to escort visitors around the station, in order to ensure compliance with the measures included in this Code of Conduct.
- The national authorities operating Decepción or Gabriel de Castilla Stations will inform Antarctic Treaty Secretariat, COMNAP and IAATO in case of a clear risk of volcanic eruption. The stations shall notify any ships in the area of any immediate danger.

10. Co-operation and sharing of resources

- Both stations will co-ordinate and periodically conduct joint emergency evacuation, oil spill response and fire-fighting exercises.

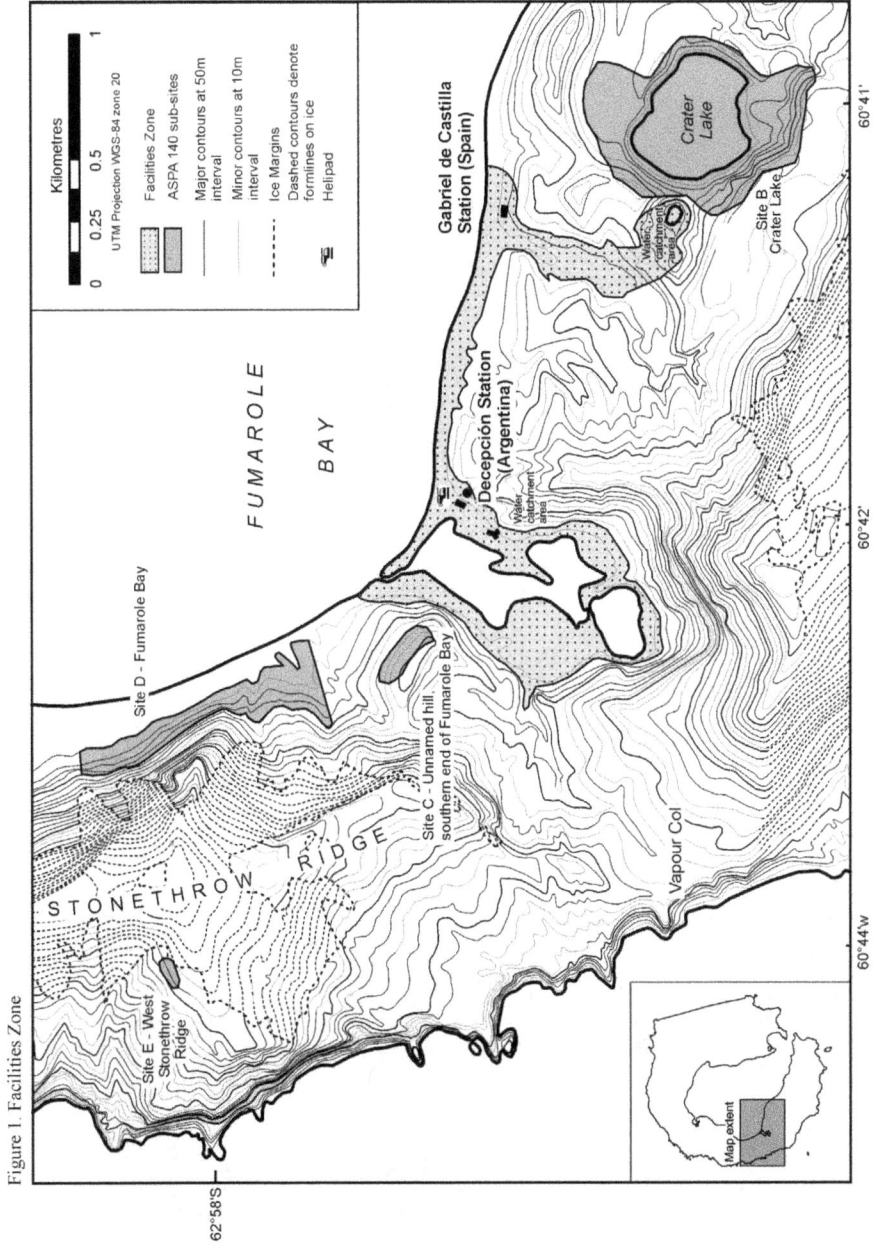

Figure 1. Facilities Zone

Figure 2. Argentinian Antarctic Base Decepción

Figure 3. Spanish Antactic Base Gabriel de Castilla

Appendix 5: Visitor Sites Code of Conduct

Code of Conduct for Visitors to Deception Island

1.   Introduction

This code of conduct has been produced for commercial tour operators (IAATO and non-IAATO affiliated), private expeditions and National Antarctic Programme staff when undertaking recreational visits to Deception Island.

There are four sites on Deception Island which may generally be visited: Whalers Bay, Baily Head, Pendulum Cove, and Telefon Bay (east). Stancomb Cove, in Telefon Bay, is also used as an anchorage for yachts. Visits to Decepción Station (Argentina) and Gabriel de Castilla Station (Spain) are only permitted by prior agreement with the respective Station Leaders. Tourist or recreational visits to other sites on the island are discouraged.

2.   General Guidelines

The following general guidelines apply to all the above sites visited on Deception Island:

- Visits are to be undertaken in line with the Management Plan for Deception Island ASMA 4, the general guidelines for visitors to the Antarctic (Resolution 3 (2011) and with Recommendation XVIII-1.

- All visits must be planned and conducted taking into account the significant risk to human life posed by the threat of volcanic eruption.

- Expedition Leaders of cruise ships and Masters of national programme support vessels are encouraged to exchange itineraries in order to avoid two ships unintentionally converging on a site simultaneously.

- Vessels approaching or departing from Port Foster must announce over VHF Marine Channel 16 the intended time and direction of passage through Neptunes Bellows.

- For commercial cruise operators, no more than 100 passengers may be ashore at a site at any time, accompanied by a minimum of one member of the expedition staff for every 20 passengers.

- Do not walk on vegetation such as moss or lichen. The flora of Deception Island is of exceptional scientific importance. Walking on the alga *Prasiola crispa* (associated with penguin colonies) is permissible as it will not cause it any adverse disturbance.

- Maintain an appropriate distance from birds or seals which is safe and does not cause them disturbance. As a general rule, maintain a distance of 5 metres. Where practicable, keep at least 15 metres away from fur seals.

- In order to prevent biological introductions, carefully wash boots and clean clothes, bags, tripods and walking sticks before landing.

- Do not leave any litter.

- Do not take biological or geological souvenirs or disturb artefacts.

- Do not write or draw graffiti on any man-made structure or natural surface.

- Scientific equipment is routinely deployed during the austral summer by National Antarctic Programmes at a number of locations on Deception Island. The Spanish Antarctic Programme deploy equipment for important and necessary seismic monitoring. Such equipment is highly sensitive to disturbance. At least 20 metres must be maintained from seismic monitoring equipment, which will be marked with a red flag. This distance is under examination - any revisions will be provided as necessary.

- Do not touch or disturb other types of scientific instruments or markers (e.g. wooden stakes marking botanical plots).

- Do not touch or disturb field depots or other equipment stored by National Antarctic Programmes.

3. Site Specific Guidelines

3.1 Whalers Bay (latitude 62°59'S, longitude 60°34'W)

Whalers Bay is the most visited site on Deception Island, and one of the most visited sites in the Antarctic. It is a small bay immediately to the east after passing into Port Foster through Neptunes Bellows. It was named by the French explorer Jean-Baptiste Charcot because of the whaling activity that took place there. The site includes the remains of the Norwegian Hektor Whaling Station, the site of the cemetery and the abandoned British 'Base B', as well as the whaling remains along the length of the beach, some of which pre-date the whaling station. Appendix 3, Conservation Strategy for Whalers Bay Historic Site and Monument No. 71, contains further information about Whalers Bay.

- Visits to Whalers Bay must be undertaken in line with Visitor Site Guide for Whalers Bay (Appendix 8).

3.2 Pendulum Cove (latitude 62°56'S, longitude 60°36'W)

Pendulum Cove (see figure 1) is a small cove on the north east side of Port Foster. It was named by Henry Foster of the British Royal Naval vessel HMS

Chanticleer who, in 1828, undertook magnetic observations there using pendulums. The gently sloping ash and cinder beach leads to the remains of the abandoned Presidente Pedro Aguirre Cerda Station (Chile), Historic Site and Monument No. 76, which was destroyed by a volcanic eruption in 1967. Thermal springs along the shallow shoreline of Pendulum Cove offer visitors the opportunity to 'bathe' in warm water.

Visits to Pendulum Cove must be undertaken in line with Visitor Site Guide for Pendulum Cove (Appendix 10).

-

3.3   Baily Head (latitude 62°58'S, longitude 60°30'W)

Baily Head (see figure 2) is a rocky headland exposed to the Bransfield Strait on the south east coast of Deception Island. It was named after Francis Baily, the English astronomer who reported on Foster's magnetic observations at Pendulum Cove. The site comprises the southern end of a long linear beach which runs along most of the eastern side of Deception Island, and a narrow valley that rises steeply inland to a semi-circular ridgeline, giving the impression of a natural 'amphitheatre'. It is bounded to the north by a large glacier and to the south by the cliffs of Baily Head. A substantial melt-stream runs through the centre of the valley during the austral summer.

Within this unnamed valley, and to the south of it, is one of the largest colonies of chinstrap penguins (*Pygoscelis antarctica*) in Antarctica - although recent studies indicate a significant reduction in the population here. Brown skuas (*Catharacta antarctica lonnbergi*), cape petrels (*Daption capensis*) and snowy sheathbills (*Chionis alba*) also nest at Baily Head. Antarctic fur seals (*Arctocephalus gazella*) haul out along the beach in large numbers during the austral summer.

Visits to Baily Head must be undertaken in line with Visitor Site Guide for Baily Head (Appendix 9).

-

3.4   Telefon Bay (east) (latitude 62°56'S, longitude 60°40'W)

Telefon Bay (see figure 3) was named after the whaling vessel *Telefon* which was moored in the bay for repairs in 1909 by Adolfus Amandus Andresen, founder of the company Sociedad Ballenera de Magallanes. At the easternmost end of Telefon Bay a gently sloping beach leads to a shallow valley which rises sharply to the rim of an unnamed volcanic crater.

Visits to Telefon Bay must be undertaken in line with Visitor Site Guide for Telefon Bay (Appendix 7).

3.5 Decepción Station (Argentina) and Gabriel de Castilla Station (Spain)

Visits to Decepción Station (Argentina) and Gabriel de Castilla Station (Spain) may only be undertaken with the prior agreement of the appropriate Station Leader. Visits to the stations must be undertaken in line with the Code of Conduct for the Deception Island Facilities Zone (Appendix 4).

Appendix 6: Volcanic Alert and Escape

Alert Scheme and Escape Strategy for volcanic eruptions on Deception Island

The volcanism in Deception Island

Within the area that encompasses the South Shetland Island, Antarctic Peninsula and Bransfield Sea, only Deception Island has experienced recent eruptive processes (i.e. in 1842, 1967, 1969 and 1970, with other non-verified events in 1912 and 1917).

Between 1967 and 1970, the intense volcanic activity in Deception Island caused the destruction of the scientific stations of Chile, in Pendulum Cove, and the United Kingdom, in Whalers Bay. The intense volcanic activity changed the island's morphology; a small island was created in Port Foster which, with time, was joined to the rest of Deception Island in the Telefon Bay area. The great amount of ejected volcanic ash, rock and debris covered some of the surroundings islands, which can still be observed at Johnson Glacier on Livingston Island.

An immediate consequence of the volcanic activity in 1967-1970, was the temporary end of scientific activity on the island, with only a limited number of studies looking at the post eruptive period taking place

At present, the only evidence of surface volcanic activity on Deception Island is the presence of areas where there is significant seismic activity, due to the tectonic expansion of the Bransfield rift and local volcanic activity that generates, when measured during the summer field season, an average of 1000 low energy surface quakes (magnitudes lower than 2 on the Richter Scale).

Higher magnitude tectonic-volcanic earthquakes, measuring between 3 and 4 on the Richter Scale, were recorded during two particularly active seismic-volcanic periods (1991-92 and 1998-99). During these periods, seismic events were felt, recorded and described by scientific groups on Gabriel de Castilla Station.

Between 31 December 1991 and 25 January 1992, the island experienced an important increase in seismic activity with up to 900 earthquakes recorded, four of which were directly felt by personnel on the island. These activities were interpreted as a reactivation process, probably due to a small intrusion located in Fumarole Bay.

After the periods of increased volcanic activity in 1994-95 and 1995-96, on 3 January 1999, a further important period of seismic-volcanic activity commenced with two earthquakes of magnitude 2.9 (January 11) and 3.4 (January 20) . These seismic-volcanic activities were located between Fumarole Bay and Whalers Bay. They included volcano-tectonics quakes that liberated a significant amount of energy, the like of which had never been recorded previously..

Following this period of more intense seismic activity, the multi-disciplinary geophysical and geodetic studies were increased within the island. Activities included:

resurveying of the geodetic net, establishing a new seismometer display, sampling of gases in the fumaroles and maintaining geomagnetic, gravimetric and bathymetric data records. An important geophysical study was performed that produced a tomography model of speed and attenuation in wave propagation, including a model to explain the relationship between the seismic activity recorded and dynamics of the volcano.

At present, volcanic activity on Deception Island could be considered typical of an andesitic volcano model (basaltic), with an effusive eruptive mechanism of surseyane type, with low magmatic volume and activity, mainly concentrated in Fumarole Bay, Telefon Bay, Pendulum Cove and Whalers Bay.

Present surface volcanic activity on Deception Island is related to important geothermal anomaly areas where a great number of zones with significant low energy (less than magnitude 2) surface seismic-volcanic activities are recorded.

Alert System

Every year, for approximately four months in the austral summer, Spanish and Argentinean scientists record continuously the volcanic activity on the island (typically between the end of November and the beginning of March). These periods are also coincident with the maximum human presence in the island.

The instruments deployed on Deception Island include a local network of seismometers and seismic array, telemetric seismographs, thermometric stations and a geodetic net maintained and recorded by Gabriel de Castilla Station. Geochemical data is collected and equipment maintained by Decepción Station.

Captains of ships entering Port Foster, and pilots of aircraft or helicopters, overflying the island, must pay attention to the volcanic activity bulletin broadcasts from Gabriel de Castilla (Spain) and Decepción (Argentina) Stations on VHF Channel 16 Marine.

To communicate this information it is considered useful to use a traffic light system that describes in a simple and accessible way, the present volcanic risk of the Deception Island volcano (Table 1).

Table I

Alert system for volcanic eruptions in Deception Island as recommended by AVCEI (International Association of Volcanology and Chemistry of the Earth's Interior)

Colour Code	Alert State	Description	Operative Actions
GREEN	No eruption expected	Normal volcanic parameters recorded. This is the normal island status	Control
YELLOW	Some anomalies in the volcanic system. A volcanic crisis could arise at some point in the future	There are small but significant anomalies in the volcanic parameters recorded	Control. Increase volcanic parameters recordings. Verify the parameters
ORANGE	Increased probability of volcanic eruption	Significant increase in volcanic parameters anomalies recorded. New changes in volcanic parameters appears	Increase readiness to respond. Start preparing the evacuation plan. Recommend restricting access to the island. Recommend temporaryevacuation of the island including ships and helicopters
RED	High probability of an imminent volcanic eruption	High probability of volcanic eruption confirmed with a significant change in the number of volcanic parameters anomalies	Personnel on the island to move to emergency camps or evacuate the island entirely depending on the location of the eruption. Forbid ships and helicopters to enter the island..

Note: The recording and evaluation of the volcanic risk should be on-going, at least during the time the bases are operating. Volcanologists must update the state of the traffic lights system, according to the variability ofvolcanic parameters recorded.

Escape strategy in case of a volcanic eruption on Deception Island

The present evacuation strategy is based in the assumption that future eruptions will be similar to the ones in 1967-1970 and that the volcanic activity will have a geographically limited impact in the island.

A sudden slump of the whole caldera could result in a most serious event with lethal effects for all personnel on the island. Evacuation under this scenario is unlikely to be possible. The likelihood of such event is probably low and would likely be preceded by many warning events such as an increase in surface altitude and and increase in earthquake frequency and intensity forseveral days or weeks before the event. Nevertheless, an event could arise suddenly, without any warning signs.

If an orange state of alert is declared all ships should leave Port Foster immediately after taking on board all crew and passengers that are ashore.

Captains and Masters of ships must take extreme caution when crossing Neptune Bellows taking into account the possibility of strong currents, Ravn rock in the middle of the narrow strait and any material that may have fallen from the steep cliffs on either side of the channel.

If an eruption is considered likely, some precautionary actions could be taken.

Firstly, ships should be advised not to access Port Foster in order to reduce future evacuation problems.. These measures would be temporary.

Although the island is small, it may be large enough to have areas where small groups may be relatively safe during a volcanic event. When considering recent eruptions on Deception Island, locations at distances from 7 to 10 kilometres from the centre of volcanic activity could be relatively safe.

It should be noted that evacuating all personnel from existing research stations could be more problematic, and have worse consequences, than moving personnel to selected emergency camps during a volcanic event. Timely use of previously assessed emergency camp locations could reduce the risk associated with a fast and full evacuation of personnel from the island during a volcanic event.

Consequently it is important to have selected locations *a priori* for emergency camps, taking into consideration the different possible locations of volcanic eruptions and other processes. As a general rule different options should therefore be considered before initiating an evacuation.

Evacuation routes

During a volcanic event all interior coastal areas may be considered dangerous, because of the fall of pyroclasts, rocks and other materials and the possibility of high, fast and irregular waves produced by seiches in Port Foster, that could put in danger ships sailing or anchoring in the island's lagoon.

Before evacuation it should be understood, that evacuation routes may be over difficult terrain and that the descent to the beaches on the outer coastline of the island may be steep and difficult to follow.

In addition, because of the substantial difficulties associated with crossing glaciers (broken and slippery surfaces, sudden lahars possible), it is advisable to avoid these areas, unless the support of specialists guides and adequate equipment is provided. However, it is recognised that such support may not always be available under emergency conditions.

Evacuation in helicopters may be the best solution, taken into account that external beaches are steep and narrow, with large boulders and are adjacent to deep waters with large waves that are often present even under good weather conditions. Some beaches (for example near Punta de la Descubierta) havesubmerged rocks which may be dangerous for small boats.

If the weather is good it could be possible to try helicopter evacuation from some locations around Port Foster, although helicopters working in any evacuation must avoid flying through volcanic clouds, because the fall of pyroclasts and ash could damage their engines.

These factors increase the danger of evacuation from Port Foster beaches, and it should be considered likely that evacuations may only be possible from external beaches or from some specific areas that could allow safe helicopters operation

To estimate the likely difficulties that could be encountered by evacuating personnel, most of the recommended evacuation routes were trialled previously by experienced personnel. The general conclusion of these surveys was that only three of the island's external beaches are available during bad weather: north side of Kendall Terrace, Macaroni Point and Baily Head. All of the other beaches identified were rocky and with access available only with helicopters. The route toward Punta de la Descubierta could be used, but only when the tide is very low.

As a result of these studies the main available evacuation routes are:

- From the facilities zone (Gabriel de Castilla, Decepcion Stations) toward Descubierta Point (1)
- From the facilities zone towards Entrance Point (the proposed route would entail evacuation from the beach) (2)
- From the facilities zone towards Entrance Point (helicopter extraction) (2)
- From Whalers Bay towards Baily Head (3)
- From the facilities zone towards Kendall Terrace (through the Pass at 168 m altitude above Telefon Bay) (4)
- From the facilities zone towards Kendall Terrace (through the Pass at 158 m altitude near Obsidians) (5)
- From the facilities zone towards Escondido Lake beach to Kendall Terrace (6)

Table 2 includes details of the evacuation routes, including distance, height gain and estimated journey time.

Table 2. Evacuation routes

Evacuation route	Total distances	Maximum altitude[9]	Estimated time
•Facilities zone to Punta de la Descubierta (figure 2)	3920 m	130 m in Espolon	1 hours 11 minutes

[9] The given altitudes refer to the highest point of the route.

• Facilities zone to Entrance Point (beach extraction area);	6800m	180 in Espolon	2 hours 9 minutes
• Facilities zone to Entrance Point (helicopter extraction area)	7237 m	172 m	2 hours
• Whalers Bayto Baily Head	3954 m	295 m in Collado crossing	1 hour 37 minutes
• Facilities zone to Kendall Terrace (by Collado crossing 168 of Telefon Bay)	9400 m	168 m in Collado	2 hours 31 minutes
• Facilities zone to Kendall Terrace (by Collado 158 in Obsidianas	6400 m	169 m in Collado	1 hour 46 minutes
Lago Escondido to Kendall Terrace	5980 m	180 m Vaguada crossing	1 hour 30 minutes

Figure 1 Suggested escape routes on Deception Island during a volcanic crisis corresponding to no more than a code orange alert state

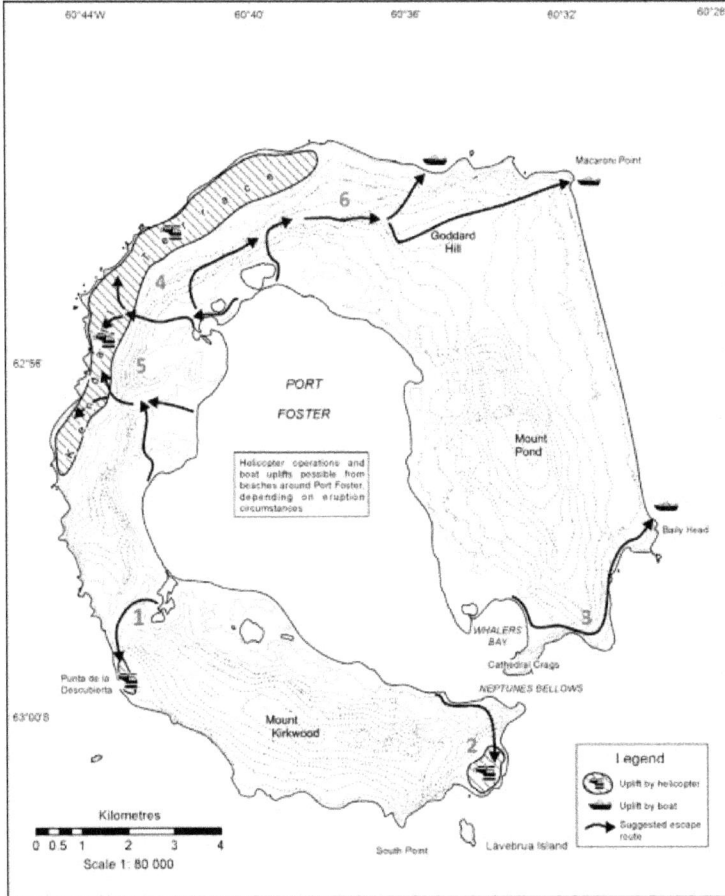

Appendix 7: Visitor Site Guide: Telefon Bay

Current guidelines at http://www.ats.aq/siteguidelines/documents/Telefon_bay_e.pdf

Appendix 8: Visitor Site Guide: Whalers Bay

Current guidelines at http://www.ats.aq/siteguidelines/documents/Whalers_bay_e.pdf

Appendix 9: Visitor Site Guide: Baily Head

Current guidelines at http://www.ats.aq/siteguidelines/documents/baily_head_e.pdf

Appendix 10: Visitor Site Guide: Pendulum Cove

Guidelines submitted to CEP XV/ATCM XXXV for approval and adoption. Link to adopted guidelines will be updated as soon as available.

Appendix 11: Practical biosecurity measures

Guidelines to reduce the risk of non-native species introductions to Deception Island (Antarctic Specially Managed Area No. 4)

Introduction

Deception Island, South Shetland Islands (Antarctic Specially Managed Area No. 4) is exceptionally vulnerable to the impacts of introduced non-native species. The high level of human occupation and visitation means the likelihood of unintentional introduction of non-native species is high. The mild climate, relative to other areas of Antarctica, and the presence of geothermally-heated sites may make establishment of introduced marine and terrestrial species more likely than at other Antarctic locations. Deception Island has already been subject to non-native introductions: six species of non-native invertebrates have been recorded on the island and one introduced plant has also been found and subsequently eradicated.

Acknowledging:

(i)   the value of the Area's unique and isolated biological assemblies; and

(ii)   the exceptional vulnerability of terrestrial and marine ecosystems within Deception Island to the potential impacts of non-native species due to the island's mild climate, geothermally-heated ground and high level of human presence;

the following guidelines aim to minimize the unintentional introduction of non-native species and material likely to carry such species (i.e. soils and untreated wood bark) to Deception Island, and describe appropriate monitoring and response activities.

Protection measures

AWARENESS

Programmes, operators and organisations active in Deception Island shall:

1. Educate personnel (including station personnel, scientists, contractors, landing ship crews, tour operator staff and tourists) about the potential risks to the environment through the introduction of non-native species.

2. Remind personnel that the introduction of non-sterile soil into the Antarctic Treaty area is prohibited as stipulated within the Protocol on Environmental Protection to the Antarctic Treaty. Similarly, that cultivated plants and their reproductive propagules may only be imported for controlled use and in accordance with a permit.

3. Remind personnel that, in accordance with the Protocol on Environmental Protection to the Antarctic Treaty, food waste must be incinerated or removed from the Antarctic Treaty area

(Annex III) or disposed of at sea not less than 12 nautical miles from the nearest land or ice shelf (Annex IV).

OPERATIONAL PROCEDURES

Programmes, operators and organizations active in Deception Island shall furthermore:

4. Consider application of biosecurity guidelines concerning: (a) ships travelling to Deception Island, (b) stores supplying food and cargo to the island and (c) visitors' clothing and personal and scientific equipment. More specifically:

   • As far as is practicable, ensure that personnel entering and leaving the ASMA have clean footwear, for example, through boot cleaning procedures (preferably completed before departure for Antarctica as well as on entering and leaving the ASMA). Similar attention should be paid to clothes and other personal gear on which seeds and other non-native species propagules may be attached, such as bags, walking poles and camera tripods.

   • Reduce, to the maximum extent practical, the importation of untreated sand, aggregate and gravel to the ASMA.

   • Reduce, to the maximum extent practical, the importation of untreated wood to the ASMA.

   • Prohibit the importation of untreated wood to which bark is attached, as it is likely to contain many resilient non-native species such as micro-invertebrates, micro-algae, mosses, lichens and microorganisms.

   • Prevent food and food waste from being accessed by wildlife.

   • Prohibit the cultivation of plants for food, for example through hydroponics, within Deception Island station buildings.

   • Collect and incinerate or remove from the region any soil or biological material that is known not to have originated from within the ASMA.

   • Take particular care to reduce the risk of transfer of soils and biological material between spatially distinct geothermally-heated sites (e.g. ensure footwear is clean).

   • Take steps to reduce the risk of the biological contamination, or cross-contamination, of the island's fresh water bodies.

   • Implement measures to prevent intra-regional transfer of non-native species that are already present on Deception Island to other parts of Antarctica (e.g. by preventing transfer of Deception Island soils to other Antarctic locations).

The above guidance is based on advice provided in the CEP *Non-native species manual*, where two central resources are the COMNAP/SCAR *Checklists for supply chain managers of National Antarctic Programmes for the reduction in risk of transfer of non-native species* and the SCAR *environmental code of conduct for terrestrial scientific field research in Antarctica.*

RECORDING, MONITORING AND RESPONSE

Programmes, operators and organizations active in Deception Island shall furthermore:

5. Undertake monitoring for introduced species through terrestrial and marine biodiversity surveys, including the establishment of baseline survey data, ideally as part of a multi-national research programme.

6. Inform the Deception Island Management Group and other Parties, as appropriate, of the discovery of any non-native species within the ASMA. Inform SCAR of the discovery through the SCAR Aliens Species Database: http://data.aad.gov.au/aadc/biodiversity/index.cfm.

7. Share new information concerning any non-native species found on the Island with the Deception Island Management Group and other Parties, as appropriate, with a view to co-ordinating a rapid management response (e.g. eradication or containment measures).

8. Undertake the response to an introduction as a priority, to prevent an increase in the species' distribution range and to make eradication simpler, cost effective and more likely to succeed[10].

9. Assess regularly the efficacy of control or eradication programmes, including follow-up surveys.

COOPERATION & FUTURE PROTECTION

Programmes, operators and organizations active in Deception Island shall furthermore:

10. Consider the exceptional vulnerability of Deception Island to non-native species introductions in all Environmental Impact Assessments undertaken for activities occurring place within the ASMA.

11. Consider joint implementation of these guidelines through the Deception Island Management Group and other relevant Parties, as appropriate.

12. Commit to continuous improvement and revision of these guidelines.

---

[10]Note in this context the *Guidance for visitors and environmental managers following the discovery of a suspected non-native species in the terrestrial and freshwater Antarctic environment* referred to in the *CEP Non-native species manual*

PART III

Opening and Closing Addresses and Reports

1. Reports by Depositaries and Observers

The Scientific Committee on Antarctic Research (SCAR) Annual Report 2011/12

1. Background

The Scientific Committee on Antarctic Science (SCAR) is a non-governmental, Interdisciplinary Scientific Body of the International Council of Science (ICSU), and Observer to the Antarctic Treaty and the United Nations Framework Convention on Climate Change.

SCAR's Mission is to be the leading, independent, non-governmental facilitator, coordinator, and advocate of excellence in Antarctic and Southern Ocean science and research. Secondly, SCAR's Mission is to provide independent, sound, scientifically-based advice to the Antarctic Treaty System and other policy makers including the use of science to identify emerging trends and bring these issues to the attention of policy makers.

2. Introduction

SCAR's scientific research adds value to national efforts by enabling national researchers to collaborate on large-scale scientific programmes to accomplish objectives not easily obtainable by any single country. SCAR's members currently include scientific academies of 36 nations and 9 ICSU scientific unions.

SCAR provides independent scientific advice in support of the wise management of the Antarctic environment, in partnership with the Antarctic Treaty Parties and other bodies such as the CEP, CCAMLR and COMNAP.

SCAR's success depends on the quality and timeliness of its scientific outputs. Descriptions of SCAR's research programmes and scientific outputs are available at www.scar.org. This short paper summarises past (since the last annual report) highlights and future meetings we believe will be of interest to Treaty Parties.

SCAR produces an electronic quarterly Newsletter highlighting relevant science and other SCAR related issues (http://www.scar.org/news/newsletters/). Please email info@scar.org if you would like to be added to the mailing list. As well as the web (www.scar.org) SCAR is also available on Facebook, LinkedIn and Twitter.

3. SCAR Highlights (2011/12)

3.1 The next Generation of SCAR Research Programmes

In July 2012 SCAR Delegates will be asked to approve five new Scientific Research Programmes (SRPs). The new SRPs will continue the important scientific foci of SCAR, whilst expanding into newly identified high priority areas for research, including a stronger emphasis on scientific advice to the Treaty. For further details see http://www.scar.org/researchgroups/progplanning/. The proposed new SRPs are:

- **State of the Antarctic Ecosystem (AntECO)**

Biological diversity is the sum of all those organisms that are present in an ecosystem, that dictate how ecosystems function, and that underpin the life-support system of our planet. This programme has been designed to focus on patterns of biodiversity across terrestrial, limnological, glacial and marine environments within the Antarctic, sub-Antarctic and Southern Ocean regions, and to provide the scientific knowledge on biodiversity that can be also used for conservation and management. In essence we propose to explain what biodiversity is there, how it got there, what it does there, and what threatens it. A primary product of this programme would be recommendations for its management and conservation.

- **Antarctic Thresholds - Ecosystem Resilience and Adaptation (AnT-ERA)**

AnT-ERA will examine the current biological processes in Antarctic ecosystems, to define their thresholds and thereby determine resistance and resilience to change. Such processes depend on a cascade of responses from the genomic and physiological through organismic and population to the ecosystem level. The extreme environment and marked difference in community complexity between the polar regions and much of the rest of the planet may mean that consequences of stress for ecosystem function and services, and their resistance and resilience, will differ from elsewhere. Polar ecosystem processes are therefore key to informing wider ecological debate about the nature of stability and change in ecosystems. The main goal of AnT-ERA is to define and facilitate the science required to determine the resistance, resilience and vulnerability to change of Antarctic biological systems. In particular, the science needs to determine the likelihood of cataclysmic shifts or "tipping points" in Antarctic ecosystems.

- **Antarctic Climate Change in the 21st Century (AntClim21)**

The goals of AntClim21 are to deliver improved regional predictions of key elements of the Antarctic atmosphere, ocean and cryosphere for the next 20 to 200 years and to understand the responses of the physical and biological systems to natural and anthropogenic forcing factors. A primary form of data that we see being used by AntClim21 are the global coupled atmosphere-ocean model runs that form the basis of the Fifth Assessment Report (AR5) of the IPCC. Palaeo-reconstructions of selected time periods, recognised as past analogues for future climate predictions, will be used to validate model performances for the Antarctic region.

- **Past Antarctic Ice Sheet Dynamics (PAIS)**

PAIS aims to improve our understanding of ice sheet dynamics during past warm world conditions by:

- targeting the study of vulnerable areas around the continent (both on the West and East Antarctic margin);
- linking ice-proximal records with coastal and offshore records including far field paleoceanographic and sea level records;
- integrating data into the latest generation of coupled Glacial Isostatic Adjustment (GIA)-Ice Sheet-Climate models.

- **Solid Earth Response and Cryosphere Evolution (SERCE)**

SERCE aims to improve understanding of the solid earth response to cryospheric and tectonic forcing. SERCE will:

- Identify and develop key disciplinary and interdisciplinary science components of a science programme aimed at advancing understanding of the interactions between the solid earth and the cryosphere;
- Communicate and coordinate with other international groups investigating ice mass change, ice sheet contributions to global sea level rise, glacial isostatic adjustment models of Greenland and other ice caps etc.;
- Work with SCAR action/expert groups and research programmes to promote interdisciplinary science using POLENET data;
- Provide an international framework for maintaining, and potentially augmenting, the remote autonomous POLENET infrastructure after the International Polar Year (IPY).

3.2   The Southern Ocean Observing System (SOOS)

The Southern Ocean plays a key role in the climate and ecosystem functioning of the whole planet, but understanding has long been hampered by lack of data. The science community, led by SCAR and SCOR (the Scientific Committee on Oceanic Research), has established the Southern Ocean Observing System (SOOS) to address this. An International Project Office, established in Australia and supported by the new Institute for Marine and Antarctic Studies at the University of Tasmania in Hobart was established in August 2011. This is a crucial step in implementing the SOOS. For further details, including a pdf of the initial Science and Implementation plan, see: www.soos.aq or see the accompanying paper.

3.3 The Ice Sheet Mass Balance and Sea Level (ISMASS) group

The Ice Sheet Mass Balance and Sea Level group, which is co-sponsored by the International Arctic Science Committee, will be holding a workshop in conjunction with the Climate and Cryosphere project of the World Climate Research Programme and other organisations on July the 14th. The workshop has many aims (See http://www.climate-cryosphere.org/en/events/2012/ISMASS/Home.html) but with the overreaching goal to assess the current knowledge of the contribution of the Antarctic and Greenland Ice Sheets to global and regional sea-level rise, taking into account ongoing and proposed projects.

3.4 Antarctic Conservation in the 21st Century

SCAR, in association with several partners, held a meeting and horizon scanning activity in South Africa to start the process of producing a new strategy for Antarctic Conservation in the 21st Century. For further details see the accompanying paper.

3.5 Medals and Awards

- Dr. José Xavier, from the Institute of Marine Research of the University of Coimbra in Portugal has been awarded the prestigious 2011 Martha T. Muse Prize for Science and Policy in Antarctica. Dr Xavier has conducted outstanding research on the predator-prey dynamics that sustain populations of albatrosses, penguins and other top predators in the Southern Ocean. The Selection Committee of leading Antarctic scientists and policy makers also cited his leadership in the establishment of a new and thriving Antarctic research programme in Portugal during the International Polar Year (IPY, 2007-2008).

- Professor Diana H Wall will be awarded the 2012 SCAR President's Medal for Excellence in Antarctic Research. Professor Wall has conducted more than twenty years of research in the Antarctic Dry Valleys examining the response of soil biodiversity and ecosystem processes to environmental change. She is an active member of the SCAR Standing Scientific Group on Life Sciences and has been involved in the development of SCAR's next generation of Scientific Research Programmes and the 21st Century Conservation initiative.

3.6 New SCAR Project Officer

Dr Eoghan Griffin was hired for a period one year, 1 day a week to work on the Climate Communications. The funds to hire Dr Griffin were kindly supplied by the UK, Norway and ASOC. See accompanying paper.

4. SCAR: Future Meetings

SCAR is involved in several major meetings over the next year (http://www.scar.org/events/), including:

- IPY Montreal. April 2012. SCAR is actively involved in the 3rd and final International Polar Year Conference, with the theme "From Knowledge to Action"

- SCAR Open Science Conference, Business and Delegates' Meetings. July 2012. (see http://scar2012.geol.pdx.edu/). Almost a 1000 abstracts were submitted to the SCAR Open Science Conference, which has as its theme "Antarctic Science and Policy Advice in a

Changing World". Several Treaty Observers and Experts are actively involved in the various symposia and sessions, which promises to help make it an exciting meeting.

- SCAR Biology Symposium. SCAR will hold its four yearly biology symposium in Barcelona, Spain, in summer 2013.

For further details on SCAR activities see www.scar.org or email info@scar.org.

The Annual Report for 2011 of the Council of Managers of National Antarctic Programs (COMNAP)

COMNAP is the organisation of National Antarctic Programs which brings together, in particular, the Managers of those Programs, that is, the national officials responsible for planning, conducting and managing support to science in Antarctica on behalf of their respective governments, all Consultative Parties to the Antarctic Treaty.

COMNAP has grown into an international association whose Members are the 28 National Antarctic Programs from Antarctic Treaty Consultative Parties from Argentina, Australia, Belgium, Brazil, Bulgaria, Chile, China, Ecuador, Finland, France, Germany, India, Italy, Japan, Republic of Korea, Netherlands, New Zealand, Norway, Peru, Poland, Russian Federation, South Africa, Spain, Sweden, United Kingdom, Ukraine, Uruguay and USA.

COMNAP's Constitution asserts its purpose: to develop and promote best practice in managing the support of scientific research in the Antarctic. As an organisation, COMNAP acts to add value to National Antarctic Program's efforts by serving as a forum to develop practices that improve effectiveness of activities in an environmentally responsible manner, by facilitating and promoting international partnerships, and by providing opportunities and systems for information exchange.

COMNAP also strives to provide the Antarctic Treaty System with objective, practical, technical and non-political advice drawn from the National Antarctic Programs' extensive pool of expertise and their first-hand knowledge of the Antarctic.

Increasingly complex science questions are being poised which can only be answered by multi-disciplinary and often multi-national science teams. This complexity, along with more demanding environmental measures and, in some cases, a reduced funding stream, contributes to added pressure on National Antarctic Programs and to an even greater need for international collaboration. COMNAP works in support of greater collaboration between National Antarctic Programs and recognises the need for robust partnerships with organisations with similar goals. COMNAP has also progressively assumed responsibility for the production of a number of practical tools related to safety and information exchange.

At the COMNAP Annual General Meeting in August 2011 in Stockholm, Sweden, Dr. Jose Retamales (INACH) completed his four year term as COMNAP Chair and Dr. Heinrich Miller (AWI) was elected as Chair for a three year term of office.

COMNAP Highlights and Achievements for 2011

New COMNAP Website Launched

Information sharing and provision of guidelines and practical advice is core business for COMNAP. Therefore we updated and launched a new website in February 2012 as a tool to do so. The website has both public and members-only areas and is structured to allow for ease of access to information. The website address remains the same at www.comnap.aq. The new website makes publically available many documents of interest to the Antarctic community such as the proceedings from each of the COMNAP/SCALOP Symposiums, the COMNAP Antarctic facilities list and will soon provide information on each COMNAP Member National Antarctic Program from the "Our Members" page.

Management Implications of a Changing Antarctica Workshop

Considering the discussion that took place at ATCM XXXIII and CEP XIII and the discussions and recommendations of the ATME on climate change and implications for Antarctic management and governance (Svolvær, Norway, 7-9 April 2010), COMNAP convened The Management Implications of a Changing Antarctica Workshop, which was open to COMNAP members and invited participants, on Sunday 31 July 2011 on the margins of the COMNAP AGM in Stockholm, Sweden. The topic is one that the Managers of National Antarctic Programs think about every day, since National Antarctic Program's must monitor and respond to change in order to successfully support their science in Antarctica. Key points from the workshop discussions are contained in a COMNAP Information Paper to this ATCM.

Inland Traversing in Antarctica Workshop

COMNAP Executive Committee Vice Chairs, Kazuyuki Shiraishi (NIPR) and Yuansheng Li (PRIC) convened the COMNAP Inland Traverses in Antarctica Workshop on Sunday, 31 July 2011, on the margins of the COMNAP AGM in Stockholm, Sweden. The workshop provided an opportunity to share experiences with members and to learn practical techniques to ensure traverses are safe and successful. Ten presentations were made and a range of posters were exhibited. Representatives from operations and logistics industry were also in attendance.

COMNAP Antarctic Research Fellowship

Noting that education and capacity-building was an area of mutual interest to both SCAR and COMNAP, and in recognition of the depth and breadth of talent within National Antarctic Programs, COMNAP announced the inaugural COMNAP Antarctic Research Fellowship in May 2011. The award went to Ms Amelia Marks of the UK to undertake research with the Italian Antarctic Program at Mario Zucchelli Station. The 2012 COMNAP Antarctic Research Fellow will be announced in July 2012 as part of the COMNAP AGM in Portland.

COMNAP Participation in ICGs 2011-2012

COMNAP was pleased to participate in the ATCM ICG convened by the AT Secretariat on the Review of Recommendations of an Operational Nature. We also were pleased to make suggestions as part of the informal discussions facilitated by SCAR on the SCAR paper on measures to reduce the risk of introduction of non-native species.

COMNAP Products and Tools

Accident, Incident and Near-Miss Reporting (AINMR)

Information on problems encountered in Antarctica has always been exchanged. The very first ATCM agreed in Recommendation I-VII Exchange *of Information on Logistics Problems* that this should be so (effective 30 April 1962). COMNAP Annual General Meetings offer an opportunity for Members to exchange such information and also an on-line, comprehensive AINMR System was launched this year with resources from the Australian Antarctic Division (AAD). This on-line system allows COMNAP members to report accidents and incidents in a timely manner. The AINMR's primary objective is: to capture outline information about events that had, or could have had, serious consequences; and/or reveal lessons to be learned; and/or are novel, very unusual events. So that National Antarctic Programs can learn from each other to reduce the risk of serious consequences occurring in the course of their activities. With the launch of the new COMNAP website, the on-line system will be transferred from AAD to that new website which will be available at www.comnap.aq/membersonly/AINMR/SitePages/Home.aspx.

COMNAP Ship Position Reporting System (SPRS)

The SPRS (www.comnap.aq/sprs) is an optional, voluntary system for exchange of information about National Antarctic Program ship operations. Its primary purpose is to facilitate collaboration between National Antarctic Programs. It can also, however, make a very useful contribution to safety with all SPRS information made available to the Rescue Coordination Centres (RCCs) which cover the Antarctic region, as an additional source of information complementing all other national and international systems in place.

The Antarctic Flight Information Manual (AFIM)

AFIM is a handbook of aeronautical information published by COMNAP as a tool towards safe air operations in Antarctica as recommended by the ATCM Recommendation XV-20 *Air safety in Antarctica*. An in-depth review of the AFIM has resulted in a wish to deliver the AFIM in electronic format. The AFIM will continue to be updated via information from National Antarctic Programs and revisions will be regularly prepared and distributed. COMNAP signalled its plan to reformat AFIM via the ICG discussions on Review of Recommendations of an Operational Nature.

Antarctic Telecommunications Operators Manual (ATOM)

ATOM is an evolution of the handbook of telecommunications practices to which ATCM Recommendation X-3 *Improvement of Telecommunications in Antarctica and the Collection and Distribution of Antarctic Meteorological Data* refers. COMNAP members and Search and Rescue authorities have access to the latest version (Feb 2012) via the COMNAP website.

———

For more information, please visit COMNAP's web site at www.comnap.aq or email us at info@comnap.aq. Also, see attachments to this Annual Report: Appendix 1 and Appendix 2

Appendix 1. COMNAP officers, projects and expert groups

Executive Committee (EXCOM)

The COMNAP Chair and Vice-Chairs are elected officers of COMNAP. The elected officers plus the Executive Secretary, compose the COMNAP Executive Committee as follows:

Position	Officer	Term expires
Chair	Heinrich Miller (AWI) heinrich.miller@awi.de	AGM 2014
Vice-Chairs	Maaike Vancauwenberghe (BELSPO) maaike.vancauwenberghe@belspo.be	AGM 2012
	Yuansheng Li (PRIC) lysh@pric.gov.cn	AGM 2013
	Mariano Memolli (DNA) drmemolli@gmail.com	AGM 2013
	Juan Jose Dañobeitia (CSIC) jjdanobeitia@cmima.csic.es	AGM 2014
	Brian Stone (USAP/NSF) bstone@nsf.gov	AGM 2014
Executive Secretary	Michelle Rogan-Finnemore michelle.finnemore@comnap.aq	30 Sept 2015

Table 1 – COMNAP Executive Committee.

Projects

Project	Project Manager	EXCOM officer (oversight)
Antarctic Glossary	Valerie Lukin	Mariano Memolli
Antarctic Flight Information Manual (AFIM) – Implementation of new format		Brian Stone
Accident, Incident & Near-miss Reporting (AINMR) System & on-line implementation	Robert Culshaw	Maaike Vancauwenberghe
Risk to Antarctic Operations from Volcanic Ash	Robert Culshaw	Maaike Vancauwenberghe
Antarctic Peninsula Advanced Science Information (APASI)	Jose Retamales	Heinz Miller
COMNAP 25th Anniversary Book	Christo Pimpirev	EXCOM All
Energy Management Guidelines and their application – Survey; Database of preferred suppliers	David Blake	Yuansheng Li & Juan Jose Dañobeitia
Oil Spill Contingency Planning & Response - Survey	Veronica Vlasich	Mariano Memolli

Table 2 – COMNAP Projects currently in progress.

Expert Groups

Expert Group (topic)	Expert Group leader	EXCOM officer (oversight)
Science	Jose Retamales	Heinz Miller
Outreach	Eva Gronlund	Maaike Vancauwenberghe
Air	Giuseppe De Rossi	Brian Stone
Environment	Sandra Potter	Maaike Vancauwenberghe
Training	Veronica Vlasich	Mariano Memolli
Medical	Jeff Ayton	Mariano Memolli
Shipping	Miki Ojeda	Juan Jose Dañobeitia
Safety	Robert Culshaw	Maaike Vancauwenberghe
Energy & Technology	David Blake	Yuansheng Li & Juan Jose

		Dañobeitia
Data Management	Michelle Rogan-Finnemore	Heinz Miller
External Relationships	Michelle Rogan-Finnemore	EXCOM All
Strategic Framework	Michelle Rogan-Finnemore	Heinz Miller

Table 3 – COMNAP Expert Groups.

Appendix 2. Meetings

Previous 12 months

31 July 2011, COMNAP Workshop "Management Implications of a Changing Antarctica", Stockholm, Sweden.

31 July 2011, COMNAP Workshop "Inland Traversing in Antarctica", Stockholm, Sweden.

1 – 3 August, 2011, COMNAP Annual General Meeting (COMNAP XXIII), Stockholm, Sweden, hosted by the Swedish Polar Research Secretariat.

17 – 18 October, 2011, COMNAP Executive Committee (EXCOM) Meeting, Barcelona, Spain, hosted by COMNAP Vice Chair, Juan Jose Dañobeitia at the Centro Mediterráneo de Investigaciones Marinas y Ambientales (CMIMA, CSIC).

Upcoming 12 months

14 July 2012, COMNAP/SCAR Joint Executive Meeting, Portland, Oregon, USA.

15 July, 2012, COMNAP Symposium "Sustainable Solutions to Antarctic Challenges: Supporting Polar Research in the 21st Century".

16 - 19 July, 2012, COMNAP Annual General Meeting (COMNAP XXIV), Portland, Oregon, USA.

Report Submitted to Antarctic Treaty Consultative Meeting XXXV by the Depositary Government for the Convention for the Conservation of Antarctic Seals in Accordance with Recommendation XIII-2, Paragraph 2(D)

Submitted by the United Kingdom

This report covers events regarding the Convention for the Conservation of Antarctic Seals (CCAS) for the reporting year 1 March 2010 to 28 February 2011.

The summary at Annex A lists all capturing and killing of Antarctic seals by Contracting Parties to CCAS during the reporting period. A report of events in the 2011 – 2012 year will be submitted to ATCM XXXVI, once the June 2012 deadline for exchange of information has passed.

The United Kingdom would like to remind Contracting Parties to CCAS that the reporting period for the Exchange of Information is from 1 March to the end of February each year. The reporting period was changed to the above dates during the September 1988 Meeting to Review the Operation of the Convention. This is documented in Paragraph 19(a) of the Report of that Meeting.

The Exchange of Information, referred to in Paragraph 6(a) in the Annex to the Convention, should be submitted to other Contracting Parties and to SCAR by **30 June** each year, including nil returns. The UK would like to thank all Contracting Parties to CCAS for providing this information in time to enable the UK to submit a complete report to ATCM XXXV. The UK would, however, continue to encourage all Contracting Parties to CCAS to submit returns by the 30 June deadline to ensure that all relevant information has been provided.

Since ATCM XXXIII, there have been no accessions to CCAS. However, the UK understands that Pakistan wishes to accede to the Convention. In line with the provisions of Article 12, the UK will seek the consent of the Contracting Parties to invite Pakistan to accede. A list of countries which were original signatories to the Convention, and countries which have subsequently acceded is attached to this report (Annex B).

April 2012

ANNEX A

CONVENTION FOR THE CONSERVATION OF ANTARCTIC SEALS (CCAS)

Synopsis of reporting in accordance with Article 5 and the Annex of the Convention: Capturing and killing of seals during the period 1 March 20010 to 28 February 2011.

Contracting Party	Antarctic Seals Captured	Antarctic Seals Killed
Argentina	49 [a]	Nil
Australia	67 [b]	2 [c]
Belgium	Nil	Nil
Brazil	Nil	Nil
Canada	Nil	Nil
Chile	Nil	Nil
France	600 [d]	Nil
Germany	Nil	Nil
Italy	Nil	Nil
Japan	Nil	Nil
Norway	Nil	Nil
Poland	Nil	Nil
Russia	Nil	Nil
South Africa	Nil	Nil
United Kingdom	24 [e]	1 [f]
United States of America	3760 [g]	2 [h]

[a] 10 Elephant Seals, 20 Southern Elephant Seals, 19 Leopard seals
[b] 21 Elephant Seals, 28 Leopard Seals, 20 Weddell Seals
[c] 1 Weddell Seal and 1 Leopard Seal
[d] 160 Weddell Seals, 275 Elephant Seals, 165 Antarctic Fur seals
[e] 24 Weddell Seals
[f] 1 Weddell Seal
[g] 600 Antarctic fur seals 50 Leopard seals, 50 southern elephant seals, 1430 Weddell Seals
[h] 2 Weddell Seals

All reported capturing was for scientific research.

ANNEX B

CONVENTION FOR THE CONSERVATION OF ANTARCTIC SEALS (CCAS)

London, 1 June – 31 December 1972

(The Convention entered into force on 11 March 1978)

State	Date of Signature	Date of deposit (Ratification or Acceptance)
Argentina[1]	9 June 1972	7 March 1978
Australia	5 October 1972	1 July 1987
Belgium	9 June 1972	9 February 1978
Chile[1]	28 December 1972	7 February 1980
France[2]	19 December 1972	19 February 1975
Japan	28 December 1972	28 August 1980
Norway	9 June 1972	10 December 1973
Russia[1,2,4]	9 June 1972	8 February 1978
South Africa	9 June 1972	15 August 1972
United Kingdom[2]	9 June 1972	10 September 1974[3]
United States of America[2]	28 June 1972	19 January 1977

ACCESSIONS

State	Date of deposit of Instrument of Accession
Brazil	11 February 1991
Canada	4 October 1990
Germany, Federal Republic of	30 September 1987
Italy	2 April 1992
Poland	15 August 1980

[1] Declaration or Reservation
[2] Objection
[3] The instrument of ratification included the Channel Islands and the Isle of Man
[4] Former USSR

Report of the Depositary Government for the Convention on the Conservation of Antarctic Marine Living Resources (CCAMLR)

Information Paper submitted by Australia

Abstract

A report is provided by Australia as Depositary of the Convention on the Conservation of Antarctic Marine Living Resources 1980.

Background

Australia, as Depositary of the Convention on the Conservation of Antarctic Marine Living Resources 1980 (Convention) is pleased to report to the Thirty-fifth Antarctic Treaty Consultative Meeting on the status of the Convention.

Australia advises the Antarctic Treaty Parties that, since the Thirty-fourth Antarctic Treaty Consultative Meeting, Pakistan acceded to the Convention on 24 January 2012. The Convention entered into force for Pakistan on 22 February 2012.

A copy of the status list for the Convention is available via the internet on the Australian Treaties Database at the following address:
http://www.austlii.edu.au/au/other/dfat/treaty_list/depository/CCAMLR.html

The status list is also available upon request to the Treaties Secretariat of the Australian Government Department of Foreign Affairs and Trade. Requests can be conveyed through Australian diplomatic missions.

Report of the Depositary Government for the Agreement on the Conservation of Albatrosses and Petrels (ACAP)

Information Paper submitted by Australia

Abstract

A report is provided by Australia as Depositary of the Agreement on the Conservation of Albatrosses and Petrels 2001.

Background

Australia, as Depositary of the Agreement on the Conservation of Albatrosses and Petrels 2001 (Agreement) is pleased to report to the Thirty-fifth Antarctic Treaty Consultative Meeting on the status of the Agreement.

Australia advises the Antarctic Treaty Parties that, since the Thirty-fourth Antarctic Treaty Consultative Meeting, no States have acceded to the Agreement.

A copy of the status list for the Agreement is available via the internet on the Australian Treaties Database at the following address:

http://www.austlii.edu.au/au/other/dfat/treaty_list/depository/consalbnpet.html

The status list is also available upon request to the Treaties Secretariat of the Australian Government Department of Foreign Affairs and Trade. Requests can be conveyed through Australian diplomatic missions.

Report of the Depositary Government of the Antarctic Treaty and its Protocol in accordance with Recommendation XIII-2

Information Paper submitted by the United States

This report covers events with respect to the Antarctic Treaty and the Protocol on Environmental Protection.

In the past year, there have been two accessions to the Antarctic Treaty. Malaysia acceded to the Antarctic Treaty on October 31, 2011, and Pakistan acceded to the Treaty on March 1, 2012.

There was one accession to the Protocol on Environmental Protection to the Antarctic Treaty. Pakistan acceded on March 1, 2012, and the Protocol entered into force for Pakistan on March 31, 2012. There are fifty (50) Parties to the Treaty and thirty-five (35) Parties to the Protocol.

The following countries have provided notification that they have designated the persons so noted as Arbitrators in accordance with Article 2(1) of the Schedule to the Protocol on Environmental Protection:

Bulgaria	Mrs. Guenka Beleva	30 July 2004
Chile	Amb. María Teresa Infante	June 2005
	Amb. Jorge Berguño	June 2005
	Dr. Francisco Orrego	June 2005
Finland	Amb. Holger Bertil Rotkirch	14 June 2006
India	Prof. Upendra Baxi	6 October 2004
	Mr. Ajai Saxena	6 October 2004
	Dr. N. Khare	6 October 2004
Japan	Judge Shunji Yanai	18 July 2008
Rep. of Korea	Prof. Park Ki Gab	21 October 2008
United States	Prof. Daniel Bodansky	1 May 2008
	Mr. David Colson	1 May 2008

Lists of Parties to the Treaty, to the Protocol, and of Recommendations/Measures and their approvals are attached.

Date of most recent action: March 1, 2012

The Antarctic Treaty

Done: Washington; December 1, 1959

Entry into force: June 23, 1961
In accordance with Article XIII, the Treaty was subject to ratification by the signatory States and is open for accession by any State which is a Member of the United Nations, or by any other State which may be invited to accede to the Treaty with the consent of all the Contracting Parties whose representatives are entitled to participate in the meetings provided for under Article IX of the Treaty; instruments of ratification and instruments of accession shall be deposited with the Government of the United States of America. Upon the deposit of instruments of ratification by all the signatory States, the Treaty entered into force for those States and for States which had deposited instruments of accession to the Treaty. Thereafter, the Treaty enters into force for any acceding State upon deposit of its instrument of accession.

Legend: (no mark) = ratification; a = accession; d = succession; w = withdrawal or equivalent action

Participant	Signature	Consent to be bound		Other Action	Notes
Argentina	December 1, 1959	June 23, 1961			
Australia	December 1, 1959	June 23, 1961			
Austria		August 25, 1987	a		
Belarus		December 27, 2006	a		
Belgium	December 1, 1959	July 26, 1960			
Brazil		May 16, 1975	a		
Bulgaria		September 11, 1978	a		
Canada		May 4, 1988	a		
Chile	December 1, 1959	June 23, 1961			
China		June 8, 1983	a		
Colombia		January 31, 1989	a		
Cuba		August 16, 1984	a		
Czech Republic		January 1, 1993	d		i
Denmark		May 20, 1965	a		
Ecuador		September 15, 1987	a		
Estonia		May 17, 2001	a		
Finland		May 15, 1984	a		
France	December 1, 1959	September 16, 1960			
Germany		February 5, 1979	a		ii
Greece		January 8, 1987	a		
Guatemala		July 31, 1991	a		
Hungary		January 27, 1984	a		
India		August 19, 1983	a		
Italy		March 18, 1981	a		
Japan	December 1, 1959	August 4, 1960			

Korea (DPRK)		January 21, 1987	a		
Korea (ROK)		November 28, 1986	a		
Malaysia		October 31, 2011	a		
Monaco		May 31, 2008	a		
Netherlands		March 30, 1967	a		iii
New Zealand	December 1, 1959	November 1, 1960			
Norway	December 1, 1959	August 24, 1960			
Pakistan		March 1, 2012	a		
Papua New Guinea		March 16, 1981	d		iv
Peru		April 10, 1981	a		
Poland		June 8, 1961	a		
Portugal		January 29, 2010	a		
Romania		September 15, 1971	a		v
Russian Federation	December 1, 1959	November 2, 1960			vi
Slovak Republic		January 1, 1993	d		vii
South Africa	December 1, 1959	June 21, 1960			
Spain		March 31, 1982	a		
Sweden		April 24, 1984	a		
Switzerland		November 15, 1990	a		
Turkey		January 24, 1996	a		
Ukraine		October 28, 1992	a		
United Kingdom	December 1, 1959	May 31, 1960			
United States	December 1, 1959	August 18, 1960			
Uruguay		January 11, 1980	a		viii
Venezuela		March 24, 1999	a		

---

[i] Effective date of succession by the Czech Republic. Czechoslovakia deposited an instrument of accession to the Treaty on June 14, 1962. On December 31, 1992, at midnight, Czechoslovakia ceased to exist and was succeeded by two separate and independent states, the Czech Republic and the Slovak Republic.

[ii] The Embassy of the Federal Republic of Germany in Washington transmitted to the Department of State a diplomatic note, dated October 2, 1990, which reads as follows:

"The Embassy of the Federal Republic of Germany presents its compliments to the Department of State and has the honor to inform the Government of the United States of America as the depositary Government of the Antarctic Treaty that, t[h]rough the accession of the German Democratic Republic to the Federal Republic of Germany with effect from October 3, 1990, the two German states will unite to form one sovereign state which, as a contracting party to the Antarctic Treaty, will remain bound by the provisions of the Treaty and subject to those recommendations adopted at the 15 consultative meetings which the Federal Republic of Germany has approved. From the date of German unity, the Federal Republic of Germany will act under the designation of "Germany" within the framework of the [A]ntarctic system.
"The Embassy would be grateful if the Government of the United States of America could inform all contracting parties to the Antarctic Treaty of the contents of this note.
"The Embassy of the Federal Republic of Germany avails itself of this opportunity to renew to the Department of State the assurances of its highest consideration."

Prior to unification, the German Democratic Republic deposited an instrument of accession to the Treaty, accompanied by a declaration, on November 19, 1974, and the Federal Republic of Germany deposited an instrument of accession to the Treaty, accompanied by a statement, on February 5, 1979.

[iii] The instrument of accession to the Treaty by the Netherlands states that the accession is for the Kingdom in Europe, Suriname and the Netherlands Antilles; as of January 1, 1986, Aruba as a separate entity.

[iv] Date of deposit of notification of succession by Papua New Guinea; effective September 16, 1975, the date of its independence.

[v] The instrument of accession to the Treaty by Romania was accompanied by a note of the Ambassador of the Socialist Republic of Romania to the United States of America, dated September 15, 1971, which reads as follows:
"Dear Mr. Secretary:
"Submitting the instrument of adhesion of the Socialist Republic of Romania to the Antarctic Treaty, signed at Washington on December 1, 1959, I have the honor to inform you of the following:
'The Council of State of the Socialist Republic of Romania states that the provisions of the first paragraph of the article XIII of the Antarctic Treaty are not in accordance with the principle according to which the multilateral treaties whose object and purposes are concerning the international community, as a whole, should be opened for universal participation.'
"I am kindly requesting you, Mr. Secretary, to forward to all parties concerned the text of the Romanian instrument of adhesion to the Antarctic Treaty, as well as the text of this letter containing the above mentioned statement of the Romanian Government.
"I avail myself of this opportunity to renew to you, Mr. Secretary, the assurances of my highest consideration."

Copies of the Ambassador's letter and the Romanian instrument of accession to the Treaty were transmitted to the Antarctic Treaty parties by the Secretary of State's circular note dated October 1, 1971.

[vi] The Treaty was signed and ratified by the former Union of Soviet Socialist Republics. By a note dated January 13, 1992, the Russian Federation informed the United States Government that it "continues to perform the rights and fulfil the obligations following from the international agreements signed by the Union of Soviet Socialist Republics."

[vii] Effective date of succession by the Slovak Republic. Czechoslovakia deposited an instrument of accession to the Treaty on June 14, 1962. On December 31, 1992, at midnight, Czechoslovakia ceased to exist and was succeeded by two separate and independent states, the Czech Republic and the Slovak Republic.

[viii] The instrument of accession to the Treaty by Uruguay was accompanied by a declaration, a Department of State English translation of which reads as follows:
"The Government of the Oriental Republic of Uruguay considers that, through its accession to the Antarctic Treaty signed at Washington (United States of America) on December 1, 1959, it helps to affirm the principles of using Antarctica exclusively for peaceful purposes, of prohibiting any nuclear explosion or radioactive waste disposal in this area, of freedom of scientific research in Antarctica in the service of mankind, and of international cooperation to achieve these objectives, which are established in said Treaty.
"Within the context of these principles Uruguay proposes, through a procedure based on the principle of legal equality, the establishment of a general and definitive statute on Antarctica in which, respecting the rights of States as recognized in international law, the interests of all States involved and of the international community as a whole would be considered equitably.
"The decision of the Uruguayan Government to accede to the Antarctic Treaty is based not only on the interest which, like all members of the international community, Uruguay has in Antarctica, but also on a special, direct, and substantial interest which arises from its geographic location, from the fact that its Atlantic coastline faces the continent of Antarctica, from the resultant influence upon its climate, ecology, and marine biology, from the historic bonds which date back to the first expeditions which ventured to explore that continent and its waters, and also from the obligations assumed in conformity with the Inter-

American Treaty of Reciprocal Assistance which includes a portion of Antarctic territory in the zone described in Article 4, by virtue of which Uruguay shares the responsibility of defending the region. "In communicating its decision to accede to the Antarctic Treaty, the Government of the Oriental Republic of Uruguay declares that it reserves its rights in Antarctica in accordance with international law."

PROTOCOL ON ENVIRONMENTAL PROTECTION TO THE ANTARCTIC TREATY

Signed at Madrid on October 4, 1991*

State	Date of Signature	Date deposit of Ratification, Acceptance (A) or Approval (AA)	Date deposit of Accession	Date of entry into force	Date Acceptance ANNEX V**	Date of entry into force of Annex V
CONSULTATIVE PARTIES						
Argentina	Oct. 4, 1991	Oct. 28, 1993 ³		Jan. 14, 1998	Sept. 8, 2000 (A) / Aug. 4, 1995 (B)	May 24, 2002
Australia	Oct. 4, 1991	Apr. 6, 1994		Jan. 14, 1998	Apr. 6, 1994 (A) / June 7, 1995 (B)	May 24, 2002
Belgium	Oct. 4, 1991	Apr. 26, 1996		Jan. 14, 1998	Apr. 26, 1996 (A) / Oct. 23, 2000 (B)	May 24, 2002
Brazil	Oct. 4, 1991	Aug. 15, 1995		Jan. 14, 1998	May 20, 1998 (B)	May 24, 2002
Bulgaria			April 21, 1998	May 21, 1998	May 5, 1999 (AB)	May 24, 2002
Chile	Oct. 4, 1991	Jan. 11, 1995		Jan. 14, 1998	Mar. 25, 1998 (B)	May 24, 2002
China	Oct. 4, 1991	Aug. 2, 1994		Jan. 14, 1998	Jan. 26, 1995 (AB)	May 24, 2002
Ecuador	Oct. 4, 1991	Jan. 4, 1993		Jan. 14, 1998	May 11, 2001 (A) / Nov. 15, 2001 (B)	May 24, 2002
Finland	Oct. 4, 1991	Nov. 1, 1996 (A)		Jan. 14, 1998	Nov. 1, 1996 (A) / Apr. 2, 1997 (B)	May 24, 2002
France	Oct. 4, 1991	Feb. 5, 1993 (AA)		Jan. 14, 1998	Apr. 26, 1995 (B) / Nov. 18, 1998 (A)	May 24, 2002
Germany	Oct. 4, 1991	Nov. 25, 1994		Jan. 14, 1998	Nov. 25, 1994 (A) / Sept. 1, 1998 (B)	May 24, 2002
India	July 2, 1992	Apr. 26, 1996		Jan. 14, 1998	May 24, 2002 (B)	May 24, 2002
Italy	Oct. 4, 1991	Mar. 31, 1995		Jan. 14, 1998	May 31, 1995 (A) / Feb. 11, 1998 (B)	May 24, 2002
Japan	Sept. 29, 1992	Dec. 15, 1997 (A)		Jan. 14, 1998	Dec. 15, 1997 (AB)	May 24, 2002
Korea, Rep. of	July 2, 1992	Jan. 2, 1996		Jan. 14, 1998	June 5, 1996 (B)	May 24, 2002
Netherlands	Oct. 4, 1991	Apr. 14, 1994 (A) ⁶		Jan. 14, 1998	Mar. 18, 1998 (B)	May 24, 2002
New Zealand	Oct. 4, 1991	Dec. 22, 1994		Jan. 14, 1998	Oct. 21, 1992 (B)	May 24, 2002
Norway	Oct. 4, 1991	June 16, 1993		Jan. 14, 1998	Oct. 13, 1993 (B)	May 24, 2002
Peru	Oct. 4, 1991	Mar. 8, 1993		Jan. 14, 1998	Mar. 8, 1993 (A) / Mar. 17, 1999 (B)	May 24, 2002
Poland	Oct. 4, 1991	Nov. 1, 1995		Jan. 14, 1998	Sept. 20, 1995 (B)	May 24, 2002
Russian Federation	Oct. 4, 1991	Aug. 6, 1997		Jan. 14, 1998	June 19, 2001 (B)	May 24, 2002
South Africa	Oct. 4, 1991	Aug. 3, 1995		Jan. 14, 1998	June 14, 1995 (B)	May 24, 2002
Spain	Oct. 4, 1991	July 1, 1992		Jan. 14, 1998	Dec. 8, 1993 (A) / Feb. 18, 2000 (B)	May 24, 2002
Sweden	Oct. 4, 1991	Mar. 30, 1994		Jan. 14, 1998	Mar. 30, 1994 (A) / Apr. 7, 1994 (B)	May 24, 2002

Ukraine			May 25, 2001	June 24, 2001	May 25, 2001 (A)	May 24, 2002
United Kingdom	Oct. 4, 1991	Apr. 25, 1995 [5]		Jan. 14, 1998	May 21, 1996 (B)	May 24, 2002
United States	Oct. 4, 1991	Apr. 17, 1997		Jan. 14, 1998	Apr. 17, 1997 (A) May 6, 1998 (B)	May 24, 2002
Uruguay	Oct. 4, 1991	Jan. 11, 1995		Jan. 14, 1998	May 15, 1995 (B)	May 24, 2002

** The following denotes date relating either
to acceptance of Annex V or approval of Recommendation XVI-10
(A) Acceptance of Annex V   (B) Approval of Recommendation XVI-10

1. Reports by Depositaries and Observers

State	Date of Signature	Ratification Acceptance or Approval	Date deposit of Accession	Date of entry into force	Date Acceptance ANNEX V**	Date of entry into force of Annex V
NON-CONSULTATIVE PARTIES						
Austria	Oct. 4, 1991					
Belarus			July 16, 2008	Aug. 15, 2008		
Canada	Oct. 4, 1991	Nov. 13, 2003		Dec. 13, 2003		
Colombia	Oct. 4, 1991					
Cuba						
Czech Rep.[1,2]	Jan. 1, 1993	Aug. 25, 2004 [4]		Sept. 24, 2004		
Denmark	July 2, 1992					
Estonia						
Greece	Oct. 4, 1991	May 23, 1995		Jan. 14, 1998		
Guatemala						
Hungary	Oct. 4, 1991					
Korea, DPR of	Oct. 4, 1991					
Malaysia						
Monaco			July 1, 2009	July 31, 2009		
Pakistan			Mar. 1, 2012	Mar. 31, 2012		
Papua New Guinea						
Portugal						
Romania	Oct. 4, 1991	Feb. 3, 2003		Mar. 5, 2003	Feb. 3, 2003	Mar. 5, 2003
Slovak Rep.[1,2]	Jan. 1, 1993					
Switzerland	Oct. 4, 1991					
Turkey						
Venezuela						

* Signed at Madrid on October 4, 1991; thereafter at Washington until October 3, 1992.
The Protocol will enter into force initially on the thirtieth day following the date of deposit of instruments of ratification, acceptance, approval or accession by all States which were Antarctic Treaty Consultative Parties at the date on which this Protocol was adopted. (Article 23)

** Adopted at Bonn on October 17, 1991 at XVIth Antarctic Consultative Meeting.

1. Signed for Czech & Slovak Federal Republic on Oct. 2, 1992 - Czechoslovakia accepts the jurisdiction of the International Court of Justice and Arbitral Tribunal for the settlement of disputes according to Article 19, paragraph 1. On December 31, 1992, at midnight, Czechoslovakia ceased to exist and was succeeded by two separate and independent states, the Czech Republic and the Slovak Republic.
2. Effective date of succession in respect of signature by Czechoslovakia which is subject to ratification by the Czech Republic and the Slovak Republic.

3. Accompanied by declaration, with informal translation provided by the Embassy of Argentina, which reads as follows: "The Argentine Republic declares that in as much as the Protocol to the Antarctic Treaty on the Protection of the Environment is a Complementary Agreement of the Antarctic Treaty and that its Article 4 fully respects what has been stated in Article IV, Subsection 1, Paragraph A) of said Treaty, none of its stipulations should be interpreted or be applied as affecting its rights, based on legal titles, acts of possession, contiguity and geological continuity in the region South of parallel 60, in which it has proclaimed and maintained its sovereignty."

4. Accompanied by declaration, with informal translation provided by the Embassy of the Czech Republic, which reads as follows: "The Czech Republic accepts the jurisdiction of the International Court of Justice and of the Arbitral Tribunal under Article 19, paragraph 1, of the Protocol on Environmental Protection to the Antarctic Treaty, done at Madrid on October 4, 1991."

5. Ratification on behalf of the United Kingdom of Great Britain and Northern Ireland, the Bailiwick of Jersey, the Bailiwick of Guernsey, the Isle of Man, Anguilla, Bermuda, the British Antarctic Territory, Cayman Islands, Falkland Islands, Montserrat, St. Helena and Dependencies, South Georgia and the South Sandwich Islands, Turks and Caicos Islands and British Virgin Islands.

6. Acceptance is for the Kingdom in Europe. At the time of its acceptance, the Kingdom of the Netherlands stated that it chooses both means for the settlement of disputes mentioned in Article 19, paragraph 1 of the Protocol, i.e. the International Court of Justice and the Arbitral Tribunal. A declaration by the Kingdom of the Netherlands accepting the Protocol for the Netherlands Antilles was deposited on October 27, 2004 with a statement confirming that it chooses both means for the settlement of disputes mentioned in Article 19, paragraph 1 of the Protocol.

Department of State, Washington, April 10, 2012.

Approval, as notified to the Government of the United States of America, of measures relating to the furtherance of the principles and objectives of the Antarctic Treaty

	16 Recommendations adopted at First Meeting (Canberra 1961) Approved	10 Recommendations adopted at Second Meeting (Buenos Aires 1962) Approved	11 Recommendations adopted at Third Meeting (Brussels 1964) Approved	28 Recommendations adopted at Fourth Meeting (Santiago 1966) Approved	9 Recommendations adopted at Fifth Meeting (Paris 1968) Approved	15 Recommendations adopted at Sixth Meeting (Tokyo 1970) Approved
Argentina	ALL	ALL	ALL	ALL	ALL	ALL
Australia	ALL	ALL	ALL	ALL	ALL	ALL
Belgium	ALL	ALL	ALL	ALL	ALL	ALL
Brazil (1983)+	ALL	ALL	ALL	ALL	ALL	ALL (except 10)
Bulgaria (1998)+						
Chile	ALL	ALL	ALL	ALL	ALL	ALL
China (1985)+	ALL	ALL	ALL	ALL	ALL	ALL (except 10)
Ecuador (1990)+						
Finland (1989)+						
France	ALL	ALL	ALL	ALL	ALL	ALL
Germany (1981)+	ALL	ALL	ALL (except 8)	ALL (except 16-19)	ALL (except 6)	ALL (except 9)
India (1983)+	ALL	ALL	ALL (except 8***)	ALL (except 18)	ALL	ALL (except 9 & 10)
Italy (1987)+	ALL	ALL	ALL	ALL	ALL	ALL
Japan	ALL	ALL	ALL	ALL	ALL	ALL
Korea, Rep. (1989)+						
Netherlands (1990)+	ALL (except 11 & 15)	ALL (except 3, 5, 8 & 10)	ALL (except 3, 4, 6 & 9)	ALL(except 20, 25, 26 & 28)	ALL (except 1, 8 & 9)	ALL (except 15)
New Zealand	ALL	ALL	ALL	ALL	ALL	ALL
Norway	ALL	ALL	ALL	ALL	ALL	ALL
Peru (1989)+	ALL	ALL	ALL	ALL	ALL	ALL
Poland (1977)+	ALL	ALL	ALL	ALL	ALL	ALL
Russia	ALL	ALL	ALL	ALL	ALL	ALL
South Africa	ALL	ALL	ALL	ALL	ALL	ALL
Spain (1988)+	ALL	ALL	ALL	ALL	ALL	ALL
Sweden (1988)+	ALL	ALL	ALL	ALL	ALL	ALL
U.K.	ALL	ALL	ALL	ALL	ALL	ALL
Uruguay (1985)+	ALL	ALL	ALL	ALL	ALL	ALL
U.S.A.	ALL	ALL	ALL	ALL	ALL	ALL

* IV-6, IV-10, IV-12, and V-5 terminated by VIII-2

*** Accepted as interim guideline

+ Year attained Consultative Status. Acceptance by that State required to bring into force Recommendations or Measures of meetings from that year forward.

Approval, as notified to the Government of the United States of America, of measures relating to the furtherance of the principles and objectives of the Antarctic Treaty

	9 Recommendations adopted at Seventh Meeting (Wellington 1972) Approved	14 Recommendations adopted at Eighth Meeting (Oslo 1975) Approved	6 Recommendations adopted at Ninth Meeting (London 1977) Approved	9 Recommendations adopted at Tenth Meeting (Washington 1979) Approved	3 Recommendations adopted at Eleventh Meeting (Buenos Aires 1981) Approved	8 Recommendations adopted at Twelfth Meeting (Canberra 1983) Approved
Argentina	ALL	ALL	ALL	ALL	ALL	ALL
Australia	ALL	ALL	ALL	ALL	ALL	ALL
Belgium	ALL	ALL	ALL	ALL	ALL	ALL
Brazil (1983)+	ALL (except 5)	ALL	ALL	ALL	ALL	ALL
Bulgaria (1998)+						
Chile	ALL	ALL	ALL	ALL	ALL	ALL
China (1985)+	ALL (except 5)	ALL	ALL	ALL	ALL	ALL
Ecuador (1990)+						
Finland (1989)+						
France	ALL	ALL	ALL	ALL	ALL	ALL
Germany (1981)+	ALL (except 5)	ALL (except 2 & 5)	ALL	ALL	ALL	ALL
India (1983)+	ALL	ALL	ALL	ALL (except 1 & 9)	ALL	ALL
Italy (1987)+	ALL (except 5)	ALL	ALL	ALL (except 1 & 9)		
Japan	ALL	ALL	ALL	ALL	ALL	ALL
Korea, Rep. (1989)+	ALL	ALL	ALL	ALL	ALL	ALL
Netherlands (1990)+	ALL	ALL	ALL (except 3)	ALL (except 9)	ALL (except 2)	ALL
New Zealand	ALL	ALL	ALL	ALL	ALL	ALL
Norway	ALL	ALL	ALL	ALL	ALL	ALL
Peru (1989)+	ALL	ALL	ALL	ALL	ALL	ALL
Poland (1977)+	ALL	ALL	ALL	ALL	ALL	ALL
Russia	ALL	ALL	ALL	ALL	ALL	ALL
South Africa	ALL	ALL	ALL	ALL	ALL	ALL
Spain (1988)+	ALL	ALL	ALL	ALL (except 1 & 9)	ALL (except 1)	ALL
Sweden (1988)+						
U.K.	ALL	ALL	ALL	ALL	ALL	ALL
Uruguay (1985)+	ALL	ALL	ALL	ALL	ALL	ALL
U.S.A.	ALL	ALL	ALL	ALL	ALL	ALL

* IV-6, IV-10, IV-12, and V-5 terminated by VIII-2

*** Accepted as interim guideline

+ Year attained Consultative Status. Acceptance by that State required to bring into force Recommendations or Measures of meetings from that year forward.

Approval, as notified to the Government of the United States of America, of measures relating to the furtherance of the principles and objectives of the Antarctic Treaty

	16 Recommendations adopted at Thirteenth Meeting (Brussels 1985) Approved	10 Recommendations adopted at Fourteenth Meeting (Rio de Janeiro 1987) Approved	22 Recommendations adopted at Fifteenth Meeting (Paris 1989) Approved	13 Recommendations adopted at Sixteenth Meeting (Bonn 1991) Approved	4 Recommendations adopted at Seventeenth Meeting (Venice 1992) Approved	1 Recommendation adopted at Eighteenth Meeting (Kyoto 1994) Approved
Argentina	ALL	ALL	ALL	ALL	ALL	ALL
Australia	ALL	ALL	ALL	ALL	ALL	ALL
Belgium	ALL	ALL	ALL	ALL	ALL	ALL
Brazil (1983)+	ALL	ALL	ALL	ALL	ALL	ALL
Bulgaria (1998)+				XVI-10		
Chile	ALL	ALL	ALL	ALL	ALL	ALL
China (1985)+	ALL	ALL	ALL	ALL	ALL	ALL
Ecuador (1990)+				XVI-10		
Finland (1989)+			ALL	ALL	ALL	ALL
France	ALL	ALL	ALL (except 3, 8, 10, 11&22)	ALL	ALL	ALL
Germany (1981)+	ALL	ALL	ALL	ALL	ALL	ALL
India (1983)+	ALL	ALL	ALL	ALL	ALL	ALL
Italy (1987)+	ALL	ALL	ALL	ALL	ALL	ALL
Japan	ALL	ALL	ALL (except 1-11, 16, 18, 19)	ALL (except 1, 3-9, 12&13)	ALL (except 1-2 & 4)	ALL
Korea, Rep. (1989)+			ALL (except 22)	ALL (except 12)	ALL (except 1)	ALL
Netherlands (1990)+				ALL	ALL	ALL
New Zealand	ALL	ALL (except 9)	ALL (except 22)	ALL	ALL	ALL
Norway	ALL	ALL	ALL	ALL	ALL	ALL
Peru (1989)+			ALL (except 22)	ALL (except 13)	ALL	ALL
Poland (1977)+	ALL	ALL	ALL	ALL	ALL	ALL
Russia	ALL	ALL	ALL	ALL	ALL	ALL
South Africa	ALL	ALL	ALL	ALL	ALL	ALL
Spain (1988)+	ALL	ALL	ALL	ALL	ALL	ALL
Sweden (1988)+	ALL	ALL	ALL	ALL	ALL	ALL
U.K.	ALL	ALL (except 2)	ALL (except 3, 4, 8, 10, 11)	ALL (except 4, 6, 8, & 9)	ALL	ALL
Uruguay (1985)+	ALL	ALL	ALL	ALL	ALL	ALL
U.S.A.	ALL	ALL	ALL (except 1-4, 10, 11)	ALL	ALL	ALL

* IV-6, IV-10, IV-12, and V-5 terminated by VIII-2

*** Accepted as interim guideline

+ Year attained Consultative Status. Acceptance by that State required to bring into force Recommendations or Measures of meetings from that year forward.

Approval, as notified to the Government of the United States of America, of measures relating to the furtherance of the principles and objectives of the Antarctic Treaty

	5 Measures adopted at Nineteenth Meeting (Seoul 1995) Approved	2 Measures adopted at Twentieth Meeting (Utrecht 1996) Approved	5 Measures adopted at Twenty-First Meeting (Christchurch 1997) Approved	2 Measures adopted at Twenty-Second Meeting (Tromso 1998) Approved	1 Measure adopted at Twenty-Third Meeting (Lima 1999) Approved
Argentina	ALL	ALL	ALL	ALL	ALL
Australia	ALL	ALL	ALL	ALL	ALL
Belgium	ALL	ALL	ALL	ALL	ALL
Brazil (1983)+	ALL	ALL	ALL	ALL	ALL
Bulgaria (1998)+					
Chile	ALL	ALL	ALL	ALL	ALL
China (1985)+	ALL	ALL	ALL	ALL	ALL
Ecuador (1990)+					
Finland (1989)+	ALL	ALL	ALL	ALL	ALL
France	ALL	ALL	ALL	ALL	ALL
Germany (1981)+	ALL	ALL	ALL	ALL	ALL
India (1983)+	ALL	ALL	ALL	ALL	ALL
Italy (1987)+	ALL	ALL	ALL	ALL	ALL
Japan	ALL (except 2&5)	ALL (except 1)	All (except 1-2 & 5)		
Korea, Rep. (1989)+	ALL	ALL	ALL	ALL	ALL
Netherlands (1990)+	ALL	ALL	ALL	ALL	ALL
New Zealand	ALL	ALL	ALL	ALL	ALL
Norway	ALL	ALL	ALL		
Peru (1989)+	ALL	ALL	ALL	ALL	ALL
Poland (1977)+	ALL	ALL	ALL	ALL	ALL
Russia	ALL	ALL	ALL	ALL	ALL
South Africa	ALL	ALL	ALL	ALL	ALL
Spain (1988)+	ALL	ALL	ALL	ALL	ALL
Sweden (1988)+	ALL	ALL	ALL	ALL	ALL
U.K.	ALL	ALL	ALL	ALL	ALL
Uruguay (1985)+	ALL	ALL	ALL	ALL	ALL
U.S.A.	ALL	ALL	ALL	ALL	ALL

"+Year attained Consultative Status. Acceptance by that state required to bring into force Recommendations or Measures of meetings from that Year forward."

Approval, as notified to the Government of the United States of America, of measures relating to the furtherance of the principles and objectives of the Antarctic Treaty

	2 Measures adopted at Twelfth Special Meeting (The Hague 2000) Approved	3 Measures adopted at Twenty-Fourth Meeting (St. Petersburg 2001) Approved	1 Measure adopted at Twenty-Fifth Meeting (Warsaw 2002) Approved	3 Measures adopted at Twenty-Sixth Meeting (Madrid 2003) Approved	4 Measures adopted at Twenty-Seventh Meeting (Cape Town 2004) Approved
Argentina			*	XXVI-1, XXVI-2 *, XXVI-3 **	XXVII-1 *, XXVII-2 *, XXVII-3 **
Australia	ALL	ALL	ALL	XXVI-1, XXVI-2 *, XXVI-3 **	XXVII-1 *, XXVII-2 *, XXVII-3 **
Belgium	ALL	ALL	ALL	ALL	ALL
Brazil (1983)+	ALL	ALL	ALL	ALL	XXVII-1, XXVII-2, XXVII-3
Bulgaria (1998)+			*	XXVI-1, XXVI-2 *, XXVI-3 **	XXVII-1 *, XXVII-2 *, XXVII-3 **
Chile	ALL	ALL	ALL	ALL	ALL
China (1985)+	ALL	ALL	ALL	ALL	XXVII-1 *, XXVII-2 *, XXVII-3 **
Ecuador (1990)+			*	XXVI-1, XXVI-2 *, XXVI-3 **	XXVII-1 *, XXVII-2 *, XXVII-3 **
Finland (1989)+	ALL	ALL		XXVI-1, XXVI-2 *, XXVI-3 **	XXVII-1 *, XXVII-2 *, XXVII-3 **, XXVII-4
France	ALL (except SATCM XII-2)	ALL	*	XXVI-1, XXVI-2 *, XXVI-3 **	XXVII-1, XXVII-2 *, XXVII-3, XXVII-4
Germany (1981)+	ALL	ALL	ALL	ALL	XXVII-1 *, XXVII-2 *, XXVII-3 **
India (1983)+	ALL	ALL	ALL	ALL	XXVII-1 *, XXVII-2 *, XXVII-3 **
Italy (1987)+	ALL	ALL		XXVI-1, XXVI-2 *, XXVI-3 **	XXVII-1 *, XXVII-2 *, XXVII-3 **
Japan	ALL	ALL	*	ALL	XXVII-1 *, XXVII-2 *, XXVII-3 **, XXVII-4
Korea, Rep. (1989)+	ALL	ALL		XXVI-1, XXVI-2 *, XXVI-3 **	XXVII-1 *, XXVII-2 *, XXVII-3 **
Netherlands (1990)+	ALL	ALL	ALL	XXVI-1, XXVI-2 *, XXVI-3 **	XXVII-1 *, XXVII-2 *, XXVII-3 **, XXVII-4
New Zealand	ALL	ALL	ALL	ALL	ALL
Norway		ALL	*	XXVI-1, XXVI-2 *, XXVI-3 **	XXVII-1 *, XXVII-2 *, XXVII-3 **, XXVII-4
Peru (1989)+	ALL	ALL	ALL	XXVI-1, XXVI-2 *, XXVI-3 **	XXVII-1 *, XXVII-2 *, XXVII-3 **
Poland (1977)+		ALL	ALL	ALL	ALL
Russia	ALL	ALL	ALL	XXVI-1, XXVI-2, XXVI-3 **	XXVII-1 *, XXVII-2 *, XXVII-3 **
South Africa	ALL	ALL	ALL	ALL	ALL
Spain (1988)+		ALL	*	XXVI-1, XXVI-2 *, XXVI-3 **	XXVII-1 *, XXVII-2 *, XXVII-3 **
Sweden (1988)+	ALL			ALL	XXVII-1 *, XXVII-2 *, XXVII-3 **
Ukraine (2004)+			ALL		XXVII-1 *, XXVII-2 *, XXVII-3 **
U.K.	ALL (except SATCM XII-2)	ALL (except XXIV-3)	ALL	ALL	XXVII-1 *, XXVII-2 *, XXVII-3 **, XXVII-4
Uruguay (1985)+	ALL	ALL	*	XXVI-1, XXVI-2 *, XXVI-3	XXVII-1 *, XXVII-2 *, XXVII-3 **, XXVII-4
U.S.A.	ALL	ALL	*	XXVI-1, XXVI-2 *, XXVI-3 **	XXVII-1 *, XXVII-2 *, XXVII-3 **

"+=Year attained Consultative Status. Acceptance by that state required to bring into force Recommendations or Measures of meetings from that Year forward."

* Management Plans annexed to this Measure were deemed to have been approved in accordance with Article 6(1) of Annex V to the Protocol on Environmental Protection to the Antarctic Treaty and the Measure not specifying a different approval method.

** Revised and updated List of Historic Sites and Monuments annexed to this Measure was deemed to have been approved in accordance with Article 8(2) of Annex V to the Protocol on Environmental Protection to the Antarctic Treaty and the Measure not specifying a different approval method.

Approval, as notified to the Government of the United States of America, of measures relating to the furtherance of the principles and objectives of the Antarctic Treaty

	5 Measures adopted at Twenty-Eighth Meeting (Stockholm 2005) Approved	4 Measures adopted at Twenty-Ninth Meeting (Edinburgh 2006) Approved	3 Measures adopted at Thirtieth Meeting (New Delhi 2007) Approved	14 Measures adopted at Thirty-first Meeting (Kyiv 2008) Approved	16 Measures adopted at Thirty-second Meeting (Baltimore 2009) Approved
Argentina	XXVIII-2*, XXVIII-3*, XXVIII-4*, XXVIII-5**	XXIX-1*, XXIX-2*, XXIX-3**, XXIX-4***	XXX-1*, XXX-2*, XXX-3**	XXXI-1*, XXXI-2*, … XXXI-14*	XXXII-1*, XXXII-2*, … XXXII-14**
Australia	XXVIII-2*, XXVIII-3*, XXVIII-4*, XXVIII-5**	XXIX-1*, XXIX-2*, XXIX-3**, XXIX-4***	XXX-1*, XXX-2*, XXX-3**	XXXI-1*, XXXI-2*, … XXXI-14*	XXXII-1*, XXXII-2*, … XXXII-14**
Belgium	ALL except Measure 1	ALL	ALL		
Brazil (1983)+	ALL except Measure 1	XXIX-1*, XXIX-2*, XXIX-3**, XXIX-4***	XXX-1*, XXX-2*, XXX-3**	XXXI-1*, XXXI-2*, … XXXI-14*	XXXII-1*, XXXII-2*, … XXXII-14**
Bulgaria (1998)+	XXVIII-2*, XXVIII-3*, XXVIII-4*, XXVIII-5**	XXIX-1*, XXIX-2*, XXIX-3**, XXIX-4***	XXX-1*, XXX-2*, XXX-3**	XXXI-1*, XXXI-2*, … XXXI-14*	XXXII-1*, XXXII-2*, … XXXII-14**
Chile	ALL except Measure 1	XXIX-1*, XXIX-2*, XXIX-3**, XXIX-4***	XXX-1*, XXX-2*, XXX-3**	XXXI-1*, XXXI-2*, … XXXI-14*	XXXII-1*, XXXII-2*, … XXXII-14**
China (1985)+	XXVIII-2*, XXVIII-3*, XXVIII-4*, XXVIII-5**	XXIX-1*, XXIX-2*, XXIX-3**, XXIX-4***	XXX-1*, XXX-2*, XXX-3**	XXXI-1*, XXXI-2*, … XXXI-14*	XXXII-1*, XXXII-2*, … XXXII-14**
Ecuador (1990)+	XXVIII-2*, XXVIII-3*, XXVIII-4*, XXVIII-5**	XXIX-1*, XXIX-2*, XXIX-3**, XXIX-4***	XXX-1*, XXX-2*, XXX-3**	XXXI-1*, XXXI-2*, … XXXI-14*	XXXII-1*, XXXII-2*, … XXXII-14**
Finland (1989)+	XXVIII-1, XXVIII-2*, XXVIII-3*, XXVIII-5**	XXIX-1*, XXIX-2*, XXIX-3**, XXIX-4***	XXX-1*, XXX-2*, XXX-3**	XXXI-1*, XXXI-2*, … XXXI-14*	XXXII-1*, XXXII-2*, … 14**, XXXII-16
France	XXVIII-2*, XXVIII-3*, XXVIII-4*, XXVIII-5**	XXIX-1*, XXIX-2*, XXIX-3**, XXIX-4***	XXX-1*, XXX-2*, XXX-3**	XXXI-1*, XXXI-2*, … XXXI-14*	XXXII-1*, XXXII-2*, … 14**, XXXII-15
Germany (1981)+	XXVIII-2*, XXVIII-3*, XXVIII-4*, XXVIII-5**	XXIX-1*, XXIX-2*, XXIX-3**, XXIX-4***	XXX-1*, XXX-2*, XXX-3**	XXXI-1*, XXXI-2*, … XXXI-14*	XXXII-1*, XXXII-2*, … XXXII-14**
India (1983)+	XXVIII-2*, XXVIII-3*, XXVIII-4*, XXVIII-5**	XXIX-1*, XXIX-2*, XXIX-3**, XXIX-4***	XXX-1*, XXX-2*, XXX-3**	XXXI-1*, XXXI-2*, … XXXI-14*	XXXII-1*, XXXII-2*, … XXXII-14**
Italy (1987)+	XXVIII-2*, XXVIII-3*, XXVIII-4*, XXVIII-5**	XXIX-1*, XXIX-2*, XXIX-3**, XXIX-4***	XXX-1*, XXX-2*, XXX-3**	XXXI-1*, XXXI-2*, … XXXI-14*	XXXII-1*, XXXII-2*, … XXXII-14**
Japan	XXVIII-2*, XXVIII-3*, XXVIII-4*, XXVIII-5**	XXIX-1*, XXIX-2*, XXIX-3**, XXIX-4***	XXX-1*, XXX-2*, XXX-3**	XXXI-1*, XXXI-2*, … XXXI-14*	XXXII-1*, XXXII-2*, … 14**, XXXII-15
Korea, Rep. (1989)+	ALL except Measure 1	ALL	ALL	ALL	XXXII-1, XXXII-2, … XXXII-14
Netherlands (1990)+	XXVIII-2*, XXVIII-3*, XXVIII-4*, XXVIII-5**	XXIX-1*, XXIX-2*, XXIX-3**, XXIX-4***	XXX-1*, XXX-2*, XXX-3**	XXXI-1*, XXXI-2*, … XXXI-14*	XXXII-1*, XXXII-2*, … XXXII-14**
New Zealand	XXVIII-2*, XXVIII-3*, XXVIII-4*, XXVIII-5**	XXIX-1*, XXIX-2*, XXIX-3**, XXIX-4***	XXX-1*, XXX-2*, XXX-3**	XXXI-1*, XXXI-2*, … XXXI-14*	XXXII-1*, XXXII-2*, … XXXII-14**
Norway	XXVIII-1, XXVIII-2*, XXVIII-3*, XXVIII-5**	XXIX-1*, XXIX-2*, XXIX-3**, XXIX-4***	XXX-1*, XXX-2*, XXX-3**	XXXI-1*, XXXI-2*, … XXXI-14*	XXXII-1*, XXXII-2*, … XXXII-14**
Peru (1989)+	XXVIII-4*, XXVIII-5**	XXIX-1*, XXIX-2*, XXIX-3**, XXIX-4***	XXX-1*, XXX-2*, XXX-3**	XXXI-1*, XXXI-2*, … XXXI-14*	XXXII-1*, XXXII-2*, … XXXII-14**
Poland (1977)+	ALL	ALL	ALL	XXXI-1*, XXXI-2*, … XXXI-14*	XXXII-1*, XXXII-2*, … XXXII-14**
Russia	XXVIII-2*, XXVIII-3*, XXVIII-4*,	XXIX-1*, XXIX-2*, XXIX-3**,	XXX-1*, XXX-2*, XXX-3**	XXXI-1*, XXXI-2*, … XXXI-14*	XXXII-1*, XXXII-2*, … XXXII-14**

	XXVIII	XXIX	XXX	XXXI	XXXII
South Africa	XXVIII-2*, XXVIII-3*, XXVIII-4*, XXVIII-5**	XXIX-4***	XXX-1*, XXX-2*, XXX-3**	XXXI-1*, XXXI-2*, ...XXXI-14*	XXXII-1*, XXXII-2*, ...XXXII-14**, XXXII-
Spain (1988)+	XXVIII-1, XXVIII-2*, XXVIII-3*, XXVIII-4*, XXVIII-5**	ALL XXIX-1*, XXIX-2*, XXIX-3**, XXIX-4***	XXX-1*, XXX-2*, XXX-3**	XXXI-1*, XXXI-2*, ...XXXI-14*	XXXII-1*, XXXII-2*, ...XXXII-14**, XXXII-
Sweden (1988)+	XXVIII-1, XXVIII-2*, XXVIII-3*, XXVIII-4*, XXVIII-5**	XXIX-1*, XXIX-2*, XXIX-3**, XXIX-4***	XXX-1*, XXX-2*, XXX-3**	XXXI-1*, XXXI-2*, ...XXXI-14*	XXXII-1*, XXXII-2*, ...XXXII-14**, XXXII-
Ukraine (2004)+	XXVIII-2*, XXVIII-3*, XXVIII-4*, XXVIII-5**	XXIX-1*, XXIX-2*, XXIX-3**, XXIX-4***	XXX-1*, XXX-2*, XXX-3**	XXXI-1*, XXXI-2*, ...XXXI-14*	XXXII-1*, XXXII-2*, ...XXXII-14**, XXXII-
U.K.	XXVIII-2*, XXVIII-3*, XXVIII-4*, XXVIII-5**	XXIX-1*, XXIX-2*, XXIX-3**, XXIX-4***	XXX-1*, XXX-2*, XXX-3**	XXXI-1*, XXXI-2*, ...XXXI-14*	XXXII-1*, XXXII-2*, ...XXXII-14**, XXXII-
Uruguay (1985)+	XXVIII-2*, XXVIII-3*, XXVIII-4*, XXVIII-5**	XXIX-1*, XXIX-2*, XXIX-3**, XXIX-4***	XXX-1*, XXX-2*, XXX-3**	XXXI-1*, XXXI-2*, ...XXXI-14*	XXXII-1*, XXXII-2*, ...XXXII-14***, XXXII-15
U.S.A.	XXVIII-2*, XXVIII-3*, XXVIII-4*, XXVIII-5**	XXIX-1*, XXIX-2*, XXIX-3**, XXIX-4***	XXX-1*, XXX-2*, XXX-3**	XXXI-1*, XXXI-2*, ...XXXI-14*	XXXII-1*, XXXII-2*, ...XXXII-14**, XXXII-

---

‾+Year attained Consultative Status. Acceptance by that state required to bring into force Recommendations or Measures of meetings from that Year forward."

* Management Plans annexed to this Measure deemed to have been approved in accordance with Article 6(1) of Annex V to the Protocol on Environmental Protection to the Antarctic Treaty and the Measure not specifying a different approval method.

** Revised and updated List of Historic Sites and Monuments annexed to this Measure deemed to have been approved in accordance with Article 8(2) of Annex V to the Protocol on Environmental Protection to the Antarctic Treaty and the Measure not specifying a different approval method.

*** Modification of Appendix A to Annex II to the Protocol on Environmental Protection to the Antarctic Treaty deemed to have been approved in accordance with Article 9(1) of Annex II to the Protocol on Environmental Protection to the Antarctic Treaty and the Measure not specifying a different approval method.

Approval, as notified to the Government of the United States of America, of measures relating to the furtherance of the principles and objectives of the Antarctic Treaty

	15 Measures adopted at Thirty-third Meeting (Punta del Este 2010) Approved	12 Measures adopted at Thirty-fourth Meeting (Buenos Aires 2011) Approved
Argentina	XXXIII-1 - XXXIII-14* and XXXIII-15**	XXXIV-1 - XXXIV-10* and XXXIV-11 - XXXIV-12**
Australia	XXXIII-1 - XXXIII-14* and XXXIII-15**	XXXIV-1 - XXXIV-10* and XXXIV-11 - XXXIV-12**
Belgium	XXXIII-1 - XXXIII-14* and XXXIII-15**	XXXIV-1 - XXXIV-10* and XXXIV-11 - XXXIV-12**
Brazil (1983)+	XXXIII-1 - XXXIII-14* and XXXIII-15**	XXXIV-1 - XXXIV-10* and XXXIV-11 - XXXIV-12**
Bulgaria (1998)+	XXXIII-1 - XXXIII-14* and XXXIII-15**	XXXIV-1 - XXXIV-10* and XXXIV-11 - XXXIV-12**
Chile	XXXIII-1 - XXXIII-14* and XXXIII-15**	XXXIV-1 - XXXIV-10* and XXXIV-11 - XXXIV-12**
China (1985)+	XXXIII-1 - XXXIII-14* and XXXIII-15**	XXXIV-1 - XXXIV-10* and XXXIV-11 - XXXIV-12**
Ecuador (1990)+	XXXIII-1 - XXXIII-14* and XXXIII-15**	XXXIV-1 - XXXIV-10* and XXXIV-11 - XXXIV-12**
Finland (1989)+	XXXIII-1 - XXXIII-14* and XXXIII-15**	XXXIV-1 - XXXIV-10* and XXXIV-11 - XXXIV-12**
France	XXXIII-1 - XXXIII-14* and XXXIII-15**	XXXIV-1 - XXXIV-10* and XXXIV-11 - XXXIV-12**
Germany (1981)+	XXXIII-1 - XXXIII-14* and XXXIII-15**	XXXIV-1 - XXXIV-10* and XXXIV-11 - XXXIV-12**
India (1983)+	XXXIII-1 - XXXIII-14* and XXXIII-15**	XXXIV-1 - XXXIV-10* and XXXIV-11 - XXXIV-12**
Italy (1987)+	XXXIII-1 - XXXIII-14* and XXXIII-15**	XXXIV-1 - XXXIV-10* and XXXIV-11 - XXXIV-12**
Japan	XXXIII-1 - XXXIII-14* and XXXIII-15**	XXXIV-1 - XXXIV-10* and XXXIV-11 - XXXIV-12**
Korea, Rep. (1989)+	XXXIII-1 - XXXIII-14* and XXXIII-15**	XXXIV-1 - XXXIV-10* and XXXIV-11 - XXXIV-12**
Netherlands (1990)+	ALL	XXXIV-1 - XXXIV-10* and XXXIV-11 - XXXIV-12**
New Zealand	XXXIII-1 - XXXIII-14* and XXXIII-15**	XXXIV-1 - XXXIV-10* and XXXIV-11 - XXXIV-12**
Norway	XXXIII-1 - XXXIII-14* and XXXIII-15**	XXXIV-1 - XXXIV-10* and XXXIV-11 - XXXIV-12**
Peru (1989)+	XXXIII-1 - XXXIII-14* and XXXIII-15**	XXXIV-1 - XXXIV-10* and XXXIV-11 - XXXIV-12**
Poland (1977)+	XXXIII-1 - XXXIII-14* and XXXIII-15**	XXXIV-1 - XXXIV-10* and XXXIV-11 - XXXIV-12**
Russia	XXXIII-1 - XXXIII-14* and XXXIII-15**	XXXIV-1 - XXXIV-10* and XXXIV-11 - XXXIV-12**
South Africa	XXXIII-1 - XXXIII-14* and XXXIII-15**	XXXIV-1 - XXXIV-10* and XXXIV-11 - XXXIV-12**
Spain (1988)+	XXXIII-1 - XXXIII-14* and XXXIII-15**	XXXIV-1 - XXXIV-10* and XXXIV-11 - XXXIV-12**
Sweden (1988)+	XXXIII-1 - XXXIII-14* and XXXIII-15**	XXXIV-1 - XXXIV-10* and XXXIV-11 - XXXIV-12**
Ukraine (2004)+	XXXIII-1 - XXXIII-14* and XXXIII-15**	XXXIV-1 - XXXIV-10* and XXXIV-11 - XXXIV-12**
U.K.	XXXIII-1 - XXXIII-14* and XXXIII-15**	XXXIV-1 - XXXIV-10* and XXXIV-11 - XXXIV-12**
Uruguay (1985)+	XXXIII-1 - XXXIII-14* and XXXIII-15**	XXXIV-1 - XXXIV-10* and XXXIV-11 - XXXIV-12**
U.S.A.	XXXIII-1 - XXXIII-14* and XXXIII-15**	XXXIV-1 - XXXIV-10* and XXXIV-11 - XXXIV-12**

"+Year attained Consultative Status. Acceptance by that state required to bring into force Recommendations or Measures of meetings from that Year forward." not specifying a different approval method.

Office of the Assistant Legal Adviser for Treaty Affairs
Department of State
Washington, April 10, 2012.

Report by the CCAMLR Observer to the Thirty-Fifth Antarctic Treaty Consultative Meeting

(Submitted by the CCAMLR Secretariat in the four official languages)

1.　The Thirtieth Annual Meeting of the Commission for the Conservation of Antarctic Marine Living Resources was held in Hobart, Tasmania, Australia, from 24 October to 4 November 2011. It was chaired by Mr T. Løbach (Norway). The Report of the Meeting is available at: http://www.ccamlr.org/pu/e/e_pubs/cr/drt.htm.

Report of the Chair

2.　The Chair reported that the Commission had 25 Members and that nine other States are party to the Convention.

3.　During the 2010/11 season, CCAMLR Members participated in 14 fisheries in the Convention Area. Vessels fishing in fisheries managed under conservation measures in force in 2010/11 had reported, by 24 September 2011, a total catch of 179 131 tonnes of krill, 11 254 tonnes of toothfish, and 11 tonnes of icefish. A number of other species were taken as by-catch.[1]

Finance and administration

4.　The Commission adopted a budget for the Commission and recommendations relating to:

- a strategic plan for the Secretariat
- revised financial regulations.

Scientific committee

5.　Notifications for krill fishing in 2011/12 were received from seven Members and 15 vessels with a notified total predicted catch of 401 000 tonnes.

6.　The Commission noted that fishing for krill had taken place inside ASMA 1 in Admiralty Bay in 2010 and that this may be inconsistent with the management objectives of the ASMA.

7.　In addition to the 11 254 tonnes of toothfish reported from within the Convention Area, catches reported under the Catch Document Scheme (CDS) indicated that 9 190 tonnes of *Dissostichus* spp. were taken outside the Convention Area in 2010/11 (to 26 September 2011) compared with 12 441 tonnes in 2009/10.

8.　In 2010/11, one Member fished for icefish in Subarea 48.3 with a reported catch of 10 tonnes and one Member fished in Division 58.5.2 and reported a total catch of 1 tonne.

9.　The Commission welcomed the Scientific Committee's deliberation on climate change and noted the recommendations of the EU/Netherlands-sponsored workshop on 'Antarctic Krill and Climate Change'.

---

[1]　Total catches reported at the end of the 2010/2011 fishing season (30 November 2011) were: 181,511 t of krill, 14,572 t of toothfish and 12 t of icefish.

Chair and Vice-Chair

10.   Dr C. Jones (USA) was elected as Scientific Committee Chair and Dr X. Zhao (China) was elected Vice-Chair.

Bottom fishing

11.   The Commission endorsed the advice of the Scientific Committee including the prohibition of bottom fishing in Subarea 88.1 (SSRU G) to provide protection of registered VMEs from direct effects of interactions with fishing gear.

Assessment of incidental mortality

12.   The Commission noted that the total extrapolated mortalities of seabirds within Subarea 58.6 and Division 58.5.1 was estimated to be 220 and that incidental mortalities elsewhere in the Convention Area were similar to the near-zero levels of recent years.

Marine protected areas

13.   The Commission noted the outcomes of the Workshop on Marine Protected Areas and expressed its gratitude to France for hosting the workshop.

14.   The Commission welcomed the development of planning domains for representative systems of MPAs to replace the priority areas defined in 2008 as the basis for planning MPAs in the Convention Area.

Ross Sea region

15.   The Commission thanked New Zealand and the USA for two scenarios for an MPA in the Ross Sea planning domain, noting the advice of the Scientific Committee that the scenarios are based on the best scientific evidence available and that no further scientific analysis and debate is needed in that Committee.

16.   New Zealand and the USA confirmed their intention of bringing forward proposals for the formal establishment of an MPA in 2012.

East Antarctica

17.   The Commission thanked Australia and France which jointly presented a proposal for a representative system of MPAs (RSMPA) for the whole East Antarctic planning domain.

18.   Australia and France expressed their intention to prepare a conservation measure for consideration in 2012.

Protection of habitats newly exposed by the collapse of ice shelves

19.   The Commission noted the proposal from the UK concerning the protection of marine habitats that may be newly exposed as a consequence of ice-shelf collapse.

Proposal for a general conservation measure on MPAs

20.   The Commission adopted a general conservation measure for the adoption of MPAs.

Implementation and compliance

System of Inspection

21. No cases of non-compliance with conservation measures were reported as a result of any at-sea inspections undertaken under the System of Inspection.

Environmental and mitigation measures

22. The Commission noted that reports of non-compliance with all the requirements of CMs 26-01 and 25-02 in 2010/11 had been investigated and no violations had been found.

Compliance evaluation procedure

23. The Commission noted that a compliance evaluation procedure will be developed for possible adoption at CCAMLR-XXXI.

Catch Documentation Scheme

24. The Commission revoked Singapore's status as a Non-Contracting Party cooperating with CCAMLR. The Commission requested that the Chair write to Singapore in relation to this matter.

25. The Commission requested the Chair to write to the ATS Secretariat to outline CCAMLR's efforts in engaging with Malaysia to combat IUU. The letter will request that the matter be formally raised with Malaysia at the next opportunity.

Iuu fishing in the convention area

26. Five vessels were reported to have engaged in IUU fishing activities in the Convention Area and three IUU-listed vessels were sighted outside the Convention Area during 2010/11. Six of the identified vessels were reported to be using gillnets.

27. The Commission noted that there is no evidence to suggest that IUU fishing has declined and that it continued at a relatively low level, although it was possible it was increasing and that the spatial distribution of IUU fishing may be changing.

28. The Commission included the Iranian-flagged vessel, the *Koosha 4*, on the NCP-IUU Vessel List in 2011.

29. The Commission removed the vessels *West Ocean* and *North Ocean* from the CP-IUU Vessel List.

Scheme of international scientific observation

30. In accordance with the CCAMLR Scheme of International Scientific Observation, scientific observers were deployed on all vessels in all finfish fisheries in the Convention Area in 2010/11.

Conservation measures

31. Conservation measures and resolutions adopted at CCAMLR-XXX have been published in the *Schedule of Conservation Measures in Force 2011/12*.

Krill fisheries

32. The Commission agreed that krill fishing vessels must ensure that an observer has access to sufficient samples to enable a target coverage rate of at least 20% of hauls or haul units during the period that the observer is on board the vessel per fishing season.

33. The Commission agreed to retain the interim distribution of the trigger level in the fishery for *E. superba* in Subareas 48.1 to 48.4 (CM 51-07) for a further three seasons, until the

Scientific Committee and WG-EMM complete the development of a feedback management procedure for this fishery.

New conservation measures

Gear regulations and bottom fishing

34.   The Commission agreed that all bottom fishing activities shall be prohibited within the defined area of the registered VMEs, with the exception of scientific research activities agreed by the Commission for monitoring or other purposes on advice from the Scientific Committee.

Fishing seasons, closed areas and prohibition of fishing

35.   Directed fishing for *Dissostichus* spp. in Subarea 48.5 was prohibited in 2011/12.

By-catch limits

36.   The Commission carried forward the existing by-catch limits in Division 58.5.2 in 2011/12.

37.   The Commission carried forward the by-catch limits for exploratory fisheries in 2011/12, taking account of the revised catch limits for *Dissostichus* spp. in Subareas 88.1 and 88.2, and revised boundaries of SSRUs in Subarea 88.2.

Toothfish

38.   The Commission revised the catch limits, by-catch limits, vessel numbers, move-on rules, research plans, including tagging rates, gear restrictions and fishery prohibitions for the fishery for *D. eleginoides* in each Subarea.

Icefish

39.   The Commission revised the limits on the fishery for *C. gunnari* in Subarea 48.3 and Division 58.5.2 for 2011/12 to 0 tonnes, with a 30-tonne research and by-catch limit.

Crab

40.   Noting that crabs were not harvested during 2010/11 the Commission closed the fishery.

Other

41.   The Commission adopted a resolution which encourages Members and their flagged vessels to provide relevant vessel information to the appropriate Maritime Rescue Coordination Centre in advance of the vessels entering the Convention Area.

42.   The Commission also adopted a resolution to enhance the safety of fishing vessels in the Convention Area.

Fishing capacity and effort in exploratory fisheries

43.   The Commission agreed on the need to discuss capacity management and called for restraint in exploratory fisheries while this issue was being developed.

Cooperation with other elements of the antarctic treaty system

44.   The Commission agreed that CCAMLR be represented at ATCM XXXV by the Executive Secretary. The Chair of the Scientific Committee and the Science Officer will represent the Commission and Scientific Committee at CEP XIV.

Implementation of convention objectives

Future structure of Commission Meetings

45.   The Commission agreed to trial an eight-day meeting in 2012 and 2013.

Election of vice chair

46.   The Commission elected the USA as Vice-Chair.

Date and location of the next meeting

47.   The Thirty-first Meeting of the Commission will be held from 23 October to 1 November 2012 in Hobart. The Thirty-first Meeting of the Scientific Committee will be held in Hobart from 22 to 26 October 2012.

Global Environment Facility proposal

48.   South Africa advised it is seeking GEF support to improve the capacity of Developing State Members of CCAMLR to engage in CCAMLR processes.

Adoption of the report

49.   The Report of the Meeting was adopted.

2. Reports by Experts

Report of the International Association of Antarctica Tour Operators 2011-2012

Under Article III (2) of the Antarctic Treaty

Introduction

The International Association of Antarctica Tour Operators (IAATO) is pleased to report its activities to ATCM XXXV, under Article III (2) of the Antarctic Treaty.

IAATO continues to focus activities in support of its mission statement to ensure:
- Effective day-to-day management of Member activities in Antarctica;
- Educational outreach, including scientific collaboration; and
- Development and promotion of Antarctic tourism industry best practices.

A detailed description of IAATO, its mission statement, primary activities and recent developments can be found in the *2012-13 Fact Sheet*, and on the IAATO website: www.iaato.org.

IAATO Membership and Visitor Levels during 2011-12

IAATO comprises 111 Members, Associates and Affiliates. Member offices are located worldwide, representing 57% of the Antarctic Treaty Consultative Party countries, and carrying nationals from nearly all Treaty Parties annually to Antarctica.

During the 2011-12 Antarctic tourism season, the overall number of visitors decreased nearly 22% to 26,519 from the previous season (33,824 visitors in 2010-2011). These numbers reflect only those travelling with IAATO member companies. Details on tourism statistics can be found in ATCM XXXIV IP39 *IAATO Overview of Antarctic Tourism: 2011-12 Season and Preliminary Estimates for 2012-13*. The Membership Directory and additional statistics on IAATO member activities can be found at ***www.iaato.org***.

Recent Work and Activities

In line with IAATO's Strategic Plan, progress was made on a number of initiatives. These included:

- Strengthening the Secretariat through a reorganisation of Director's roles and responsibilities and the creation of an additional half-time position.

- Launch of a new interactive website and web-based content management system to facilitate access for both Members and Public. Unique access to the field operations areas of the website is available to Treaty Party representatives on request.

- The Yacht Outreach Campaign continued during the season, with IAATO yacht operators dedicating considerable effort at departure gateways to inform non-IAATO yacht operators.

- All IAATO SOLAS Passenger ships participated in the web-based satellite tracking system, which is shared with Rescue Coordination Centres. This effort continues to be useful not only for enhancing contingency response but also for day-to-day management.

- Trials of the three-step IAATO Enhanced Observer Scheme (See ATCM XXXIV/IP107 for additional details) were conducted, providing useful feedback on the scheme and also on the various competent authority authorisation processes. The scheme will continue to be trialled, on a voluntary basis, for the next three seasons.

- Field Staff Online Assessment and Certification was further developed to include different activities, staff levels, and geographic areas. To date, 77 Field Staff have been certified.

IAATO Meeting and Participation at Other Meetings during 2011-12

IAATO Secretariat staff and member representatives participated in internal and external meetings, liaising with National Antarctic Programs, governmental, scientific, environmental and industry organisations.

- The IAATO 23rd Meeting (May 1-3, 2012, Providence, USA) hosted over 100 participants. Treaty Party representatives from Canada, Chile, Germany, Norway, UK and USA and COMNAP attended. In addition to reporting the progress listed above, notable outcomes included:
    - Adoption of Rules of Procedure for Compliance and Dispute Resolution;
    - Establishing IAATO Safety Advisories (See ATCMXXXV/IP38)
    - Establishing a Hydrographic Working Group;
    - Developing a generic IAATO lecture on climate change for all IAATO operators by the Climate Change Working Group (see ATCM XXXIV/IP103). Additionally, further steps to assess and mitigate Members CO_2 footprint were tabled, and the commitment to continue this work renewed.

- As before, IAATO Members and representatives from Treaty Parties participated in an informal round table discussion following IAATO 23rd Meeting. This annual discussion is held under Chatham House rules and provides an invaluable opportunity to have a free-flowing discussion on issues relating to Antarctic tourism. A summary report will be forthcoming.

- IAATO welcomed the opportunity to participate at COMNAPXXIII in Stockholm, Sweden (August, 2012). The meeting also provided a forum for IAATO and their deep field operators to meet with NSF to ensure good communication and collaboration at South Pole Station in anticipation of the high profile Centenary season. IAATO places great merit in good cooperation and collaboration between its Members and National Antarctic Programs.

- IAATO representatives attended the 11th International Hydrographic Organization / Hydrographic Commission on Antarctica (IHO/HCA) Meeting in Hobart, Australia. In addition to supporting the ongoing work of the HCA, IAATO was pleased to start working with the UKHO and HCA in the development of a crowd-sourcing scheme, using technological advances, to improve the viability of IAATO vessels as ships of opportunity.

- As an advisor to Cruise Lines International Association (CLIA), IAATO continues to be active in the development of the International Maritime Organization's (IMO) mandatory Polar Code. This included participation in the Norwegian-sponsored workshop on Environmental Aspects of the Polar Code; the dedicated working group during the 56th session of the IMO's Design and Equipment (DE) Subcommittee meeting; and the intercessional correspondence group discussions. Additionally, IAATO has continued to work with an independent maritime safety consultant on an in-depth risk assessment study, and is now commencing development of a voyage risk assessment framework to assist Members in applying the code once adopted.

- IAATO 24th Meeting is scheduled for April 22-25, 2013 either in Punta Arenas, Chile or Providence, Rhode Island, USA. Interested Treaty Parties are welcome to attend and should contact IAATO at iaato@iaato.org.

Environmental Monitoring

IAATO continues to provide ATCM and CEP with detailed information on member activities in Antarctica. For details see ATCM XXXV/IP39 *IAATO Overview of Antarctic Tourism: 2011-12 Season and Preliminary Estimates for 2012-13 Antarctic Season* and ATCM XXXV IP37 *Report on IAATO Operator use of Antarctic Peninsula Landing Sites and ATCM Visitor Site Guides, 2011-12 Season.*

IAATO continues to work collaboratively with scientific institutions to address specific issues on environmental monitoring. This includes working with Oceanites, Antarctic Site Inventory, London Zoological Society and the IPY Aliens in Antarctica study.

Additionally, effort continues to be made to ensure educational outreach through both educational media and institutions (e.g BBC Frozen Planet / Open University, UK and University of Edinburgh, UK)

IAATO welcomes opportunities for future collaboration with other organisations.

Tourism Incidents 2011-12; Update on Tourism Incidents 2008-09

IAATO continues to follow a policy of disclosing incidents to ensure risks are understood and appropriate lessons are learned for all Antarctic operators. Incidents during the 2011-12 season included:

- MV *Sea Spirit* temporarily grounded in Whalers Bay, Deception Island on 9 Dec. 2011, floating free at the next high water. Reports indicated no threat to human life and no damage to the environment. A subsequent diving inspection indicated no damage to the vessel. The incident was reported to the Deception Island Management Group (DIMG), and subsequently the IAATO Marine Committee issued an IAATO Safety Advisory on Whalers Bay (See ATCMXXXV/IP38).

- Despite having attended the mandatory code of conduct briefing, two members of a gospel group on board MS *Expedition* were seen dispersing barley seeds on a hike at Telefon Bay on 14 Dec. 2011. The dispersed seeds were collected and the severity of the offense explained to the passengers. Additional seeds were confiscated. The group was carefully monitored during future landings. The DIMG was informed.

- During an Antarctic Logistics and Expeditions staff crevasse rescue exercise on 17 Jan. 2012, a Piston-Bully Tractor broke through a snow bridge into a crevasse. Two personnel received minor abrasions. Analysis of the incident is being undertaken by the operator to see what lessons can be learned.

- During a visit to Neko Harbour 11 Feb. 2012, a Gentoo penguin chick that had approached a passenger was injured when a tripod was knocked over. After monitoring the chick for some time during which the chick could no longer walk and was being repeatedly attacked by conspecifics, the field staff euthanised the chick. As a USA authorised expedition, the incident is under investigation in the USA.

Updates on previous season incidents:

IAATO Marine Committee reviewed the 2011 flag state summary report from Bahamas on the *MV Ocean Nova* grounding in 2009. On the basis of the report and the subsequent mitigation actions that were enacted by the operator, the Marine Committee issued additional Recommendations to Enhance Marine Safety.

Scientific and Conservation Support

During the 2011-12 season, IAATO Members cost-effectively or on *pro bono* basis transported more than 150 scientific, support and heritage conservation staff, as well as equipment and supplies used by these personnel, to and from stations, field sites and gateway ports.

In addition, IAATO Members and their passengers contributed US$478,848 to scientific and conservation organisations active in Antarctica and the sub-Antarctic (e.g. Save the Albatross, Antarctic Heritage Trust, Last Ocean, Mawson's Huts Foundation, Oceanites and World Wildlife Fund). Over the past eight years, these donations have totalled more than US$2.5 million in cash donations.

With Thanks

IAATO appreciates the opportunity to work cooperatively with Antarctic Treaty Parties, COMNAP, SCAR, CCAMLR, IHO/HCA, ASOC and others toward the long-term protection of Antarctica.

Report by the International Hydrographic Organization (IHO) on "Cooperation in Hydrographic Surveying and Charting of Antarctic waters"

Introduction

The International Hydrographic Organization (IHO) is an intergovernmental consultative and technical organization that was established in 1921. The IHO enjoys observer status at the UN and is recognized as the competent international authority regarding hydrography and nautical charting. Its competence is also referred in the United Nations Convention on the Law of the Sea. The Organization coordinates on a worldwide basis the setting of standards for the production of hydrographic data and the provision of hydrographic services to support safety of navigation and the protection and sustainable use of the marine environment. The IHO's mission is to create a global environment in which States provide adequate and timely hydrographic data, products and services for their widest possible use.

The IHB has encouraged the establishment of Regional Hydrographic Commissions (RHCs) to coordinate hydrographic activity and cooperation at the regional level. The RHCs are made up predominantly of IHO Member States with interests in a particular region. RHCs work in close harmony with the Organization to help further its ideals and program. RHCs meet at regular intervals to discuss such things as mutual hydrographic and chart production problems, plan joint survey operations, and resolve schemes for medium and large scale International Chart coverage in their regions.

One of these Commissions is the Hydrographic Commission on Antarctica (HCA) dedicated to promoting technical co-operation in the domains of hydrographic surveying, marine cartography, and nautical information within the Antarctic region.

The IHO and particularly the HCA works closely with different organizations concerned with and interested in Antarctica, aiming at strengthening cooperation to improve safety of life at sea, safety of navigation, protection of the marine environment and contribute to marine scientific research in Antarctica.

This Report provides a brief summary of the key coordination activities since the last ATCM.

The 11th Meeting of the IHO Hydrographic Commission on Antarctica

The 11th Meeting of the Hydrographic Commission on Antarctica (HCA) took place in Hobart, Tasmania, Australia, from 5 to 7 October 2011. The meeting was organised by the Australian Hydrographic Service (AHS) with the support of the Australian Antarctic Division (AAD). Fifteen HCA Member States[2], out of 23, were represented at this meeting, plus observers from COMNAP, IAATO, IALA, GEBCO and SCAR, and one expert contributor (Fugro-Pelagos). In total, 29 delegates were in attendance.

Participants were welcomed by Dr. Tony FLEMING, AAD Director, highlighting the strong involvement of AAD in environment protection in Antarctica and climate change.

Opening Remarks were provided by Commodore Rod NAIRN, AHS Director and HCA Vice-Chair, stressing the need for better charts and improved chart coverage in Antarctica. He emphasized that the HCA work is critical to best support shipping operations and advancing science knowledge in Antarctica.

He thanked AAD for their support in organizing this meeting and reported that apologies for absence had been received from Japan and the Antarctic Treaty Secretariat.

The HCA currently comprised 23 IHO Members States and there have been no changes since the last report. (**See Annex A**).

The Commission re-elected Commodore NAIRN (Australia) as Vice-Chairman of HCA and reviewed all actions arising from the 10th HCA meeting concluding that most of the actions had been completed. The following subjects merit special attention:

---

[2] Australia, Brazil, Chile, Ecuador, France, Germany, Korea (Rep. of), New Zealand, Norway, South Africa, Spain, United Kingdom, USA, Uruguay and Venezuela.

- HCA Members from Brazil, Chile, France, Germany, South Africa, Spain and UK reported that they have briefed their ATCM National delegates on the importance of improving hydrography and nautical charting for safety of navigation in Antarctica. The meeting agreed that improving coordination at a national level should be an ongoing practice.

- Noting the unique status of Antarctica and the imminent introduction of the IMO Polar Code, the Commission agreed that there was a need to define how safety of navigation, including hydrography and aids to navigation, should be administered in Antarctica.

- The Commission felt that a new strategic approach was needed for raising awareness on safety of navigation and environmental protection in Antarctica, through the submission of a set of recommendations to the XVIII International Hydrographic Conference. This was done and the IHO 2013-2017 Work Program includes the following relevant tasks:

  a) to conduct a risk assessment for the Antarctic region and develop a Work Program to improve Antarctic charting. (2013/2014)

  b) to submit through the IHB to ATCM the risk assessment conducted by HCA for the Antarctic Region together with a proposed HCA work program to improve Antarctic charting, for consideration, endorsement and support from ATCM. (2015)

- The Commission instructed the HCA Chair to approach ATCM explaining that SOLAS obligations (limited to Chap V, Reg. 2, 4, 9, 27) [and environmental protection mechanisms] and related efforts in Antarctica rely on the efforts of the nations that are party to the Antarctic Treaty in meeting those obligations. The Commission also instructed the HCA Chair to seek support from the ATCM for the IMO to encourage voluntary participation in data collection activities to be included into the Polar Code (IMO's mandatory code for ships operating in polar waters), noting that the remote nature and environmental constraints of the Antarctic region coupled with the limited suitable resources available to conduct surveying and charting drives a focus on investigating alternate methods for data gathering.

- Following a kind invitation from the Servicio Oceanografico, Hidrografico y Meteorologico de la Armada del Uruguay, the Commission decided to have the 12th HCA meeting in Uruguay, (venue to be determined) on 10 – 12 October 2012.

The Status of Hydrographic Surveys

Out of the 15 National Reports submitted to the last HCA meeting, 8 indicated that some systematic hydrographic surveys had taken place during the 2010/2011 season. There is no assessment yet with respect to the 2011/2012 season.

The HCA Hydrographic Survey Prioritizing Working Group with cooperation from COMNAP and IAATO, have revised and produced new versions of the HCA Long Term Survey Plan and the HCA Survey Short List to reflect new survey requirements arising from IAATO input based on previous season tourist statistics.

HCA has been proactive in complying with the scope of ATCM Resolution 2/2010 and at least 9 HCA members have established links and arrangements *with relevant national scientific institutions for the collection of bathymetric information.* Another 4 HCA Members, having a direct responsibility for the collection of bathymetric data information, indicated that such links do not seem relevant to be established. Nevertheless as soon as new data is available, the IHB stands ready to receive such data and further disseminate it to the relevant HOs.

IAATO has released some past bathymetric data to the IHB that then made it available to the producer nation of the charts that could benefit from such data. The HCA encourages IAATO members to continue this practice that enables the improvement of the Antarctic chart coverage

Following experiences so far gathered the HCA agreed to further develop guidelines for IAATO ships of opportunity willing to collect hydrographic data and for the Hydrographic Offices visiting IAATO ships so that a visit process and participation schemes be facilitated. Despite of the feeling of little concrete results from such visits to date, due to the difficulties in their implementation, the meeting agreed to continue arranging the visit of hydrographic surveyors to IAATO ships when calling in ports on her way to Antarctica, or in Antarctica, to advice on the collection and rendering of hydrographic data.

The Commission took note of a project involving the UKHO and a hydrographic company aiming to improve data coverage in Antarctica (predominately the Peninsula) for all shipping. The system is known as ARGUS (Autonomous Remote Global Underwater Surveillance) and will provide cooperative surveying through the acquisition and collective processing of vessel GPS and Echo Sounder data via a black box recorder. The cost of a box should be about USD 2.000.

The Status of Nautical Chart Production

Six new INT charts have been approved for inclusion in the scheme, to be produced by Ecuador (INT 9129), Spain (INT 9128), Australia (INT 9022 and INT 9038) and UK (INT 9117 and INT 9133). As a result, the total number of INT charts in the scheme is 108. Of these, 67 INT charts had been published as of April 2012; 27 are planned for publication by 2014 as either new publication or new edition. (**See Annex B**).

The key element for progressing INT chart production is the availability of good quality hydrographic survey data for the areas concerned. In many areas not yet covered, there is either no data or it is old data of unsatisfactory quality. Any significant progress towards completion of production for the whole scheme will therefore depend upon the capability of conducting hydrographic surveys to modern standards.

Hydrographic operations in Antarctica are highly costly. This fact and the priority given by IHO Member States to surveying their own national waters are both limiting factors to the progression of INT chart production for Antarctica.

The production of Electronic Navigational Charts (ENC) of Antarctica has continued to grow. So far 60 ENCs cells are available (**See Annex C**) based on various national charts and on 32 INT charts. These ENCs include 13 "overview", 7 "general", 15 "coastal", 13 "approach", 11 "harbour" and 1 "berthing".

The current production program covers mainly the same areas covered by the paper charts and that looks promising, but at the end, ENC production will be governed by the availability of new surveys data. Therefore if real progress is to be achieved, an increase in the hydrographic surveys operations seems necessary.

The IHO/HCA has already agreed on a small and medium scale scheme for ENCs covering Antarctic waters and it is working together with the IHB on the development of a large scale ENC scheme, based on existing paper charts and other requirements.

Others

The IHO has contributed to the ATCM work participating with comments on the work conducted by :

a) ICG on "Yachting guidelines for Antarctic cruises"
b) ICG on "Outstanding Questions on Antarctic Tourism" and
c) ICG on "Review of ATCM Recommendations on Operational Matters"

Conclusions

- While several Hydrographic Offices are progressing in the production of INT Charts and ENC covering Antarctic waters, this activity is dependent on the availability of reliable hydrographic data. The IHO/HCA acknowledges and appreciates the cooperation and contribution received from several international organizations, particularly from IAATO, COMNAP and research institutions, which have made ancient collections of bathymetric informative data available. This collective effort goes in direct support of the production of INT Charts and ENC covering Antarctic waters.

- Improving coordination at a national level between the ATCM National delegates and their respective National Hydrographers facilitates the understanding of the importance of improving hydrography and nautical charting for safety of navigation and protection of the marine environment in Antarctica.

- Noting the unique status of Antarctica and the imminent introduction of the IMO Polar Code, there is a need to define within the ATCM how safety of navigation, including hydrography and aids to navigation, should be administered in Antarctica.

- SOLAS obligations (limited to Chap V, Reg. 2, 4, 9, 27) and related efforts in Antarctica rely on the efforts of the nations that are party to the Antarctic Treaty in meeting those obligations. It is important that ATCM invites IMO to encourage voluntary participation in data collection activities to be included into the Polar Code (IMO's mandatory code for ships operating in polar waters).

- The approved IHO 2013-2017 Work Program includes the following relevant tasks to be developed by the HCA, the result of which shall contribute the ATCM objectives :

  a) to conduct a risk assessment for the Antarctic region and develop a Work Program to improve Antarctic charting (2013/2014)

  b) to submit through the IHB to ATCM the risk assessment conducted together with a proposed HCA work program to improve Antarctic charting, for consideration, endorsement and support from ATCM. (2015)

Recommendations

It is recommended that the XXXV ATCM:

a) Takes note of the IHO Report.

b) Consider adopting the required administrative provisions to implement SOLAS obligations (limited to Chap V, Reg. 2, 4, 9, 27)

c) Consider inviting IMO to encourage voluntary participation in data collection activities to be included into the Polar Code and consider the way the implementation of the provisions contained in the mentioned IMO Polar Code will be handle in Antarctica.

Monaco, May 2012.

ANNEXES (IN ENGLISH ONLY):

A: HCA Membership.

B: INT Chart Production Status (April 2012).

C: ENC Production Status (April 2012)

ANNEX A

HCA MEMBERSHIP

(March 2012)

MEMBERS:

Argentina		Korea, Republic of
Australia		New Zealand
Brazil		Norway
Chile		Peru
China		Russian Federation
Ecuador		South Africa
France	Spain	
Germany		United Kingdom
Greece		Uruguay
India		USA
Italy		Venezuela
Japan		

===

OBSERVER ORGANIZATIONS:

Antarctic Treaty Secretariat (ATS)

Council of Managers of National Antarctic Programmes (COMNAP)

Standing Committee on Antarctic Logistics and Operations (SCALOP)

International Association of Antarctic Tour Operators (IAATO)

Scientific Committee on Antarctic Research (SCAR)

International Maritime Organization (IMO)

Intergovernmental Oceanographic Commission (IOC)

General Bathymetric Chart of the Oceans (GEBCO)

International Bathymetric Chart of the Southern Ocean (IBCSO)

IHO Data Center for Digital Bathymetry (DCDB)

Australian Antarctic Division

Antarctica New Zealand

ANNEX B

INT CHART PRODUCTION STATUS

(April 2012)

STATUS OF INTERNATIONAL CHART PRODUCTION IN ANTARCTICA
(1 of 2)

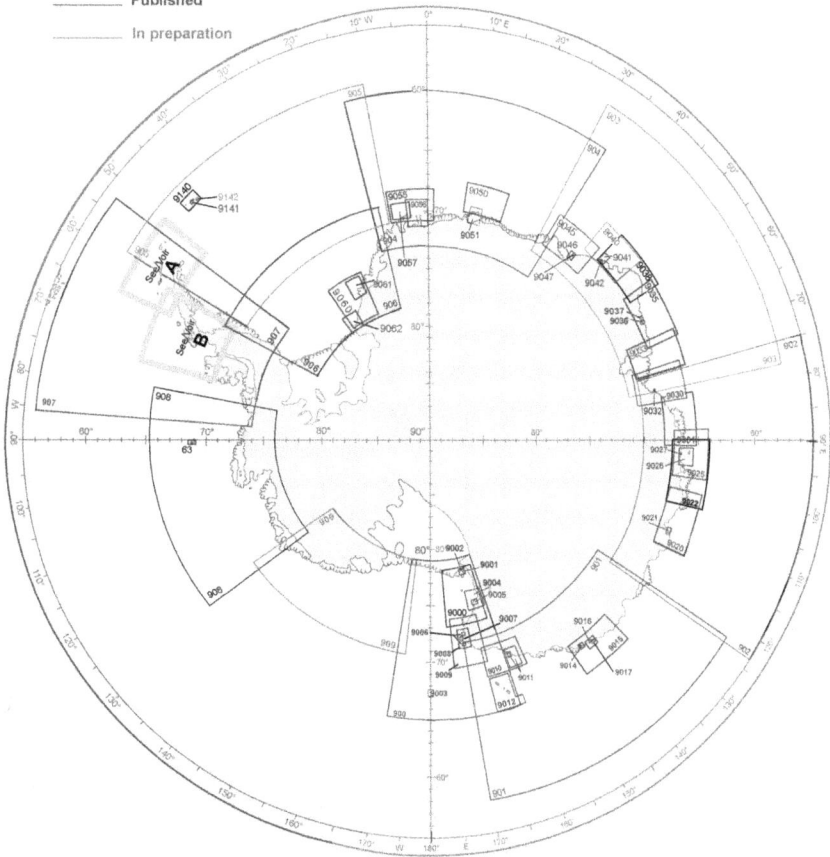

STATUS OF INTERNATIONAL CHART PRODUCTION IN ANTARCTICA
(2 of 2)

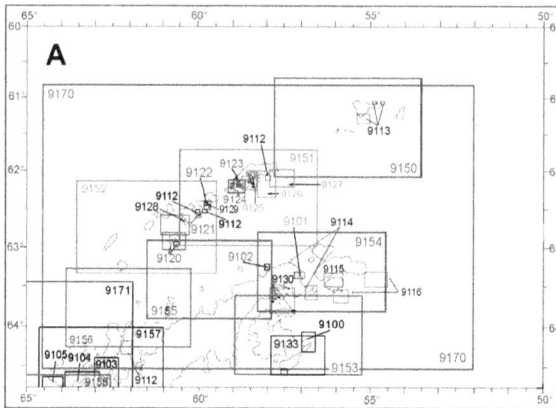

Not published
Published
In preparation

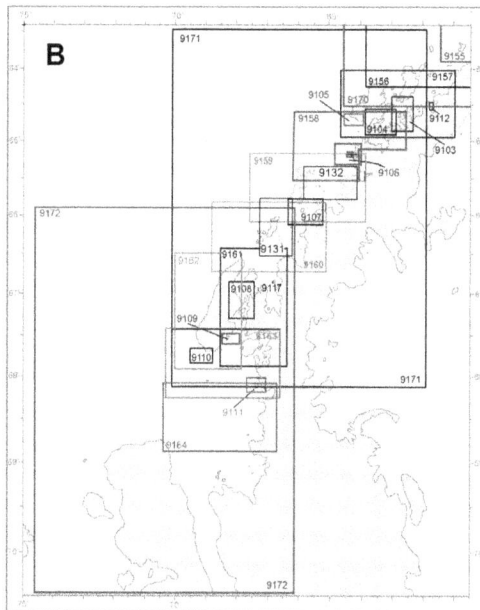

ANNEX C

ENC PRODUCTION STATUS

(April 2012)

STATUS OF ENC PRODUCTION IN ANTARCTICA
«OVERVIEW» ENCs
(based on the 1: 10M and 1: 2M INT Chart Series)

10M & 2M
NAVIGATIONAL PURPOSE 1
(OVERVIEW)

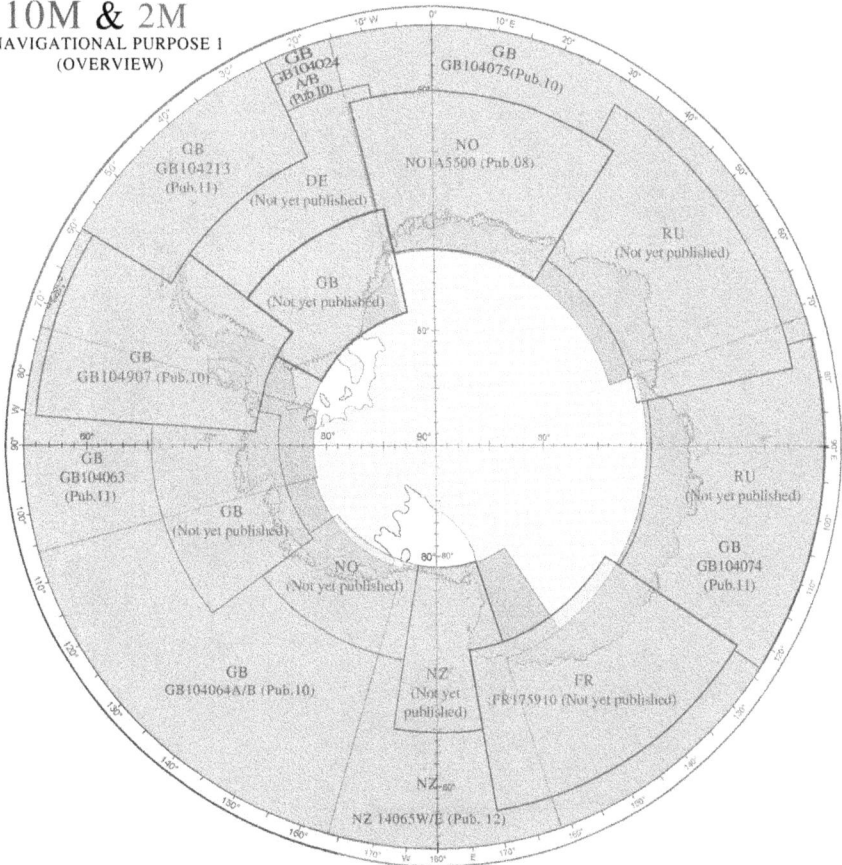

GB
GB104024
A/B
(Pub.10)

GB
GB104075(Pub.10)

GB
GB104213
(Pub.11)

NO
NO1A5500 (Pub.08)

DE
(Not yet published)

RU
(Not yet published)

GB
(Not yet published)

GB
GB104907 (Pub.10)

GB
GB104063
(Pub.11)

RU
(Not yet published)

GB
(Not yet published)

GB
GB104074
(Pub.11)

NO
(Not yet published)

GB
GB104064A/B (Pub.10)

NZ
(Not yet published)

FR
FR175910 (Not yet published)

NZ

NZ 14065W/E (Pub.12)

STATUS OF ENC PRODUCTION IN ANTARCTICA (2 of 3)
MEDIUM-SCALE « GENERAL» and «COASTAL» ENCs

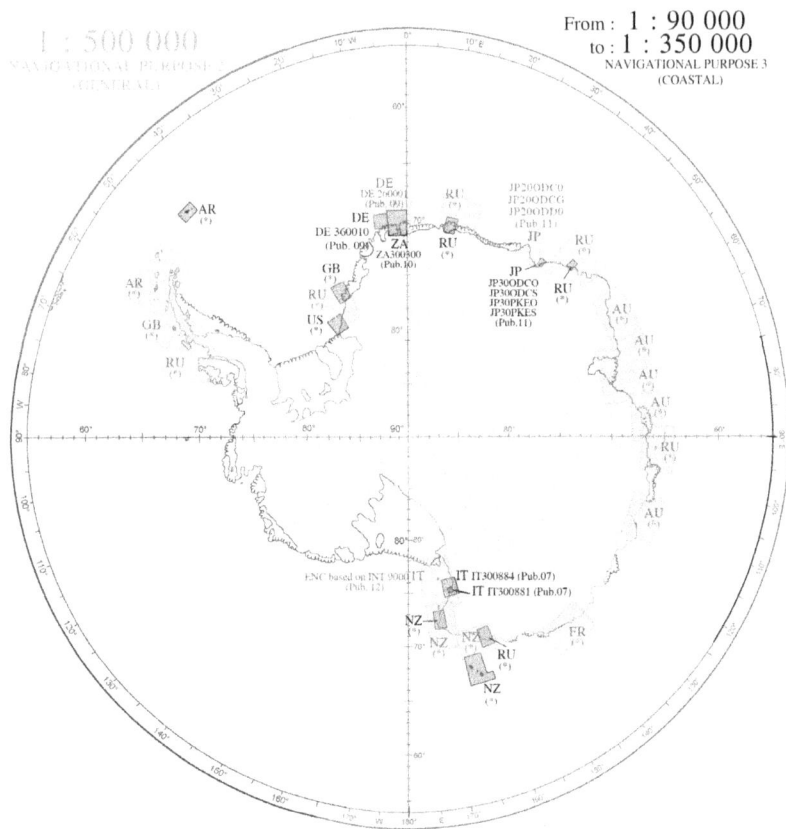

(*) Not yet published

STATUS OF ENC PRODUCTION IN ANTARCTICA (3 of 3)
MEDIUM-SCALE «COASTAL» ENCs
(based on the medium-scale INT Chart Series)

Antarctic Peninsula

From :1 : 90 000
to : 1 : 350 000
NAVIGATIONAL PURPOSE 3
(COASTAL)

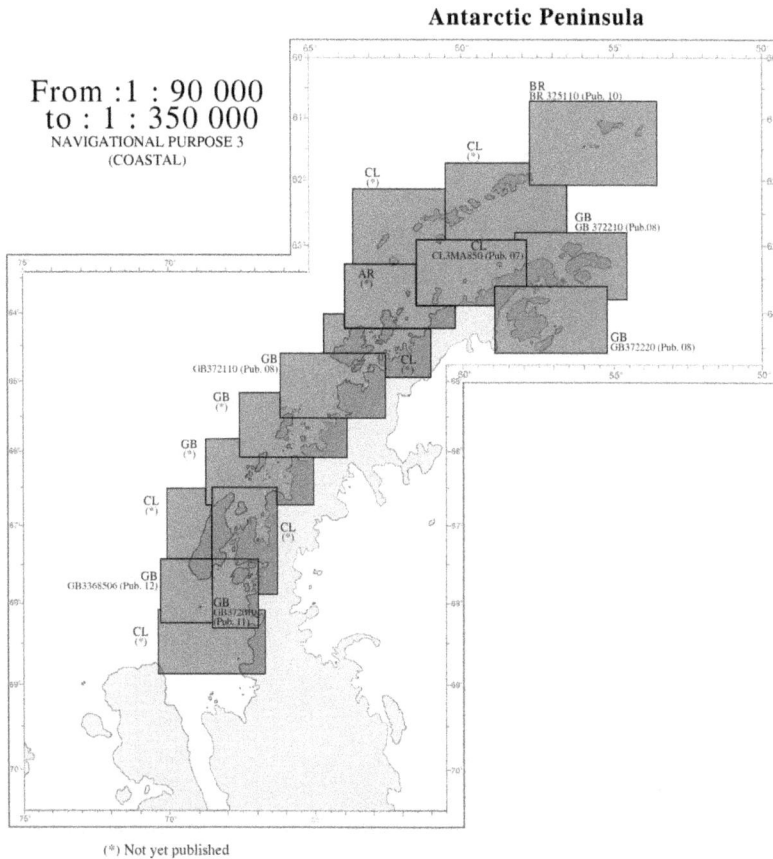

(*) Not yet published

Note: Additionally, 25 large-scale ENCs have been published by Australia (3 ENCs), Brazil (2 ENCs), Chile (3 ENCs), France (3 ENCs), Italy (1 ENC), Japan (6 ENCs), United Kingdom (6 ENCs) and USA (1 ENC).

Report of the Antarctic and Southern Ocean Coalition

1. *Introduction*

ASOC is pleased to be in Australia for the Antarctic Treaty Consultative Meeting. This report briefly describes ASOC's work over the past year, and outlines some key issues for this ATCM.

ASOC's Secretariat is in Washington DC, USA and its website is http://www.asoc.org). ASOC has 20 full member groups in 8 countries and supporting groups in those and several other countries. ASOC campaigns are carried out by teams of experts in Argentina, Australia, Brazil, Chile, France, Japan, The Netherlands, New Zealand, Norway, South Africa, South Korea, Spain, Russia, Ukraine, UK and USA.

2. *ASOC Intersessional Activities Since XXXIV ATCM*

Since XXXIV ATCM ASOC and its member groups' representatives participated in intersessional discussions in the ATCM and CEP fora, monitoring all ICGs and contributing actively to the discussions. In addition, ASOC and member group representatives attended the:

- IWC Commission meeting (St. Helier, Jersey July 11-14, 2011).
- Sixth Meeting of ACAP's Advisory Committee and working group meetings (Guayaquil, Ecuador August 25-September 2, 2011.
- CCAMLR MPA Workshop (Brest, France August 29-September 2, 2011).
- Polar Code workshop hosted by the IMO (Cambridge, UK September 27-30, 2011).
- CCAMLR's 30th Meeting, introducing papers on krill management, Marine Protected Areas and the Ross Sea marine reserve, IUU fishing, and impacts of climate change. (Hobart, Australia October 24-November 4, 2011
- Willem Barentsz Polar Institute Symposium (Utrecht, The Netherlands, December 14, 2011)
- International Maritime Organization meetings, including the 62nd and 63rd Marine Environment Protection Committee sessions, the 56th session of the Ship Design and Equipment sub-committee and a Polar Code Hazard Identification Workshop.
- Southern Ocean Whales Symposium (Puerto Varas, Chile March 27-29, 2012).
- Fourth Session of the Meeting of the Parties to ACAP (Lima, Peru April 23-27, 2012.
- Workshop on identification of priority areas for MPA designations in domain No. 1,- the Antarctic Peninsula and the Scotia Sea (Valparaíso, Chile May 28-June 1, 2012)

3. *Information Papers for XXXV ATCM*

ASOC has introduced 11 Information Papers, which contain recommendations for the ATCM and CEP that will help achieve more effective environmental protection and conservation of Antarctica:

Annex V Inviolate and Reference Areas: Current Management Practices (IP 49). Setting aside inviolate areas to preserve reference areas for future research is a tool specifically called for in Annex V of the Protocol but it is under-used, with inviolate areas covering only a very small proportion of the Treaty area. The designation of inviolate areas of significant size will provide reference sites that remain pristine and available for different fields of scientific interest in the future and contribute to protection of Antarctica's wilderness values.

Antarctic Ocean Legacy: A Marine Reserve for the Ross Sea (IP 50) summarises this Antarctic Ocean Alliance (AOA) report). The report, appended to this IP, describes AOA's proposal and the rationale for designation.

Data Sources for Mapping the Human Footprint in Antarctica (IP 52). The first step in constructing a model of the human footprint in Antarctica and the Southern Ocean is to compile data from the different information repositories in a common format. This would help to fulfill the CEP's obligation to advise the ATCM on the state of the Antarctic environment and facilitate Treaty Parties and CCAMLR Members taking coherent steps through time to limit the human footprint.

Antarctic Treaty System Follow-up to Vessel Incidents in Antarctic Waters (IP 53) undertakes a preliminary assessment of reporting following vessel incidents. It identifies shortcomings in the current system and recommends that the ATCM and CCAMLR address these as a matter of urgency. Annex 1 provides a list of incidents in Antarctic waters in the past 6 years involving cruise ships, fishing vessels and yachts.

Implications of Antarctic krill fishing in ASMA No.1 - Admiralty Bay (IP 54) reviews the cooperation framework between the ATCM and CCAMLR in the light of krill fishing that took place that is not envisioned in the Management Plan. The paper offers a series of recommendations to the CEP, ATCM and CCAMLR to prevent future such events.

Key Issues on a Strategic Approach to Review Tourism Policies (IP 55) concludes that increased supervision of tourism, through inspections or other means, is necessary to match the scale of this activity. Some aspects of tourism, particularly expansion, diversification and new site occupation, should be addressed in a proactive manner through legally binding regulation. Identifying tourism impacts requires additional monitoring efforts. Failing to address these issues in a timely manner will jeopardize the values the Protocol seeks to protect.

Progress on the Development of a Mandatory Polar Code (IP 56) provides an update on development of the Polar Code by the International Maritime Organization. It highlights areas where further work is required, identifies the next steps towards completion of the Code, and raises concerns about the possible minimal impact of the Code on Antarctic vessels if there is insufficient leadership by Antarctic Treaty states at the IMO. It recommends that Antarctic Treaty Parties ensure that the Code includes an Environmental Protection Chapter, is applied to both new and existing vessels, and requires polar class standards for all vessels likely to encounter ice.

Repair or Remediation of Environmental Damage (IP 57) reviews several key issues associated with the repair and remediation of environmental damage. The paper concludes that there is a general understanding of what constitutes environmental damage in Antarctica, that repairing or remediation of environmental damage should be carried out to the extent possible, and that at minimum assessment and monitoring of damage and suitable reporting should be done.

Earth Hour Antarctica 2013 (IP 58). WWF's Earth Hour is the world's largest environmental initiative in which people, businesses and governments around the world turn out lights for one hour to take a stand against climate change and show that everyone can act to change the world they live in. ASOC, Australia and the UK propose a coordinated continent–wide switch off of all non-essential lights at Antarctic research stations for Earth Hour on March 30, 2013, within operational and safety constraints.

Review of the Implementation of the Madrid Protocol: Inspections by Parties (Article 14) (IP 59). This joint paper with UNEP reviews the practice of inspections undertaken by Parties carried out under Article 14 of the Madrid Protocol. Fourteen inspections have been conducted since 1998, of 83 different facilities or sites. Of the 101 facilities on the COMNAP list, 56 (55%) have been inspected and 45 (45%) have never been inspected. Seven vessels, of which six were tourist vessels, were inspected during the same period.

Antarctic Ocean Legacy: A Vision for Circumpolar Protection (IP 90). In October 2011 the AOA proposed the creation of a network of marine protected areas and no-take marine reserves in 19 specific areas in the Southern Ocean around Antarctica. The report, attached to this IP, elaborates that vision. The report covers areas that collectively capture a wide, representative range of habitats and ecosystems, including seafloor and pelagic ecoregions, different environmental types, rare and unusual biological features, and areas critical for ecosystem and species protection.

4. *Other Important Issues for XXXV ATCM*

- **Climate change:** It is imperative for the ATCM to inform the rest of the world about the effects of what is happening in Antarctica and its implications for the global climate system, and to do more to reduce the impacts of its activities in the Antarctic.

- **Annex VI on Liability Arising from Environmental Emergencies:** Bringing this important Annex into force as rapidly as possible should be a high priority. ASOC urges all Parties to redouble their efforts over the next year to solve the remaining implementation problems, so that Annex VI can be ratified and enter into force as quickly as possible.

- **Biological prospecting:** ASOC supports a framework that includes more transparent sharing of data and information by Parties, based on full compliance with Resolution 9 (2009). ASOC urges the Parties to resume substantive discussion of bio-prospecting based on the information flowing from Treaty and Protocol information sharing requiring requirements as well as the data and information provided by the UN University, the Belgian database, and SCAR's reports.

- **Strategic planning:** ASOC supports the development of a multiyear strategic plan for the ATCM, which will help Parties in managing human activities sustainably over the longer term.

- **Search and Rescue:** Improving search and rescue coordination and capacity, including the development of a real-time information exchange communications system, should be an important priority for the Parties.

- **Sub-glacial lakes:** ASOC continues to be concerned about the fate of pristine Lake Vostok, and urges Parties to discuss the activities carried out in the past year in the attempt to penetrate the lake, and the next steps, with a view to minimizing risks to the lake's ecosystem as well as providing lessons for exploring other sub-glacial lakes in Antarctica.

5. *Concluding Remarks*

Antarctica is facing many pressures from global climate change and a wide range of human activities. ASOC looks forward to the ATCPs having the vision and taking concrete actions in Hobart that will help protect Antarctica's ecosystems and intrinsic values over the longer term.

PART IV

Additional Documents from XXXV ATCM

1. Additional Documents

Abstract of SCAR Lecture: "Aliens in Antarctica"

One of the primary goals of the Scientific Committee for Antarctic Research (SCAR) is to co-ordinate and facilitate international Antarctic research that will contribute to conservation and management of the region. Two recent examples highlight the recent success that SCAR has had in achieving this goal.

The first is the Aliens in Antarctic program, which was initiated in 2007-08 as an International Polar Year Program and culminated in 2012 with a highly publicised, continent-wide risk assessment of the establishment of non-native species. The Aliens in Antarctica program was an international collaboration that involved over 20 nations, and had the support of both the Council of Managers of National Antarctic Programs (COMNAP) and the International Association of Antarctica Tour Operators (IATTO). In this study, numbers of landings made by each visitor class was obtained, the mean number of seeds was calculated, the most likely pathways were determined and the likelihood of propagules establishing was quantified. Using this information together with a measure of the environmental suitability of the receiving environment allowed the continent-wide risk assessment to be undertaken. This was the first risk assessment of this nature to encompass an entire continent. Furthermore, much of the data and associated recommendations from the Aliens in Antarctic project have been instrumental in developing, refining and improving biosecurity protocols for both scientists and tourists visiting Antarctica.

The second example of successful SCAR coordinated research is the recent bioregionalisation analyses of terrestrial Antarctica. This study began in 2008 and culminated in the recent publication of the paper 'Conservation Biogeography of the Antarctic'. In this study, an international team of researchers utilised existing spatial frameworks together with tens of thousands of biodiversity records, to delineate the terrestrial biodiversity of Antarctica into 15 bioregions or Antarctic Conservation Biogeographic Regions. These areas not only have important implications for the consideration of movement within Antarctica, but also provide a framework for assessment and development of the Antarctic Specially Protected Area network.

These programs were discussed in detail in the SCAR lecture, and the implications of them were described, particularly in the context of developing Antarctic policies. The importance of feeding good, reliable, science into such policy development was emphasised.

2. List of Documents

2. List of Documents

Working Papers								
Number	**Ag. Items**	**Title**	**Submitted By**	**E**	**F**	**R**	**S**	**Attachments**
WP001	ATCM 5	Antarctic Treaty Consultative Meeting Communiqué	Australia					
WP002	CEP 7a	Revised Management Plan for Antarctic Specially Protected Area (ASPA) No. 151 Lions Rump, King George Island, South Shetland Islands	Poland					ASPA 151 Map 1 ASPA 151 Map 2 ASPA 151 Map 3 ASPA 151 Map 4 ASPA 151 Revised Management Plan
WP003	CEP 7a	Revised Management Plan for Antarctic Specially Protected Area (ASPA) No. 128 Western Shore of Admiralty Bay, King George Island, South Shetland Islands	Poland					ASPA 128 Map 1 ASPA 128 Map 2 ASPA 128 Revised Management Plan
WP004	ATCM 10	The Assessment of Land-Based Activities in Antarctica	United Kingdom					
WP005	CEP 8a	Outcomes of the International Polar Year Programme: Aliens in Antarctica	SCAR					Continent-wide risk assessment for the establishment of nonindigenous species in Antarctica
WP006	CEP 8a	Reducing the risk of inadvertent non-native species introductions associated with fresh fruit and vegetable importation to Antarctica	SCAR					
WP007	CEP 9	Remote sensing for monitoring Antarctic Specially Protected Areas: use of multispectral and hyperspectral data for monitoring Antarctic vegetation	United Kingdom					
WP008	CEP 7a	Revision of the Management Plan for Antarctic Specially Protected Area (ASPA) No. 129 Rothera Point, Adelaide Island	United Kingdom					ASPA 129 Revised Management Plan
WP009	CEP 7a	Revision of the Management Plan for Antarctic Specially Protected Area (ASPA) No. 109 Moe Island, South Orkney Islands	United Kingdom					ASPA 109 Revised Management Plan
WP010	CEP 7a	Revision of the Management Plan for Antarctic Specially Protected Area (ASPA) No. 111 Southern Powell Island and adjacent islands, South Orkney Islands	United Kingdom					ASPA 111 Revised Management Plan
WP011	CEP 7a	Revision of the Management Plan for Antarctic Specially Protected Area (ASPA) No. 115 Lagotellerie Island, Marguerite Bay, Graham Land	United Kingdom					ASPA 115 Revised Management Plan
WP012	CEP 7a	Revision of the Management Plan for Antarctic Specially Protected Area (ASPA) No. 110 Lynch Island, South Orkney Islands	United Kingdom					ASPA 110 Revised Management Plan
WP013	ATCM 10	Understanding Risk to National Antarctic Program Operations and Personnel in Coastal Antarctica from Tsunami Events	COMNAP SCAR					COMNAP Preliminary Research Report: Understanding Risk to National Antarctic Program Operations and Personnel in Coastal Antarctica from Tsunami Events.

Working Papers								
Number	Ag. Items	Title	Submitted By	E	F	R	S	Attachments
WP014	CEP 7a	Subsidiary Group on Management Plans -- Report on 2011/12 Intersessional Work	Australia					ASPA 140 Revised Management Plan
WP015	CEP 7c	Site Guidelines for D'Hainaut Island, Mikkelsen Harbour, Trinity Island	United Kingdom Argentina United States					Site Guidelines for D'Hainaut Island
WP016	CEP 7c	Site Guidelines for Port Charcot, Booth Island	United Kingdom Argentina France Ukraine United States					Site Guidelines for Port Charcot
WP017 rev.1	ATCM 11	Compiling yacht guidelines to complement safety standards of ship traffic around Antarctica	Germany United Kingdom United States					Checklist of yacht specific items for preparing safe Antarctic voyages Contact details of national competent authorities Yachting guidelines for Antarctic cruises
WP018	CEP 9	Penguin monitoring via remote sensing	Germany					
WP019	CEP 7a	The proposed designation of an Antarctic Specially Protected Area (ASPA) for high altitude geothermal areas of the Ross Sea region	New Zealand					Draft ASPA YYY Management Plan
WP020	CEP 9	Establishing a monitoring programme to assess changes in vegetation at two Antarctic Specially Protected Areas	New Zealand					
WP021	CEP 12	An Antarctic Clean-Up Manual	Australia United Kingdom					Committee for Environmental Protection Clean-Up Manual
WP022	CEP 6b	Environmental Aspects and Impacts of Tourism and Non-governmental Activities in Antarctica	New Zealand					
WP023 rev.1	CEP 7f	Antarctic Conservation Biogeographic Regions	Australia New Zealand SCAR					Antarctic Conservation Biogeographic Regions
WP024	ATCM 6	A guide for Secretariat systems and information sources	Australia					
WP025 rev.1	CEP 8a	Guidelines to minimise the risks of non-native species and disease associated with Antarctic hydroponics facilities	Australia France					
WP026	CEP 12	Environmental issues related to the practicality of repair or remediation of environmental damage	Australia					
WP027 rev.1	ATCM 11	Report of the Intersessional Contact Group 'Outstanding Questions' on Antarctic Tourism	Netherlands					
WP028	ATCM 5	Jurisdiction in Antarctica (updated version)	France					
WP029	ATCM 17	Improving the Functioning of the Electronic Information Exchange	France					

Working Papers								
Number	**Ag. Items**	**Title**	**Submitted By**	**E**	**F**	**R**	**S**	**Attachments**
		System (EIES) for Non-Governmental Activities in Antarctica (Updated version)						
WP030	ATCM 7	The Development of a Multi-Year Strategic Work Plan for the Antarctic Treaty Consultative Meeting	Australia Belgium Netherlands New Zealand Norway South Africa Sweden United Kingdom United States	⬚	⬚	⬚	⬚	Multi-Year Strategic Work Plan - Format Multi-Year Strategic Work Plan - Principles
WP031	ATCM 5	Strengthening Support for the Protocol on Environmental Protection to the Antarctic Treaty	Australia France Spain	⬚	⬚	⬚	⬚	
WP032	ATCM 14	ATCM interests in international climate change discussions – options for enhanced engagement	Australia	⬚	⬚	⬚	⬚	
WP033	CEP 5	RACER1 - 'Rapid Assessment of Circum-Arctic Ecosystem Resilience': a tool from the Arctic to assess ecosystem resilience and areas of conservation importance, and its possible application to Antarctica	**United Kingdom** Norway	⬚	⬚	⬚	⬚	
WP034	CEP 6b	Technology for investigating the water layer of subglacial Lake Vostok through the ice borehole 5G at the Russian Antarctic Vostok station	Russian Federation	⬚	⬚	⬚	⬚	
WP035	CEP 7f	Proposals on preparation of revised management plans of Antarctic Specially Protected and Antarctic Specially Managed Areas	Russian Federation	⬚	⬚	⬚	⬚	
WP036	CEP 7b	Proposal on revision of Historic Sites and Monuments under management of the Russian Federation	Russian Federation	⬚	⬚	⬚	⬚	
WP037	ATCM 11	Coastal Camping Considerations	**United States** Norway	⬚	⬚	⬚	⬚	
WP038	CEP 7f	Developing Protection for a Geothermal Area; Volcanic Ice Caves at Mount Erebus, Ross Island	**United States** New Zealand	⬚	⬚	⬚	⬚	
WP039	ATCM 14	Invitation to the WMO	Norway United Kingdom	⬚	⬚	⬚	⬚	
WP040	CEP 7a	Proposal for a new Antarctic Specially Protected Area at Cape Washington and Silverfish Bay Terra Nova Bay, Ross Sea	Italy United States	⬚	⬚	⬚	⬚	ASPA XYZ Cape Washington & Silverfish Bay Management Plan ASPA XYZ Cape Washington & Silverfish Bay Map 1 ASPA XYZ Cape Washington & Silverfish Bay Map 2
WP041	CEP 7a	Proposal for a new Antarctic Specially Protected Area at Taylor Glacier and Blood Falls, Taylor Valley, McMurdo Dry Valleys Victoria Land	United States	⬚	⬚	⬚	⬚	ASPA 172 Lower Taylor Glacier and Blood Falls Management Plan ASPA 172 Lower Taylor Glacier and Blood Falls Map 1

Working Papers								
Number	Ag. Items	Title	Submitted By	E	F	R	S	Attachments
								ASPA 172 Lower Taylor Glacier and Blood Falls Map 2
WP042	CEP 7a	Review of the Management Plan for ASMA No 4: Deception Island	Argentina Chile Norway Spain United Kingdom United States					ASMA 4 Revised Management Plan
WP043	ATCM 11	Final Report of the Intersessional Contact Group on Supervision of Antarctic Tourism	Argentina					Attachment: Checklist for Visitor's In-field Activities
WP044	CEP 7a	Revised Management Plan for Antarctic Specially Protected Area No. 132 (Potter Peninsula)	Argentina					Revised Management Plan for ASPA 132
WP045	CEP 7c	Site Guidelines for Visitors Pendulum Cove, Deception Island, South Shetland Islands	Argentina Chile Norway Spain United Kingdom United States					Site Guidelines for Pendulum Cove
WP046	CEP 7b	Final Report of the Informal Discussions on Historic Sites and Monuments	Argentina					
WP047	ATCM 7	Prioritisation of Issues in an ATCM Multi-Year Strategic Work Plan	New Zealand					
WP048	ATCM 11	Repeat Unauthorised Commercial Expedition: Nilaya/Berserk	New Zealand					
WP049	ATCM 10	ATCM Response to CCAMLR Fishing Vessel Incidents	New Zealand					
WP050	CEP 7d	Concepts for Wilderness protection in Antarctica using tools in the Protocol	New Zealand Netherlands					
WP051	ATCM 10	Coordination of Maritime and Aeronautical Search and Rescue (SAR) – Proposal for Considering Means to Improve Antarctic SAR Coordination	United States					
WP052	CEP 7a	Revision of Management Plan for Antarctic Specially Protected Area No. 133 Harmony Point	Argentina Chile					ASPA 133 Revised Management Plan
WP053	CEP 6b	Comandante Ferraz Station: Proposed Plan for the Demolition and Construction of Antarctic Emergency Modules	Brazil					
WP054	CEP 7a	Revised Management Plan for Antarctic Specially Protected Area No. 145, Port Foster, Deception Island, South Shetland Islands	Chile					Map 1 Revised Management Plan for ASPA 145
WP055	CEP 9	New records of the Presence of Human Associated Microorganisms in the Antarctic Marine Environment	Chile					
WP056 rev.1	CEP 7b	Proposed Modification to Historic Site N° 37	Chile					
WP057	CEP 3	Antarctic Environments Portal	New Zealand Australia					

Working Papers								
Number	**Ag. Items**	**Title**	**Submitted By**	**E**	**F**	**R**	**S**	**Attachments**
			SCAR					
WP058	CEP 7a	Management Plan for Antarctic Specially Protected Area No. 112, Coppermine Peninsula, Robert Island, South Shetland Islands	Chile					ASPA 112 Revised Management Plan ASPA 112 Table toponyms in four languages
WP059	CEP 7c	Revised Visited Site Guidelines: Aitcho Islands	Ecuador Spain					Mapa Isla Barrientos Revised Visited Site Guidelines: Aitcho Islands
WP060	CEP 7a	Management Plan for Specially Protected Area No. 146, South Bay, Doumer Island, Palmer Archipelago	Chile					Revised Management Plan for ASPA 146
WP061	CEP 7a	Management Plan for Antarctic Specially Protected Area No. 144, Chile Bay (Discovery Bay), Greenwich Island, South Shetland Islands	Chile					Revised Management Plan for ASPA 144
WP062	CEP 12	Repair or Remediation of Environmental Damage: COMNAP report on its experience	COMNAP					List of Papers
WP063	ATCM 17	Exchange of real time information of the maritime traffic in Antarctica	Chile					
WP064	ATCM 5	Establishing a Working Group on Antarctic Cooperation	Chile					

Information Papers								
Number	Ag. Items	Title	Submitted By	E	F	R	S	Attachments
IP001	ATCM 4 CEP 11	The Scientific Committee on Antarctic Research (SCAR) Annual Report 2011/12	SCAR	⌞	⌞	⌞	⌞	
IP002	ATCM 13 CEP 9	The Southern Ocean Observing System (SOOS)	SCAR	⌞				
IP003	ATCM 4 CEP 11	The Annual Report for 2011 of the Council of Managers of National Antarctic Programs (COMNAP)	COMNAP	⌞	⌞	⌞	⌞	
IP004	ATCM 14	Management Implications of a Changing Antarctica - COMNAP Workshop	COMNAP	⌞	⌞	⌞	⌞	
IP005	ATCM 4	Report Submitted to Antarctic Treaty Consultative Meeting XXXV by the Depositary Government for the Convention for the Conservation of Antarctic Seals in Accordance with Recommendation XIII-2, Paragraph 2(D)	United Kingdom	⌞	⌞	⌞	⌞	
IP006	CEP 12	Topic Summary: CEP Discussions on Clean-Up	Australia	⌞	⌞	⌞	⌞	
IP007	ATCM 15	Review of COMNAP Working Papers and Information Papers presented to the ATCM 1988 - 2011	COMNAP	⌞	⌞	⌞	⌞	Attachments 1 and 2: Lists of COMNAP papers 1988-2011
IP008	ATCM 5	Contemporary opportunities for weather and related Polar Observations, Research and Services - leading to improved mitigation of risk	WMO	⌞				
IP009 rev.1	ATCM 4	Report of the Depositary Government for the Convention on the Conservation of Antarctic Marine Living Resources (CCAMLR)	Australia	⌞	⌞	⌞	⌞	
IP010	ATCM 4	Report of the Depositary Government for the Agreement on the Conservation of Albatrosses and Petrels (ACAP)	Australia	⌞	⌞	⌞	⌞	
IP011	ATCM 7	Topic Summary: The Development of a Multi-Year Strategic Work Plan for the Antarctic Treaty Consultative Meeting	Australia	⌞	⌞	⌞	⌞	
IP012	ATCM 7	Examples to illustrate the proposed application of a Multi-Year Strategic Work Plan	Australia	⌞	⌞	⌞	⌞	
IP013	CEP 8a	Colonisation status of the non-native grass Poa pratensis at Cierva Point, Danco Coast, Antarctic Peninsula	Spain Argentina United Kingdom	⌞				
IP014	CEP 7b	Brief Introduction of the Maintenance and Conservation Project of No.1 Building at Great Wall Station	China	⌞				
IP015	ATCM 10	The Crash and Rescue of Chinese Ka-32 Helicopter	China	⌞				

Information Papers

Number	Ag. Items	Title	Submitted By	E	F	R	S	Attachments
IP016	ATCM 7	Prioritisation of ATCM Issues: Illustrative Table	New Zealand	📄	📄	📄	📄	
IP017	ATCM 10	Search and Rescue Incidents in the 2011/12 Season: FV SPARTA and FV JEONG WOO 2	New Zealand	📄	📄	📄	📄	
IP018	ATCM 13	Contribuciones chilenas al conocimiento científico de la Antártica: Expedición 2011/12	Chile				📄	
IP019	ATCM 4	Report of the Depositary Government of the Antarctic Treaty and its Protocol in accordance with Recommendation XIII-2	United States	📄	📄	📄	📄	Antarctic Treaty Status table List of Recommendations/Measures and their approvals Protocol Status table
IP020	CEP 8c	Evaluation of the "Strategic assessment of the risk posed to marine mammals by the use of airguns in the Antarctic Treaty area"	Germany	📄				
IP021	ATCM 13 CEP 8c	Anthropogenic Sound in the Southern Ocean: an Update	SCAR	📄				
IP022	ATCM 18	Report on the bioprospecting activities carried out by Belgian scientists since 1998	Belgium	📄				
IP023	CEP 6b	Final Comprehensive Environmental Evaluation (CEE) for the Proposed Construction and Operation of the Jang Bogo Station, Terra Nova Bay, Antarctica	Korea (ROK)	📄				
IP024	CEP 7a	Management Report of Narębski Point (ASPA 171) and Ardley Island (ASPA 150) during the 2011/2012 period	Korea (ROK)	📄				
IP025	CEP 12	Examples to illustrate key environmental issues related to the practicality of repair or remediation of environmental damage	Australia	📄				
IP026	CEP 7f	Analyses of the Antarctic protected areas system using spatial information	Australia	📄				
IP027	ATCM 4	Report by the CCAMLR Observer to the Thirty-Fifth Antarctic Treaty Consultative Meeting	CCAMLR	📄	📄	📄	📄	
IP028	CEP 11	Report by the SC-CAMLR Observer to the Fifteenth Meeting of the Committee for Environmental Protection	CCAMLR	📄	📄	📄	📄	
IP029	CEP 8a	Colonisation status of known non-native species in the Antarctic terrestrial environment (updated 2012)	United Kingdom	📄				
IP030	CEP 6b	The Final Comprehensive Environmental Evaluation (CEE) for the Proposed Exploration of Subglacial Lake Ellsworth, Antarctica	United Kingdom	📄				Proposed Exploration of Subglacial Lake Ellsworth, Antarctica - Final Comprehensive Environmental Evaluation

Information Papers

Number	Ag. Items	Title	Submitted By	E	F	R	S	Attachments
IP031	ATCM 14 CEP 5	Best Practice for Energy Management – Guidance and Recommendations	COMNAP	⚲				Survey questions and summary of results
IP032	ATCM 10 CEP 13	COMNAP Survey of National Antarctic Programs on Oil Spill Contingency Planning	COMNAP	⚲				
IP033	CEP 6b	Environmental Aspects and Impacts of Tourism and Non-governmental Activities in Antarctica	New Zealand	⚲				CEP Tourism Study Tourism and Non-governmental Activities in the Antarctic: Environmental Aspects and Impacts Tourism Study Supporting Tables and Data Sets
IP034	CEP 7e	Using ASMAs and ASPAs when necessary to complement CCAMLR MPAs	IUCN	⚲				
IP035	ATCM 13 CEP 8c	Antarctic Conservation for the 21st Century: Background, progress, and future directions	SCAR IUCN New Zealand	⚲				
IP036	ATCM 4	Report of the International Association of Antarctica Tour Operators 2011-12	IAATO	⚲	⚲	⚲	⚲	
IP037	ATCM 11 CEP 7c	Report on IAATO Operator use of Antarctic Peninsula Landing Sites and ATCM Visitor Site Guidelines, 2011-2012 Season	IAATO	⚲				
IP038	ATCM 11 CEP 7a	Establishing IAATO Safety Advisories	IAATO	⚲				
IP039	ATCM 11	IAATO Overview of Antarctic Tourism: 2011-12 Season and Preliminary Estimates for 2012-13 Season	IAATO	⚲				
IP040 rev.1	ATCM 13 CEP 9	SCAR Products available to support the deliberations of the ATCM	SCAR	⚲				
IP041	CEP 6b	Starting a feasibility study for the realization of a gravel runway near Mario Zucchelli Station	Italy	⚲				
IP042	ATCM 11	Data Collection and Reporting on Yachting Activity in Antarctica in 2011-12	United Kingdom IAATO	⚲				
IP043	CEP 6b	Establishment and Operation of New Indian Research Station "Bharati" at Larsemann Hills	India	⚲				
IP044	ATCM 16 CEP 5	Communicating the Science of Climate Change	SCAR	⚲				
IP045	ATCM 14 CEP 5	Antarctic Climate Change and the Environment: an Update	SCAR	⚲				
IP046	CEP 9	Pilot study on monitoring climate-induced changes in penguin colonies in the Antarctic using satellite images	Germany	⚲				

Information Papers

Number	Ag. Items	Title	Submitted By	E	F	R	S	Attachments
IP047	ATCM 12 CEP 10	United States-Russian Federation Report of Inspection	United States Russian Federation					U.S.-Russian Federation Report of Inspection
IP048	ATCM 13	Japan's Antarctic Research Highlights in 2011–2012	Japan					
IP049	CEP 7f	Annex V Inviolate and Reference Areas: Current Management Practices	ASOC					
IP050	CEP 7e	Antarctic Ocean Legacy: A Marine Reserve for the Ross Sea	ASOC					Report "Antarctic Ocean Legacy: A Marine Reserve for the Ross Sea"
IP051	CEP 7e	Antarctic Ocean Legacy: A Vision for Circumpolar Protection	ASOC					Report "Antarctic Ocean Legacy: A Vision for Circumpolar Protection"
IP052	CEP 7d	Data Sources for Mapping the Human Footprint in Antarctica	ASOC					
IP053	ATCM 10 CEP 9	Follow-up to Vessel Incidents in Antarctic Waters	ASOC					
IP054	CEP 7e	Implications of Antarctic krill fishing in ASMA No. 1 - Admiralty Bay	ASOC					
IP055	ATCM 11	Key Issues for a Strategic Approach to Review Tourism Policies	ASOC					
IP056	ATCM 10	Progress on the Development of a Mandatory Polar Code	ASOC					
IP057	CEP 12	Repair or Remediation of Environmental Damage	ASOC					
IP058 rev.1	CEP 5	Earth Hour Antarctica (2013)	ASOC Australia United Kingdom					
IP059	ATCM 12 CEP 10	Review of the Implementation of the Madrid Protocol: Inspections by Parties (Article 14)	UNEP ASOC					
IP060	CEP 7d	Further information about wilderness protection in Antarctica and use of tools in the Protocol	New Zealand Netherlands					
IP061	CEP 7a	Report of the Larsemann Hills Antarctic Specially Managed Area (ASMA) Management Group	Australia China India Romania Russian Federation					
IP062	ATCM 15	The Dirck Gerritsz Laboratory at the UK's Rothera Research Station	Netherlands United Kingdom					
IP063	ATCM 18	An Update on Biological Prospecting in Antarctica and Recent Policy Developments at the International Level	Netherlands Belgium Finland Sweden UNEP					
IP064	ATCM	Brazilian Yacht Accident	Brazil					

Information Papers

Number	Ag. Items	Title	Submitted By	E	F	R	S	Attachments
	10							
IP065	ATCM 10	Comandante Ferraz Station: Oil Barge Incident	Brazil	🔒				
IP066	CEP 7a	Working Plan Proposal for the Review of the Admiralty Bay Antarctic Specially Managed Area Management Plan (ASMA No. 1)	Brazil	🔒				
IP067	ATCM 11	'Outstanding Questions' on Antarctic Tourism: An Inventory and Discussion	Netherlands	🔒				
IP068	CEP 7e	Progress of Ukraine on Designation of Broad-scale Management System in the Vernadsky Station Area	Ukraine	🔒		🔒		
IP069	ATCM 15	Proyecto para que la Estación Científica Ecuatoriana "Pedro Vicente Maldonado", tenga el carácter de permanente	Ecuador				🔒	
IP070	ATCM 4	Report by the International Hydrographic Organization (IHO) on "Cooperation in hydrographic surveying and charting of Antarctic waters"	IHO	🔒	🔒	🔒	🔒	
IP071	ATCM 9	On preparation for ratification of Annex VI of the Protocol on Environmental Protection to the Antarctic Treaty	Russian Federation	🔒		🔒		
IP072	ATCM 11	Activity of the international air program DROMLAN and its interaction with non-governmental activity in the Antarctic	Russian Federation	🔒		🔒		
IP073	ATCM 10	Russian experience of applying automatic aids to approach of heavy transport aircraft at the Antarctic aerodromes using satellite navigation systems	Russian Federation	🔒		🔒		
IP074	CEP 6b	Results of Russian activity for penetrating subglacial Lake Vostok in the season 2011–12	Russian Federation	🔒		🔒		
IP075	ATCM 11	Relation of activities performed by Chile regarding Nilaya / berserk yacht situation	Chile	🔒			🔒	
IP076	CEP 9	Antarctic Environmental Monitoring Centre	Chile	🔒			🔒	
IP077	ATCM 10	Maritime support tasks performed by Chile in the Antarctic area during season 2011/2012	Chile	🔒			🔒	
IP078	CEP 7a	Amundsen-Scott South Pole Station. South Pole Antarctica Specially Managed Area (ASMA No. 5) 2012 Management Report	United States	🔒				
IP079	ATCM 10	Apoyo aéreos efectuados por Chile en la Antártica durante los años 2011 y 2012	Chile				🔒	
IP080	CEP 7e	Report of The CEP Observer To The CCAMLR Workshop On	CCAMLR	🔒				

Information Papers								
Number	Ag. Items	Title	Submitted By	E	F	R	S	Attachments
		Marine Protected Areas.Brest, France, 29 August to 2 September 2011						
IP081	ATCM 11	The Nilaya/Berserk Expedition	Norway	☑				
IP082	CEP 7a	Deception Island Specially Managed Area (ASMA) Management Group Report	Argentina Chile Norway Spain United Kingdom United States	☑				
IP083	ATCM 13	Medical scientific cooperation between Romania and UK within the SCAR for the study of biometeorological human adaptation in a changing climate	Romania	☑				
IP084	ATCM 18	Management Plan for Romanian Biological Prospecting Activities in Antarctica	Romania	☑				
IP085	ATCM 4	Report of the Antarctic and Southern Ocean Coalition	ASOC	☑	☑	☑	☑	
IP086	ATCM 11	Areas of tourist interest in the Antarctic Peninsula and Orcadas del Sur Islands (South Orkney Islands) region. 2011/2012 austral summer season	Argentina	☑			☑	
IP087	ATCM 11	Antarctic tourism through Ushuaia. Comparison of the last four Austral summer seasons	Argentina	☑			☑	
IP088	ATCM 11	Report on Antarctic tourist flows and cruise ships operating in Ushuaia during the 2011/2012 austral summer season	Argentina	☑			☑	

Secretariat Papers								
Number	Ag. Items	Title	Submitted By	E	F	R	S	Attachments
SP001 rev.1	ATCM 1 CEP 1	ATCM XXXV and CEP XV Agenda and Schedule	ATS	🔒	🔒	🔒	🔒	
SP002 rev.1	ATCM 6	Secretariat Report 2011/12	ATS	🔒	🔒	🔒	🔒	Audited Financial Report 2010/11 Contributions Received by the Antarctic Treaty Secretariat 2011/12 Estimate of Income and Expenditures 2011/12
SP003 rev.1	ATCM 6	Secretariat Programme 2012/13	ATS	🔒	🔒	🔒	🔒	Contribution scale 2013/14 Provisional Statement 2011/12, Forecast 2012/13, Budget 2012/13, Forecast Budget 2013/14 Salaries Scale 2012/13 Secretariat Programme 2012/13
SP004	ATCM 6	Contributions Received by the Antarctic Treaty Secretariat 2009-2012	ATS	🔒	🔒	🔒	🔒	
SP005	ATCM 6	Five Years Forward Budget 2012 - 2017	ATS	🔒	🔒	🔒	🔒	Appendix 1: Scenario 1 Appendix 2: Scenario 2
SP006 rev.1	CEP 6b	Annual list of Initial Environmental Evaluations (IEE) and Comprehensive Environmental Evaluations (CEE) prepared between April 1st 2011 and March 31st 2012	ATS	🔒	🔒	🔒	🔒	
SP007	CEP 7a	Status of Antarctic Specially Protected Area and Antarctic Specially Managed Area Management Plans	ATS	🔒	🔒	🔒	🔒	
SP008	ATCM 14 CEP 5	Actions taken by the CEP and the ATCM on the ATME Recommendations on Climate Change	ATS	🔒	🔒	🔒	🔒	
SP009	ATCM 5	Report of the Intersessional Contact Group on Review of ATCM Recommendations on Operational Matters	ATS	🔒	🔒	🔒	🔒	Annex to Decision 1 (2012)
SP010	ATCM 17 CEP 4	Report on the Informal Contact Group on the improvement of the EIES and other Information Exchange Matters	ATS	🔒	🔒	🔒	🔒	
SP012	ATCM 1	Summary of Papers - Legal & Insitutional Working Group	ATS	🔒				
SP013	ATCM 11	Annotated Agenda and Summary of Papers Tourism Working Group	ATS	🔒				
SP014	ATCM 15	Operations WG - Summary of Papers	ATS	🔒				
SP015	CEP 1	CEP XV: Summary of Papers	ATS	🔒				Work of the CEP during the 2011-2012 intersession period
SP016	ATCM 10	Joint Session Operations WG and Tourism WG Summary of Papers	ATS	🔒				

Secretariat Papers								
Number	Ag. Items	Title	Submitted By	E	F	R	S	Attachments
SP017 rev.1	ATCM 19	ATCM XXXVI and CEP XVI - Preliminary Agenda and Draft Schedule	ATS					

Background Papers								
Number	Ag. Items	Title	Submitted By	E	F	R	S	Attachments
BP001	CEP 8a	Continent-wide risk assessment for the establishment of nonindigenous species in Antarctica	SCAR	♪				
BP002	ATCM 16	Estrategias para acercar la Antártica a los ciudadanos	Chile				♪	
BP003	ATCM 11 CEP 7c	Antarctic Site Inventory: 1994-2012	United States	♪				
BP004	ATCM 13	Report on Scientific Activity of Ukraine for 2011/2012 Season	Ukraine	♪				
BP005	ATCM 15	Renaming of an Argentine Antarctic Base	Argentina	♪			♪	
BP006	ATCM 13	La base Belgrano II, un punto aventajado para observaciones científicas en el extremo austral del Mar de Weddell	Argentina				♪	
BP007	ATCM 13	Evaluación institucional del Instituto Antártico Argentino	Argentina				♪	
BP008	ATCM 15	The Second Antarctic Expedition of Araon (2011/2012)	Korea (ROK)	♪				
BP009	ATCM 13	Scientific & Science-related Collaborations with Other Parties During 2011-2012	Korea (ROK)	♪				
BP010	CEP 9	Assessment of Environmental impacts arising from sewage discharge at Davis Station	Australia	♪				Marine Environment and Survey Design
BP011	CEP 12	Clean-up Techniques for Antarctica	Australia	♪				
BP012	CEP 12	Clean-up of a fuel spill near Lake Dingle, Vestfold Hills	Australia	♪				
BP013	CEP 12	Development of environmental quality standards for the management of contaminated sites in Antarctica	Australia	♪				
BP014	CEP 12	Assessment, monitoring and remediation of old Antarctic waste disposal sites: the Thala Valley example at Casey station	Australia	♪				
BP015	CEP 9	Summary information on improvements and modernizations done on Polish Antarctic Station "Arctowski"	Poland	♪				
BP016	ATCM 11	Natación en aguas antárticas	Chile				♪	
BP017	ATCM 14 CEP 5	Energy Efficiency and Carbon Reduction Initiatives	New Zealand	♪				
BP018	ATCM 9	Australia's progress on the implementation of Measure 4 (2004), Measure 1 (2005), and Measure 15 (2009)	Australia	♪				

Background Papers

Number	Ag. Items	Title	Submitted By	E	F	R	S	Attachments
BP019	ATCM 20	Minimising the environmental impacts of the 35th Antarctic Treaty Consultative Meeting	Australia	▣				
BP020	ATCM 16	Australia's Antarctic Centenary celebrations	Australia	▣				
BP021	ATCM 13	Icebreaker Oden and her Southern Ocean missions	Sweden	▣				
BP022	CEP 10	Measures Adopted at Maitri Station on the Recommendations of Recent Visit of Japanese Inspection Team	India	▣				
BP023	ATCM 16	A Hundred Years of the South Pole Conquest: events organized by Uruguay	Uruguay	▣			▣	
BP024	ATCM 16	Educational, cultural and outreach activities of the Uruguayan Antarctic Institute in 2011-2012	Uruguay	▣			▣	
BP025	ATCM 14	Energy Efficiency project in Antarctic Research Station Artigas	Uruguay	▣			▣	
BP026	ATCM 13	XI Meeting of Iberoamerican Antarctic Historians Playa Hermosa, Piriápolis-Uruguay – November 24 - 25th 2011	Uruguay	▣			▣	
BP027	ATCM 13	Actividades de investigación y proyectos científicos coordinados por el Instituto Antártico Uruguayo en la campaña 2011 - 2012	Uruguay				▣	
BP028	ATCM 15	Renovación del Parque de Tanques de combustible de la Base Científica Antártica Artigas (BCAA)	Uruguay				▣	
BP029	ATCM 15	Maintenance of the Scientific Station T/N Ruperto Elichiribehety, Hope Bay, Antarctica Peninsula	Uruguay	▣			▣	
BP030	ATCM 16	Re-Edición del "Acta Antártica Ecuatoriana", publicación científica oficial del Ecuador sobre investigación antártica	Ecuador				▣	
BP031	ATCM 16	II Concurso Intercolegial sobre Temas Antárticos, CITA2011	Ecuador				▣	
BP032	ATCM 16	Seminario Taller "Ecuador en la Antártida: Historia, Perspectivas y Proyecciones"	Ecuador				▣	
BP033	ATCM 13	Programa de cooperación binacional en asuntos antárticos "Ecuador-Venezuela"	Ecuador				▣	
BP034	ATCM 18	Paleo-ecología de las diatomeas en el Río Culebra y Puntas: Fort William y Hermosilla, Isla Greenwich (Islas Shetland del Sur)-Antártida y el comportamiento climático	Ecuador				▣	
BP035	ATCM 13	Biorremediación con microorganismos antárticos	Ecuador				▣	
BP036	CEP 6b	Resumen de la Auditoría Ambiental de Cumplimiento de la Estación Científica Ecuatoriana	Ecuador				▣	

Background Papers								
Number	Ag. Items	Title	Submitted By	E	F	R	S	Attachments
		Pedro Vicente Maldonado						
BP037	ATCM 13	Scientific results of Russian studies in the Antarctic in 2011	Russian Federation	⌐ 丸		⌐ 丸		
BP038	ATCM 15 CEP 12	Retiro de chatarra desde la base Presidente Eduardo Frei Montalva, isla Rey Jorge	Chile				⌐ 丸	
BP039	ATCM 13	Law-Racovita-Negoita Base. An example of cooperation in Antarctica	Romania	⌐ 丸				
BP040	ATCM 13	ERICON Aurora Borealis Icebreaker. A new era in the polar research	Romania	⌐ 丸				
BP041	CEP 7b	Antarctic Heritage Trust Conservation Update	New Zealand	⌐ 丸				
BP042	ATCM 13	Report on the Research Activities: Czech Research Station J. G. Mendel, James Ross Island, January - March 2012	Czech Republic	⌐ 丸				

3. List of Participants

3. List of Participants

Participants: Consultative Parties				
Party	Title	Contact	Position	Email
Argentina	Sr.	Castro Lacroze, Gustavo	Advisor	gacastrolacroze@ara.mil.ar
Argentina	Sr.	Conde Garrido, Rodrigo	Delegate	xgr@mrecic.gov.ar
Argentina	Lic.	Daverio, María Elena	Advisor	medaverio@arnet.com.ar
Argentina	Sr.	Mansi, Ariel	Head of Delegation	digea@mrecic.gov.ar
Argentina	Dr	Marenssi, Sergio	Delegate	smarenssi@dna.gov.ar
Argentina	Dr	Memolli, Mariano A.	CEP Representative	drmemolli@gmail.com
Argentina	Mrs	Ortúzar, Patricia	Delegate	portuzar@dna.gov.ar
Argentina	Lic.	Vereda, Marisol	Advisor	marisol.vereda@speedy.com.ar
Argentina	Ms	Vlasich, Verónica	Delegate	veronicavlasich@hotmail.com
Australia	Ms	Broweleit, Jane	Advisor	jane.broweleit@ona.gov.au
Australia	Mr	Clifton, Robb	Delegate	robb.clifton@aad.gov.au
Australia	Ms	Curtis, Rebecca	Delegate	rebecca.curtis@dfat.gov.au
Australia	Dr	Fleming, Tony	Alternate	tony.fleming@aad.gov.au
Australia	Dr	French, Greg	Head of Delegation	greg.french@dfat.gov.au
Australia	Dr	Gales, Nick	Delegate	nick.gales@aad.gov.au
Australia	Mr	Graham, Alistair	Advisor	alistairgraham1@bigpond.com
Australia	Ms	Matley, Holly	Delegate	holly.matley@ag.gov.au
Australia	Mr	McIvor, Ewan	CEP Representative	ewan.mcivor@aad.gov.au
Australia	Dr	Miller, Denzil	Advisor	denzil.miller@development.tas.gov.au
Australia	Mr	Mundy, Jason	Delegate	Jason.Mundy@aad.gov.au
Australia	Mr	Parker, David	Advisor	david.parker@environment.gov.au
Australia	Dr	Potter, Sandra	Delegate	sandra.potter@aad.gov.au
Australia	Ms	Ralston, Kim	Delegate	Kim.Ralston@dfat.gov.au
Australia	Dr	Riddle, Martin	Delegate	martin.riddle@aad.gov.au
Australia	Mr	Rowe, Richard	ATCM Chairman	Richard.Rowe@dfat.gov.au
Australia	Mr	Rudkin, Tobin	Delegate	tobin.rudkin@amsa.gov.au
Australia	Mr	Sulikowski, Edward	Delegate	edward.sulikowski@dfat.gov.au
Australia	Ms	Taylor, Hannah	Delegate	hannah.taylor@aad.gov.au
Australia	Dr	Tracey, Phillip	Delegate	phil.tracey@aad.gov.au
Australia	Ms	Trousselot, Chrissie	Advisor	chrissie.trousselot@development.tas.gov.au
Australia	Ms	Werner, Stephanie	Delegate	Stephanie.Werner@dfat.gov.au
Australia	Dr	Wooding, Rob	Delegate	rob.wooding@aad.gov.au
Belgium	Mr	Andre, François	CEP Representative	francois.andre@environnement.belgique.be
Belgium	Mr.	Jordens, David	Staff	david.jordens@diplobel.fed.be
Belgium	Mr	Marsia, Luc	Staff	luc.marsia@diplobel.fed.be
Belgium	Mr	Régibeau, Jean-Arthur	Head of Delegation	jean-arthur.regibeau@diplobel.fed.be
Belgium	H.E.	Renault, Patrick	Delegate	patrick.renault@diplobel.fed.be
Belgium	Ms	Vancauwenberghe, Maaike	Delegate	maaike.vancauwenberghe@belspo.be
Belgium	Ms	Wilmotte, Annick	Advisor	awilmotte@ulg.ac.be
Brazil	Comander	Corrêa Paes Filho, José	Delegate	paes@secirm.mar.mil.br
Brazil	Comander	do Amaral Silva, Marco Antonio	Delegate	amaral.silva@secirm.mar.mil.br
Brazil	Ms	Leal Madruga, Jaqueline	CEP Representative	jaqueline.madruga@mma.gov.br
Brazil	PhD	S.Campos, Lucia	Delegate	campos-lucia@biologia.ufrj.br
Brazil	Rear Admiral	Silva Rodrigues, Marcos	Alternate	proantar@secirm.mar.mil.br
Brazil	Minister	Vaz Pitaluga, Fábio	Head of Delegation	dmae@itamaraty.gov.br
Bulgaria	Prof.	Pimpirev, Christo	Alternate	polar@gea.uni-sofia.bg
Bulgaria	Amb.	Stefanov, Krassimir	Head of Delegation	stefanovkd@yahoo.com
Chile	Mr.	Cariceo Yutronic, Yanko Jesús	Delegate	ycariceo.12@mma.gob.cl
Chile	Ms.	Carvallo, María Luisa	Delegate	mlcarvallo@minrel.gov.cl
Chile	Mr.	Ferrada, Luis Valentín	Delegate	lferrada@ssdefensa.gov.cl
Chile	Mr.	Figueroa, Miguel	Delegate	mfigueroa@fach.cl
Chile	Mr.	Prado, Carlos	Delegate	prado.antartica@gmail.com
Chile	Dr.	Retamales, José	Alternate	jretamales@inach.cl
Chile	Mr.	Sainz, Manuel	Delegate	msainz@fach.cl

Participants: Consultative Parties				
Party	Title	Contact	Position	Email
Chile	Counsellor	Sanhueza, Camilo	Head of Delegation	csanhueza@minrel.gov.cl
Chile	Mr.	Sepulveda, Victor	Delegate	vsepulveda@armada.cl
Chile	Mr.	Soto, Juan Luis	Delegate	jsoto@inach.cl
Chile	Ms.	Vallejos, Verónica	CEP Representative	vvallejos@inach.cl
Chile	Mr.	Velasquez, Ricardo	Delegate	rvelasquezo@dgtm.cl
China	Mr.	Gao, Feng	Head of Delegation	gao_feng@mfa.gov.cn
China	Second Secretary	Kong , Xiangwen	Delegate	kong_xiangwen@mfa.gov.cn
China	Director-General	Qu, Tanzhou	Delegate	chinare@263.net.cn
China	Mr.	Wei, Long	Delegate	chinare@263.net.cn
China	Program Officer	Yang, Lei	Delegate	chinare@263.net.cn
China	Director	Zhu, Jiangang	Delegate	chinare@263.net.cn
Ecuador	CPFG-EM	Gomez, Humberto	Delegate	mhgomezp@yahoo.com
Ecuador	Captain	Olmedo Morán, José	Head of Delegation	pinguino.olmedo@gmail.com
Ecuador	Amb	Suarez, Alejandro	Delegate	cartografia@mmrree.gob.ec
Finland	Ms.	Mähönen, Outi	CEP Representative	outi.mahonen@ely-keskus.fi
Finland	Ms	Pohjanpalo, Maria	Alternate	maria.pohjanpalo@formin.fi
Finland	Ms.	Valjento, Liisa	Head of Delegation	liisa.valjento@formin.fi
France	Mrs	Belna, Stéphanie	CEP Representative	stephanie.belna@developpement-durable.gouv.fr
France	Dr.	Choquet, Anne	Delegate	annechoquet@orange.fr
France		Dalmas, Dominique	CEP Representative	dominique.dalmas@interieur.gouv.fr
France	Dr	Frenot, Yves	CEP Representative	yves.frenot@ipev.fr
France	Mr.	Lebouvier, Marc	CEP Representative	marc.lebouvier@univ-rennes1.fr
France	Mr	Maxime, Reynaud	Delegate	maxime.reynaud@diplomatie.gouv.fr
France	Mr	Mayet, Laurent	Advisor	laurent.mayet@diplomatie.gouv.fr
France	Mr	Reuillard, Emmanuel	Delegate	emmanuel.reuillard@taaf.fr
France	Ambassador	Rocard, Michel	Head of Delegation	laurent.mayet@diplomatie.gouv.fr
France	Mr.	Segura, Serge	Head of Delegation	serge.segura@diplomatie.gouv.fr
France	M.	Trouyet, Marc	Delegate	marc.trouyet@diplomatie.gouv.fr
Germany	Dr.	Hain, Stefan	Advisor	Stefan.Hain@awi.de
Germany	Dr.	Herata, Heike	CEP Representative	heike.herata@uba.de
Germany	Ms.	Heyn, Andrea	Delegate	Andrea.Heyn@bmbf.bund.de
Germany	Dr.	Läufer, Andreas	Advisor	andreas.laeufer@bgr.de
Germany		Liebschner, Alexander	Delegate	alexander.liebschner@bfn-vilm.de
Germany		Lindemann, Christian	Delegate	christian.lindemann@bmu.bund.de
Germany	Mr	Lorenz, Sönke	Head of Delegation	504-0@diplo.de
Germany	Prof. Dr.	Miller, Heinrich	Delegate	heinrich.miller@awi.de
Germany	Dr.	Nixdorf, Uwe	Delegate	Uwe.Nixdorf@awi.de
India	Dr	Bhat, Kajal	Delegate	bhatkajal@yahoo.com
India	Dr.	Gupta, Vasudha	Delegate	vasudha.gupta@nic.in
India	Dr	Ravindra, Rasik	Head of Delegation	rasik@ncaor.org
India	Dr	Tiwari, Anoop	Delegate	anooptiwari@ncaor.org
Italy	Amb.	Fornara, Arduino	Head of Delegation	arduino.fornara@esteri.it
Italy	Dr.sa	Mecozzi, Roberta	Delegate	roberta.mecozzi@enea.it
Italy	Professor	Moze, Oscar	Alternate	adscien.canberra@esteri.it
Italy	Dr.	Tamburelli, Gianfranco	Advisor	gtamburelli@pelagus.it
Italy	Ms.	Tomaselli, Maria Stefania	Delegate	tomaselli.stefania@minambiente.it
Italy	Dr.	Torcini, Sandro	Delegate	sandro.torcini@casaccia.enea.it
Japan	Mr	Amada, Shinichi	Delegate	shinichi_amada@env.go.jp
Japan	Ms.	Fujimoto, Masami	Delegate	masami.fujimoto@mofa.go.jp
Japan	Mr.	Hasegawa, Shuichi	CEP Representative	SHUICHI_HASEGAWA@env.go.jp
Japan	Mr	Kawashima, Tetsuya	Delegate	tetsuya_kawashima@nm.maff.go.jp
Japan	Mr	Sasaki, Hideki	Delegate	ssk@mext.go.jp
Japan	Prof.	Shiraishi, Kazuyuki	Head of Delegation	kshiraishi@nipr.ac.jp

Participants: Consultative Parties				
Party	Title	Contact	Position	Email
Japan	Prof.	Watanabe, Kentaro	Delegate	kentaro@nipr.ac.jp
Korea (ROK)	Dr	Ahn, In-Young	CEP Representative	iahn@kopri.re.kr
Korea (ROK)	Ms.	An, Heeyoung	Delegate	1234567@korea.kr
Korea (ROK)	Ms.	Cho, Ji I	Delegate	jicho07@mofat.go.kr
Korea (ROK)	Dr.	Choi, Jaeyong	CEP Representative	jaychoi@cnu.ac.kr
Korea (ROK)	Dr	Chung, Hosung	Advisor	hchung@kopri.re.ke
Korea (ROK)	Dr.	Jin, Dongmin	Delegate	dmjin@kopri.re.kr
Korea (ROK)	Mr.	Kang, Jiwon	Delegate	jwkang515@gmail.com
Korea (ROK)	Dr.	Kim, Ji Hee	Advisor	jhalgae@kopri.re.kr
Korea (ROK)	Dr.	Kim, Yeadong	Delegate	ydkim@kopri.re.kr
Korea (ROK)	Mr	Kim, Young-won	Head of Delegation	youngwon05@hotmail.com
Korea (ROK)	Dr.	Lee, Yoo Kyung	Delegate	yklee@kopri.re.kr
Korea (ROK)	Dr	Seo, Hyun kyo	Delegate	shkshk@kopri.re.kr
Korea (ROK)	Mr.	Shin, Maengho	Head of Delegation	mhshin85@mofat.go.kr
Korea (ROK)	Dr.	Shin, Hyoung Chul	Delegate	hcshin@kopri.re.kr
Netherlands	Prof. dr.	Bastmeijer, Kees	Advisor	c.j.bastmeijer@uvt.nl
Netherlands		Elstgeest, Marlynda	Advisor	marlynda@waterproof-expeditions.com
Netherlands	Mr	Hernaus, Reginald	Alternate	Reggie.hernaus@minienm.nl
Netherlands	Prof. dr.	Lefeber, René J.M.	Head of Delegation	rene.lefeber@minbuza.nl
Netherlands	drs. ir.	Martijn, Peijs	Delegate	w.f.peijs@minInv.nl
New Zealand	Ms	Bird, Rebecca	Delegate	rbird@wwf.org.nz
New Zealand	Mr.	Gaston, David	Advisor	david.gaston@mfat.govt.nz
New Zealand	Dr.	Gilbert, Neil	Alternate	n.gilbert@antarcticanz.govt.nz
New Zealand	Dr.	Keys, Harry	Advisor	hkeys@doc.govt.nz
New Zealand	Mr	Kingston, Charles	Advisor	charles.kingston@mfat.govt.nz
New Zealand	Mr	MacKay, Don	Advisor	don_maria_mackay@msn.com
New Zealand	Ms	Newman, Jana	Advisor	j.newman@antarcticanz.govt.nz
New Zealand	Ms	Ng, Jocelyn	Advisor	jocelyn.ng@mfat.govt.nz
New Zealand	Mr.	Sanson, Lou	Advisor	l.sanson@antarcticanz.govt.nz
New Zealand	Mrs.	Schwalger, Carolyn	Head of Delegation	carolyn.schwalger@mfat.govt.nz
New Zealand	Dr	Sharp, Ben	Advisor	ben.sharp@mpi.govt.nz
New Zealand	Mr	Zuur, Bob	Delegate	bzuur@wwf.org.nz
Norway	Ms	Gaalaas, Siv Christin	Advisor	scg@nhd.dep.no
Norway	Mr.	Halvorsen, Svein Tore	Advisor	sth@md.dep.no
Norway	Ms.	Njaastad, Birgit	CEP Representative	njaastad@npolar.no
Norway	Ms	Nygaard, Kristina	Advisor	krny@mfa.no
Norway	Mr	Rognhaug, Magnus H.	Advisor	mar@md.dep.no
Norway	Mr	Rosenberg, Stein Paul	Head of Delegation	stro@mfa.no
Peru	AMB	Quesada, Luis	Head of Delegation	lquesada@embaperu.org.au
Peru	Dr	Sueldo, Jaime	Advisor	jaimesueldo@yahoo.com
Poland	Dr	Kidawa, Anna	Delegate	akidawa@arctowski.pl
Poland	Director	Sarkowicz, Ryszard	Head of Delegation	ryszard.sarkowicz@msz.gov.pl
Poland	Dr.	Tatur, Andrzej	Delegate	tatura@interia.pl
Poland	Amb.	Wolski, Jakub T.	Alternate	jakub.wolski@msz.gov.pl
Russian Federation	Ms	Antonova, Anna	Delegate	avant71@yandex.ru
Russian Federation	Mr	Gonchar, Dmitry	Head of Delegation	dp@mid.ru
Russian Federation	Mr.	Lukin, Valery	CEP Representative	lukin@aari.nw.ru
Russian Federation	Mr.	Pomelov, Victor	Delegate	pom@aari.nw.ru
Russian Federation	Ms	Stetsenko, Ksenia	Delegate	dp@mid.ru
South Africa	ADv	Dwarika, Yolande	Delegate	DwarikaY@dirco.gov.za
South Africa	Ms	Jacobs, Carol	CEP Representative	cjacobs@environment.gov.za
South Africa	Mr	Janse Van Noordwyk, Christo	Alternate	JanseVanNoordwykC@dirco.gov.za
South Africa	Dr	Mphepya, Jonas	Delegate	jmphepya@environment.gov.za
South Africa	Dr	Siko, Gilbert	Delegate	Gilbert.Siko@dst.gov.za
South Africa	Mr.	Valentine, Henry	Head of Delegation	hvalentine@environment.gov.za
Spain	Mr.	Catalan, Manuel	CEP Representative	cpe@mineco.es

Participants: Consultative Parties

Party	Title	Contact	Position	Email
Spain	Dr	Dañobeitia, Juan Jose	Advisor	jjdanobeitia@cmima.csic.es
Spain	Ambassador	Gomez Martinez, Marcos	Head of Delegation	marcos.gomez@maec.es
Spain	Mrs	Puig, Roser	Advisor	rpuigmar@ub.edu
Spain	Mrs	Ramos, Sonia	Advisor	sonia.ramos@mineco.es
Sweden	Research Coordinator	Jonsell, Ulf	Alternate	ulf.jonsell@polar.se
Sweden	Ambassador	Ödmark, Helena	Head of Delegation	helena.odmark@foreign.ministry.se
Sweden	Mrs.	Selberg, Cecilia	CEP Representative	cecilia.selberg@polar.se
Ukraine		Fedchuk, Andrii	CEP Representative	andriyf@gmail.com
Ukraine	Dr	Gurzhii, Andrii	Head of Delegation	valery_sav@ukr.net
United Kingdom	Mr	Burgess, Henry	CEP Representative	henry.burgess@fco.gov.uk
United Kingdom	Ms	Clarke, Rachel	Delegate	racl@bas.ac.uk
United Kingdom	Mr.	Downie, Rod	Delegate	rhd@bas.ac.uk
United Kingdom	Mr	Drakeford, Jonathan	Delegate	jonathan.drakeford@fco.gov.uk
United Kingdom	Dr	Hughes, Kevin	Delegate	kehu@bas.ac.uk
United Kingdom	Mr	Madden, Paul	Delegate	paul.madden@fco.gov.uk
United Kingdom	Ms.	Rumble, Jane	Head of Delegation	Jane.Rumble@fco.gov.uk
United Kingdom	Dr.	Shears, John	Delegate	jrs@bas.ac.uk
United States	Mr.	Bloom, Evan T.	Head of Delegation	bloomet@state.gov
United States	Ms	Cooper, Susannah	Alternate	cooperse@state.gov
United States	Ms.	Dahood, Adrian	Delegate	adahood@nsf.gov
United States	Mr.	Edwards, David	Delegate	david.l.edwards@uscg.mil
United States	Dr.	Falkner, Kelly	Delegate	kfalkner@nsf.gov
United States	Mr.	Gilanshah, Bijan	Delegate	bgilansh@nsf.gov
United States	Ms.	Hessert, Aimee	Delegate	hessert.aimee@epamail.epa.gov
United States	Mr.	Israel, Brian	Delegate	israelbr@state.gov
United States	Dr.	Karentz, Deneb	Advisor	karentzd@usfca.edu
United States	Mr.	Naveen, Ron	Advisor	oceanites.mail@verizon.net
United States	Dr.	Penhale, Polly A.	CEP Representative	ppenhale@nsf.gov
United States	Mr.	Smith, Lowell	Advisor	lowsmith@mail2Scientist.com
United States	Mr.	Stone, Brian	Delegate	bstone@nsf.gov
United States	Ms.	Toschik, Pamela	Delegate	pamela.toschik@noaa.gov
United States	Mr.	Watters, George	Delegate	George.Watters@noaa.gov
United States	Ms.	Wheatley, Victoria	Advisor	vewheatley@gmail.com
Uruguay	Mr	Abdala, Juan	CEP Representative	jabdala@iau.gub.uy
Uruguay	Mr	Alonzo, Ismael	Head of Delegation	presidente@iau.gub.uy
Uruguay	Amb	Fajardo, Alberto	Alternate	urucan@iimetro.com.au
Uruguay	Mr	Fontes, Waldemar	Delegate	dirsecretaria@iau.gub.uy
Uruguay	Mr	González Otero, Alvaro	Delegate	politica@mrree.gub.uy
Uruguay	Mr	Saravia, Ricardo	Delegate	rsaravia@iau.gub.uy
Uruguay	Mr	Vignali, Daniel	Advisor	dvignal@adinet.com.uy

Participants: Non-Consultative Parties

Party	Title	Contact	Position	Email
Canada		Sadar, Kamuran	Head of Delegation	kamuran.sadar@ec.gc.ca
Colombia		Bula, Olga	Head of Delegation	olenabula@gmail.com
Czech Republic	Mr.	Prošek, Pavel	Advisor	prosek@geogr.muni.cz
Czech Republic	Mr.	Venera, Zdenek	Head of Delegation	zdenek.venera@geology.cz
Malaysia	Prof.	Abu Samah, Azizan	Alternate	azizans@um.edu.my
Malaysia	Dr	Goh, Hong Ching	Delegate	gohhc@um.edu.my
Malaysia	Dr	Hamzah, B.Ahmad	Delegate	bahamzah@pd.jaring.my
Malaysia	Mr	Hashim, Eldeen	Delegate	ehusaini@hotmail.com
Malaysia	Mr.	Leman, Wan Ashbi	Delegate	ashbi@mosti.gov.my
Malaysia	Dr	Mohd Nor, Salleh	Delegate	salleh.mohdnor@gmail.com
Malaysia	Prof.	Mohd Shah, Rohani	Delegate	rohanimohdshah@yahoo.com
Malaysia	Dr.	Syed Ahmad, Sharifah	Head of Delegation	zarah@mosti.gov.my

Participants: Non-Consultative Parties

Party	Title	Contact	Position	Email
		Zarah		
Monaco	Del.	Van Klaveren, Céline	Delegate	cevanklaveren@gouv.mc
Slovak Republic	Ing.	Petrasova, Anna	Delegate	anna.petrasova@mzv.sk

Participants: Observers

Party	Title	Contact	Position	Email
CCAMLR	Dr	Jones, Christopher	CEP Representative	chris.d.jones@noaa.gov
CCAMLR	Mr	Kremzer, Ed	Advisor	ed.kremzer@ccamlr.org
CCAMLR		Nilsson, Jessica	Advisor	Jessica.nilsson@ccamlr.org
CCAMLR	Dr	Reid, Keith	Advisor	keith@ccamlr.org
CCAMLR	Mr	Wright, Andrew	Head of Delegation	andrew_wright@ccamlr.org
COMNAP	Ms.	Rogan-Finnemore, Michelle	Head of Delegation	michelle.finnemore@comnap.aq
SCAR	Prof.	Chown, Steven L.	CEP Representative	slchown@sun.ac.za
SCAR	Prof	Kennicutt, Mahlon (Chuck)	Delegate	m-kennicutt@tamu.edu
SCAR	Dr	Newman, Louise	Delegate	Louise.Newman@utas.edu.au
SCAR	Dr	O'Brien, Philip	Delegate	phil.obrien.ant@gmail.com
SCAR	Dr.	Sparrow, Mike	Head of Delegation	mds68@cam.ac.uk
SCAR	Dr	Terauds, Aleks	Delegate	aleks.terauds@gmail.com

Participants: Experts

Party	Title	Contact	Position	Email
ACAP	Dr	Misiak, Wieslawa	Advisor	wieslawa.misiak@acap.aq
ACAP	Mr.	Papworth, Warren	Head of Delegation	warren.papworth@acap.aq
ASOC	Mr.	Barnes, James	Head of Delegation	james.barnes@asoc.org
ASOC	Ms	Barrett, Jill	Advisor	j.barrett@biicl.org
ASOC	Mr	Campbell, Steve	Advisor	steve@antarcticocean.org
ASOC	Ms.	Christian, Claire	Advisor	Claire.Christian@asoc.org
ASOC	Mr	Harte, Michael	Advisor	MHarte@wwf.org.au
ASOC	Mr	Keey, Geoff	Advisor	geoff.keey@gmail.com
ASOC	Mr	Kennedy, Michael	Advisor	michael@hsi.org.au
ASOC	Mr.	Nicoll, Rob	Advisor	rnicoll@wwf.org.au
ASOC	Dr.	Roura, Ricardo	CEP Representative	ricardo.roura@worldonline.nl
ASOC	Ms	Smith, Elyse	Advisor	elysedav@aol.com
ASOC	Dr.	Tin, Tina	Advisor	tinatintk@gmail.com
ASOC	Mr	Werner Kinkelin, Rodolfo	Advisor	rodolfo.antarctica@gmail.com
IAATO	Dr.	Crosbie, Kim	Head of Delegation	kimcrosbie@iaato.org
IAATO	Ms.	Hohn-Bowen, Ute	Delegate	ute@antarpply.com
IAATO	Ms	Holgate, Claudia	Delegate	cholgate@iaato.org
IAATO	Mr	Ledingham, Rod	Advisor	rod.ledingham@bigpond.com
IAATO	Mr.	Rootes, David	Delegate	david.rootes@antarctic-logistics.com
IAATO	Ms.	Schillat, Monika	Delegate	Monika@antarpply.com
IAATO	Mr.	Wellmeier, Steve	Alternate	swellmeier@iaato.org
IHO	Capt.	Gorziglia, Hugo	Head of Delegation	hgorziglia@ihb.mc
UNEP	Mr.	Johnston, Sam	Advisor	johnston@ias.unu.edu
WMO	Mr	Ondras, Miroslav	Head of Delegation	mondras@wmo.int
WMO	Mr	Pendlebury, Steve	Delegate	s.pendlebury@bom.gov.au

Participants: Secretariats

Party	Title	Contact	Position	Email
ATS	Mr.	Acero, José Maria	Staff	tito.acero@antarctictreaty.org
ATS	Mr.	Agraz, José Luis	Staff	pepe.agraz@antarctictreaty.org
ATS	Ms.	Balok, Anna	Staff	anna.balok@antarctictreaty.org
ATS	Mr.	Davies, Paul	Staff	littlewest2@googlemail.com
ATS	Ms	Guretskaya, Anastasia	Staff	a.guretskaya@googlemail.com

Participants: Secretariats				
Party	Title	Contact	Position	Email
ATS	Dr.	Reinke, Friederike	Staff	friederike.reinke@uni-bremen.de
ATS	Dr.	Reinke, Manfred	Head of Delegation	manfred.reinke@antarctictreaty.org
ATS	Mr.	Wainschenker, Pablo	Staff	pablo.wainschenker@antarctictreaty.org
ATS	Mr	Walton, David W H	Staff	dwhw@bas.ac.uk
ATS	Mr.	Wydler, Diego	Staff	diego.wydler@antarctictreaty.org
HC Secretariat	Ms	Bartley, Rhonda	Staff	rhonda.bartley@aad.gov.au
HC Secretariat	Ms	Bourke, Deborah	Staff	deborah.bourke@aad.gov.au
HC Secretariat	Ms	Chapman, Fiona	Staff	Fiona.Chapman@development.tas.gov.au
HC Secretariat	Ms	Chin, Mey	Staff	Mey.Chin@development.tas.gov.au
HC Secretariat	Ms	Coad, Lizzy	Staff	lizzy.coad@aad.gov.au
HC Secretariat	Mr	Cooper, Jamie	Staff	Jamie.Cooper@dfat.gov.au
HC Secretariat	Mr	Cullen, Paul	Staff	Cullen254@hotmail.com
HC Secretariat	Mr	Davis, Bob	Staff	bob.davis@dfat.gov.au
HC Secretariat	Ms	Eldershaw, Jane	Staff	Jane.Eldershaw@development.tas.gov.au
HC Secretariat	Ms	Erceg, Diane	Staff	dzerceg@gmail.com
HC Secretariat	Ms	Forman, Catherine	Staff	Catherine.Forman@development.tas.gov.au
HC Secretariat	Ms	Foster, Phillipa	Staff	Phillipa.Foster@tmag.tas.gov.au
HC Secretariat	Ms	Goldworthy, Lyn	Staff	lyn.goldsworthy@ozemail.com.au
HC Secretariat	Mr.	Gonzalez Vaillant, Joaquín	Staff	joacogv@hotmail.com
HC Secretariat	Ms	Hamilton, Katie	Staff	Katie.hamilton@dfat.gov.au
HC Secretariat	Mr	Hanson, Paul	Staff	paul.hanson@aad.gov.au
HC Secretariat	Ms	Hwang, Eugenie	Staff	Eugenie.hwang@dfat.gov.au
HC Secretariat	Ms.	Idiens, Melissa	Staff	melissa.idiens@canterbury.ac.nz
HC Secretariat	Mr.	Jackson, Andrew	HC Executive Secretary	andrew.jackson@aad.gov.au
HC Secretariat	Ms	Jacobs, Linda	Staff	linda.jacobs@aad.gov.au
HC Secretariat	Ms	Johnson, Constance	Staff	constancemgj2003@yahoo.com.au
HC Secretariat	Ms	Leaney, Tara	Staff	tara.leaney@dfat.gov.au
HC Secretariat	Ms	Leeson, Karin	Staff	Karin.Leeson@development.tas.gov.au
HC Secretariat	Ms	Lloyd, Megan	Staff	megan.lloyd@aad.gov.au
HC Secretariat	Ms	Lovell, Georgia	Staff	Georgia.Lovell@dfat.gov.au
HC Secretariat	Ms	Malcolm, Rebecca	Staff	Rebecca.malcolm@aad.gov.au
HC Secretariat	Ms	Marshall, Rebecca	Staff	Rebecca.marshall@dfat.gov.au
HC Secretariat	Mr	Moles, Nick	Staff	Nick.Moles@tourism.tas.gov.au
HC Secretariat	Ms	Pike, Melanie	Staff	Melanie.pike@aad.gov.au
HC Secretariat	Mr	Powell, Stephen	Staff	stephen.powell@environment.gov.au
HC Secretariat	Ms	Raw, Kristin	Staff	kristin.raw@aad.gov.au
HC Secretariat	Miss	Sulikowski, Chavelli	Staff	chavelli.sulikowski@utas.edu.au
HC Secretariat	Ms	Swift, Isabella	Staff	Isabella.swift@dfat.gov.au
HC Secretariat	Ms	Tisdall, Amy	Staff	Amy.tisdall@dfat.gov.au
HC Secretariat	Ms	Wallace, Heather	Staff	Heather.wallace@environment.gov.au
HC Secretariat	Ms	Woolnough, Mary	Staff	Mary.Woolnough@development.tas.gov.au
HC Secretariat		x, x	Staff	xxx@xxx.xxx
HC Secretariat	y	y, y	Staff	yyy@yyy.yyy
Trans. & Interp.	Ms	Alal, Cecilia	Staff	conference@oncallinterpreters.com
Trans. & Interp.	Mr	Aroustian, Aramais	Staff	conference@oncallinterpreters.com
Trans. & Interp.	Mr	Avella, Alex	Staff	conference@oncallinterpreters.com
Trans. & Interp.	Ms	Avila, Patricia	Staff	conference@oncallinterpreters.com
Trans. & Interp.	Ms	Barua, Lucy	Staff	conference@oncallinterpreters.com
Trans. & Interp.	Ms	Blundo-Grimison, Rosemary	Staff	conference@oncallinterpreters.com
Trans. & Interp.	Ms	Boury, Marjorie	Staff	conference@oncallinterpreters.com
Trans. & Interp.	Ms	Christopher, Vera	Staff	conference@oncallinterpreters.com
Trans. & Interp.	Ms	Coussaert, Joelle	Staff	conference@oncallinterpreters.com
Trans. & Interp.	Mr	Giglio, Daniel	Staff	conference@oncallinterpreters.com
Trans. & Interp.	Mr	Hulusi, Hulus	Staff	conference@oncallinterpreters.com
Trans. & Interp.	Mr	Iatsenko, Viktor	Staff	conference@oncallinterpreters.com

Participants: Secretariats

Party	Title	Contact	Position	Email
Trans. & Interp.	Mr	Ivacheff, Alexey	Staff	conference@oncallinterpreters.com
Trans. & Interp.	Ms	Kasimova, Zouchra-Katerina	Staff	conference@oncallinterpreters.com
Trans. & Interp.	Ms	Lacey, Roslyn	Staff	conference@oncallinterpreters.com
Trans. & Interp.	Ms	Lieve, Marisol	Staff	conference@oncallinterpreters.com
Trans. & Interp.	Ms	Lira, Isabel	Staff	conference@oncallinterpreters.com
Trans. & Interp.	Mrs.	McGrath, Peps	Staff	peps.mcgrath@oncallinterpreters.com
Trans. & Interp.	Mr	Merlot, Christian	Staff	conference@oncallinterpreters.com
Trans. & Interp.	Ms	Mullova, Ludmila	Staff	conference@oncallinterpreters.com
Trans. & Interp.	Mr	Orlando, Marc	Staff	conference@oncallinterpreters.com
Trans. & Interp.	Ms	Poblete, Verónica	Staff	conference@oncallinterpreters.com
Trans. & Interp.	Ms	Radetskaya, Maria	Staff	conference@oncallinterpreters.com
Trans. & Interp.	Mr	Tanguy, Philippe	Staff	conference@oncallinterpreters.com
Trans. & Interp.	Dr	Watt, Emy	Staff	conference@oncallinterpreters.com
Trans. & Interp.	Mr	Yeo, Anson	Staff	conference@oncallinterpreters.com

www.ingramcontent.com/pod-product-compliance
Lightning Source LLC
Chambersburg PA
CBHW080719220326

41520CB00056B/7149